Soviet Government

A Selection of Official Documents
on Internal Policies

MERVYN MATTHEWS

Soviet Government

A Selection of Official Documents
on Internal Policies

Jonathan Cape Thirty Bedford Square London

FIRST PUBLISHED 1974
INTRODUCTION, COMMENTARY AND COMPILATION © 1974 BY MERVYN MATTHEWS

JONATHAN CAPE LTD, 30 BEDFORD SQUARE, LONDON WCI

ISBN 0 224 00923 0

K
.M441 so
1974

PRINTED AND BOUND IN GREAT BRITAIN
BY RICHARD CLAY (THE CHAUCER PRESS) LTD
BUNGAY, SUFFOLK

Contents

Part III Legality, the Courts and the Police

Acknowledgements

For permission to reproduce copyright material, I gratefully acknowledge the following: Compton Press, Compton, California, for document 11; The Controller, Her Majesty's Stationery Office, for documents 45, 48, 84, 85; *Current Digest of the Soviet Press* and the American Association for the Advancement of Slavic Studies, Columbus, Ohio, for documents 17, 21, 28, 33, 34, 35, 36, 38, 40, 41, 53, 54, 56, 57, 60, 76, 77, 79, 92. Translation copyright by the *Current Digest of the Soviet Press*, published weekly at the Ohio State University by the American Association for the Advancement of Slavic Studies, reprinted by permission of *The Digest*; Foreign Languages Publishing House, Moscow, for documents 15, 24, 29, 52, 65, 66, 68; George Wahr Publishing Company, Ann Arbor, Mich., for document 88; *International Conciliation* and the Carnegie Endowment for International Peace, New York, for documents 42, 43; Johns Hopkins University Press, Baltimore, Md., for documents 63, 81; Lawrence and Wishart, Ltd, London, for documents 1, 2, 7, 9, 10, 27, 62, 80; The Macmillan Company, New York, for documents 25, 26; Michigan Legal Publications, Ann Arbor, Mich., for documents 70, 71, 72, 73; *The Nation*, New York, for documents 4, 5, 6; Parker School of Foreign and Comparative Law, Columbia University, New York, for documents 58, 59, 89; *Slavonic and East European Review* and Cambridge University Press, for documents 14, 31, 49, 50, 86, 87; Sweet and Maxwell, Ltd, London, for document 47; and University of Notre Dame Press, Notre Dame, Ind., for document 8.

Introduction

A major obstacle to the reader who wishes to understand the nature of Soviet government is, more often than not, the inaccessibility of many laws and decrees which mould it. This collection of official documents in translation is an attempt to ease this problem. The reader will, I believe, find in these pages many items which are essential for understanding the development and texture of Soviet polity.

The choice of such documents inevitably presents enormous difficulties. The definition of 'official' must of necessity be vague. In a totalitarian, one-party state with a controlled press, an informal utterance by a leader or a small, strategically placed article by an unknown correspondent may be just as significant, or 'official', as an authoritative text put together in the Central Committee of the CPSU. Although some of the published documents are obviously designed to deal effectively with a specific problem, others, like the constitutions, may be mainly demonstrative or propagandistic in character. Sometimes important legislation seems to stem directly from the speeches of Soviet leaders, and may contain quotations from them. The volume of material from which a small selection has to be made is thus practically immeasurable.

Paradoxically, the difficulties of selection are exacerbated by the Soviet leadership's frequent failure to publish key enactments which could be used to pinpoint important developments. There is no doubt that even at 'all-union' level only a small proportion of all laws passed are brought to public notice. The same is true of the union and autonomous republics, not to mention individual ministries and administrations. Many exceedingly significant documents are circulated through official channels only, and must be returned for the head-office archives in Moscow after perusal. Every state has its confidential sector, but in the Soviet Union the principle of state secrecy is stretched to an alarming degree. One explanation of this is the actual illegality of many state documents in constitutional terms.

The system of censorship in the USSR provides a good example of what the editor has to contend with in this respect. The RSFSR constitution, which was approved in July 1918, stated in clear and unequivocal terms that Soviet citizens had the right to genuine freedom of expression, and were to be granted facilities for the publication and circulation of printed matter throughout the country. There is a similar clause in the present constitution. In fact freedom of the press was abolished by decree only two days after the Bolsheviks took power. This decree itself proved to be self-contradictory, for it stated that the suppression of 'counter-revolutionary' organs would be only a temporary expedient. The state-run system of censorship which was subsequently established in the RSFSR was important enough to warrant its own (illegal) statute in 1922. This was revised somewhat in 1931. Since state censorship still exists (it appears under its old name, 'Glavlit', in a number of Soviet handbooks) we may presume that the 1931 statute, or more likely a later one, is still in force.

This is not, however, the end of the story. The Soviet censorship, like all organizations, has sets of instructions for its own internal use: a bound and published list of some 10,000 titles of books 'subject to exclusion from libraries and the trading network' is known to have existed in 1958, and this was evidently only one part of a two-volume work. There is, therefore, a large body of documentation which is not only illegal under the terms of the constitution, but also secret. As far as the censorship is concerned, obviously we know of only a very few items from a sizeable archive.

The last major difficulty is of an individual character. Everyone views Soviet government in his own way, attributing more or less importance to the various elements which comprise it. All perspectives change with time, and no two persons have the same view of Soviet history at a given moment. The present selection of documents inevitably reflects my own personal proclivities. In an endeavour to introduce other viewpoints I have asked experienced colleagues to comment on my choice, and I have adopted many of their suggestions. My approach has been to pick items which seem to embody permanent elements of the Soviet system or which characterized government policy over long periods of time. Most of these documents are well known to specialist observers, and fairly obvious choices. In cases where many variants are to hand I have tended to go for the most informative or longest-standing ones. I have avoided abridgement whenever it was practicable to do so.

It has, of course, proved impossible to cover all spheres of Soviet government, and five have in fact been chosen for illustration. The section on *state administration* contains the 1918 and 1924 constitutions (the 1936 version being easily available elsewhere), documents on the Supreme and local Soviets, and decrees which illustrate the subordination of the latter to party rule. Additional material on the passport system, the censorship, and the electoral system has been included. The documents on the *Party* illustrate its structural development, and the more striking schisms which have occurred in the leadership. This material is intended to throw light on the functioning of the all-important Politburo, or Presidium as it was from 1952 to 1966.

Next comes a section on *law*, *justice* and the *police*. The documents chosen here concern the aspects of law most akin to politics: thus the development of the secret police, and the laws on state crimes are given prominence. The state provisions for extra-legal bodies and a few smaller items of undoubted interest have also been put in.

The *peasantry*, which until recently made up the bulk of the labour force, and the land which they tilled, have always presented a problem to the Bolsheviks. For this reason they have been given separate treatment. I

12

have here endeavoured to illustrate some aspects of the rural question, collectivization, and the efforts of post-Stalin leadership to improve the peasant's lot.

Labour legislation in the Soviet Union is extremely extensive, probably because the state has, since the late 'twenties, been the only employer outside the collective farm, and has controlled all aspects of people's working lives. In this last section I have picked out elements illustrating primarily workers' rights (or the absence of them) during the years of the New Economic Policy (NEP), the period of enforced industrialization, and again after Stalin's death.

The introductory commentaries on the documents have been kept short. Many of the items translated would require literally a volume of explanation: the main aim here has been to present as many original sources as possible, leaving the reader to look for fuller explanation in the numerous works on Soviet history and politics which have been written over the last half century. The sources given for the Russian texts refer, whenever possible, to recently published Soviet works, since these are often easier to find than original legislative series.

A proportion of the translations (including those of most of the documents which appeared after 1948) have been taken from the *Current Digest of the Soviet Press* and the kindred publication *Soviet Current Policies*. I am extremely grateful to Mr Leo Gruliow, the editor, for permission to use this valuable material. It would have been more difficult for me to undertake this venture without this body of competently translated documentation to fall back on. Some of the earlier documents were chosen through the medium of *Materials for the Study of the Soviet System*, by J. Meisel and E. S. Kozera (George Wahr Publishing Co., Ann Arbor, 1950). This work, which warranged a second edition in 1953, contained a very useful selection of documents, particularly from the earlier years of Soviet power.

A number of publishers in Great Britain and America have willingly co-operated, and allowed me to use their copyright material: full details are given in the Acknowledgements, p. 9. Professor J. M. Hazard of Columbia University was kind enough to let me use a few of the translations from *The Soviet Legal System*, which he wrote with Mr Isaac Shapiro (Oceana Publications, New York, 1962). Two of my students, Miss Margot Light and Mr Michael Colenso, did outline translations of documents 16 and 32.

The reader will find small discrepancies of terminology between one text and another. I decided not to strive for complete uniformity in work from so many different hands: this would have been a laborious and hardly worthwhile task. At the same time I have modified some of the more unexpected variants. A glossary of terms and abbreviations has been added to facilitate comprehension and comparison in doubtful cases.

A number of experienced teachers have given their opinion on the contents of this book. My particular thanks are due to Andrew Threipland of the London School of Economics for taking a keen interest in the manuscript, especially in its early stages. Mr Martin Dewhurst, Mr Everett Jacobs, Dr Ivo Lapenna, Professor Leonard Schapiro and Professor Marcus Wheeler all looked through sections most germane to their interests. I have tried, as far as space permitted, to take their comments into account. From an early stage the Nuffield Foundation provided some useful financial assistance for the research involved.

A collection of this kind cannot do more than provide an impression of what Soviet government is. But if the documents presented here serve to improve the reader's knowledge of the Soviet system, or recall some half-forgotten facts, then the effect which has gone into the selection will not have been in vain.

MERVYN MATTHEWS

14

Part I

Government and Administration

1. The Bolshevik Appeal to the Citizenry after Taking Power

25 October 1917, OS

This brief document, drafted by Lenin, announced the advent of the Bolsheviks to power. By the time it appeared most of the key installations of Petrograd had fallen into their hands. There had in fact been very little resistance: the take-over of government was completed that evening, with the seizure of the Winter Palace, where the remnants of the Provisional Government were still holding out. The Bolshevik Military Revolutionary Committee, which led the coup, was headed by Trotsky, who made an equally brief official announcement in the Petrograd Soviet that afternoon.

1. To the Citizens of Russia

Appeal of the Petrograd Military Revolutionary Committee, 25 October 1917, OS

The Provisional Government has been deposed. State power has passed into the hands of the organ of the Petrograd Soviet of Workers' and Soldiers' Deputies—the Military Revolutionary Committee, which heads the Petrograd proletariat and the garrison.

The cause for which the people have fought, namely, the immediate offer of a democratic peace, the abolition of landed proprietorship, workers' control over production, and the establishment of Soviet power—this cause has been secured.

Long live the revolution of workers, soldiers and peasants!

> Military Revolutionary Committee of the Petrograd Soviet
> of Workers' and Soldiers' Deputies.

10 a.m., 25 October 1917.

Source: G. D. Obichkin, i drugie, *Dekrety sovetskoi vlasti*, Vol. I (Moscow, 1957), p. 2.
Translation: Yuri Akhapkin, *First Decrees of Soviet Power*, (Lawrence and Wishart, London, 1970), p. 37.

2. The Suppression of the Non-Bolshevik Press

27 October 1917, OS

This decree, passed two days after the Bolsheviks had seized power, was the basis of Lenin's suppression of the non-Bolshevik press. It foreshadowed many other measures leading to censorship of all information media (see for instance document 13). The insistence on the decree's temporary character, repeated several times in the text, is now nothing more than a historical curiosity. The promulgation of this decree was followed, a few days later, by a major debate in the Central Executive Committee; the Leninist faction were in a majority, but a number of prominent figures, including Zinoviev, Kamenev and Rykov, resigned in protest against it. The measure, as everyone realized, concerned the very nature of Bolshevik rule.

2. Decree on the Press

Issued by the Council of People's Commissars, 27 October 1917, OS

In the trying critical period of the revolution and the days that immediately followed it the Provisional Revolutionary Committee was compelled to take a number of measures against the counter-revolutionary press of different shades.

Immediately outcries were heard from all sides that the new, socialist power had violated a fundamental principle of its programme by encroaching upon the freedom of the press.

The Workers' and Peasants' Government calls the attention of the population to the fact that what this liberal façade actually conceals is freedom for the propertied classes, having taken hold of the lion's share of the entire press, to poison, unhindered, the minds and obscure the consciousness of the masses.

Everyone knows that the bourgeois press is one of the most powerful weapons of the bourgeoisie. Especially at the crucial moment when the new power, the power of workers and peasants, is only affirming itself, it was impossible to leave this weapon wholly in the hands of the enemy, for in such moments it is no less dangerous than bombs and machine-guns. That is why temporary extraordinary measures were taken to stem the torrent of filth and slander in which the yellow and green press would be only too glad to drown the recent victory of the people.

As soon as the new order becomes consolidated, all administrative pressure on the press will be terminated and it will be granted complete freedom within the bounds of legal responsibility, in keeping with a law that will be broadest and most progressive in this respect.

However, being aware that a restriction of the press, even at critical moments, is permissible only within the limits of what is absolutely necessary, the Council of People's Commissars resolves:

General Provisions on the Press

1. Only those publications can be suppressed which (1) call for open resistance or insubordination to the Workers' and Peasants' Government; (2) sow sedition through demonstrably slanderous distortion of facts; (3) instigate actions of an obviously criminal, i.e. criminally punishable, nature.
2. Publications can be proscribed, temporarily or permanently, only by decision of the Council of People's Commissars.
3. The present ordinance is of a temporary nature and will be repealed by a special decree as soon as normal conditions of social life set in.

Chairman of the Council of People's Commissars,
VLADIMIR ULYANOV (LENIN).

Petrograd, 27 October 1917.

Source: G. D. Obichkin, i drugie, *Dekrety sovetskoi vlasti*, Vol. I (Moscow, 1957), p. 24.
Translation: Yuri Akhapkin, *First Decrees of Soviet Power* (Lawrence and Wishart, London, 1970), p. 29.

3. The Tsarist System of Ranks Abolished

11 November 1917, OS

The tsarist regime had been characterized, since the time of Peter the Great, by a system of estates and ranks which in many respects governed the legal rights of most social groups. The Bolsheviks abolished this by the decree translated below. But service to the state, on which the rank system had been based, was to remain a key element in determining the Soviet citizen's social status and material privileges. This could hardly be otherwise under conditions of extensive state ownership of the means of production, and the existence of a single party-state bureaucracy. The official concept of social structure approved by Stalin in 1936 stipulated two friendly classes — the workers and peasants — with a cross-stratum of the intelligentsia, and this scheme has been retained ever since.

3. Decree on the Abolition of Classes and Civil Ranks

Approved by the Central Executive Committee and the Council of People's Commissars, 11 November 1917, OS

ARTICLE 1. All the classes of society existing up to now in Russia, and all divisions of citizens, all class distinctions and privileges, class organizations and institutions and also civil grades are abolished.

ARTICLE 2. All ranks (nobleman, merchant, peasant, etc.), titles (prince, count, etc.) and denominations of civil grades (private, state, and other councillors) are abolished and only one denomination is established for all the population of Russia, that of citizens of the Russian Republic.

ARTICLE 3. The property of the class institutions of the nobility is to be immediately handed over to the *zemstvo* self-governing organizations.

ARTICLE 4. All property of the merchants and bourgeois corporations is to be immediately transferred to the corresponding municipal self-governing organizations.

ARTICLE 5. All the institutions of corporations, affairs, proceedings and archives are to be handed over immediately to the corresponding town and *zemstvo* organizations.

ARTICLE 6. All the corresponding articles of the laws in force up to now are revoked.

ARTICLE 7. The present decree shall enter in force on the day of its publication, and it shall be immediately put into execution by the local soviets of workers', soldiers' and peasants' deputies.

The present decree is confirmed by the Central Executive Committee of the soviets of workers' and soldiers' Deputies at the meeting of 10 November 1917 [OS].

> Chairman of the Central Executive Committee, IA. SVERDLOV.
>
> Chairman of the Council of People's Commissaries, V. ULIANOV (LENIN).
>
> Director of the Affairs of the Council of People's Commissaries, BONCH-BRUYEVICH.
>
> Secretary to the Council, N. GORBUNOV.

Source: G. D. Obichkin, i drugie, *Dekrety sovetskoi vlasti*, Vol. I (Moscow, 1957), p. 72.

Translation: Bolshevik Propaganda, Hearings before a Subcommittee of the Committee on the Judiciary, United States Senate, 65th Congress, 3rd Session, 11 February 1919, Washington D.C., p. 1174. Text slightly modernized.

4. The Rights and Duties of the Post-Revolutionary Soviets

24 December 1917, *OS*

5. Lenin on the Provincial Soviets

5 January 1918, *OS*

6. The Structure of Local Government

9 January 1918, *OS*

When the Bolsheviks came to power the soviets were already very much in evidence, but the activities of these bodies were largely unco-ordinated and their structures often informal. The three documents which follow illustrate the first attempts of the leadership to define the competence of the soviets and introduce some order into the chaos: naturally, the soviets inherited many of their functions directly from the old tsarist zemstva, *but organizational traits which were to become characteristic of them under the Bolsheviks are here made quite clear. In view of the extreme centralization envisaged by the 1918 constitution, and the imminent dominance of the Party, Lenin's provisions for elections to and within the soviets ring rather hollow.*

Local government in Russia virtually collapsed during the Civil War, and had to be re-established in the mid-'twenties. These early instructions are not, however, the less interesting for that.[1]

4. Instructions on the Rights and Duties of the Soviets

Published on 24 December 1917, *OS*

1. The soviets of workmen's, soldiers', and poor peasants' deputies are, as local organs, quite independent in matters of a local character, but they always act in accordance with the decrees of both the central Soviet Government and of the larger units (*uzed, gubernia* and *oblast* soviets) of which they form part.
2. Upon the soviets, as organs of government, devolve the tasks of administering and servicing all spheres of life in the locality — administrative, economic, financial and educational.
3. In their administrative work the soviets carry out all decrees and decisions of the central government, take measures for providing the people with the

[1] It has not, unfortunately, been possible to trace the Soviet sources of documents 5 and 6, but given their content, it is reasonable to suppose they are genuine.

most extensive information about those decisions, issue obligatory ordinances, make requisitions and confiscations, impose fines, close down counter-revolutionary press organs, make arrests, and dissolve public organizations which incite active opposition to, or the overthrow of, the Soviet Government.

NOTE. The soviets submit to the central Soviet Government a report on all measures undertaken by them and on important local events.

4. The soviets elect from their number an executive organ (an executive committee or presidium) which is charged with carrying out their decisions and doing the current administrative work.

NOTE 1. The Military-Revolutionary Committees, as fighting organs which came into existence during the revolution, are abolished.
NOTE 2. It is permitted, as a temporary measure, to appoint commissaries in those provinces and districts where the power of the soviet is not sufficiently well established, or where the Soviet Government is not exclusively recognized.

5. The soviets, as organs of government, are granted credit from state funds for three months upon the presentation of detailed budgets.

Source: Sobranie uzakonenii i rasporyazhenii raboche-krestyanskogo pravitelstva, 1917, No. 12, statya 180.
Translation: The Nation, New York, 28 December 1919, with the editor's modifications.

5. The Organization of Provincial Soviets
[5] January 1918, OS

The scheme of the general statutes of soviets of workers', soldiers', peasants', and Cossacks' deputies, as a representative organ, is needed as much in obscure places in our provinces as is the scheme of the soviet's departments and sub-departments ...

The statutes of the soviets may be divided into sections, covering: (1) the purpose of the organization of soviets; (2) the basis of representation; (3) the departments of the soviet; (4) elections to the presidium and executive committee; (5) the functions of the presidium; (6) the executive committee and its functions; (7) general sessions; (8) committees.

1. The purpose of the organization of the soviet

The soviet of workmen's, soldiers', peasant, and Cossack deputies is a sovereign state organ of revolutionary democracy, as well as the repository of governmental authority in the provinces. The soviet pursues the following objects:

(a) The organization of the labouring masses of workmen, peasants, soldiers, and Cossacks;
(b) The struggle against counter-revolutionary currents, the consolidation of the Soviet Republic and all the liberties gained by the October revolution.

2. The basis and order of representation in the soviets

(a) A soviet of workers', soldiers', peasant, and Cossack deputies is constituted of one or two representatives each of all workers', soldiers', peasant, and Cossack organizations (parties, trade unions, committees, etc.) in the towns, villages and settlements.
(b) The peasants elect two representatives from each town to the district soviet (a town soviet has one or two representatives from each settlement, village, or hamlet).
(c) The Cossacks elect two (or three) representatives from each village to the Regional Soviet of Workers', Soldiers', Peasant, and Cossack Deputies, and one representative each from a forepost (small settlement), hamlet, or small town to the village soviet. (In Cossack territories the peasant representation in the regional soviet is proportional, according to the village.)
(d) The workers and all the proletarian labouring masses in towns where the urban proletariat does not exceed 5,000 or 6,000 persons are represented on the following basis:

(1) Every enterprise employing 100 persons sends one representative.
(2) Enterprises employing from 100 to 200 persons send two representatives; those employing from 200 to 300 persons — three representatives, etc.
(3) Enterprises employing less than fifty persons, combine, if possible, with other small kindred enterprises and send a common representative to the soviet. Those unable to combine may send their representative independently.

(e) The soldiers of a local garrison (Cossacks, sailors) send to the soviet their representatives on the following principle: each company, squadron, command, etc., elects two representatives to the soviet; clerks, hospital attendants, horse reserves, and other small units send one representative each.

Addenda to paragraph 2. (1) Every member newly elected to the soviet must present a certificate from his constituents which is examined by the credentials committee; (2) if a member of the soviet deviates from the instructions of his constituents then the constituents have the right to recall him and elect another in his place; (3) each section (workers' section, soldiers', etc.) of the soviet has the right to co-opt into its membership experienced and needed workers to up to one-fifth of its entire membership. Persons added by co-option have the right of a consultative voice at general sessions of the soviet, in its committees and sections.

3. The sections of the soviet

(a) A soviet has four sections: one each for peasants, workers, soldiers, and Cossacks;

(b) Each section elects from its membership a presidium consisting of a chairman, two vice-chairmen, and two secretaries, and this presidium directs all the business of the section;

(c) Representation in the presidium is proportional to the membership of the given party groups.

4. The election of the presidium and executive committee

(a) The members in each section of the soviet elect a presidium, which is chosen at a general meeting by a universal, direct, equal and secret vote, in the proportions and numbers indicated in paragraph 3 (The sections of the soviet);

(b) The presidiums of all sections of the soviet constitute the general presidium of the soviet, which elects from among its members a general chairman of all sections, two vice-chairmen, and two secretaries;

(c) Besides the presidium, the general assembly of the soviet elects from its members an executive committee proportionate to the membership of each party group (not section); this is so arranged that the membership of the executive committee shall not exceed one-fourth of the entire membership of the soviet;

(d) The members of the presidium form a part of the membership of the executive committee on an equal basis with the other members.

5. The functions of the presidium

(a) The presidium is the directing organ of the entire soviet and decides independently all matters which cannot suffer delay;

(b) The presidium meets not less than four times a week;

(c) The presidium submits an account of its activity to the executive committee and the entire soviet, which have the right to recall and replace them at any time and period;

(d) The presidium must, in its work, abide strictly by the instructions of the executive committee and the general assembly.

6. The executive committee and its functions

(a) The executive committee of the soviet is an organ formed from among the members of the soviet (paragraph 4). The president, or one of the vice-presidents of the soviet, is the chairman of the executive committee (paragraph 4);

(b) All the current business of the soviet is decided and carried on by the executive committee, and only matters of particular importance are submitted for the decision of the general assembly of the soviet;

(c) Questions considered by the executive committee are passed or rejected by a relative majority of votes. On questions of extraordinary importance a minority report may be accepted, entered in the records, and passed to the general assembly;

(d) Questions are decided by an open vote, and only in matters of extraordinary importance, at the request of members of the executive committee, by secret ballot;

(e) A session of the executive committee is considered legal when not less than one-half of its membership is present;

(f) Members of the executive committee who for one reason or another cannot attend a session of the executive committee must notify the duty member of the executive committee to that effect not later than half an hour before the opening of the session;

(g) Members of the executive committee who have been absent from three sessions without sufficient reason are deprived of the right to vote at two sessions, and the presidium brings the matter to the notice of their constituents;

(h) The executive committee meets once a week (irrespective of special sessions);

(i) Special sessions to consider questions of extraordinary importance are called by the chairman or the vice-chairmen or by three members of the executive committee;

(j) Members of the executive committee must be notified of a special session by a summons not later than two hours before the session is due to begin;

(k) A special session is legal when any number of members is present;

(l) The sessions of the executive committee may be open or executive;

(m) Members of the executive committee, one from each section, take turns at duty in the reception rooms of the soviet.

7. The general sessions

(a) General sessions of the soviets are called by the presidium whenever the necessity arises, but not less than twice a month;

(b) General sessions may be regarded as legal when half of the entire membership of the soviet is present; special sessions are so when any number are present;

(c) All questions submitted for the consideration of the general assembly must first be approved either by the executive committee or by the presidium;

(d) A general session may also be called at the request of one-fifth of the membership of the soviet;

(e) Admission to the sessions of the soviet is by ticket only;

(f) The sessions may be open or executive by decision of the presidium or of the assembly itself.

8. Committees

(a) Committees are elected in each case by the general assembly, by the executive committee, or by the presidium;

(b) The membership of a committee is determined by the assembly;

(c) The chairman of each committee makes a report about the work of the committee to the general assembly of the soviet, the executive committee, and the presidium;

(d) Auditing committees, control committees, etc., concerned with the examination of the soviet's affairs are selected only by the general assembly of the soviet;

(e) Each committee has the right to co-opt independently learned persons with the privilege of a consultative voice.

> IV. [VL. ?] ULIANOV (LENIN) [President of the Council of People's Commissars].

Translation: The Nation, New York, 28 December 1919, with some terms modified by the editor.

6. Instruction on the Organization of Soviets of Workers', Soldiers' and Peasants' Deputies

Approved by the collegium of the People's Commissary for Internal Affairs, 9 January 1918, OS

On 9 January 1918, at the session of the collegium attached to the People's Commissary for Internal Affairs, instructions on the organization of soviets of workers', soldiers', and peasants' deputies were voted as follows:

In all soviets, in place of the old, outdated government institutions, the following departments or commissariats must be organized first:

1. An administration department, which is in charge of the domestic and foreign relations of the Republic and technically unites all the other departments.
2. A finance department, which has the duty of compiling the local budget, collecting local and state taxes, carrying out measures for the nationalization of the banks, administrating the People's Bank, controlling the disbursements of national funds, etc.
3. A Board of the National Economy, which organizes the manufacture of essential products of factory, mill, and home industries, determines the amount of raw materials and fuel required, obtains and distributes them, organizes and supplies agriculture, etc.
4. A department of land, whose duty is to make an exact survey of the land, forests, water and other resources, and their distribution for purposes of utilization.
5. A department of labour, which has to organize and unite trade unions, factory and mill committees, peasant associations, etc., and also create insurance organizations of all kinds.
6. A department of means of communication, whose duty is to take measures for the nationalization of the railways and steamship enterprises, direct this most important branch of the national economy, build new roads of local importance, etc.
7. A post, telegraph, and telephone department, which must aid and develop these state enterprises.
8. A public education department, which looks after the education and instruction of the population in and out of school, establishes new schools, kindergartens, universities, libraries, clubs, etc., carries out measures for the nationalization of printing-shops, the publication of necessary periodicals and books and their circulation among the population, etc.
9. A legal department, which has to liquidate the old courts, organize people's and arbitration courts, take charge of places of detention, reform them, etc.
10. A medical-sanitary department, whose duty is the supervision of sanitation and hygiene, the organization of medical aid which is accessible to all, the equipping of urban and rural settlements with sanitary facilities, etc.
11. A public estates department, whose duty is the regulation of the housing problem, supervision of confiscated and public buildings, the construction of new ones, etc.

NOTE. Soviets are advised to utilize the organizational apparatus of *zemstvo* and municipal institutions, with appropriate changes, when forming these departments.

At the same session the draft of a decree fixing the boundaries of provinces, districts, etc., was passed as follows:

1. Questions of changes of boundaries of provinces, districts, or townships are to be settled entirely by the local soviets of workers', soldiers', peasants', and poor peasants' deputies.
2. When parts of one province or territory are included in another, any technical questions and misunderstandings to arise are dealt with by mixed commissions of the interested provincial soviets or their congress.
3. A similar procedure is followed when the boundaries of one district or town are rectified at the expense of another.
4. Territories, provinces, districts, and towns may also be divided into parts, so as to form new administrative economic units.
5. Detailed data regarding all such changes are reported to the Commissar for Internal Affairs.

> President of the Council of People's Commissars, V. ULIANOV (V. LENIN).
> People's Commissars: PETROVSKY, A. SHLIAPNIKOV, V. TRUTOVSKY, M. URITSKY.
> Director of the Affairs of the Council of People's Commissars, BONCH-BRUYEVICH.
> Secretary, N. GORBUNOV.

Translation: The Nation, New York, 28 December 1919, with some terms modified by the editor.

7. The Constituent Assembly Dissolved
7 January 1918, *OS*

It was evident from the 'Theses on the Constituent Assembly' published in Pravda *in mid-December that the Bolsheviks were contemplating the dispersal of that body. When it met on 5 January, OS, the Bolsheviks and Left Social Revolutionaries, who commanded about 30 per cent of the votes, proposed that the Assembly pass a 'Declaration of the Rights of the Toiling and Exploited People', drafted by Lenin. This would have specifically limited its competence to working out the generalities of what was termed 'the socialist reconstruction of society'.[1] The refusal of the majority to accept this was the pretext for a Bolshevik walk-out. On the following day Red Guards refused to admit the delegates, and the Constituent Assembly ceased to exist: its power was formally assumed by the Third Congress of Soviets. The decree translated below was intended to be an official justification for this step.*

7. Decree on the Dissolution of the Constituent Assembly
Passed by the All-Russian Central Executive Committee, 7 January 1918, *OS*

At its very inception, the Russian revolution produced the soviets of workers', soldiers' and peasants' deputies as the only mass organization of all the working and exploited classes capable of giving leadership to the struggle of these classes for their complete political and economic emancipation.

Throughout the initial period of the Russian revolution the soviets grew in number, size and strength, their own experience disabusing them of the illusions regarding compromise with the bourgeoisie, opening their eyes to the fraudulence of the forms of bourgeois-democratic parliamentarism, and leading them to the conclusion that the emancipation of the oppressed classes was unthinkable unless they broke with these forms and with every kind of compromise. Such a break came with the October Revolution, with the transfer of power to the Soviets.

The Constituent Assembly, elected on the basis of lists drawn up before the October Revolution, was expressive of the old correlation of political forces, when the conciliators and Constitutional-Democrats were in power.

Voting at that time for candidates of the Socialist-Revolutionary Party, the people were not in a position to choose between the Right-Wing Socialist-Revolutionaries, supporters of the bourgeoisie, and the Left-Wing Socialist-

---

[1] The Declaration was incorporated, in a slightly amended form, in the 1918 constitution.

Revolutionaries, supporters of Socialism. Thus the Constituent Assembly, which was to have crowned the bourgeois parliamentary republic, was bound to stand in the way of the October Revolution and Soviet power.

The October Revolution, which gave power to the soviets and through them to the working and exploited classes, aroused frantic resistance on the part of the exploiters, and in putting down this resistance it fully revealed itself as the beginning of the socialist revolution.

The working classes learned through experience that old bourgeois parliamentarism had outlived its day, that it was utterly incompatible with the tasks of socialism, and that only class institutions (such as the soviets) and not national ones were capable of overcoming the resistance of the propertied classes and laying the foundations of socialist society.

Any renunciation of the sovereign power of the soviets, of the Soviet Republic won by the people, in favour of bourgeois parliamentarism and the Constituent Assembly would now be a step backwards and would cause a collapse of the entire October Workers' and Peasants' Revolution.

By virtue of generally known circumstances the Constituent Assembly, opening on 5 January, gave the majority to the Party of Right-Wing Socialist-Revolutionaries, the party of Kerensky, Avsentyev and Chernov. Naturally, this party refused to discuss the absolutely precise, clear-cut and unambiguous proposal of the supreme body of Soviet power, the Central Executive Committee of the Soviets, to recognize the programme of Soviet power, to recognize the Declaration of Rights of the Working and Exploited People, to recognize the October Revolution and Soviet power. By doing so the Constituent Assembly severed all ties with the Soviet Republic of Russia. The withdrawal from such a Constituent Assembly of the groups of Bolsheviks and Left-Wing Socialist-Revolutionaries, who now are in an indisputably vast majority in the soviets and enjoy the confidence of the workers and the majority of the peasants, was inevitable.

Outside the Constituent Assembly, the parties which have the majority there, the Right-Wing Socialist-Revolutionaries and the Mensheviks, are waging an open struggle against Soviet power, calling in their press for its overthrow and thereby objectively supporting the exploiters' resistance to the transition of land and factories into the hands of the working people.

Obviously, under such circumstances the remaining part of the Constituent Assembly can only serve as a cover for the struggle of the bourgeois counter-revolution to overthrow the power of the soviets.

In view of this, the Central Executive Committee resolves:

The Constituent Assembly is hereby dissolved.

Source: G. D. Obichkin, i drugie, *Dekrety sovetskoi vlasti*, Vol. I (Moscow, 1957), p. 335. *Translation*: Yuri Akhapkin, *First Decrees of Soviet Power* (Lawrence and Wishart, London, 1970), p. 74.

8. The Separation of the Church from the State and the School

20 January 1918, OS

The Bolsheviks had always viewed religion with profound hostility. Apart from their Marxist premises — which alone were sufficient to explain this — there was the fact that religion in Russia was an integral part of tsarist despotism, and a basically anti-communist force.

The law of 20 January 1918, which nationalized church property and deprived religious bodies of most of their former rights and privileges, was thus central to Bolshevik policy. It was a first step: a great deal of legislation was passed in the following months and years (see document 12) with the object of restricting freedom of worship as far as was practicable.

It is hardly coincidental that the day before this decree was passed Tikhon, the Orthodox Patriarch of Moscow and All Russia, pronounced an anathema against the Bolsheviks in general.

8. Decree on the Freedom of Conscience, and of Church and Religious Societies

Approved by the Council of People's Commissars, 20 January 1918, OS

1. The Church is separated from the state.
2. Within the confines of the Republic it shall be prohibited to issue any local by-laws or regulations restricting or limiting freedom of conscience, or establishing privileges or preferential rights of any kind based on the religious creed of citizens.
3. Every citizen may profess any religious belief, or profess no belief at all. All restrictions of rights, involved by professing one or another religious belief, or by professing no belief at all, are cancelled and void.

> NOTE: All reference to the professing or non-professing of religious creeds by citizens shall be expunged from all official documents.

4. State or other public functions binding in law shall not be accompanied by the performance of religious rites or ceremonies.
5. Free performance of religious rites is permissible as long as it does not disturb public order, or interfere with the rights of the citizens of the Soviet Republic. The local authorities shall be entitled in such cases to adopt all necessary measures for maintenance of public order and safety.
6. Nobody is entitled to refuse to perform his duties as a citizen on the basis of his religious belief. Exceptions to this rule, on the condition that one civic

duty be replaced by another, may be granted in each individual case by the verdict of the People's Court.

7. The official taking or administering of religious oaths is cancelled. In necessary cases merely a solemn promise is given.

8. Births, marriages, and deaths are to be registered and solemnized solely by civic (secular) authorities: marriage and birth registration offices.

9. The School is separated from the Church. Instruction in any religious creed or belief shall be prohibited in all state, public, and also private educational establishments in which general instruction is given. Citizens may give or receive religious instruction in a private way.

10. All church and religious associations are subject to the ordinary legislation concerning private associations and unions. They shall not enjoy special privileges, nor receive any subsidies from the state or from local autonomous or self-governing institutions.

11. Compulsory collection of imposts and taxes in favour of church and religious associations, also measures of compulsion or punishment adopted by such associations in respect to their members, shall not be permitted.

12. No church or religious associations have the right to own property. They do not possess the rights of juridical persons.

13. The property of all church and religious associations existing in Russia is pronounced the property of the People. Buildings and objects especially used for the purposes of worship shall be let, free of charge, to the respective religious associations, by resolution of the local, or central state authorities.

> Signed: President of the Soviet Commissars, ULIANOV (LENIN).
> People's Commissars: PODVOISKII, ALGASOV, TRUTOV-SKII, SHLIKHTER, PROSHIN, MENZHINSKII, SHLIA-PNIKOV, and PETROVSKII.
> Director of Affairs of the Soviet of Commissars, VL. BONCH-BRUEVICH.

Source : G. D. Obichkin, i drugie, *Dekrety sovetskoi vlasti*, Vol. I (Moscow, 1957), p. 373.
Translation : B. Szczesniak, *The Russian Revolution and Religion*, 1917–25 (University of Notre Dame Press, Paris, 1959), p. 34.

9. Large-Scale Industry Nationalized

28 June 1918

The nationalization of Soviet industry was an untidy process involving dozens of decrees at the RSFSR level alone. Nationalization supplemented the establishment of the Supreme Economic Council and the committees for workers' control.

First to be nationalized were the banks; these were brought under a state monopoly on 14 December 1917, OS. The most comprehensive measure was, however, the decree of 28 June 1918, which nationalized all the main branches of industry. By the end of the year all important concerns had been taken out of private hands.

This has remained a central characteristic of Soviet government. Even during the NEP period of the 'twenties the private and co-operative sector, under temporary reprieve, was contributing only about 8 per cent of the value of Soviet national industrial production.

9. On the Nationalization of Enterprises in a Number of Industries, Railway Transport Enterprises, Public Utilities, and Steam Mills

Decree of the Council of People's Commissars of 28 June 1918

In order to overcome economic dislocation and food shortages, and to consolidate the dictatorship of the working class and the village poor, the Council of People's Commissars has resolved:

I. To declare the following industrial and commercial-industrial enterprises situated on the territory of the Soviet Republic, with all their capital and properties in whatever form, the property of the Russian Socialist Federative Soviet Republic:

In the mining industry
In the metallurgical and metalworking industries
In the textile industry
In the electrical engineering industry
In the timber and woodworking industry
In the tobacco industry
In the rubber industry
In the glass and ceramic industry
In the leather and shoe-making industry
In the cement industry

Steam mills
Public utilities
Railway transport
In other industries

[*This heading covers thirty-two clauses in all — Ed.*]

II. The appropriate departments of the Supreme Economic Council are instructed urgently to organize management of the nationalized enterprises, with observance of all the previously issued relevant decrees and under the general guidance of the presidium of the Supreme Economic Council.

With respect to the enterprises mentioned in Section I, Paragraph 24 of this Decree (steam mills), this commission is entrusted to the Commissariat for Food Supply with full observance of all the previously issued decrees on the management of nationalized enterprises.

With respect to the enterprises mentioned in Section I, Paragraph 25 of this Decree (public utilities), the same commission is entrusted, on the same condition, to the local soviets of workers' and peasants' deputies.

With respect to the enterprises mentioned in Section I, Paragraph 26 of this Decree (railways and subsidiary lines), the same commission is entrusted to the Commissariat of Railways, subject to ultimate approval by the Council of People's Commissars.

III. Pending a special decision of the Supreme Economic Council regarding each particular enterprise, the enterprises declared under this Decree to be the property of the Russian Soviet Federative Socialist Republic are regarded as leased to their former owners gratis; their boards and former owners continue to finance them and receive profits in the usual manner.

IV. From the moment of the issue of this Decree, the board members, directors and other executives of nationalized enterprises are accountable to the Soviet Republic for their safety and normal operation.

Those who abandon their offices without the consent of the appropriate agencies of the supreme Economic Council, or inexcusably mismanage the affairs of the enterprise, not only answer to the Republic with all their property but will be prosecuted in the courts of the Republic as for a grave criminal offence.

V. The entire office, technical and operative personnel of a nationalized enterprise, as well as the directors, board members and other executives, are declared to be in the service of the Soviet Socialist Federative Republic, and are paid according to the rates that existed prior to nationalization, out of the profits and working capital of the enterprise.

Members of the technical and managerial personnel of nationalized enterprises who abandon their offices are answerable to a revolutionary tribunal, with all the severity of the law.

VI. The personal means of board members, shareholders and owners of nationalized enterprises are sequestered until the relationship of the sums involved to the working capital and resources of the enterprises is ascertained.

VII. The boards of all nationalized enterprises are instructed to draw up without delay balance-sheets as on 1 July 1918.

VIII. The Supreme Economic Council is instructed to work out in the shortest time possible, and to dispatch to all nationalized enterprises, detailed instructions on the organization of management and on the tasks of the workers' organizations stemming from this decree.

IX. Enterprises belonging to consumers' co-operative societies and partnerships and their associations are not subject to conversion into the property of the Republic.

X. This Decree becomes effective from the day of its signing. Moscow, 28 June 1918.

> Chairman of the Council of People's Commissars, V. ULYANOV (LENIN).
> People's Commissars, TSYURUPA, NOGIN.
> Business Manager of the Council of People's Commissars, V. BONCH-BRUYEVICH.
> Secretary of the Council, N. GORBUNOV.

Source: G. D. Obichkin, i drugie, *Dekrety sovetskoi vlasti*, Vol. II (Moscow, 1959), p. 498.

Translation: Yu. Akhapkin, *First Decrees of Soviet Power*, (Lawrence and Wishart, London, 1970), p. 147.

10. The 1918 RSFSR Constitution

10 *July* 1918

This constitution was approved by the Fifth All-Union Congress of Soviets on 10 July 1918. It was worked out by a commission under the direction of Ia. Sverdlov and I. Stalin, and examined by the Central Committee on 3 July, prior to its submission to the Congress. It bears a hasty and improvised character, and, significantly, Lenin is said to have shown little interest in it. It may have been intended only as a stop-gap until, as many Bolsheviks believed, political developments would make states and constitutions obsolete. As an exposition of state aims and structure it is, of course, far removed from liberal Western traditions.

10. Constitution (Fundamental Law) of the RSFSR Adopted by the Fifth All-Russia Congress of Soviets

Adopted by the decree of the Fifth All-Russia Congress of Soviets, 10 July 1918

The Declaration of Rights of the Working and Exploited People, approved by the Third All-Russia Congress of Soviets in January 1918, together with the constitution of the Soviet Republic approved by the Fifth Congress, make up the single fundamental law of the Russian Socialist Federative Soviet Republic.

This fundamental law becomes effective from the moment of its publication in final form in *Izvestia Vserossiiskogo Tsentralnogo Ispolnitelnogo Komiteta*. It shall be published by all local organs of Soviet government and prominently displayed in all Soviet institutions.

The Fifth Congress instructs the People's Commissariat for Public Education to introduce in all schools and other educational establishments of the Russian Republic, without exception, the study of the basic provisions of the present constitution, as well as their explanation and interpretation.

Part One: Declaration of Rights of the Working and Exploited People[1]

CHAPTER ONE

1. Russia is hereby proclaimed a Republic of Soviets of Workers', Soldiers' and Peasants' Deputies. All power, centrally and locally, is vested in these Soviets.

[1] The Declaration was published separately in almost identical form on 12 January 1918, OS. The sections are here numbered as in the constitution.

2. The Russian Soviet Republic is established on the principle of a free union of free nations, as a federation of Soviet national republics.

CHAPTER TWO

3. Its fundamental aim being abolition of all exploitation of man by man, complete elimination of the division of society into classes, merciless suppression of the exploiters, socialist organization of society, and victory of socialism in all countries, the Third All-Russia Congress of Soviets of Workers', Soldiers' and Peasants' Deputies further resolves:

(a) Pursuant to the socialization of land, private land ownership is hereby abolished, and all land is proclaimed the property of the entire people and turned over to the working people without any redemption, on the principles of egalitarian land tenure.

(b) All forests, mineral wealth and waters of national importance, as well as all live and dead stock, model estates and agricultural enterprises are proclaimed the property of the nation.

(c) The Soviet laws on workers' control and on the Supreme Economic Council are hereby confirmed in order to guarantee the power of the working people over the exploiters and as a first step towards the complete conversion of factories, mines, railways and other means of production and transportation into the property of the Soviet Workers' and Peasants' Republic.

(d) The Third Congress of Soviets regards as a first blow at international banking, financial capital, the Soviet law on the annulment of loans negotiated by the governments of the tsar, the landlords and the bourgeoisie and expresses confidence that Soviet power will be advancing steadfastly along this road until the complete victory of an international workers' uprising against the rule of capital.

(e) The conversion of all banks into the property of the workers' and peasants' state is hereby confirmed as a prerequisite of the emancipation of the working people from the rule of capital.

(f) In order to eliminate parasitic sections of society, universal labour conscription is hereby instituted.

(g) To ensure the sovereign power of the working people and to rule out any possibility of restoration of the power of the exploiters, the arming of the working people, the creation of a socialist Red Army of workers and peasants, and the complete disarming of the propertied classes are hereby decreed.

CHAPTER THREE

4. Expressing firm determination to wrest mankind from the clutches of finance capital and imperialism, which have in this most criminal of wars drenched the world in blood, the Third Congress of Soviets unreservedly

endorses Soviet policy of denouncing the secret treaties, organizing most extensive fraternization with the workers and peasants of the combatant armies and achieving at all costs by revolutionary means a democratic peace for the working people, without annexations of indemnities, on the basis of free self-determination of nations.

5. With the same aim in view, the Third Congress of Soviets insists on a complete break with the barbarous policy of bourgeois civilization, which has built the prosperity of the exploiters in a few chosen nations through the enslavement of hundreds of millions of working people in Asia, in the colonies in general, and in small countries.

6. The Third Congress of Soviets supports the policy of the Council of People's Commissars which has proclaimed the complete independence of Finland, commenced the withdrawal of troops from Persia, and proclaimed freedom of self-determination for Armenia.

CHAPTER FOUR

7. The Third All-Russia Congress of Soviets holds that now, in the hour of the people's resolute struggle against the exploiters, there should be no room for exploiters in any governmental agency. Power must belong fully and exclusively to the working people and their plenipotentiary representatives — the soviets of workers', soldiers' and peasants' deputies.

8. At the same time, endeavouring to create a genuinely free and voluntary, and therefore all the more firm and stable, union of the working classes of all the nations of Russia, the Third Congress of Soviets confines itself to promulgating the fundamental principles of a federation of Soviet republics of Russia, leaving it to the workers and peasants of each nation to decide independently at their own representative congresses of soviets whether they wish to participate in the federal government and in the other federal Soviet institutions, and on what terms.

Part Two: General Provisions of the Constitution of the RSFSR

CHAPTER FIVE

9. The main objective of the constitution of the Russian Socialist Federative Soviet Republic, designed for the present transitional period, is to establish the dictatorship of the urban and rural proletariat and the poorest peasantry in the form of a powerful All-Russia Soviet Government, with a view to completely suppressing the bourgeoisie, abolishing exploitation of man by man, and establishing socialism, under which there will be neither division into classes nor state power.

10. The Russian Republic is a free socialist society of all the working people of Russia. All power in the Russian Socialist Federative Soviet Republic belongs to the entire working population of the country united in urban and rural soviets.

11. The soviets of regions with a distinct mode of living and national composition can unite in autonomous regional unions at the head of which, as at the head of all regional unions that can be eventually formed, stand regional congresses of Soviets and their executive agencies.

These autonomous regional unions form, on a federal basis, component parts of the Russian Socialist Federative Soviet Republic.

12. Supreme power in the Russian Socialist Federative Soviet Republic is exercised by the All-Russia Congress of Soviets, and in the intervals between Congresses by the All-Russia Central Executive Committee.

13. In order to ensure genuine freedom of conscience for the working people, the church is separated from the State, and the school from the church: and freedom of religious and anti-religious propaganda is recognized for all citizens.

14. In order to ensure genuine freedom of expression for the working people, the Russian Socialist Federative Soviet Republic abolishes the dependence of the press on capital, and places at the disposal of the working class and the poor peasantry all the technical and material requisites for the publication of newspapers, pamphlets, books and all other printed matter, and guarantees their unhindered circulation throughout the country.

15. In order to ensure genuine freedom of assembly for the working people, the Russian Socialist Federative Soviet Republic, recognizing the right of citizens of the Soviet Republic freely to hold assemblies, meetings, processions, etc., places at the disposal of the working class and the poor peasantry all buildings suitable for the holding of public gatherings, complete with furnishing, lighting and heating.

16. In order to ensure genuine freedom of association for the working people, the Russian Socialist Federative Soviet Republic, having destroyed the economic and political rule of the propertied classes and thereby removed all the obstacles which heretofore, in bourgeois society, prevented the workers and peasants from enjoying freedom of organization and action, renders material and all other assistance to the workers and poorest peasants for purposes of their association and organization.

17. In order to ensure access to knowledge for the working people, the Russian Socialist Federative Soviet Republic makes its aim to give the workers and poorest peasants complete all-round and free education.

18. The Russian Socialist Federative Soviet Republic declares labour to be the duty of all citizens of the Republic, and proclaims the slogan: 'He who does not work, neither shall he eat!'

19. In order to safeguard the gains of the great workers' and peasants' revolution, the Russian Socialist Federative Republic declares defence of the socialist Fatherland to be the duty of all the citizens of the Republic and introduces universal military service. The honourable right of bearing arms in defence of the revolution is granted only to working people; non-working elements are enlisted for other military duties.

20. Proceeding from the principle of solidarity of the working people of all nations, the Russian Socialist Federative Soviet Republic grants full political rights of Russian citizens to foreigners residing in the territory of the Russian Republic for purposes of employment, and belonging to the working class or to the peasantry not employing the labour of others: and it empowers the local soviets to grant to such foreigners, without any cumbersome formalities, Russian citizenship rights.

21. The Russian Socialist Federative Soviet Republic grants the right of asylum to all foreigners subjected to persecution for political and religious crimes.

22. The Russian Socialist Federative Soviet Republic, recognizing the equality of rights of all citizens, irrespective of their race or nationality, declares the establishment or toleration on this basis of any privileges or advantages, or any oppression of national minorities or restriction of their equality, to be contraventions of the fundamental laws of the Republic.

23. Guided by the interests of the working class as a whole, the Russian Socialist Federative Soviet Republic deprives individuals and groups of rights which they utilize to the detriment of the socialist revolution.

Part Three: The Structure of Soviet Government

A. Organization of the central authority

CHAPTER SIX: THE ALL-RUSSIA CONGRESS OF SOVIETS OF WORKERS', PEASANTS', COSSACKS' AND RED ARMY MEN'S DEPUTIES

24. The All-Russia Congress of Soviets is the supreme authority of the Russian Socialist Federative Soviet Republic.

25. The All-Russia Congress of Soviets is composed of representatives of urban soviets on the basis of one deputy for every 25,000 electors, and representatives of *gubernia* congresses of soviets on the basis of one deputy for every 125,000 of the population.

> NOTE 1. In the event of a *gubernia* congress of soviets not preceding the All-Russia Congress, delegates to the latter are sent directly by *uyezd* congresses.
> NOTE 2. In the event of a regional congress of soviets directly preceding the All-Russia Congress, delegates to the latter can be sent by the regional congress.

26. The All-Russia Congress of Soviets is convened by the All-Russia Central Executive Committee at least twice a year.

27. An extraordinary All-Russia Congress of Soviets is convened by the All-Russia Central Executive Committee on its own initiative, or on the

demand of the soviets of localities inhabited by at least one-third of the population of the Republic.

28. The All-Russia Congress of Soviets elects the All-Russia Central Executive Committee, to consist of not more than 200 members.

29. The All-Russia Central Executive Committee is fully accountable to the All-Russia Congress of Soviets.

30. In the intervals between Congresses the All-Russia Central Executive Committee is the supreme authority of the Republic.

CHAPTER SEVEN: THE ALL–RUSSIA CENTRAL EXECUTIVE COMMITTEE

31. The All-Russia Central Executive Committee is the highest legislative, administrative and supervisory body of the Russian Socialist Federative Soviet Republic.

32. The All-Russia Central Executive Committee gives general directives for the activity of the Workers' and Peasants' Government and all organs of Soviet power in the country; unites and co-ordinates legislative and administrative activities, and supervises the implementation of the Soviet constitution and of the decisions of All-Russia Congresses of Soviets and the central bodies of Soviet power.

33. The All-Russia Central Executive Committee examines and approves draft decrees and other proposals submitted by the Council of People's Commissars or by separate departments, and issues its own decrees and ordinances.

34. The All-Russia Central Executive Committee convenes the All-Russia Congress of Soviets, to which it submits an account of its activity and reports on general policy and particular matters.

35. The All-Russian Central Executive Committee appoints the Council of People's Commissars for general management of the affairs of the Russian Socialist Federative Soviet Republic, and departments (People's Commissariats) to be in charge of particular branches of the administration.

36. The members of the All-Russia Central Executive Committee work in the departments (People's Commissariats) or carry out special commissions of the All-Russia Central Executive Committee.

CHAPTER EIGHT: THE COUNCIL OF PEOPLE'S COMMISSARS

37. The Council of People's Commissars exercises general management of the affairs of the Russian Socialist Federative Soviet Republic.

38. In pursuance of this task the Council of People's Commissars issues decrees, ordinances, instructions and generally takes what measures are necessary to ensure the proper course of life of the State.

39. The Council of People's Commissars immediately notifies the All-Russia Central Executive Committee of all its orders and decisions.

40. The All-Russia Central Executive Committee has the right to cancel or suspend any order or decision of the Council of People's Commissars.

41. All decisions and orders of the Council of People's Commissars which are of major general political importance are submitted to the All-Russia Central Executive Committee for consideration and approval.

NOTE. Urgent measures can be taken by the Council of People's Commissars directly.

42. Members of the Council of People's Commissars head the People's Commissariats.

43. Eighteen People's Commissariats are formed: (a) Foreign Affairs; (b) Military Affairs; (c) Maritime Affairs; (d) Interior; (e) Justice; (f) Labour; (g) Social Security; (h) Public Education; (i) Post and Telegraph; (j) Nationalities Affairs; (k) Finance; (l) Transport; (m) Agriculture; (n) Trade and Industry; (o) Food Supply; (p) State Control; (q) the Supreme Economic Council; (r) Public Health.

44. Under the chairmanship of every People's Commissar a board is constituted whose members are confirmed by the Council of People's Commissars.

45. The People's Commissar has the right personally to take decisions on all matters that come within the competence of his commissariat. In the event of its disagreement with a decision of the People's Commissar the board can, without suspending the implementation of the decision, appeal against it to the Council of People's Commissars or the Presidium of the All-Russia Central Executive Committee.

The same right of appeal belongs to individual members of the board.

46. The Council of People's Commissars is fully accountable to the All-Russia Congress of Soviets and the All-Russia Central Executive Committee.

47. The People's Commissars and the boards of the People's Commissariats are fully accountable to the Council of People's Commissars and the All-Russia Central Executive Committee.

48. The rank of People's Commissar is given exclusively to members of the Council of People's Commissars, which manages the general affairs of the Russian Socialist Federative Soviet Republic, and cannot be conferred on any other representative of Soviet government either in the centre or in the provinces.

CHAPTER NINE: THE JURISDICTION OF THE ALL-RUSSIA CONGRESS OF SOVIETS AND THE ALL-RUSSIA CENTRAL EXECUTIVE COMMITTEE

49. Within the jurisdiction of the All-Russia Congress of Soviets and the Central Executive Committee come all matters of State importance, viz:

(a) Approval and amendment of the Constitution of the Russian Socialist Federative Soviet Republic.

(*b*) General guidance of the foreign and domestic policy of the Russian Socialist Federative Soviet Republic.

(*c*) Delimitation and modification of frontiers, as well as alienation of parts of the territory of the Russian Socialist Federative Soviet Republic or of rights belonging to it.

(*d*) Delimitation of the boundaries and spheres of jurisdiction of the regional unions of soviets forming part of the Russian Socialist Federative Soviet Republic, as well as settlement of disputes between them.

(*e*) Admission of new members into the Russian Socialist Federative Soviet Republic and confirmation of secession of parts of the Russian Federation.

(*f*) General determination of the administrative divisions of the territory of the Russian Socialist Federative Soviet Republic, and confirmation of regional formations.

(*g*) Establishment and modification of the system of weights and measures and the monetary system on the territory of the Russian Socialist Federative Soviet Republic.

(*h*) Relations with foreign states, declaration of war and conclusion of peace.

(*i*) Contracting and granting of loans, conclusion of customs and trade treaties and financial agreements.

(*j*) Determination of the fundamentals and the general plan of the national economy and its branches on the territory of the Russian Socialist Federative Soviet Republic.

(*k*) Approval of the budget of the Russian Socialist Federative Soviet Republic.

(*l*) Establishment of federal taxes and duties.

(*m*) Definition of the basic principles of organization of the armed forces of the Russian Socialist Federative Soviet Republic.

(*n*) Federal legislation, the judicial system and judicial procedure, civil and criminal legislation, etc.

(*o*) Appointment and dismissal of individual members of the Council of People's Commissars and of the Council of People's Commissars as a whole, as well as confirmation of the Chairman of the Council of People's Commissars.

(*p*) General regulations on the acquisition and loss of Russian citizenship rights and on the rights of foreigners on the territory of the Republic.

(*q*) The right of amnesty, general and partial.

50. In addition to the matters listed above, the All-Russian Congress of Soviets and the All-Russia Central Executive Committee decide all questions which they find coming within their competence.

51. It is the exclusive prerogative of the All-Russian Congress of Soviets to:

(*a*) define and amend the basic principles of the Soviet constitution;
(*b*) ratify peace treaties.

52. The All-Russia Central Executive Committee may decide matters indicated in paragraphs (*c*) and (*h*) of Article 49 only when an All-Russian Congress of Soviets cannot be convened.

B. Organization of Local Soviet Authority

CHAPTER TEN: CONGRESSES OF SOVIETS

53. Congresses of soviets are composed as follows:

(*a*) *Oblast* (regional) congresses — of representatives of city soviets and *uyezd* congresses, on the basis of one delegate per 25,000 residents, and from cities, one delegate per 5,000 electors, with not more than 500 delegates from the region as a whole; or of representatives of *gubernia* congresses of soviets, elected on the same basis, if such congresses directly precede the regional congress.

(*b*) *Gubernia* (area) congresses — of representatives of city soviets and *volost* congresses, on the basis of one delegate per 10,000 residents and from cities, one deputy per 2,000 electors, with not more than 300 delegates from the *gubernia* (area) as a whole. If *uyezd* congresses of soviets directly precede the *gubernia* congress, elections are conducted on the same basis, by *uyezd* rather than *volost* congresses.

(*c*) *Uyezd* (district) congresses — of representatives of village soviets, on the basis of one delegate per 1,000 residents, with not more than 300 delegates from the *uyezd* (district) as a whole.

(*d*) *Volost* congresses — of representatives of all village soviets of the *volost*, on the basis of one delegate for every ten members of a soviet.

NOTE 1. *Uyezd* congresses are attended by representatives of the soviets of towns whose population does not exceed 10,000; village soviets of localities with a population of less than 1,000 unite to elect delegates to the *uyezd* congress.

NOTE 2. Village soviets having less than ten members send to the *volost* congress one representative each.

54. Congresses of soviets are convened by the respective local executive bodies of Soviet authority (executive committees) at their discretion, or on the demand of the soviets of localities accounting for not less than one-third of the population of the given territorial unit: but in any event at least twice a year in a region, once in every three months in a *gubernia* or *uyezd*, and once a month in a *volost*.

55. The region, *gubernia*, *uyezd* or *volost* congress of soviets elects its executive committee, to consist of not more than: (*a*) 25 members in a region or

gubernia; (*b*) 20 in an *uyezd*, and (*c*) 10 in a *volost*. The executive committee is fully accountable to the congress of soviets that elected it.

56. Within the boundaries of its region, *gubernia*, *uyezd* or *volost*, the congress of soviets is the highest authority; in the intervals between congresses this authority is vested in the executive committee.

CHAPTER ELEVEN: SOVIETS OF DEPUTIES

57. The soviets of deputies are composed as follows:

(*a*) In cities — on the basis of one deputy per 1,000 of the population, but with not less than 50 and not more than 1,000 members.

(*b*) In rural localities (villages, Cossack settlements, towns with less than 10,000 residents, auls, hamlets, etc.) — on the basis of one deputy per 100 of the population, but with not less than three and not more than 50 deputies per locality.

The term of office of deputies is three months.

Note. In those rural localities where this is recognized as practicable, matters of administration are decided directly by a general meeting of the electors.

58. For day-to-day work, the soviets of deputies elect, from among their members, executive bodies (executive committees) consisting of not more than five members in villages, and on the basis of one member per fifty deputies, but with not less than three and not more than fifteen members, in cities (not more than forty members in Petersburg and Moscow). The executive committee is fully accountable to the Soviet which elected it.

59. Sessions of the soviet of deputies are convened by the executive committee at its discretion, or on the demand of not less than half of the deputies to the soviet: but at least once a week in cities and twice a week in rural areas.

60. Within the boundaries of the given locality the soviet or, in the event envisaged in Article 57 (Note), the general meeting of electors, is the highest authority.

CHAPTER TWELVE: THE JURISDICTION OF LOCAL BODIES
OF SOVIET RULE

61. The regional, *gubernia*, *uyezd* and *volost* bodies of Soviet rule and the soviets of deputies:

(*a*) Put into effect all decisions of the corresponding higher bodies of soviet rule;

(*b*) Take all measures to promote the cultural and economic development of the given territory;

(*c*) Decide all questions of purely local importance (for the given territory);

(*d*) Co-ordinate all soviet activity within the boundaries of the given territory.

62. The congress of soviets and their executive bodies have the right of control over the activities of the local soviets (i.e. those of regions have the right of control over all the soviets of the given region; those of *gubernii*, over all the soviets of the given *gubernia*, with the exception of city soviets not forming parts of *uyezd* congresses, etc.); the regional and *gubernia* congresses and their executive committees have, in addition, the right to cancel decisions of the soviets functioning in their localities, notifying, in the most important instances, the central Soviet authority.

63. To ensure fulfilment of the tasks devolving on the organs of Soviet authority, city and village soviets and regional, *gubernia*, *uyezd* and *volost* executive committees set up corresponding departments and appoint their heads.

Part Four: Active and Passive Suffrage

CHAPTER THIRTEEN

64. The right to elect and to be elected to soviets is enjoyed, irrespective of religion, nationality, sex, domicile, etc. by the following citizens of the Russian Socialist Federative Soviet Republic who have reached the age of eighteen by polling day:

(*a*) All those who earn a living by productive and socially useful labour (as well as persons engaged in housekeeping which enables the former to work productively), viz. wage and salaried workers of all groups and categories engaged in industry, trade, agriculture, etc. and peasants and Cossack farmers who do not employ hired labour for profit;
(*b*) Soldiers of the Soviet army and navy;
(*c*) Citizens belonging to categories listed in Paragraphs (*a*) and (*b*) of the present article who have been to any degree incapacitated.

NOTE 1. The local soviets may, subject to approval by the central authority, lower the age limit established in the present article.
NOTE 2. As far as resident foreigners are concerned, active and passive suffrage is enjoyed by persons indicated in Article 20 (Part Two, Chapter V).

65. The right to elect and to be elected is denied to the following persons, even if they belong to one of the categories listed above:

(*a*) Persons who employ hired labour for profit;
(*b*) Persons living on unearned income, such as interest on capital, profits from enterprises, receipts from property, etc.;
(*c*) Private traders and commercial middle-men;

(*d*) Monks and ministers of religion;

(*e*) Employees and agents of the former police, the special corps of gendarmerie and the secret political police department, as well as members of the former imperial family;

(*f*) Persons declared insane by legal proceeding, as well as persons in ward;

(*g*) Persons condemned for pecuniary and infamous crimes to terms established by law or by a court decision.

CHAPTER FOURTEEN: THE CONDUCT OF ELECTIONS

66. Elections are held, according to established customs, on days appointed by local soviets.

67. Elections are conducted in the presence of an electoral commission and a representative of the local soviet.

68. In instances when the presence of a representative of Soviet authority is technically impossible, he is replaced by the electoral commission chairman or, in the absence of the latter, by the chairman of the electoral assembly.

69. The proceedings and results of the election are recorded in a minute signed by the members of the electoral commission and the representative of the soviet.

70. The detailed procedure for the conduct of elections, and for the participation in them of trade unions and other workers' organizations, is determined by the local soviets in keeping with instructions issued by the All-Russia Central Executive Committee.

CHAPTER FIFTEEN: VERIFICATION AND REVOCATION OF ELECTION RETURNS: RECALL OF DEPUTIES

71. All material pertaining to the conduct of elections is forwarded to the respective soviet.

72. The soviet appoints a credentials committee to verify the results of the elections.

73. The credentials committee reports to the soviet on its findings.

74. The soviet decides the question of confirming disputed candidates.

75. Should the soviet reject a candidate, it appoints re-elections.

76. Should the elections as a whole be found faulty, the question of quashing them is decided by the higher body of soviet rule.

77. The final instance for quashing elections to soviets is the All-Russia Central Executive Committee.

78. The electors who have sent a deputy to the soviet have the right to recall him at any time, and to hold new elections, in keeping with the general rules.

Part Five: Budgetary Law

CHAPTER SIXTEEN

79. The main objective of the fiscal policy of the Russian Socialist Federative Soviet Republic in the current transitional period of the dictatorship of the working people is expropriation of the bourgeoisie and preparation of conditions for the universal equality of the citizens of the Republic in the sphere of production and distribution of values. It is therefore aimed at placing at the disposal of the organs of Soviet power all the means necessary for satisfying the local and national needs of the Soviet Republic, in the pursuit of which tasks it will not stop at invading the sphere of the right of private ownership.

80. The state revenues and expenditures of the Russian Socialist Federative Soviet Republic are united in the state budget.

81. The All-Russian Congress of Soviets or the All-Russia Central Executive Committee determine which revenues and duties accrue to the state budget and which are placed at the disposal of the local soviets, and establish the limits of taxation.

82. The soviets collect taxes and rates for exclusively local economic needs. The requirements of the state as a whole are met out of resources allocated by the State Treasury.

83. No expenditures can be made out of the resources of the State Treasury unless provided for in the state budget, or without a special decision of the central authority

84. To meet needs of national importance, local soviets are allotted credits by the appropriate People's Commissariats out of State Treasury funds.

85. All State Treasury credits, and credits approved for local needs, are expanded by soviets strictly as provided for in their budgets, and cannot be used for other purposes without a special decision of the All-Russian Central Executive Committee and the Council of People's Commissars.

86. Local soviets draw up half-yearly and yearly estimates of revenues and expenditures for local needs. The estimates of village and *volost* soviets and soviets of cities participating in *uyezd* congresses, and those of the *uyezd* organs of Soviet power, are approved by the respective *gubernia* and *oblast* congresses or their executive committees; the estimates of city, *gubernia* and regional bodies of Soviet power are approved by the All-Russia Central Executive Committee and the Council of People's Commissars.

87. Should the need arise for expenditures insufficiently provided for in the estimates, or not provided for at all, the soviets apply for additional allocations to the respective People's Commissariats.

88. In the event of local resources proving insufficient to satisfy local needs, the issue of subsidies or loans to local soviets necessary to cover urgent expenditures is authorized by the All-Russia Central Executive Committee and the Council of People's Commissars.

Part Six: The Arms and the Flag of the Russian Socialist Federative Soviet Republic

89. The Arms of the Russian Socialist Federative Soviet Republic consist of a sickle and a hammer with their handles crossed, pointing downwards, gold upon a red field in the sun's rays, and surrounded by a wreath of ears of grain, with the inscriptions:

(*a*) 'Russian Socialist Federative Soviet Republic', and
(*b*) 'Proletarians of all Countries, Unite!'

90. The flag and ensign of the Russian Socialist Federative Soviet Republic is of red cloth with the gold letters 'RSFSR' or the words 'Russian Socialist Federative Soviet Republic' in the left upper corner near the staff.

> Chairman of the Fifth All-Russia Congress of Soviets and of the All-Russia Central Executive Committee, Y. A. SVERDLOV.
>
> Members of the Presidium of the All-Russia Central Executive Committee, G. I. TEODOROVICH, F. A. ROZIN, A. K. MITROFANOV, K. G. MAXIMOV.
>
> Secretary of the All-Russia Central Executive Committee, V. A. AVANESOV.

Source: G. D. Obichkin, i drugie, *Dekrety sovetskoi vlasti*, Vol. I (Moscow, 1957), p. 341; Vol. II (Moscow, 1959), p. 550.
Translation: Yuri Akhapkin, *First Decrees of Soviet Power* (Lawrence and Wishart, London, 1970), pp. 76 ff., 154 ff.

11. The 1924 USSR Constitution

13 January 1924

The formation of a Union of Soviet Socialist Republics was first formally proposed on 13 December 1922 at the First Transcaucasian Congress of Soviets, comprising Georgia, Armenia and Azerbaijan. On 30 December 1922 these republics, together with the RSFSR, the Ukraine and White Russia, sent their representatives to the First All-Union Congress of Soviets. (Delegates from the border areas had, however, attended sessions of the All-Russian Congresses of Soviets from 1921.) This constitution was approved by the VTsIK in mid-1923, on the instructions of the Twelfth Party Congress, and ratified by the Second All-Union Congress of Soviets on 31 January 1924. It was in many respects based on the RSFSR constitution of 1918, but contained significant additions, including a chapter on the judiciary.

11. Fundamental Law (Constitution) of the Union of Soviet Socialist Republics

Ratified by the decree of the Second Congress of Soviets, USSR, 13 January 1924

Part I: Declaration

Since the foundation of the Soviet Republics, the states of the world have been divided into two camps; the camp of capitalism and the camp of socialism.

There, in the camp of capitalism: national hate and inequality, colonial slavery and chauvinism, national oppression and massacres, brutalities and imperialistic wars.

Here, in the camp of socialism: reciprocal confidence and peace, national liberty and equality, the pacific co-existence and fraternal collaboration of peoples.

The attempts made by the capitalistic world during the past ten years to decide the question of nationalities by bringing together the principle of the free development of peoples with a system of exploitation of man by man have been fruitless. In addition, the number of national conflicts becomes more and more confusing, even menacing the capitalistic regime. The bourgeoisie has proven itself incapable of realizing a harmonious collaboration of the peoples.

It is only in the camp of the soviets; it is only under the conditions of the dictatorship of the proletariat that has grouped around itself the majority of the people, that it has been possible to eliminate the oppression of

51

nationalities, to create an atmosphere of mutual confidence and to establish the basis of a fraternal collaboration of peoples.

It is only thanks to these circumstances that the Soviet Republics have succeeded in repulsing the imperialistic attacks both internally and externally; it is only thanks to them that the Soviet Republics have succeeded in satisfactorily ending a civil war, in assuring their existence and in dedicating themselves to pacific economic reconstruction.

But the years of the war have not passed without leaving their trace. The devastated fields, the closed factories, the forces of production destroyed and the economic resources exhausted, this heritage of the war renders insufficient the isolated economic efforts of the several republics. National economic re-establishment is impossible as long as the Republics remain separated.

On the other hand, the instability of the international situation and the danger of new attacks make inevitable the creation of a united front of the Soviet Republics in the presence of capitalistic surroundings.

Finally, the very structure of Soviet power, international by nature of class, pushes the masses of workers of the Soviet Republics to unite in one socialist family.

All these considerations insistently demand the union of the Soviet Republics into one federated state capable of guaranteeing security against the exterior, economic prosperity internally, and the free national development of peoples.

The will of the peoples of the Soviet Republics recently assembled in Congress, where they decided unanimously to form the 'Union of Soviet Socialist Republics,' is a sure guarantee that this Union is a free federation of peoples equal in rights, that the right to freely withdraw from the Union is assured to each Republic, that access to the Union is open to all Republics already existing, as well as those that may be born in the future, that the new federal state will be the worthy crowning of the principles laid down as early as October 1917, of the pacific co-existence and fraternal collaboration of peoples, that it will serve as a bulwark against the capitalistic world and mark a new decisive step towards the union of workers of all countries in one World Wide Soviet Socialist Republic.

Part II: Treaty

The Russian Socialist Federal Soviet Republic, the Soviet Socialist Republic of Ukraine, the Soviet Socialist Republic of White Russia, and the Soviet Socialist Republic of Transcaucasia (including the Soviet Socialist Republic of Azerbaijan, the Soviet Socialist Republic of Georgia, and the Soviet Socialist Republic of Armenia) unite themselves in one federal state — 'The Union of Soviet Socialist Republics'.

ARTICLE I. The Union of Soviet Socialist Republics through its supreme organs has the following powers:

(a) To represent the Union in its international relations; to conclude all diplomatic relations; to conclude treaties, political and otherwise, with other States;

(b) To modify the exterior frontiers of the Union, as well as to regulate questions concerning the modification of frontiers between the member republics;

(c) To conclude treaties concerning the reception of new republics into the Union;

(d) To declare war and to conclude peace;

(e) To conclude internal and external loans of the Union and to authorize internal and external loans of the member republics;

(f) To ratify international treaties;

(g) To direct commerce with foreign countries and to determine the system of internal commerce;

(h) To establish the bases and the general plan of all national economy of the Union; to define the domains of industry and industrial enterprises that are of federal interest; to conclude treaties of concession both federal and in the name of the member republics;

(i) To direct transportation and the postal and telegraphic services;

(j) To organize and direct the armed forces of the Union;

(k) To approve the budget of the Federal State which includes the budgets of the member republics; to establish duties and federal revenues, making additions and reductions in order to balance the member republics' budgets; to authorize duties and supplementary taxes to meet the member republics' budgets;

(l) To establish a uniform system of money and credit;

(m) To establish general principles of exploitation and use of the earth, as well as those of the sub-soil, the forests, and the waters of the territories of the Union;

(n) To establish federal legislation on the emigration from the territory of one of the republics to the territory of another and to set up a fund for such emigration;

(o) To establish principles of the judicial organization and procedure, as well as civil and criminal legislation for the Union;

(p) To establish the fundamental laws regarding work;

(q) To establish the general principles regarding public instruction;

(r) To establish the general measures regarding public hygiene;

(s) To establish a standard system of weights and measures;

(t) To organize federal statistics;

(u) To fix the fundamental legislation regarding federal nationality, with reference to the rights of foreigners;

(v) To exercise the right of amnesty in all territories of the Union;

(w) To abrogate the acts of the Congresses of the Soviets and the Central Executive Committees of the member Republics contrary to the present constitution;

(x) To arbitrate litigious questions between the member Republics.

ARTICLE 2. The approval and modification of the fundamental principles of the present Constitution belong exclusively to the Congress of Soviets of the Union of Soviet Socialist Republics.

CHAPTER II: SOVEREIGN RIGHTS OF THE MEMBER REPUBLICS

ARTICLE 3. The Sovereignty of the member Republics is limited only in the matters indicated in the present constitution, as coming within the competence of the Union. Outside of those limits, each member Republic exerts its public powers independently; the Union of SSR protects the rights of member Republics.

ARTICLE 4. Each one of the member republics retains the right to freely withdraw from the union.

ARTICLE 5. The member republics will make changes in their constitutions to conform with the present constitution.

ARTICLE 6. The territory of the member republics cannot be modified without their consent; also, any limitation or modification or suppression of Article 4 must have the approval of all the member republics of the Union.

ARTICLE 7. Just one federal nationality is established for the citizens of the member republics.

CHAPTER III: CONGRESS OF SOVIETS OF THE UNION

ARTICLE 8. The supreme organ of power of the Union of SSR is the Congress of Soviets, and, in the recesses of the Congress of Soviets — the Central Executive Committee of the Union of SSR which is composed of the Federal Soviet and the Soviet of Nationalities.

ARTICLE 9. The Congress of Soviets of the Union of SSR is composed of representatives of the urban soviets and of the soviets of the urban type on the basis of one deputy per 25,000 electors, and of representatives of the congresses of soviets of the rural districts on the basis of one deputy per 125,000 inhabitants.

ARTICLE 10. The delegates to the Congress of the Soviets of the Union of SSR are elected in the Congresses of Soviets of the rural and urban governments. In the republics where there does not exist a rural (*gubernia*) division, the delegates are elected directly to the congress of soviets of the respective republic.

ARTICLE 11. Regular sessions of the Congress of the Soviets of the Union of SSR are convoked by the Central Executive Committee of the Union once yearly; extraordinary sessions may be convoked on decision of the CEC (Central Executive Committee), or on the demand of the Federal Soviet, or of the Soviet of Nationalities, or on the demand of two member republics.

ARTICLE 12. In cases where extraordinary circumstances interfere with the meeting of the Congress of Soviets of the Union of SSR on the date set, the CEC of the Union has the power to adjourn the meeting of Congress.

CHAPTER IV: THE CENTRAL EXECUTIVE COMMITTEE OF THE UNION

ARTICLE 13. The Central Executive Committee (CEC) of the Union of SSR is composed of the Federal Soviet and the Soviet of Nationalities.

ARTICLE 14. The Congress of Soviets of the Union of SSR elects the Federal Soviet from among the representatives of the member republics in proportion to the population of each one to make a grand total of 371 members.

ARTICLE 15. The Soviet of Nationalities is composed of representatives of the member republics and associated autonomous republics of the RSFSR on the basis of five representatives for each member republic, and one representative for each associated autonomous republic. The composition of the Soviet of Nationalities in its entirety is approved by the Congress of the Union of SSR.

(The autonomous republics of Adjaria, and Abkhasia and the autonomous region of Osetia, each send a representative to the Soviet of Nationalities.)

ARTICLE 16. The Federal Soviet and the Soviet of Nationalities examine all decrees, codes, and acts that are presented to them by the Presidium of the CEC and by the Council of Commissioners of the People of the Union of SSR, by the different Commissions of the People of the Union, by the CEC of the member republics, as well as those that owe their origin to the Federal Soviet and the Soviet of Nationalities.

ARTICLE 17. The CEC of the Union publishes the codes, decrees, acts, and ordinances; orders the work of legislation and administration of the Union of SSR, and defines the sphere of activity of the Presidium of the CEC and of the Council of Commissioners of the People of the Union of SSR.

ARTICLE 18. All decrees and acts defining the general rules of the political and economic life of the Union of SSR, or making radical modifications in the existing practices of public organs of the Union of SSR must obligatorily be submitted for examination and approval to the CEC of the Union of SSR.

ARTICLE 19. All decrees, acts, and ordinances promulgated by the CEC must be immediately put into force throughout all the territory of the Union of SSR.

ARTICLE 20. The CEC of the Union of SSR has the right to suspend or abrogate the decrees, acts, and orders of the Presidium of the CEC of the Union of SSR, as well as those of the Congress of Soviets and of the CEC of the member republics, and all other organs of power throughout the territory of the Union of SSR.

ARTICLE 21. The ordinary sessions of the CEC of the Union of SSR are convoked by the Presidium of the CEC three times yearly. The extraordinary sessions are convoked by the Presidium of the CEC of the Union of SSR on the demand of the Presidium of the Federal Soviet or the Presidium of the Soviet of Nationalities, and also on demand of one of the CEC of the member republics.

ARTICLE 22. The projects of law submitted for examination to the CEC of the Union of SSR do not have the force of law until adopted by the Federal Soviet and by the Soviet of Nationalities; they are published in the name of the CEC of the Union of SSR.

ARTICLE 23. In case of disagreement between the Federal Soviet and the Soviet of Nationalities, the question is transmitted to a compromise committee chosen by the two of them.

ARTICLE 24. If an accord is not reached by the compromise committee, the question is transferred for examination to a joint meeting of the Federal Soviet and the Soviet of Nationalities; and, if neither the Federal Soviet nor the Soviet of Nationalities get a majority, then the question may be submitted, on the demand of one of these organs, to the decision of an ordinary or extraordinary Congress of the Union of SSR.

ARTICLE 25. The Federal Soviet and the Soviet of Nationalities elect for the preparation of their sessions and the direction of their work — their Presidiums, composed of seven members each.

ARTICLE 26. Between sessions of the CEC of the Union of SSR, the supreme organ of power is the Presidium of the Union of SSR, constituted by the CEC to the extent of twenty-one members, including the Presidium of the Federal Soviet and the Presidium of the Soviet of Nationalities.

To form the Presidium of the CEC and the Council of Commissioners of the People of the Union of SSR, conforming to Articles 26 and 37 of the present constitution, joint sessions of the Federal Soviet and of the Soviet of Nationalities are convoked. In the joint session of the Federal Soviet and the Soviet of Nationalities, the vote is taken separately within each group.

ARTICLE 27. The CEC elects, in accordance with the number of member Republics, four Presidents of the CEC of the Union of SSR from among the members of the Presidium of the CEC of the Union of SSR.

ARTICLE 28. The CEC of the Union of SSR is responsible before the Congress of Soviets of the Union of SSR.

CHAPTER V: THE PRESIDIUM OF THE CEC OF THE UNION

ARTICLE 29. Between sessions of the CEC of the Union of SSR, the Presidium of the CEC of the Union of SSR is the supreme organ of legislative, executive, and administrative power of the Union of SSR.

ARTICLE 30. The Presidium of the CEC of the Union of SSR oversees the enforcement of the constitution of the Union of SSR and the execution of all decisions of the Congress of Soviets and the CEC of the Union of SSR by all the public agents.

ARTICLE 31. The Presidium of the CEC of the Union of SSR has the right to suspend and abrogate the orders of the Council of Commissioners of the People and of the different Councils of the People of the Union of the SSR as well as those of the CEC and CCP (Councils of Commissioners of the People) of the member Republics.

ARTICLE 32. The Presidium of the CEC of the Union of SSR has the right to suspend the acts of the congresses of soviets of the member republics submitting afterwards these acts for the examination and approval of the CEC of the Union of SSR.

ARTICLE 33. The Presidium of the CEC of the Union of SSR promulgates the decrees, acts, and orders; examines and approves the projects of decrees and acts deposited by the CCP, by the different authorities of the Union of SSR, by the CEC of the member republics, by their presidiums and by other organs of power.

ARTICLE 34. The decrees and decisions of the CEC, of its Presidium, and the CCP of the Union of SSR are printed in the languages generally employed in the member republics: Russian, Ukrainian, White Russian, Georgian, Armenian, Turko-Tartarian.

ARTICLE 35. The Presidium of the CEC of the Union of SSR decides questions regarding the relationships between the CCP of the Union of SSR and the Commissioners of the People of the Union of SSR, for one part and the CEC of the member republics and their presidiums, for the second part.

ARTICLE 36. The Presidium of the CEC of the Union of SSR is responsible before the CEC of the Union of SSR.

CHAPTER VI: COUNCIL OF COMMISSIONERS OF THE PEOPLE OF THE UNION

ARTICLE 37. The Council of Commissioners of the People (CCP) of the Union of SSR is the executive and administrative organ of the CEC of the Union of SSR and is constituted by the CEC as follows:

(a) The President of the Council of Commissioners of the People of the Union of SSR,
(b) The Vice-Presidents,
(c) The Commissioner of the People for Foreign Affairs,

(d) The Commissioner of the People for Military and Naval Affairs,

(e) The Commissioner of the People for Foreign Commerce,

(f) The Commissioner of the People for Ways of Communication,

(g) The Commissioner of the People for Postal and Telegraphic Service,

(h) The Commissioner of the People for the Inspection of Workers and Peasants,

(i) The President of the Supreme Council of National Economy,

(j) The Commissioner of the People for Labour,

(k) The Commissioner of the People for Finances,

(l) The Commissioner of the People for Supplies.

ARTICLE 38. The Council of Commissioners of the People of the Union of SSR, in the limits of the powers granted to it by the CEC of the Union of SSR, and on the basis of rules regulating the CCP of the Union of SSR, publishes the decrees and decisions that must become effective throughout the territory of the Union of SSR.

ARTICLE 39. The CCP of the Union of SSR examines the decrees and decisions given it by the various Commissions of the People as well as those from the CEC of the member republics and by their presidiums.

ARTICLE 40. The CCP of the Union of SSR is responsible for all its work before the CEC of the Union of SSR and before its Presidium.

ARTICLE 41. The orders and acts of the CCP of the Union of SSR may be suspended and abrogated by the CEC of the Union of SSR and by its Presidium.

ARTICLE 42. The Central Executive Committees of the member republics and their presidiums may object to the decrees and orders of the CCP of the Union of SSR to the Presidium of the CEC of the Union of SSR, without suspending the execution of these orders.

CHAPTER VII: THE SUPREME COURT OF THE UNION

ARTICLE 43. In order to maintain revolutionary legality within the territory of the Union of SSR, a Supreme Court under the jurisdiction of the CEC of the Union of SSR is established, competent:

(a) To give the Supreme Courts of the member republics the authentic interpretations on questions of federal legislation;

(b) To examine, on the request of the Prosecutor of the Supreme Court of the Union of SSR, the decrees, decisions, and verdicts of the Supreme Courts of the member republics, with view of discovering any infraction of the federal laws, or harming the interests of other republics, and if such be discovered to bring them before the CEC of the Union of SSR;

(c) To render decisions on the request of the CEC of the Union of SSR as to the constitutionality of laws passed by the member republics;

(d) To settle legal disputes between the member republics;

(e) To examine the accusations brought before it of high officials against whom charges have been made relative to their performance of duties.

ARTICLE 44. The Supreme Court performs its functions in the following manner:

(a) With a full attendance of the member judges of the Supreme Court of the Union of SSR;
(b) Or, in a meeting of the Civil Judiciary College and the Criminal Judiciary College of the Supreme Court of the Union of SSR;
(c) Or, in a meeting of the Military College.

ARTICLE 45. The Supreme Court of the Union of SSR, in full session, is composed of eleven members, including its President and Vice-President, the four Presidents of the Supreme Courts of the member republics, and a representative of the Unified Political Administration of the State of the Union of SSR; the President and the Vice-President and the other five members are named by the Presidium of the CEC of the Union of SSR.

ARTICLE 46. The Prosecutor of the Supreme Court of the Union of SSR and his assistant are named by the Presidium of the CEC of the Union of SSR. The Prosecutor of the Supreme Court of the Union of SSR is charged with the duties: (1) to give the decisions of all questions in the jurisdiction of the Supreme Court of the Union of SSR, (2) to prosecute the cases brought before the Court, (3) and, in cases of lack of agreement among the judges of the Supreme Court of the Union of SSR, to bring these questions of dispute before the Presidium of the CEC of the SSR.

ARTICLE 47. The right to submit the questions referred to in Article 43 to the Supreme Court of the Union of SSR for examination belongs exclusively to the CEC of the Union of SSR, to its Presidium, to the Prosecutor of the Supreme Courts of the member republics, and to the Unified Political Administration of the State of the Union of SSR.

ARTICLE 48. The regular sessions of the Supreme Court of the Union of SSR constitute the special legal chambers to examine:

(a) The civil and criminal affairs of exceptional importance that are of interest to two or more member republics;
(b) Personal charges against members of the CEC and the CCP of the Union of SSR.

A decision of the Supreme Court of the Union of SSR to proceed to examine a case may take place only after special authority has been granted for each case by the CEC of the Union or its Presidium.

CHAPTER VIII: COMMISSIONERS OF THE PEOPLE OF THE UNION

ARTICLE 49. For the immediate direction of the several branches of public administration, attributed to the CCP of the Union of the SSR, ten Commissioners of the People are created as mentioned in Article 37 of the Present

Constitution and who act according to the regulations of the Commissioners of the People approved by the CEC of the Union of the SSR.

ARTICLE 50. The Commissioners of the People of the Union of SSR are divided into the following groups:

(a) Commissioners of the People handling strictly federal matters of the Union of SSR that are external in character;
(b) Commissioners of the People handling matters that are purely domestic in character.

ARTICLE 51. The first group of Commissioners handling matters external in character includes the following Commissioners of the People:

(a) For Foreign Affairs,
(b) For Military and Naval Affairs,
(c) For Foreign Commerce,
(d) For Ways of Communication,
(e) For Postal and Telegraphic Service.

ARTICLE 52. The second group handling matters that are strictly domestic in character includes the following Commissioners of the People:

(a) The Council of National Economy,
(b) For Supplies,
(c) For Labour,
(d) For Finances,
(e) For the Inspection of Workers and Peasants.

ARTICLE 53. The Commissioners of the People handling matters of purely external character have, in the various member republics, their delegates directly subordinate to these Commissioners.

ARTICLE 54. The Commissioners of the People handling matters of domestic concern have, as executing organs in the various member republics, the Commissioners of the People of these Republics of similar title.

ARTICLE 55. The CCP of the Union of SSR, including the individual Commissioners, are the heads of the various departments mentioned.

ARTICLE 56. Under each Commissioner of the People, and under his presidency, is formed a college, of which the members are named by the CCP of the Union of SSR.

ARTICLE 57. The Commissioner of the People has the right to personally take decisions on all questions that come within the jurisdiction of his department, on advising the College of his department of his act. In case of disagreement on any decision of the Commissioner of the People, the College, or its members separately, may bring the dispute before the CCP of the Union of SSR, without suspending the act of the Commissioner.

ARTICLE 58. The orders of the different Commissioners of the People of the Union may be abrogated by the Presidium of the CEC and by the CCP of the Union of SSR.

ARTICLE 59. The orders of the Commissioners of the People of the Union of SSR may be suspended by the CEC or by the Presidiums of the CEC of the member republics in case of evident incompatibility of these orders with the Federal Constitution, with federal legislation or with legislation of the member republic. This suspension is immediately communicated by the CEC or by the Presidiums of the CEC of the member republics to the CCP of the Union of SSR and to the proper Commissioner of the People of the Union of SSR.

ARTICLE 60. The Commissioners of the People of the Union of SSR are responsible before the CCP, the CEC of the Union of SSR and its Presidium.

CHAPTER IX: THE UNIFIED POLITICAL ADMINISTRATION OF STATE

ARTICLE 61. In view of unifying the revolutionary efforts of the member Republics in their struggle against the political and economic counter-revolution, spying and banditry, there shall be created under the jurisdiction of the CCP of the Union of SSR a Unified Political Administration of State (GPU) of which the President shall be a consulting member of the CCP of the Union of SSR.

ARTICLE 62. The GPU of the Union of SSR directs the activities of the local organs of GPU through its delegates under the jurisdiction of the CCP of the member republics, acting in virtue of a special ruling sanctioned through legislative channels.

ARTICLE 63. The overseeing of acts of the GPU as to their legality shall be in charge of the Prosecutor of the Supreme Court of the Union of SSR in virtue of a special ruling of the CEC of the Union of SSR.

CHAPTER X: THE MEMBER REPUBLICS

ARTICLE 64. Within the limits of the territory of each member republic the supreme organ of power is the Congress of Soviets of the Republic, and in Congressional recesses, its Central Executive Committee.

ARTICLE 65. The relations between the supreme organs of power of the member republics and the supreme organs of power of the Union of SSR are established by the present constitution.

ARTICLE 66. The CEC of the member republics elect from among their own membership the presidiums that in the recesses between sessions of the CEC are the supreme organs of power.

ARTICLE 67. The CEC of the member republics will form their executive organs—the Councils of Commissioners of the People—as follows:

(a) The President of the Council of Commissioners of the People,
(b) The Vice-Presidents,
(c) The President of the Supreme Council for National Economy,

(d) The Commissioner of the People for Agriculture,

(e) The Commissioner of the People for Finances,

(f) The Commissioner of the People for Supplies,

(g) The Commissioner of the People for Labour,

(h) The Commissioner of the People for the Interior,

(i) The Commissioner of the People for Justice,

(j) The Commissioner of the People for the Inspection of the Workers and Peasants,

(k) The Commissioner of the People for Public Instruction,

(l) The Commissioner of the People for Public Health,

(m) The Commissioner of the People for Social Precaution,
   and in addition, and with a voice either consultative or deliberative, according to the decision of the CEC of the member republics, Delegates of the Commissioners of the People of the Union of SSR for Foreign Affairs, for Military and Naval Affairs, for Foreign Commerce, for Ways of Communication, for Postal and Telegraphic Service.

ARTICLE 68. The Supreme Council of National Economy and the Commissioners of Supplies, of Finances, of Labour, of the Inspection of Workers and Peasants of the member republics, while being subordinate to the CEC and CCP of the member republics, will execute the orders of the CCP of the Union of SSR.

ARTICLE 69. The right of amnesty, as well as the right of pardon and the rehabilitation of citizens condemned by the judicial and administrative organs of the member republics belongs to the CEC of these republics.

CHAPTER XI: ARMS, FLAG AND CAPITAL OF THE UNION

ARTICLE 70. The insignia of the State of the Union of SSR is composed of a sickle and a hammer on an earthly globe, surrounded by sun rays and framed with wheat stalks, with an inscription in the six languages mentioned in Article 34: 'Proletarians of all countries, unite!' Above the insignia, there shall be a five-pointed star.

ARTICLE 71. The flag of the State of the Union of SSR shall be in red or vermilion cloth with the arms of the Union.

ARTICLE 72. The Capital of the Union of SSR is Moscow.

Source: Vestnik TsIK, SNK i STO Soyuza SSR, 1924, No. 2, statya 24.
Translation: Milton H. Andrew, *Twelve Leading Constitutions,* (American University series, Compton, California, 1931), p. 327.

12. The Status of Religious Groups Defined
8 *April* 1929

The drive against religious belief in the 'twenties, backed by repressive legislation and actively promoted by the 'League of the Godless', was much less successful than the leadership had hoped. The important law of 8 April 1929 was designed to systematize restrictive measures which had been introduced in the preceding years. It also deprived worshippers of the right to participate in valuable social and cultural activities.

The narrow legal framework within which believers have since worshipped is evident from the text. The references to old and unsafe buildings, etc., which were common, given Bolshevik neglect of the churches, have been of political, rather than architectural, significance.

On 22 May 1929 freedom of religious propaganda, as laid down in the 1918 constitution, was repealed—hence the formula 'freedom of religious worship and freedom of anti-religious propaganda' used in article 124 of the 1936 version. In 1932 amendments were introduced into the April 1929 decree to transfer responsibility for religion from the People's Commissariat of Internal Affairs to a new Permanent Commission for Religious Affairs attached to the CEC of the RSFSR.

12. On Religious Associations
Decree of the All-Russian Central Executive Committee and the RSFSR Council of People's Commissars, 8 April 1929

The All-Russian Central Executive Committee and the Council of People's Commissars of the RSFSR decree that:
1. The decree of the Council of People's Commissars of the RSFSR of 20 January 1918 [OS] on the separation of the church from the state and of the school from the church shall apply to churches, religious groups, movements, trends and all other associations for religious worship of all denominations.
2. (1) Religious associations of believers of all rites shall be registered as religious societies or as groups of believers.
   (2) No citizen shall belong to more than one religious or ritual association (society or group).
3. (1) A religious society is a local association of at least twenty believers, who have reached the age of eighteen and belong to the same denomination, rite, movement or trend, for the purpose of satisfying their religious needs together.
   (2) Believers who, because of their small number, cannot form a religious society are granted the right to form a group of believers.

(3) Neither a religious society nor a group of believers shall have the rights of a person at law.

4. A religious society or group of believers may commence its activities only after the society or group has been registered in the requisite administrative department (division, section) of the local executive committee (*ispolkom*), or of the town soviet, in the *volost ispolkom* or at a town soviet which is not the administrative centre of the district (*raion* or *uezd*).

5. In order to register as a religious society, the organizers, numbering at least twenty, shall submit to one of the above-mentioned bodies (Article 4) an application for registration in the form determined by the People's Commissariat for Internal Affairs of the RSFSR.

6. In order to register as a group of believers, the nominated representative (Article 13) shall submit to one of the above-mentioned bodies (Article 4) an application for registration in the form determined by the People's Commissariat of Internal Affairs.

7. The above-mentioned bodies (Article 4) shall, within one month of receiving the application, register the society or group, or inform the applicants that their application has been refused.

8. A list of members of the association or group, of its executive and of the administrative bodies and the clergy serving it, shall be communicated to the registering body within the period and in the form determined by the People's Commissariat of Internal Affairs.

9. No one shall be listed as a member of a religious association without his express consent.

10. (1) In order to satisfy their religious needs, believers who have formed a religious association shall have the right to enter into an agreement with the *volost* or *raion* executive committee or town soviet, granting them the free use of special religious buildings and of objects for exclusively ritual use.

(2) Furthermore, believers who make up a religious society or a group of believers may also use for their prayer meetings other premises offered by private persons or by local soviets and their executive committees on a rental basis. Regulations applying to religious buildings under the present decree shall apply in equal measure to these premises. The agreement for the use of such premises shall be made by each believer on his own responsibility. Such premises must also comply with building and sanitary regulations.

(3) No religious society or group of believers shall use more than one set of premises for its prayer meetings.

11. Arrangements connected with the administration and use of religious premises and ritual objects—such as the employment of watchmen, delivery of fuel, upkeep of religious buildings and ritual objects, acquisition of goods, or objects for use in religious rites, ceremonies, or other acts closely and directly related to the teaching and ritual order of the cult in question, the lease of premises for religious meetings — can be made individually by any

member of the executive body of the religious society or group of believers who has been thus empowered by the association.

Such arrangements shall not apply to contractual relations concerned with a trade or industry, however closely related to the cult, e.g. lease of premises for a candle factory, or for a printing press producing books on religion or morals, etc.

12. General meetings of religious societies and groups of believers may be held by permission of the *volost* executive committee or *raion* administrative division in rural settlements and of the administrative departments in towns.

13. The religious association at its general meeting elects by a show of hands an executive body, consisting of three of its members for a society or of one representative for a group. These are directly entrusted with functions connected with the administration and use of religious premises and ritual objects, (Article 11) as well as with representing the association.

14. The registering body has the right to exclude certain persons from membership of the executive body of the association.

15. The religious association has the right to elect at its general meeting a control commission of not more than three of its members for verifying ritual objects and sums accruing from members' contributions or from voluntary gifts.

16. The executive body or control commission of a religious association may hold meetings (sessions) without obtaining the permission of government authorities.

17. Religious associations are prohibited from:

(a) setting up funds for mutual aid, co-operatives or associations of producers, and from using the effects at their disposal for any purpose other than the satisfaction of their religious needs,
(b) granting material aid to their members,
(c) organizing religious or other meetings specially intended for children, young people or women, biblical or literary meetings, groups, sections, circles, or handicraft meetings, religious instruction, etc., excursions, or children's play-groups, or from opening libraries, reading rooms, sanatoria, or providing medical aid.

The only books which may be kept in religious buildings or on religious premises are those indispensable for conducting a service.

18. No teaching of religious faith of any sort shall be tolerated in state or private schools or other educational establishments. Such teaching may only form part of special theological courses opened by citizens of the USSR with the special permission of the People's Commissariat of Internal Affairs of the RSFSR, or if in an autonomous republic, with the permission of the Central Executive Committee of that republic.

19. The activities of priests, preachers, instructors, etc. are restricted to the

place of residence of the members of the religious associations which they serve and the place where the religious building used is situated.

The activities of priests, preachers and instructors serving two or more religious associations are restricted to the area in which the members of these associations reside.

20. Religious societies and groups may organize local all-Russian or all-union religious conferences or congresses provided special permission has been obtained in each case individually from:

(a) the People's Commissariat of Internal Affairs of the RSFSR if the congress is an all-Russian or all-union one on the territory of the RSFSR, or if the congress covers the territory of two or more *kraiya*, *oblasti*, or *gubernii*, or

(b) the corresponding *krai*, *oblast*, *gubernia* or *okrug* administrative department if the congress is local.

In the case of republican congresses and conferences in autonomous republics, permission must be granted by the People's Commissariat of Internal Affairs or the corresponding organ of the relevant autonomous republic.

21. Local all-Russian or all-union religious congresses or conferences may elect from among their members an executive body responsible for the execution of the decrees adopted by the congress. A list of the members of the executive body elected at the congress, as well as the proceedings of the congress, shall be communicated in duplicate, in the form determined by the People's Commissariat of Internal Affairs of the RSFSR, to the body which has granted permission for the congress to be held.

22. Neither the congress nor its elected executive body have the rights of a person at law, neither have they the right to:

(a) organize any central funds whatever to collect free donations from believers;

(b) levy forced contributions of any sort;

(c) own, lease or purchase ritual objects or rent premises for religious meetings;

(d) make contracts or agreements of any sort.

23. In dealing exclusively with matters of a purely religious character, the executive bodies of religious societies, groups and religious congresses have the right to use stamps, seals and forms stating their denomination. Such stamps, seals or letter headings shall not include any emblem or slogan established for organs or institutions of Soviet power ...

25. Ritual objects used by believers who have formed a religious association —whether granted by contract or subsequently acquired by or received by

them as gifts—are nationalized property and listed by the corresponding town soviet, the *raion* or *volost* executive committee, while remaining at the disposal of the believers ...

27. The contract granting the use of religious buildings and ritual objects to believers who have formed a religious association shall be concluded in the name of the corresponding *raion* executive committee or town soviet by the relevant administrative department (section) or division, or directly by the *volost* executive committee.

28. In accordance with the contract, the religious building and the objects which it contains are handed over by a representative of the *volost* or *raion* executive committee or town soviet to at least twenty members of the religious society, who place them at the disposal of all the believers ...

36. The transfer for other purposes of a religious building used by believers (that is, its liquidation) can be authorized only by a motivated decree of the Central Executive Committee of the autonomous republic, the *krai*, *oblast* or *gubernia* executive committee, if the building is indispensable for state or social needs. The decree must be communicated to the believers who make up the religious society.

37. Should the members of the religious society appeal to the Presidium of the All-Russian CEC within two weeks of having received notice of such a decree, the case of the liquidation of the religious building shall be referred to the Presidium of the All-Russian CEC. The contract with the believers shall not cease to be valid nor shall they be deprived of its use until the decree has been confirmed by the Presidium of the All-Russian CEC.

38. The lease of nationalized, municipalized or private premises for religious meetings (Article 10, para. 2) can be dissolved by normal legal methods before the expiration of its term.

39. The liquidation of a religious building in such cases must be carried out by the administrative department or division on the request of the corresponding *uezd* or *raion* executive committee or town soviet in the presence of representatives of the local financial department and of other offices which may be involved, as well as of a representative of the religious association.

40. When a religious building is liquidated, the ritual objects shall be apportioned as follows:

(a) objects of platinum, gold, silver or brocade, and also precious stones are subject to inclusion in state funds and are put at the disposal of the local financial authorities or of the organs of the People's Commissariat of Education, if these objects were on its list;

(b) objects of historical, artistic or collector's value are handed over to the organs of the People's Commissariat of Education;

(c) all other objects (icons, vestments, banners, robes, etc.) which are of special significance for religious services shall revert to the believers for transfer to other religious buildings of the same rite; these objects shall be included in the general list of ritual objects in the usual manner;

(d) objects of current use (bells, furniture, carpets, chandeliers, etc.) are subject to inclusion in state funds and are put at the disposal of the local financial authorities or the organs of the People's Commissariat of Education, if they are on the list of this body;

(e) objects of transitory use, such as money, and also incense, candles, oil, wine, wax, firewood and coal, which are destined for a specific use in accordance with the terms of the contract, or for the celebration of the rites of the cult, are not subject to confiscation when the existing religious society exists after the liquidation of the religious building ...

46. Should the religious building, owing to its age, be in danger of partial or total collapse, then the local administrative organs, the *raion* and *volost* executive committee or village soviet has the right to request the executive body of the religious association or the representative of the religious group to refrain from using it for religious services or meetings pending its inspection by a special technical commission ...

49. The decisions of the technical commission, as set out in its reports, are binding and must be executed ...

54. (1) Members of groups of believers and religious societies have the right to collect dues and accept voluntary donations, both within and without the religious building, but only from the members of that religious association and only for purposes related to the upkeep of the building and the ritual objects, paying the clergy and maintaining the executive body.

(2) Any obligatory levies for the benefit of religious societies are a crime punishable under the Penal Code of the RSFSR (Article 124).

55. (1) All ritual objects, whether donated or purchased out of voluntary donations, must be included in the inventory of ritual objects.

(2) All sums donated for the purpose of embellishing the religious building or decorating ritual objects must be listed in the inventory of ritual properties which are used by the religious society without payment.

(3) Donations in kind for purposes other than those mentioned above, together with donations in money for purposes connected with the use of the religious building or premises (repairs, heating, etc.) or for the upkeep of the clergy need not be listed in the inventory.

(4) Voluntary donations in money from believers shall be listed by the treasurer of the association in the accounts book.

56. Sums donated for purposes connected with the management of religious buildings and ritual objects may be spent by members of the executive bodies of religious societies or by representatives of groups of believers empowered to do so.

57. (1) The prayer meetings of believers who are united in a group or society may take place in religious buildings or in specially adapted premises which

satisfy building and sanitary norms without the prior knowledge or permission of the authorities.

(2) Should the premises not be specially adapted for this purpose, believers wishing to hold a religious meeting there must give notice to the village soviet in rural areas, to the local militia in urban settlements, and to the administrative department where there is no office of the militia.

58. Religious rites and ceremonies may not be held, and ritual objects may not be placed, in any state, social, co-operative or private institution or enterprise.

This prohibition does not apply to religious rites performed at the request of those who are gravely ill or dying in prisons and hospitals, provided such rites are performed in specially isolated rooms, or to rites performed at cemeteries and crematoria.

59. For a religious procession, rite or ceremony to be held in the open, special authorization must be obtained in each case as follows:

in towns which are administrative centres not below *raion* standing—from the corresponding administrative department or division;

in towns which are not administrative centres and also in workers' and tourist settlements—from the presidium of the town or settlement soviet;

in rural districts—from the administrative division of the *raion* executive committee or the *volost* executive committee.

Application for such authorizations must be made at least two weeks before the ceremony is due to take place. No authorization is needed for religious ceremonies connected with burials.

60. In the case of processions which form an integral part of a religious service and which proceed round the religious building, in both town and country, the authorities need not be notified, and special permission is not required, provided the procession does not impede the normal street traffic.

61. Religious processions, rites and ceremonies held outside the location of the religious society are permitted on the basis of special authorization in each case from the body which made the original contract. Such an authorization may be given with the preliminary consent of the executive committee of the district in which the procession, rite or ceremony is to be held.

62. A list of religious societies and of groups of believers in a given area must be drawn up by the registering bodies there (Article 6).

63. The bodies which register religious associations (Article 6) pass statistical information about them, in the form and periods established by the People's Commissariat of Internal Affairs of the RSFSR, to the *uezd* and *okrug* administrative departments. The People's Commissariat of Internal Affairs of autonomous republics, and the *krai*, *oblast*, and *gubernia* administrative departments, summarize the information received from the subordinate administrative departments and pass it on to the People's Commissariat of Internal Affairs of the RSFSR.

64. The registering bodies shall be responsible for surveillance of the activities of the religious associations, and also for the safety of the religious buildings and ritual objects put at the disposal of the associations by contract; in rural areas responsibility for surveillance also lies with the local village soviet.

65. All religious associations actually in existence in the RSFSR at the day of promulgation of the present decree shall register within one year at their place of residence in the form and with the bodies indicated in the present decree.

66. Religious associations which fail to fulfil the requirements of this article are considered to be closed down with the consequences envisaged by the present decree ...

> Signed: President of the All-Russian Central Executive Committee, M. KALININ.
>
> Vice-President of the Council of People's Commissars, A. SMIRNOV.
>
> Vice-Secretary of the All-Russian Central Executive Committee, A. DOSOV.

Source: Sobranie uzakonenii i rasporyazhenii raboche-krestyanskogo pravitelstva, 1929, No. 35, statya 353, reproduced with commentary in N. Orleanski, *Zakon o religioznykh ob'edineniyakh RSFSR* (Moscow, 1930), p. 6.

Editor's translation.

13. The Last Published Statute on Censorship

6 *June* 1931

This statute on censorship replaced a very comprehensive document approved as early as June 1922. The 1931 version translated here was modelled closely on the earlier one, though there were a few significant differences. Excluded were references to the links between Glavlit and the secret police (OGPU), while the term 'censorship' was replaced by 'control'. At the same time radio broadcasts, public lectures, and exhibitions were now specifically mentioned as being in Glavlit aegis. No statutes have been published since this document appeared, but the Soviet censorship remains a nation-wide organization.

13. Statute of the Main Administration for Affairs of Literature and Publishing, RSFSR (Glavlit) and its Local Organs

Decree of the Council of People's Commissars of the RSFSR, 6 June 1931

1. The Main Administration for Affairs of Literature and Publishing (Glavlit) is established inside the People's Commissariat of Instruction of the RSFSR to effect political, ideological, military, and economic control[1] of all kinds over printed works, manuscripts, photographs, pictures etc., as well as radio programmes, lectures and exhibitions, which are intended for publication or distribution.

2. Glavlit, in order to carry out the tasks with which it is charged, forbids the issue, publication, or distribution of any works which:

   (a) contain agitation or propaganda against Soviet power or the dictatorship of the proletariat;
   (b) divulge state secrets;
   (c) arouse nationalist or religious fanaticism;
   (d) are of a pornographic character.

3. Glavlit is charged with:

   (a) the general administration and inspection of local organs and representatives of Glavlit;
   (b) the preliminary and subsequent control over literature which is published, both from the political and ideological, and from the military and economic, points of view, and also over radio programmes, lectures, and exhibitions;

---

[1] For other possible meanings of the Russian word *kontrol* see the glossary.

(c) the confiscation of the works which are not for distribution;

(d) the issue of permits for opening publishing houses and periodical publications, the closure of publishing houses and banning of editions, the prohibition or licensing of the importation from abroad or export of literature, pictures, etc., in accordance with existing regulations;

(e) the publication of rules, regulations and instructions on the matters which it handles: these rules etc., are obligatory for all institutions, organizations, and individuals;

(f) the examination of complaints against decisions of the local organs and representatives of Glavlit;

(g) the compilation, in conjunction with the administrations concerned, of lists of information which are, by the nature of their contents, specially reserved state secrets and not subject to publication or disclosure;

(h) the compilation of a list of works banned from publication or distribution;

(i) the prosecution of persons who violate the requirements of Glavlit, its offices and representatives.

4. Preliminary control (see paragraph (b) of Article 3 above) is effected by Glavlit through its representatives at publishing houses, the editorial offices of periodicals, printing works, radio stations, telegraphic agencies, customs houses, central post offices and similar institutions.

These representatives are nominated and removed by Glavlit and are maintained at the expense of the organization in which they serve.

The preliminary control of the output of those state publishing houses which form part of the OGIZ[1] system is effected by the managers of these publishing houses, who are representatives of Glavlit and act on the basis of a special instruction confirmed by the People's Commissar of Instruction of the RSFSR. The managers of OGIZ publishing houses nominate responsible political editors for day-to-day control work, and these are confirmed by Glavlit.

Glavlit is, when necessary, granted the right to establish preliminary control both over the whole output, and over individual kinds of literature published by the OGIZ state publishing houses, through specially nominated representatives of Glavlit.

5. Publications of the Communist International, the Central Committee of the VKP (B), *krai*, *oblast* and *raion* committees of the VKP (B), together with the *Izvestia* of the Central Executive Committee and the All-Union Executive Committee, the works of the Communist Academy, and those of the Academy of Sciences, are freed from the political and ideological control of Glavlit.

With regard to these publications, Glavlit and its local organs are charged

[1] The Union of State Publishing Houses, which existed from 1930 to 1949.

with ensuring the complete preservation of state secrets by means of pre-liminary perusal of them.

6. Glavlit is headed by a chief under whom a collegium is set up. The membership of this collegium is confirmed by the People's Commissariat of Instruction of the RSFSR in agreement with interested administrations.

7. In *kraiya* and *oblasti*, as well as in industrial centres with a well-developed network of works newspapers and a significant amount of publishing activity, local organs of Glavlit are set up, attached to the relevant public education bodies; the former conduct their work according to directives and tasks set by Glavlit.

8. The functions indicated in Articles 1 and 2 and also in paragraphs (c), (f), (g) and (h) of Article 3 of this statute are laid upon the local organs of Glavlit.

The functions of the local organs of Glavlit in the *raion* are conducted by an official nominated by the *raiispolkom* in agreement with the corresponding organ of Glavlit.

9. The local organs of Glavlit are structured analogically to Glavlit itself, while the managers are nominated and removed by the People's Commissariat of Instruction of the RSFSR at the representation of Glavlit.

10. All printed works brought out in the RSFSR carry the imprimatur of Glavlit or its local organs (*krailit, oblit, railit, gorlit*, or of a representative of Glavlit).

11. The managers of printing works are obliged to submit to the Glavlit offices five copies of any printed work as soon as it leaves the presses and before it is published.

12. Published works which have not been authorized by Glavlit and its local organs are removed from distribution at the suggestion of Glavlit and its organs by the apparatus of the publishing, book-trading and distributing organizations (OGIZ—Knigotsentr, Soyuzpechat, etc.).

Source: L. G. Fogelevich, *Osnovnye direktivy i zakonodatelstvo o pechati* ([Moscow], 1935), p. 110.
Editor's translation.

14. The Internal Passport System Re-established

27 *December* 1932

The introduction of the Soviet passport system was part of Stalin's drive to increase state control of the individual. The Soviet passport was designed not only to improve statistical work, and get rid of loafers and criminals (as stated in the preamble to the decree) but also to prevent the unauthorized movement of the peasants—who did not have these documents—into urban settlements. It therefore complemented the strict residential provisions of the collective farm statute, and paved the way to the workbook, a kind of workers' labour passport introduced in December 1938. Internal passports had existed in tsarist Russia, and many countries outside the Soviet bloc have them today. But few systems aim to be so rigorous. There has been remarkably little change in the system over the years, though its efficiency in practice seems to have varied greatly.

14. On the Introduction of a Uniform Passport System in the USSR and on the Obligatory Registration of Passports

Decree of the Central Executive Committee of the Council of People's Commissars, 27 December 1932

In order to obtain better statistics of the population in towns, workers' settlements and the settlements built around the newly constructed factories and also in order to secure the deportation from these places of persons who are not connected with industry or with work in the offices and schools and not engaged in socially useful labour (with the exception of infirm persons and pensioners), and also in order to cleanse these places from kulak, criminal and other anti-social elements which find a refuge there, the Central Executive Committee and the Council of People's Commissaries of the USSR resolve:

1. To establish, throughout the USSR, a uniform passport system on the basis of specially issued Passport Regulations.

2. To introduce the uniform passport system with obligatory registration of passports throughout the USSR in the course of 1933, and, first of all, in Moscow, Leningrad, Kharkov, Kiev, Odessa, Minsk, Rostov-on-Don and Vladivostok.

3. To empower the Council of People's Commissaries of the USSR to fix the time-limits and order in which the passport system should be introduced in all other localities of the USSR.

74

4. To empower the governments of the allied republics to make the necessary amendments in their legal Codes in correspondence with the present Passport Regulations.

President of the Central Executive Committee of the USSR, M. KALININ.
Chairman of the Council of People's Commissaries of the USSR, V. MOLOTOV (SKRYABIN).
Secretary of the Central Executive Committee of the USSR, A. ENUKIDZE.

Moscow, Kremlin, 27 December 1932, No. 1917.

Passport Regulations

1. All citizens of the USSR above sixteen years of age who permanently reside in towns, workers' settlements or are employed at the transport undertakings, *sovkhozy* and new construction schemes must have passports.

2. In those localities where the passport system is introduced, the passport is the only document which serves as an identification of the bearer. All other documents and certificates which used to serve for identification purposes are declared non-valid. The passport must be produced: (*a*) upon the registration of the bearer; (*b*) upon entering the employment of a factory or office; (*c*) upon the request of the police and other administrative institutions.

3. The registration of the inhabitants in those localities where the passport system is introduced, is obligatory. Citizens who change their addresses within the confines of the places where the passport system is introduced, or persons arriving at such places, must submit their passports, through the house managements, for registration with the police within twenty-four hours after arrival at a new address.

4. Persons below sixteen years of age are entered on the passports of those persons in whose care they are. Persons below sixteen years of age who are cared for by the state (in children's homes, etc.) are entered on the lists compiled by the corresponding institutions.

5. For persons who are in active military service in the ranks of the Workers' and Peasants' Red Army, the documents issued by corresponding military authorities are accepted in lieu of passports.

6. Passports are issued by the organs of the police. Citizens who permanently reside in places where the passport system is introduced, receive passports without applications; citizens arriving at these places from elsewhere must apply for the passports.

7. Citizens who permanently reside in places where the passport system is introduced, receive passports for a period of three years. Organs of the police

are permitted to issue temporary certificates for a period of three months upon registration of newly arrived persons before the passport system is introduced throughout the USSR.

8. The fee for the issue of a passport is three roubles and for the issue of a temporary certificate one rouble.

9. The passport must contain the following items: (*a*) christian name, patronymic and surname, (*b*) time and place of birth, (*c*) nationality, (*d*) social position, (*e*) place of permanent residence, (*f*) place of employment, (*g*) persons entered on the bearer's passport, (*h*) list of documents upon which the passport has been issued.

NOTE. The list of the documents upon which passports are to be issued is to be determined in a special instruction.

10. Passport books and forms are to be prepared according to a specimen common form for the whole of the USSR. The text of passport books and forms for citizens of the various allied and autonomous republics is to be printed in two languages: Russian and the language commonly in use in the corresponding allied or autonomous republic.

11. Persons obliged to have passports and found without them or without temporary certificates are liable to a fine not exceeding 100 roubles imposed by administrative order. Citizens who arrive from other places without a passport or temporary certificate and who do not apply for a passport or temporary certificate within the time limit fixed in the Instructions, are liable to a fine not exceeding the sum of 100 roubles and to deportation by order of the police.

12. Persons found guilty of non-registration of their passports or temporary certificates are liable to a fine not exceeding the sum of 100 roubles imposed by administrative order, and in case of a second offence against the regulations of passport registration, to criminal prosecution.

13. Persons who are responsible for registration (house managers, porters, house-owners, householders, etc.) are liable, if found guilty of infringement of these regulations, to the penalties fixed in Article 12 of the present regulations.

14. Forgery of passport forms is to be prosecuted as a criminal offence in the same manner as forgery of state bonds in accordance with Article 22 of the Code of State Crimes (Collection of Laws of the USSR, 1929, No. 72, Article 687).

15. Forgery of a passport and possession of a forged passport or of somebody else's passport is a criminal offence prosecuted in accordance with the legislation of the USSR and of the allied republics.

16. To instruct the Chief Board of the Workers' and Peasants' Police attached to the OGPU of the USSR to present in ten days' time a draft instruction regarding the putting in effect of these Regulations

for confirmation by the Council of People's Commissaries of the USSR.

President of the Central Executive Committee of the USSR, M. KALININ.
Chairman of the Council of People's Commissaries of the USSR, V. MOLOTOV (SKRYABIN).
Secretary of the Central Executive Committee of the USSR, A. ENUKIDZE.

Moscow, Kremlin, 27 December 1932.

Source: Izvestia, 28 December 1932, No. 358.
Translation: Slavonic [and East European] Review, Vol. XI, No. 33, p. 695.

15. The 1950 Regulations on Elections to the Supreme Soviet

9 January 1950

Election statutes for the Supreme Soviet (as established by the 1936 constitution) were approved in 1937, 1945 and 1950.

In 1945 the age of candidates was raised from eighteen to twenty-three, and in 1950, Article 110, covering penalties for official negligence, was added. These, and less significant changes of wording, could easily have been effected by supplementary decree: the reissue of statutes is perhaps best explained by the sensitivity of the regime to their propaganda value.

One curious feature of the statutes has been the provision for a plurality of candidates: there is evidence that for some time in 1936 Stalin was seriously considering admitting this practice. The rules for elections to local soviets fit into the all-union framework.

15. Statute on Elections to the Supreme Soviet of the USSR

Approved by the Presidium of the Supreme Soviet of the USSR in the Edict of 9 January 1950[1]

CHAPTER I: THE ELECTORAL SYSTEM

ARTICLE 1. In accordance with Article 134 of the constitution of the USSR, deputies to the Supreme Soviet of the USSR are elected by the electors on the basis of universal, equal and direct suffrage by secret ballot.

ARTICLE 2. In accordance with Article 135 of the constitution of the USSR, elections of deputies are universal: all citizens of the USSR who have reached the age of eighteen, irrespective of race or nationality, sex, religion, standard of education, domicile, social origin, property status or past activities, have the right to vote in the election of deputies to the Supreme Soviet of the U.S.S.R. with the exception of persons certified insane in the manner prescribed by law.

ARTICLE 3. All citizens of the USSR who have reached the age of twenty-three, irrespective of race or nationality, sex, religious creed, standard of education, domicile, social origin, property status or past activities, are eligible for election to the Supreme Soviet of the USSR.

[1] Articles 2, 14, 15, 21, 28, 36, 40, 44, 48, 51, 52, 58, and 95 are given with minor textual changes introduced by the Edict of 27 December 1961 (*Vedomosti Verkhovnogo Sovets SSSR*, 1962, No. 1). The amendment made to Article 109 was more significant in that a provision for a term of imprisonment of up to two years was removed and replaced by the wording shown.

ARTICLE 4. In accordance with Article 136 of the constitution of the USSR, elections of deputies are equal: each citizen is entitled to one vote; all citizens participate in elections on an equal footing.

ARTICLE 5. In accordance with Article 137 of the constitution of the USSR, women have the right to elect and be elected on equal terms with men.

ARTICLE 6. In accordance with Article 138 of the constitution of the USSR, citizens serving in the Armed Forces of the USSR have the right to elect and be elected on equal terms with all other citizens.

ARTICLE 7. In accordance with Article 139 of the constitution of the USSR, elections of deputies are direct: deputies of the Supreme Soviet of the USSR are elected by all citizens directly.

ARTICLE 8. In accordance with Article 140 of the constitution of the USSR, elections of deputies to the Supreme Soviet are secret.

ARTICLE 9. Persons residing on Soviet territory who are not citizens of the USSR but citizens or subjects of foreign states have no right to elect or be elected to the Supreme Soviet of the USSR.

ARTICLE 10. In accordance with Article 141 of the constitution of the USSR, candidates are nominated for election according to constituencies.

ARTICLE 11. All the expenditure incurred in elections to the Supreme Soviet of the USSR is borne by the state.

CHAPTER II: THE ELECTORAL ROLLS

ARTICLE 12. The electoral rolls shall include all citizens who have reached the age of eighteen by election day, who enjoy electoral rights and reside (permanently or temporarily) on the territory of the given Soviet at the time of compilation of the rolls.

ARTICLE 13. No voter may be included in more than one roll.

ARTICLE 14. Persons certified insane in the manner prescribed by law are not entered in the electoral rolls.

ARTICLE 15. Electoral rolls shall be compiled in towns by the executive committee of town soviets of working people's deputies, in cities divided into districts, by the executive committees of the district soviets, in settlements, by the executive committees of the settlement soviets, and in rural localities, by the executive committees of rural (*stanitsa*, village, hamlet, *kishlak*, *aul*) soviets of working people's deputies.

ARTICLE 16. Electoral rolls in military units and military formations are drawn up by the headquarters and signed by the commander. All other persons on military service are entered in electoral rolls according to place of residence by the executive committees of the appropriate soviets of working people's deputies.

ARTICLE 17. The electoral role shall be drawn up in each constituency in the manner laid down by the Presidium of the Supreme Soviet of the USSR: they are compiled in alphabetical order, the surname, name, patronymic, age and address of the voter being indicated, and shall be signed by the Chairman and Secretary of the Executive Committee of the Soviet of Working People's Deputies.

ARTICLE 18. Thirty days prior to the elections, the Executive Committee of the Soviet of Working People's Deputies shall exhibit electoral rolls for public inspection or shall enable electors to study the rolls on the premises either of the soviet or the election ward.

ARTICLE 19. The original copy of the electoral roll shall be kept by the Executive Committee of the Soviet of Working People's Deputies, the military unit, or the military formation, as the case may be.

ARTICLE 20. In the event of a voter changing his place of residence in the interval between the day of publication of electoral rolls and election day, the appropriate Executive Committee of the Soviet of Working People's Deputies shall issue to him, in the form prescribed by the Presidium of the Supreme Soviet of the USSR, a 'Voting Right Certificate', and shall note against his name in the register: 'removed'; at his new place of residence— permanent or temporary—the voter shall be included in the list of voters upon presentation of the 'Voting Right Certificate' and of his identity card.

ARTICLE 21. Claims of inaccuracy in the electoral roll (non-inclusion in the rolls, exclusion from the rolls, distortion of surname, name or patronymic, incorrect inclusion) shall be lodged with the Executive Committee of the Soviet of Working People's Deputies, which published the rolls and which must examine each claim of inaccuracy in the electoral roll within a period of three days.

ARTICLE 22. After having examined a claim of inaccuracy in the electoral roll, the Executive Committee of the Soviet of Working People's Deputies must either make the necessary corrections in the electoral roll or issue to the claimant a written statement of the reasons for refusing his claim.

ARTICLE 23. Should the claimant disagree with the decision of the Executive Committee of the Soviet of Working People's Deputies, he may submit a complaint to the People's Court. The latter must within a period of three days examine the complaint of inaccuracy in the roll in open court in the presence of the claimant and a representative of the soviet and announce its decision immediately both to the claimant and to the Executive Committee of the soviet. The decision of the People's Court is final.

CHAPTER III: SOVIET OF THE UNION AND SOVIET OF NATIONALITIES CONSTITUENCIES

ARTICLE 24. In accordance with Article 34 of the constitution of the USSR, the Soviet of the Union is elected by the citizens of the USSR according to constituencies, which are formed on the principle of 300,000 inhabitants per constituency. Each Soviet of the Union constituency shall elect one deputy.

ARTICLE 25. In accordance with Article 35 of the constitution of the USSR, the Soviet of Nationalities is elected by the citizens of the USSR according to the union and autonomous republics, autonomous regions and national areas.

The Soviet of Nationalities constituencies shall be formed on the basis of twenty-five constituencies to each union republic, eleven constituencies to each autonomous republic, five constituencies to each autonomous region and one constituency to each national area. Each Soviet of Nationalities constituency shall elect one deputy.

ARTICLE 26. The Soviet of the Union constituencies and the Soviet of Nationalities constituencies shall be designated by the Presidium of the Supreme Soviet of the USSR.

The list of the Soviet of the Union and the Soviet of Nationalities constituencies shall be published by the Presidium of the Supreme Soviet of the USSR within a period of two months before the election day.

CHAPTER IV: ELECTION WARDS

ARTICLE 27. For the purpose of polling and counting the votes, the territories of the cities and districts forming part of the constituencies shall be divided into election wards, which shall be common for the elections to the Soviet of the Union and for the elections to the Soviet of Nationalities.

ARTICLE 28. Election wards in cities shall be formed by the city executive committees of the soviets of working people's deputies, in cities divided into districts by the executive committees of the district soviets of working people's deputies and in rural localities by the executive committee of the district soviets of working people's deputies.

The election wards shall be formed not later than forty-five days prior to the date of the elections.

ARTICLE 29. In towns, settlements, villages and other rural localities with more than 2,000 inhabitants, election wards are formed so that each ward comprises from 1,500 to 3,000 inhabitants.

ARTICLE 30. The territory of a rural soviet with not more than 2,000 inhabitants constitutes a single election ward; each *stanitsa*, village, *kishlak*, and *aul* with 500 or more inhabitants, but not in excess of 2,000, constitutes a separate election ward. In villages or groups of villages with about 500 inhabitants, but not less than 300, separate election wards may be set up, if the distance from these villages to the election ward centre exceeds ten kilometres.

ARTICLE 31. In remote northern and eastern regions, where small communities prevail, it is permissible to form election wards of not less than 100 inhabitants.

In the national areas in the north as well as in mountainous and nomadic regions it is permissible to form election wards even if the population is below 100, provided, however, that it is not below 50.

ARTICLE 32. Military units and military formations constitute separate election wards of not less than 50 and not more than 3,000 voters, which shall form part of the constituency where the unit or formation is stationed.

ARTICLE 33. Vessels at sea on election day, and with not less than 25 voters on board, may constitute separate election wards, to be included in the constituency of the port of registry.

ARTICLE 34. Hospitals, maternity homes, sanatoriums and invalid homes with not less than 50 voters shall constitute separate election wards.

In hospitals of several buildings election wards may be set up in each building, provided it houses not less than 50 voters.

ARTICLE 35. In long-distance trains that are running on election day, wards are arranged so that voters holding 'Voting Right Certificates' may vote.

CHAPTER V: ELECTION COMMISSIONS

ARTICLE 36. The Supreme Soviet of the USSR Central Election Commission shall consist of representatives from trade-union organizations of workers and other employees, co-operative bodies, Communist Party and youth organizations, cultural, technical, and scientific societies, and other legally registered public organizations and societies of the working people, as well as representatives elected at meetings of workers and employees in enterprises and institutions and servicemen in army units, and at meetings of peasants on collective farms, and in villages, and of farm workers and other employees on state farms.

ARTICLE 37. The Central Election Commission shall be composed of a chairman, vice-chairman, secretary and twenty-four members, and shall be endorsed by the Presidium of the Supreme Soviet of the USSR not later than fifty days prior to the date fixed for the elections.

ARTICLE 38. The Central Election Commission:

(a) Sees that the 'Regulations Governing Elections to the Supreme Soviet of the USSR' are strictly observed throughout the Soviet Union;

(b) Deals with complaints concerning irregularities on the part of election commissions and takes final decisions on the complaints;

(c) Establishes the models of ballot-boxes, the form and colour of ballot-papers, the form of the official records for the registration of candidates by the district election commissions, the form of the official records of the count, the form of the certificates of election, and the design of seals for the election commissions;

(d) Registers the deputies elected to the Supreme Soviet of the USSR;

(e) Turns over the election files and records to the credentials committees of the Soviet of the Union and of the Soviet of Nationalities.

ARTICLE 39. In each union republic, autonomous republic, autonomous region and national area, a Soviet of Nationalities Election Commission of the union republic, autonomous republic, autonomous region or national area shall be set up.

ARTICLE 40. The Soviet of Nationalities Election Commissions shall consist of representatives from trade-union organizations of workers and other employees, co-operative bodies, Communist Party and youth organizations, cultural, technical and scientific societies and other legally registered public organizations and societies of the working people, as well as representatives elected at meetings of workers and other employees in enterprises and institutions and servicemen in army units, and at meetings of peasants on collective farms, and in villages, and of farm workers and other employees on state farms.

ARTICLE 41. The Soviet of Nationalities Election Commissions of the union republics, autonomous republics, autonomous regions and national areas shall be composed of a chairman, vice-chairman, secretary and from ten to sixteen members, and shall be endorsed by the presidiums of the Supreme Soviets of the union and autonomous republics and the executive committees of the soviets of working people's deputies of the autonomous regions and the national areas not later than fifty days before the elections.

ARTICLE 42. The Soviet of Nationalities Election Commissions of union republics, autonomous republics, autonomous regions and national areas shall:

(a) See that the 'Regulations Governing Elections to the Supreme Soviet of the USSR' are strictly observed on the territory of the given republic, autonomous region or national area in the course of the elections;
(b) Deal with complaints of irregularities on the part of Soviet of Nationalities election commissions.

ARTICLE 43. In each Soviet of the Union constituency a District Soviet of the Union Election Commission shall be set up.

ARTICLE 44. The District Soviet of the Union Election Commissions shall consist of representatives from trade-union organizations of workers and other employees, co-operative bodies, Communist Party and youth organizations, cultural, technical and scientific societies, and other legally registered public organizations and societies of the working people, as well as representatives elected at meetings of workers and other employees in enterprises and institutions, and servicemen in army units, and at meetings of peasants on collective farms, and in villages, and of farm workers and other employees on state farms.

ARTICLE 45. District Soviet of the Union Election Commissions shall be composed of a chairman, vice-chairman, secretary and eight members and shall be endorsed: in republics divided into territories or regions — by the executive committees of the territorial and regional soviets of working people's deputies; and in republics not divided into territories or regions — by the presidiums of the Supreme Soviets of these republics not later than fifty days before the election day.

ARTICLE 46. District Soviet of the Union Election Commissions shall:

(a) See that the 'Regulations Governing Elections to the Supreme Soviet of the USSR' are strictly adhered to on the territory of their respective constituencies;
(b) Deal with complaints of irregularities on the part of Ward Election Commissions and take appropriate decisions;
(c) See that the executive committees of the soviets of working people's deputies form the election wards in good time;
(d) See that electoral rolls are compiled and made public in due time;
(e) Register candidates nominated in accordance with the provisions of the Constitution of the USSR and the 'Regulations Governing Elections to the Supreme Soviet of the USSR';
(f) Furnish the Ward Election Commissions with ballot-papers in the prescribed form;
(g) Count the votes cast and establish the returns;
(h) Issue certificates of election to the elected deputies;
(i) Turn over the election files and records to the Central Election Commission.

ARTICLE 47. A District Soviet of Nationalities Election Commission shall be set up in each Soviet of Nationalities constituency.

ARTICLE 48. The District Soviet of Nationalities Election Commissions shall consist of representatives from trade-union organizations of workers and other employees, co-operative bodies, Communist Party and youth organizations, cultural, technical and scientific societies, and other legally registered public organizations and societies of the working people, as well as representatives elected at meetings of workers and other employees in enterprises and institutions, and servicemen in army units, and at meetings of peasants on collective farms, and in villages, and of farm workers and other employees on state farms.

ARTICLE 49. District Soviet of Nationalities Election Commissions shall be composed of a chairman, vice-chairman, secretary and eight members. They are endorsed by the Presidiums of the Supreme Soviets of the union and autonomous republics and by the executive committees of the soviets of working people's deputies of the autonomous regions and national areas not later than fifty days prior to the date fixed for the elections.

ARTICLE 50. The District Soviet of Nationalities Election Commissions:

(a) See that the 'Regulations Governing Elections to the Supreme Soviet of the USSR' are strictly adhered to on the territory of their respective election districts;
(b) Deal with complaints of irregularities on the part of Ward Election Commissions and take appropriate decisions;
(c) See that the executive committees of the soviets of working people's deputies form the election wards in good time;

(d) See that electoral rolls are compiled and made public in due time;

(e) Register candidates nominated in accordance with the provisions of the constitution of the USSR and the 'Regulations Governing Elections to the Supreme Soviet of the USSR';

(f) Furnish the Ward Election Commissions with ballot-papers in the prescribed form;

(g) Count the votes cast and establish the returns;

(h) Issue certificates of election to the elected deputies;

(i) Turn over the election files and records respectively to the Soviet of Nationalities Election Commissions of the Union and Autonomous Republics, Autonomous Regions and National Areas.

ARTICLE 51. A Ward Election Commission common for the elections to the Soviet of the Union and the Soviet of Nationalities shall be set up in each ward.

The ward election commissions shall consist of representatives from trade-union organizations of workers and other employees, co-operative bodies, Communist Party and youth organizations, cultural, technical and scientific societies and other legally registered public organizations and societies of the working people, as well as representatives elected at meetings of workers and other employees in enterprises and institutions, and servicemen of army and naval units, and at meetings of peasants on collective farms, and in villages, and of farm workers and other employees on state farms.

ARTICLE 52. Ward election commissions shall consist of a chairman, vice-chairman, secretary and from four to eight members, and in election wards with less than 300 inhabitants, of a chairman, secretary and from one to three members. Ward election commissions in towns are endorsed by the executive committees of the town soviets of working people's deputies; in towns divided into districts—by the executive committees of the district soviets; in rural localities—by the executive committees of the district soviets not later than forty days prior to the date fixed for the elections.

ARTICLE 53. The ward election commissions:

(a) Receive claims concerning inaccuracies in electoral rolls and submit them for consideration to the executive committees of the soviets which published the rolls;

(b) Receive the ballots in the election ward;

(c) Count the votes cast for each candidate;

(d) Turn over the election files and records to the district Soviet of the Union election commissions or the district Soviet of Nationalities election commissions respectively.

ARTICLE 54. Meetings of the Central Election Commission, the Soviet of Nationalities election commissions of the union republics, autonomous republics, autonomous regions and national areas, the district Soviet of the

Union election commissions, the district Soviet of Nationalities election commissions, and the ward election commissions shall be deemed valid if attended by more than one-half of their total membership.

ARTICLE 55. All questions in the election commissions are decided by a simple majority vote; in the event of an equal division, the chairman has the casting vote.

ARTICLE 56. The Central Election Commission, the Soviet of Nationalities election commissions of the union and autonomous republics, autonomous regions and national areas, the district Soviet of the Union election commissions, the district Soviet of Nationalities election commissions, and the ward election commissions shall each have its seal of a design prescribed by the Central Election Commission.

CHAPTER VI: PROCEDURE FOR NOMINATING CANDIDATES TO
THE SUPREME SOVIET OF THE USSR

ARTICLE 57. In accordance with Article 141 of the constitution of the USSR candidates are nominated according to the constituencies.

The right to nominate candidates to the Supreme Soviet of the USSR is vested in public organizations and societies of the working people, namely, Communist Party organizations, trade unions, co-operatives, youth organizations, and cultural societies.

ARTICLE 58. The right to nominate candidates is exercised by the central bodies of public organizations and societies of the working people and by their republican, territorial, regional, and district bodies, as well as by general meetings of workers and other employees in enterprises and institutions and of servicemen in army units, and also by general meetings of peasants on collective farms, and of farm workers and other employees on state farms.

ARTICLE 59. A candidate for the Supreme Soviet of the USSR may stand for election only in one constituency.

ARTICLE 60. Candidates may not be members of district Soviet of the Union election commissions or of district Soviet of Nationalities election commissions, or of ward election commissions in the constituency in which they are nominated.

ARTICLE 61. A public organization or a society of the working people nominating a candidate for the Supreme Soviet of the USSR must submit to the district election commission the following documents:

(a) The minutes of the meeting at which the candidate was nominated, signed by the members of the presidium, and stating their addresses; the minutes must state the name of the organization nominating the candidate, the time and place of the meeting at which the candidate was nominated, and the number of persons present. The minutes shall also state the surname, name and patronymic of the candidate, his age, address, party affiliation and occupation;

(b) A declaration by the candidate of his consent to stand for election in the given constituency on behalf of the organization which nominated him.

ARTICLE 62. Not later than thirty days prior to the date of the elections, all public organizations or societies of working people nominating candidates for the Supreme Soviet of the USSR must register their candidates either with the district Soviet of the Union election commissions or with the district Soviet of Nationalities election commissions, as the case may be.

ARTICLE 63. District Soviet of the Union election commissions and district Soviet of Nationalities election commissions must register all candidates for the Supreme Soviet of the USSR who have been nominated by public organizations and societies of working people in accordance with the provisions of the Constitution of the USSR and the 'Regulations Governing Elections to the Supreme Soviet of the USSR'.

ARTICLE 64. The surname, name, patronymic, age, occupation and party affiliation of every registered candidate for the Supreme Soviet of the USSR, and the name of the public organization nominating the candidate, shall be published by the district Soviet of the Union election commission or the district Soviet of Nationalities election commission, as the case may be, not later than twenty-five days prior to the date of the elections.

ARTICLE 65. All registered candidates for the Supreme Soviet of the USSR must be included in the ballot-papers.

ARTICLE 66. The refusal of a district Soviet of the Union election commission to register a candidate may be appealed against within a period of two days to the Central Election Commission whose decision shall be final.

ARTICLE 67. The refusal of district Soviet of Nationalities election commissions to register a candidate may be appealed against within a period of two days to the election commissions of the union republic, autonomous republic, autonomous region or national area, and the decision of these bodies may be appealed against to the Central Election Commission. The decision of the Central Election Commission shall be final.

ARTICLE 68. The district Soviet of the Union election commissions and the district Soviet of Nationalities election commissions must not later than fifteen days prior to the date of the elections have the ballot-papers printed and distribute them to all ward election commissions.

ARTICLE 69. The ballot-papers must be printed in the form prescribed by the Central Election Commission, in the language of the inhabitants of the election district in question, and in quantities sufficient to supply all the voters with ballot-papers.

ARTICLE 70. Every organization which has nominated a candidate registered with a district election commission and likewise every citizen of the USSR shall be ensured the right of freely canvassing in favour of that candidate at meetings, in the press and by other means, in accordance with Article 125 of the Constitution of the USSR.

ARTICLE 71. Elections to the Supreme Soviet of the USSR shall be held in the course of one day, which shall be the same throughout the USSR.

ARTICLE 72. The day of elections to the Supreme Soviet of the USSR shall be appointed by the Presidium of the Supreme Soviet of the USSR not later than two months prior to the date of the elections. The elections shall be held on a Sunday.

ARTICLE 73. Every day for a period of twenty days prior to the elections, the ward election commissions shall publish, or otherwise make generally known to the electors, the date of the elections and the place of voting.

ARTICLE 74. Polling shall take place on election day from 6 a.m. until midnight local time.

ARTICLE 75. At 6 a.m. on election day the chairman of a ward election commission shall examine the ballot-boxes in the presence of the members of the commission and ascertain that there is an electoral roll compiled in the prescribed form, whereupon he shall close the boxes and seal them with the seal of the commission and invite the electors to vote.

ARTICLE 76. Special rooms or booths shall be set aside in the polling station for filling in ballot-papers, in which the presence of members of the ward election commissions or of any other persons except the voters, during polling time, is forbidden.

ARTICLE 77. Every elector shall vote personally, attending the polling station for this purpose. Electors shall cast their votes by dropping the ballot-papers into the ballot box.

ARTICLE 78. On appearing at the polling station, the elector shall present to the secretary or any other authorized member of the ward election commission his passport, or collective-farm or trade-union membership card, or some other evidence of identity, and after his name has been checked in the electoral roll and an entry made in the list, recording the issue of ballot-papers, he shall be given ballot-papers of the prescribed form.

ARTICLE 79. While in the room set aside for filling in ballot-papers, the elector shall leave the name of the candidate he votes for and cross out the names of the others. Thence he shall proceed to the ballot-box and drop his ballot-papers into it.

ARTICLE 80. A voter who, owing to illiteracy or physical disability, is unable to fill in the ballot-paper himself, may invite any other voter into the room set aside for filling in ballot-papers to help him to fill in his ballot-papers.

ARTICLE 81. Electioneering in the polling station on election day shall not be permitted.

ARTICLE 82. The ward election commission shall keep a special register of persons who appear at the polling station with a 'Voting Right Certificate' in accordance with Article 20 of the present 'Regulations Governing Elections to the Supreme Soviet of the USSR', which register shall be signed by the chairman and secretary of the commission.

ARTICLE 83. The chairman of the ward election commission shall be responsible for the maintenance of order in the polling station, and his orders must be complied with by everybody present.

ARTICLE 84. At midnight on election day, the chairman of the ward election commission shall declare the polling terminated and the commission shall proceed to open the ballot-boxes.

CHAPTER VIII: COUNTING THE VOTES

ARTICLE 85. The right to attend the counting of votes on the premises of the ward election commission shall be extended to representatives of public organizations and societies of working people, specially authorized for the purpose, and to representatives of the press.

ARTICLE 86. Having opened the ballot-boxes, the ward election commission shall check the number of ballots cast with the number of persons who received them and enter the result in an official record.

ARTICLE 87. The chairman of the ward election commission announces in the presence of all the members of the commission the results of the vote cast by each ballot-paper.

ARTICLE 88. Ballot-papers which contain more candidates than the number of deputies to be elected and also papers not made out in the prescribed form, shall be declared invalid.

ARTICLE 89. Should doubt arise as to the validity of a ballot-paper, the question shall be decided by the ward election commission by vote, and a note made to this effect in an official record.

ARTICLE 90. The counting and registering of the votes cast in the elections to the Soviet of the Union and of the votes cast in the elections to the Soviet of Nationalities shall be conducted separately.

ARTICLE 91. The ward election commission shall draw up in the prescribed form an official record of the voting in three copies, while the ward election commissions in the autonomous republics, autonomous regions and national areas—in four copies, which shall be signed by all the members of the ward election commission, the signatures of the chairman and secretary being indispensable.

ARTICLE 92. The official voting record of the ward election commission must indicate:

(a) The time of commencement and termination of the polling;
(b) The number of electors in the Election Ward;
(c) The number of voters who received ballot-papers;
(d) The number of electors who voted—separately for the Soviet of the Union and for the Soviet of Nationalities;

(e) The number of ballot-papers declared invalid—separately for the Soviet of the Union and for the Soviet of Nationalities;

(f) The number of ballot-papers in which the names of all candidates have been struck out—separately for the Soviet of the Union and for the Soviet of Nationalities;

(g) The number of votes cast for each candidate;

(h) A brief summary of the claims and complaints submitted to the Ward Election Commission, and the decisions adopted by the commission.

ARTICLE 93. When the count of the votes has been completed and the official record drawn up, the Chairman of the Ward Election Commission shall announce the results of the voting at a meeting of the commission.

ARTICLE 94. One copy of the official record of the voting drawn up by the ward election commission shall be dispatched by messenger within twenty-four hours to the district Soviet of the Union election commission; the second copy of the official record of the voting drawn up by the ward election commission shall be dispatched by messenger within twenty-four hours to the district Soviet of Nationalities election commission.

ARTICLE 95. All ballot-papers (the valid separately from those declared invalid) must be sealed, those relating to the Soviet of the Union separately from those relating to the Soviet of Nationalities, with the seal of the ward election commission, and together with the last copy of the official record of the voting and the seal, shall be turned over by the chairman of the ward election commission for safe keeping; in the cities to the executive committees of the city soviets of working people's deputies, in the cities divided into districts to the executive committees of the district soviets, and in rural localities to the executive committees of the district soviets of working people's deputies.

ARTICLE 96. It shall be incumbent on the executive committees of the soviets of working people's deputies to keep the ballot-papers pending a special instruction by the Presidium of the Supreme Soviet of the USSR.

ARTICLE 97. The right to be present on the premises where the votes are counted by a district election commission while the count is being made shall be extended to representatives of public organizations and of societies of working people, specially authorized for the purpose, and to representatives of the press.

ARTICLE 98. The district election commission shall make a count of the votes on the basis of the official records submitted by the ward election commissions and shall ascertain the number of votes cast for each candidate.

ARTICLE 99. The district Soviet of the Union election commission and the district Soviet of Nationalities election commission of the union republic shall draw up an official record of the voting in two copies, while the district Soviet of Nationalities election commission of the autonomous republic, autonomous region or national area shall draw up an official record of the voting in three copies, which shall be signed by the members of the District Election Commission, the signatures of the Chairman and Secretary being indispensable.

ARTICLE 100. The official voting record of the district election commission shall indicate:

(a) The number of ward election commissions in the district;
(b) The number of ward election commissions that submitted official records;
(c) The number of electors in the district;
(d) The number of voters who received ballot-papers;
(e) The number of electors who have voted;
(f) The number of ballot-papers declared invalid;
(g) The number of ballot-papers in which the names of all candidates have been struck out;
(h) The number of votes cast for each candidate;
(i) A brief summary of the applications and complaints to the district election commission, and the decisions adopted by the commission.

ARTICLE 101. After the official record has been signed, the chairman of the district election commission shall announce the result of the elections at a meeting of the commission.

ARTICLE 102. The candidate for the Supreme Soviet of the USSR who receives an absolute majority of votes, i.e., more than half the total number of valid votes cast in the district, shall be elected.

ARTICLE 103. The chairman of the district election commission shall issue a certificate of election to the candidate elected to the Supreme Soviet of the USSR.

ARTICLE 104. Not later than twenty-four hours after the count of the votes is completed, the Chairman of the district Soviet of the Union election commission and the Chairman of the district Soviet of Nationalities election commission must dispatch the first copy of the official record in a sealed package by messenger to the Central Election Commission, and the second copy of the official record to the Soviet of Nationalities election commission of the union republic, autonomous republic, autonomous region or national area.

ARTICLE 105. If none of the candidates shall have received an absolute majority of votes, the district election commission shall make a note to that effect in the official record and inform the Central Election Commission and the Soviet of Nationalities election commission of the union republic, autonomous republic, autonomous region or national area and shall simultaneously announce a reballot of the two candidates who received the largest number of votes and appoint a day for a new election, which shall be held not later than two weeks after the date of the first ballot.

ARTICLE 106. If in any district the number of votes cast shall be less than one-half the number of electors entitled to vote in that district, the district Soviet of the Union election commission or the district Soviet of Nationalities election commission, as the case may be, shall make a note to that effect in the official record and immediately inform the Central Election Commission and the Soviet of Nationalities election commission of the union republic, autonomous republic, autonomous region or national area, whereupon the Central Election Commission shall appoint new elections, which shall be held not later than two weeks after the date of the first elections.

ARTICLE 107. The re-election of candidates, as well as new elections held in place of elections declared void, shall be conducted on the basis of the electoral rolls drawn up for the first elections, and shall comply with the provisions of the present 'Regulations Governing Elections to the Supreme Soviet of the USSR'.

ARTICLE 108. In the event of a seat in the Supreme Soviet of the USSR falling vacant, the Presidium of the Supreme Soviet of the USSR shall appoint a date for the election of a new deputy in the constituency concerned, which date shall be not later than two months after the seat in the Supreme Soviet of the USSR falls vacant.

ARTICLE 109. Any person who by violence, fraud, intimidation or bribery hinders a citizen of the USSR in the free exercise of his right to elect and be elected to the Supreme Soviet of the USSR bears criminal responsibility as established by law.

ARTICLE 110. Any official of a Soviet or member of an election commission guilty of falsifying election documents, or of deliberately falsifying the count, shall be liable to a term of imprisonment of up to three years.

Source: V. I. Vasiliev, i drugie, *Sbornik Zakonov SSSR*, Vol. 1 (Moscow 1968), p. 215.
Translation: S. Belsky and M. Saifulin, in A. Denisov and M. Kirichenko, *Soviet State Law* (Moscow, 1960), p. 413.

16. Khrushchev's Criticism of Local Government under Stalin

22 January 1957

This decree may be regarded as the Khrushchev leadership's definitive comment on the weaknesses of local government under Stalin. It is noteworthy that one of the main criticisms concerned unwarranted party interference, an evil which stemmed from the very nature of party rule (see document 22). The wide range of deficiencies listed leaves little doubt that the soviets were in a sorry state. The new leadership was anxious to improve matters, without, of course, enhancing the powers of the local soviets vis-à-vis the Party to any significant degree. The decree of 22 January 1957 should be read with that of 16 November 1965, pp. 112–16 below.

16. On Improving the Work of the Soviets of Workers' Deputies and Strengthening their Ties with the Masses

Decree of the Central Committee of the CPSU, 22 January 1957

1. The soviets of workers' deputies are a great achievement of the Soviet people. Based on the indestructible union of workers and peasants under the leadership of the working class, the Soviet system has ensured the triumph of socialism, an increase in the might of our motherland, a steady improvement in the material well-being and cultural level of the workers and a strengthening of the brotherly friendship of the peoples of the USSR ...
2. At the same time the Central Committee of the CPSU notes that the practical work of the soviets of workers' deputies and their executive organs suffers from serious defects, while the standard of work of many soviets is still not up to the tasks set by the Twentieth Party Congress.

Many local soviets perform their functions as organizers of the masses in economic and cultural construction inadequately. They do not show enough concern for the vital needs of the workers, and frequently overlook serious cases of negligence in housing construction; they show little initiative or persistence in improving the work of schools, hospitals, bath-houses, child-care institutions, clubs and libraries, shops, dining-halls and other enterprises and institutions which are supposed to serve the public.

Facts show that in those places where party and soviet bodies show genuine concern for the needs of the people and get on with the work in a proper, energetic manner, rapid results are achieved. In this respect the initiative shown by party and soviet organizations in the city of Gorky deserves full approval. At the beginning of last year the city soviet, actively assisted by its deputies, standing commissions and *aktiv*, devised a detailed plan for housing, public-amenity construction and urban welfare. This plan was examined and approved at a meeting of the soviet, and large numbers of the public were brought in to assist in its practical implementation ... A great deal of work on housing construction and urban welfare is also being carried out, with the general participation of the public, by soviets of workers' deputies in Moscow, Leningrad, Kiev, Minsk, Stalingrad, Omsk, Ryazan and Irkutsk.

Positive results in this matter may be obtained not only in large cities and industrial centres, but also in any rural area; all that is required is for the soviets to organize the people's initiative more skilfully, and show more persistence in solving these problems.

The most important task for the Central Committees of the Communist parties of union republics and for party committees in the *kraiya, oblasti,* towns and *raiony* is to eliminate shortcomings in the work of local soviets, and increase the role played by the soviets and their executive organs in implementing party and government policy in economic and cultural construction. It is necessary, day by day, to direct the work of the soviets towards solving the urgent problems of economic and cultural life, to extend their ties with the people as much as possible, and help them to become the true organizers of the masses in the struggle for the further consolidation of our socialist state.

In implementing the decisions of the December Plenum of the Central Committee the local soviets and their executive organs must increase their influence and their responsibility for the work of industry and agriculture; they must strive to achieve fulfilment of production plans and targets by every plant, factory, construction site, collective farm, state farm, and machine and tractor station. It is essential that soviet organs should constantly concern themselves with the construction and repair of houses, schools, hospitals, child-care institutions and communal amenity enterprises, see that they serve the public properly, provide the necessary amenities in towns and villages, and improve the work of the urban transport and communication services. The soviets must show greater initiative in procuring and using local building materials and in encouraging individual house-construction; they must exercise effective control over the proper use of funds and materials and not allow them to be frittered away or blocked, and they must also keep a close check on all kinds of extravagance which raise construction costs.

The soviets are faced with no less responsible tasks in improving state and co-operative trade, and in providing the public with the basic necessities. The soviets of workers' deputies must skilfully regulate the work of all shops and public catering enterprises and provide for the cultural needs of the consumer; they must battle resolutely against abuses of all kinds and take positive steps to use local resources for the greatest possible development of food and consumer-goods production, in every way encouraging the initiative and resourcefulness of soviet, economic and co-operative organizations in this matter.

In order to improve further the standard of work in local soviets and increase their responsibility for economic and cultural improvement it is essential that the Central Committees of Communist parties, the Presidiums of the Supreme Soviets and the Councils of Ministers of the union republics, guided by the decisions of the December Plenum of the Central Committee, should implement as soon as possible practical measures to extend the rights of the soviets, primarily in matters of economic planning in the *krai*, *oblast*, town, and *raion*, the production and distribution of the products of local and co-operative industrial enterprises, the organization of housing, cultural and welfare projects and road construction, the extensive development of the production of building materials and fuel, and in deciding financial and budgetary matters.

3. The Central Committee of the CPSU considers that the soviets of workers' deputies are not exercising to a sufficient degree the rights granted to them by the constitution to decide matters of economic and cultural development, manage the administrative bodies and enterprises under their jurisdiction, and ensure the preservation of public order and civil rights, and the observance of socialist legality. These vital matters in the practical work of the soviets are rarely brought forward for review at their meetings. Many executive committees and managers of their administrations and departments, and likewise managers of economic organizations, do not report to the soviets on their work; this leads to a lack of control and undermines the leading role of the soviets as organs of state power in the localities. In many cases sessions of the soviets are confined to discussing trivial matters of a current character; they are conducted in a formal way, sometimes only for outward approval of draft decisions prepared by the executive committees. Consequently, the meetings are conducted sluggishly; shortcomings and errors in the work of the soviet organs and their leaders are not subject to sharp criticism; proposals which are put forward by the deputies are often left unattended, while those decisions which are taken are of little substance and full of general appeals and declarations.

The party and soviet organs must do everything to make the soviets' role more active, to give their work a militant content, and ensure that they make full use of their rights. Sessions must be convened regularly, and the range of questions discussed at them extended. Sessions must be conducted not for show or for the formal or ceremonial approval of proposed legislation, but for business-like discussion, to resolve pressing questions of the economic and cultural life of the *krai*, *oblast*, town or *raion*: these include, for example, economic plans, the budget, the working of industry, the development of agriculture, the housing situation, cultural and welfare amenities and the urban economy, the work of the state education bodies, public health, trade, public catering, the militia, the preservation of socialist property and the personal property of citizens, the fight against crime. Systematic discussion of the reports of the executive committee and heads of corresponding links in the soviet and economic apparatus, and of the reports on the fulfilment of the electorate's mandates, must take place at the meetings.

An atmosphere must be created at sessions of the soviets which ensures the extensive use of criticism and self-criticism, so that deputies may discuss the questions put before them from every angle and without haste, voice their comments and suggestions, address inquiries to the executive organs and economic managers, and receive exhaustive answers. We must establish a system whereby executive committees report to the deputies at their sessions on the main aspects of their work between sessions, and also on the fulfilment of the decisions of the soviet. The heads of executive committees, administrations and departments are required to give detailed answers and explanations of the steps they have taken as a result of the deputies' critical comments, requests and proposals.

We should put an end to the abnormal situation which arises when the public does not in effect know what questions are being considered or what decisions are being taken by local soviets and their executive organs. The task is to publicize the work of the soviets, highlight their activity in the local press and on the radio, and inform the public of the decisions which are being taken. After each session deputies must, as a rule, meet their constituents, inform them of the decisions reached and do the local organizational work involved in fulfilling them.

4. Serious failings occur in the soviets' mass organizational work. Many soviets and their executive committees do not rely on the numerous workers' *aktivy* and have little connection with the public. The heads of executive committees and their departments often do not consider it their duty to appear before the workers or report on the soviets' work; neither do they receive visitors regularly, which is why, in many cases, citizens' legitimate requests are not agreed to. For instance, the chairman and deputy chairman of the executive committee of the Ferghana *oblast* do not accept visits from many workers, fail to observe the established procedure for meeting citizens and are often not available on visiting days. The deputies of the Stavropol Krai soviet justly criticize their executive committee for its poor links with the localities and for its ignorance of the day-to-day life of the *raiony*, collective and state farms, and machine and tractor stations. Unfortunately such failings are also to be found in the work of other executive committees of local soviets. There are also many deputies of soviets who rarely meet their constituents, who do not report to them on their work, and who ignore the criticism of the masses, thereby losing their sense of responsibility towards the people.

The Central Committee calls the attention of all party and soviet organizations to the need for a considerable improvement in the mass organizational work of the soviets, and for further strengthening their ties with the public. Particular attention must be paid to improving work with deputies and increasing their activities in the soviets and among the electorate. Soviet deputies must be constantly in the midst of the people; they must be acquainted with the needs, requirements and attitudes of the masses, hold regular meetings and consultations with the electorate, carefully consider statements and complaints made by the public, and offer assistance in satisfying them. Party organizations and the executive committees of soviets must help in organizing meetings between deputies and the electorate, and in arranging the deputies' periodic reports on their own work and that of the soviet.

In view of the fact that the right to recall deputies who have not justified the confidence of the electorate as provided for by the constitution is not actually exercised—there being no established recall procedure—the Presidiums of the Supreme Soviets of the union and autonomous republics must forthwith draft regulations establishing a procedure for recalling the deputies of local soviets.

Any improvement in the work of the soviets largely depends on the proper organization of the work of the executive organs. It is the duty of the executive committees of the soviets and of their departments to exercise direct and constant control over cultural, political and economic construction, to see that the needs and requirements of the workers are satisfied, and to carry out the decisions made by the soviets and higher state organs. In all their work the executive committees must rely on the deputies and numerous activists; they must strictly adhere to the principles of collectivity in the work of the soviets, and not allow themselves to replace the soviets in deciding matters which require examination in full session.

5. The permanent commissions are important for the practical work of the soviets and for strengthening their links with the masses. In this respect the work of the permanent commissions of the Moscow City Soviet of workers' deputies deserves commendation. They actively help to implement the decisions of the soviet and higher state organs and assist the executive committee in organizing the fulfilment of the urban economy development plans. These commissions systematically check the work of the Moscow soviet executive committee's departments and administrations, and that of enterprises and institutions under its control; they reveal deficiencies in their work and help eliminate them ...

It is the duty of party organs and the executive committees of the soviets to make real improvements in the work of the permanent commissions, and to ensure an active part for them in preparing questions for sessions and meetings of the executive committee, in controlling the fulfilment of decisions made by the soviets and higher organs, and in carrying out organizational work among the masses. The permanent commissions must participate in formulating draft decisions, they must deliver collateral reports at sessions, take part in the discussion of economic plans, and exercise control over the work of enterprises and institutions subordinate to the soviet. Executive committees and their departments and administrations must examine the permanent commissions' recommendations and take appropriate practical measures with regard to them. The rights of the commissions should also be extended. It would for example, be expedient to establish a system whereby the soviets' housing commissions would consider, and make advance recommendations on, the order in which people needing homes were suited, and would participate in the allocation of living space.

6. The Central Committee of the CPSU considers that the most important task facing all party organizations, soviets of workers' deputies and their executive committees is to improve further the work of the soviet apparatus and struggle resolutely against all instances of bureaucratism, red tape and careless attitudes towards the needs of the public in the work of every institution and enterprise, especially in that of the executive committees, their administrations and departments.

The facts show that the everyday needs of the workers are often inadequately met, not because the local soviets do not have the right conditions or material backing, but on account of bureaucratism and red tape, and the irresponsibility of certain soviet employees who have lost touch with the public, and who cannot see living people for paper.

Instances of bureaucratism and red tape which are manifest in the work of the soviet apparatus, and an indifferent attitude towards people, form an evil which is detrimental to the cause of communist construction. Officials who are guilty of heartlessness, rudeness, arrogance and procrastination when investigating public complaints and requests must not go unpunished. We must cultivate a heightened sense of responsibility and personal humility in soviet officials, and demand that they treat people attentively, bearing in mind that it is by the work of the soviet apparatus and its heads that the workers judge Soviet power as a whole. The complete eradication of bureaucratism and red tape cannot be regarded as a short-term campaign; it involves a constant, persistent and unyielding struggle against this evil.

Increasing the activity of the soviets, extending their ties with the masses and strengthening their control over their executive committees and all links of the soviet and economic apparatus will doubtless help to strengthen even further the local organs of state administration and eliminate the major faults and bureaucratic distortions which still exist in Soviet institutions and organizations.

7. As the leading and directing force of Soviet society, our party is responsible for everything which is done in the country; this includes the work of the soviets, the trade unions, the Komsomol, and all mass social organizations of the workers. The party organizations also take direct responsibility for the serious shortcomings from which the work of the local soviets suffers. It is essential to recognize that as far as the practical administration of the soviets

is concerned party organs are in many cases guilty of interference in the administrative and managerial work of these organs, and take their place in deciding economic and other matters; they forget the Party's most important instruction to the effect that 'the functions of party collectives must not under any circumstances be mixed up with the functions of state organs such as the soviets ... The Party must get its decisions implemented through the soviet organs, *within the framework of the Soviet constitution.* The Party endeavours *to guide* the work of the soviets but not to replace them.'[1]

The Central Committee obliges all party organizations to put a decisive end to unnecessary guardianship and petty interference in the work of the soviets and their executive committees, and to ensure the further development of initiative and independence in the soviets' work. It should be borne in mind that the *raion*, town and *oblast* party committees cannot replace soviet organs or supplement the work of the organs of state administration with their own.

The key to the proper management of the soviets by party committees lies primarily in the reinforcement of soviet organs by officials with experience, training and initiative who are truly capable of putting the party line into effect. We must train our leading soviet personnel in a spirit of strict responsibility for the job entrusted to them, a spirit of intolerance towards any inadequacies in the work of the soviet apparatus, and one of strengthening state discipline. We must also put an end to the practice of co-opting people for elective posts in the soviets, and that of dismissing soviet officials without a decision of the soviets of workers' deputies.

Party committees must activate the work of party groups in the soviets and their executive committees, and increase their role and responsibility for the work of these organs. At present the majority of party groups in the soviets are not fulfilling the functions set down in the statutes of the CPSU satisfactorily; their work, to a significant degree, bears a formal character, they assemble rarely, and do not discuss matters relating to the Communists' work in a given soviet. Such a situation cannot be regarded as normal; it is detrimental to party guidance of soviet organs. We must ensure that all directives which are issued by party organs and concern the work of the soviets are implemented through Communists working in the soviets, and through the party groups in the soviets' executive committees and sessions.

8. The Central Committee of the CPSU instructs party and soviet organs to use the forthcoming elections to the local soviets of workers' deputies for revitalizing all soviets' work and ensuring that worthy representatives of the workers, collective farmers and intelligentsia are elected to the soviets.

Elections to the soviets will take place against a background of great political and industrial growth resulting from the decisions of the Twentieth Party Congress. The further development of socialist democratism has helped the workers to become more active and has strengthened the control

[1] *KPSS v resolyutsiakh*, chast I, p. 446. See document 22, p. 135, below. (Ed.)

of the masses over the work of the soviets, their executive committees and deputies. Under these conditions it is to be expected that criticism of the organs of state power and of our officials during the elections will be even keener, the demands made on deputies greater, and the candidates for the seats available discussed much more actively. It is essential that party organs, local soviets and their officials should accept criticism from the masses in the right spirit, and take steps to eradicate faults in the work of soviet organs.

At the same time it should be borne in mind that certain hostile anti-Soviet elements will attempt to use the election campaign for the purpose of defaming the Soviet system and claiming that existing isolated cases of bureaucratic mismanagement embrace the entire state apparatus, so as to discredit it. Party organizations must firmly rebuff these hostile and demagogic elements and protect honest and conscientious officials who have been proposed as candidates.

We must develop organizational, agitation and propaganda work extensively, and on this basis strive for the active participation of every voter in the elections. During the election campaign, mass political work must be directed to mobilizing the workers for the successful implementation of the decisions of the Twentieth Party Congress and the December Plenary Session of the CPSU. In the course of this work detailed explanations should be given of the Communist Party and Soviet Government's policy, which is directed towards the further development of industry and agriculture and a steady improvement in the material welfare and cultural level of the people.

It is necessary to demonstrate, in lectures, reports and interviews, the great advantages of the Soviet social and state structure over the capitalist system, and of Soviet over bourgeois democracy; to explain the constitution of the USSR, the constitutions of the union and autonomous republics, the Leninist national policy of the Communist Party and the rights and duties of citizens of the USSR. We must reveal the successes which our people have achieved under Communist Party leadership, and show the prospects which are opening up before our country in connection with the realization of the sixth Five-Year Plan. In describing our achievements, propagandists and agitators must not pass over in silence the existing difficulties and shortcomings, or fail in their duty to give a true explanation of the causes of these difficulties, and to mobilize the workers to overcome them.

In the forthcoming elections, as before, the Communist Party will appear jointly with the trade unions, the Komsomol, and other workers' organizations and societies. Prospective deputies must therefore be candidates for both the Communist and non-party bloc.

In proposing candidates one should not act in haste; candidates must first be discussed at workers' shop meetings and meetings of collective-farm workers' brigades, and an agreement arrived at about them; the consensus of opinion must be determined, and only afterwards a single candidate nominated at the general meeting of the collective.

It cannot, as in past years, be considered normal for few workers and collective farmers engaged directly in production to be elected to the soviets, or for a certain proportion of the candidates for these posts to be nominated only by virtue of their official standing, and elected as deputies to several soviets at once. We must rectify this situation and provide for a broader selection of workers and collective farmers to become members of the soviets.

Party organizations must ensure strict compliance with the constitution and the statutes on elections, and organize detailed discussions of candidates at meetings of the electorate. It is essential for meetings between candidates and electors to be public, and for the electors to have the opportunity to become well acquainted with every candidate and critically appraise his social and production work before he is registered in the ward electoral commissions.

The Central Committee of the CPSU feels confident that the forthcoming elections to the local soviets of workers' deputies will be a mighty new demonstration of the strength of our nation, its solidarity around the Communist Party and its readiness to go on supporting the internal and foreign policy of the Soviet state under the direction of our party. The elections will strengthen even further the bond between the working class and the peasantry, and the friendship between the peoples of the USSR; they will bring about another increase in the political and production activities of the toilers in their struggle for the construction of a Communist society.

Source: V. N. Malin, i drugie, *Spravochnik partiinogo rabotnika* (Moscow, 1957), p. 448. Editor's translation.

17. Khrushchev's Reform of Economic Administration

10 *May* 1957

By the mid-'fifties the Soviet leadership was very concerned with the falling rate of growth in Soviet industry. The establishment of 105 economic councils, or sovnarkhozy, was Khrushchev's proposed answer to the problem. This measure involved the abolition of over 140 economic ministries, the regionalization of industrial administration, and a corresponding increase in party tutelage in the localities.

Khrushchev's proposals had encountered considerable opposition in the Presidium at the end of 1956 and the beginning of 1957. The sovnarkhozy *did not, in the event, live up to his expectations. Recentralization (by reducing the number of councils and creating central co-ordinating bodies) was found to be necessary in the early 'sixties. The* sovnarkhozy *were dismantled, and the old ministerial structure restored almost unchanged, in 1965, after Khrushchev had fallen from power.*

17. Law on Further Improving the Organization of Management of Industry and Construction

Passed by the Presidium of the Supreme Soviet of the USSR, 10 *May* 1957

The USSR Supreme Soviet notes that the question of further improving the organization of the management of industry and construction submitted by the Party Central Committee and the USSR Council of Ministers for examination by the seventh session of the USSR Supreme Soviet is of great significance in the successful solution of tasks of communist construction.

The nationwide discussion of this question which preceded the USSR Supreme Soviet session and its examination at the session itself have shown that the measures worked out by the Party Central Committee and the USSR Council of Ministers have met with the unanimous support and approval of all peoples of the Soviet Union. These measures fully accord with the tasks of developing the national economy of the USSR at its present stage and with the interests of a further strengthening of the country's economic might and a steady rise in the Soviet people's well-being.

As a result of consistent implementation of the Leninist general line regarding the preponderant development of heavy industry as the very foundation of the entire Soviet economy, the peoples of the Soviet Union, under the leadership of the Communist Party, have during the years of Soviet rule once and for all put an end to the age-old economic and cultural backwardness of our country. They have created a powerful socialist industry and large-scale mechanized agriculture, and have achieved the flourishing of science and technology and a tremendous economic and cultural advance of all nations and peoples of the USSR. The Soviet Union has surpassed many capitalist countries in economic development and, in terms of the level of industrial output, has taken second place in the world. By 1957 the volume of industrial output was 30 times that of the pre-revolutionary period and the volume of machine-building and metal-processing output was 180 times as great. The generation of power has increased nearly 100 times. Thanks to the rapid development of heavy industry, many sectors of the national economy have been equipped with up-to-date machinery; this alleviates, to a tremendous extent, the labour of millions of Soviet people and raises their productivity. During the past years major successes have been achieved in the development of socialist agriculture. Sown areas have been considerably expanded by developing virgin and idle lands. The harvest yield of grain and other agricultural crops has risen sharply. Output of livestock products has increased. On the basis of the successes achieved in the development of the national economy, the working people's standard of living is steadily rising in our country.

The outstanding successes in the development of our country's socialist economy are the most convincing confirmation of the correctness of the policy pursued by the Communist Party and the Soviet government, a proof of the great vital force of the Leninist principles of socialist economic management of the entire national economy on the basis of a unified state plan and centralized guidance of economic construction with maximum development of the creative initiative of the masses and their extensive participation in production management.

At the same time, the tremendous growth of the national economy, the creation of a powerful socialist industry, the unprecedented scale of industrial construction in union and autonomous republics, territories and many provinces, and the existence locally of numerous cadres of highly qualified specialists and scientists pose ever more insistently the question of the necessity of further improving the organizational forms of the management of industry and construction in order to bring management closer to production—to enterprises and construction projects—and to make it more concrete and efficient.

At present, with more than 200,000 industrial enterprises and 100,000 construction projects in our country, it is impossible to manage production concretely and efficiently from several all-Union industrial ministries and agencies. It has become imperative to expand even more the powers of union republics in the sphere of economic construction and to transfer the centre of gravity of operational guidance of enterprises and construction projects to the localities, to economic administrative regions.

The interests of developing the USSR economy demand further improvement in the organizational forms of the management of industry and

construction, the setting up of more flexible methods of economic management that will give even wider scope to the development of the country's
production forces.

Towards this end it is necessary to make the transition from the management of industry and construction through industrial ministries and agencies,
which have played a positive role in economic construction, to new forms of
the management of industrial enterprises and construction projects on the
territorial principle, preserving their specialization by industry on the basis
of economic regions. The transition to new forms of management of industry
and construction will make it possible to improve the guidance of economic
construction by eliminating numerous departmental barriers which impede
further development of specialization and co-operation in industry and to
make the fullest use of existing reserves. Economic councils, organized in
economic administrative regions, should be the main organizational form of
the management of industry and construction.

Realization of these measures marks a new stage in implementation of the
Leninist principle of democratic centralism in the guidance of economic
construction and in further strengthening the planning principle on a nationwide scale, and makes it possible correctly to combine centralized state
guidance of the economy with development of the initiative of republic and
local agencies, with an expansion of their rights and responsibility and with
even more active participation of the broad working masses in production
management. This will ensure a steady rise in material output, successful
realization of technical progress, the fullest utilization of reserves in the
national economy, a rise in the productivity of social labour, a strengthening of
the country's economic might and an advance in the Soviet people's well-being.

The USSR Supreme Soviet resolves:

ARTICLE 1. To approve the measures for improving the organization of
the management of industry and construction which have been worked out
by the Party Central Committee and the USSR Council of Ministers, which
received unanimous support during the nationwide discussion and which
aim at ensuring a steady advance of the country's national economy, further
extension of the powers of the union republics in economic construction, the
bringing of management closer to production, still broader participation of the
masses of working people in production management and comprehensive
development of their creative initiative in communist construction.

ARTICLE 2. To establish that the management of industry and construction
is to be carried out according to the territorial principle on the basis of
economic administrative regions.

The economic administrative regions are to be formed by the Supreme
Soviets of the union republics.

ARTICLE 3. An economic council for the management of industry and construction is to be formed in each economic administrative region.

ARTICLE 4. The economic council of an economic administrative region is to be formed by the union-republic Council of Ministers and will consist of a chairman, vice-chairman and members of the economic council.

To establish that the chairmen of economic councils, on the recommendation of the chairman of the union-republic Council of Ministers to the union-republic Supreme Soviet, may be appointed Ministers and be included in the union-republic Council of Ministers.

ARTICLE 5. The economic council of an economic administrative region is to be directly subordinate in all its activities to the union-republic Council of Ministers.

The USSR Council of Ministers is to exercise direction of the economic councils through the union-republic Councils of Ministers.

ARTICLE 6. The economic council of an economic administrative region is to have a technical-economics council with the status of a consultative body.

ARTICLE 7. The structure of the economic council of an economic administrative region is to be confirmed by the union-republic Council of Ministers.

ARTICLE 8. The economic council of an economic administrative region, within the bounds of its competence, makes decisions and issues directives on the basis and in execution of the laws of the USSR and union republics and of the decrees and directives of the USSR Council of Ministers and the union-republic Council of Ministers.

The decisions and directives of an economic council can be revoked by the union-republic Council of Ministers.

The USSR Council of Ministers has the right to suspend the decisions and directives of an economic council.

ARTICLE 9. In view of the reorganization of the management of industry and construction, to abolish the following all-union USSR ministries: Automobile Industry; Machine Building; Instruments and Automation; Machine Tools; Construction Machinery and Road Machine Building; Construction for the Oil Industry; Tractor and Farm Machine Building; Transport Machine Building; Heavy Machine Building; Electrical Equipment Industry.

ARTICLE 10. To merge the USSR Ministry of Power Plants and the USSR Ministry of Power Plant Construction into an all-union USSR Ministry of Power Plants.

To merge the USSR Ministry of the Defence Industry and the USSR Ministry of General Machine Building into an all-Union USSR Ministry of the Defence Industry.

ARTICLE 11. To abolish the following union-republic USSR ministries: Paper and Wood-Processing Industry; Urban and Rural Construction; Light Industry; Lumber Industry; Oil Industry; Meat and Dairy Products Industry; Food Products Industry; Building Materials Industry; Fishing Industry; Construction; Construction for the Metallurgical and Chemical

Industries; Construction for the Coal Industry; Coal Industry; Nonferrous Metallurgy; Ferrous Metallurgy.

In connection with this, to deem it necessary to abolish the corresponding Union-republic ministries of the union republics.

ARTICLE 12. To transfer enterprises and organizations which are under ministries to be abolished to the direct jurisdiction of the appropriate economic councils of the economic administrative regions.

ARTICLE 13. To transfer enterprises and organizations which fall under the all-union Ministries of the Aviation Industry, the Defence Industry, the Radio Industry, the Shipbuilding Industry, the Chemical Industry, and Power Plants to the direct jurisdiction of the appropriate economic councils of the economic administrative regions, according to a list approved by the USSR Council of Ministers.

To assign to the USSR ministries mentioned in this article the functions of planning their industries and seeing to high technical standards in the development of production. To establish that these functions are to be carried out by the ministries through the economic councils of the economic administrative regions.

ARTICLE 14. To transfer enterprises which fall under the non-industrial USSR ministries to the direct jurisdiction of the appropriate economic councils, according to a list approved by the USSR Council of Ministers.

ARTICLE 15. To entrust the USSR Council of Ministers, in accordance with this law, with establishing the procedure and dates for transferring enterprises and organizations, as well as equipment, raw materials and other property, under the ministries to be abolished to the economic councils of the economic administrative regions.

ARTICLE 16. To entrust the USSR Council of Ministers and the union-republic Councils of Ministers with the task of providing employment, within the shortest period of time, for employees released from the apparatus of ministries and agencies, displaying in this the necessary attention and concern.

ARTICLE 17. To entrust the union-republic Councils of Ministers with submitting for consideration by the union-republic Supreme Soviets proposals for abolishing the republic economic ministries and for transferring the enterprises and organizations under these ministries to the economic Councils of the economic administrative regions or to the local Soviets.

ARTICLE 18. To reorganize the USSR Council of Ministers' State Commission for Long-Range Planning of the National Economy as the USSR Council of Ministers' State Planning Committee (USSR Gosplan).

To establish that the USSR State Planning Committee is to be a scientific economic planning agency of the country's national economy.

To entrust the USSR State Planning Committee with the comprehensive study of the national economy's requirements and the drafting of current and long-range plans for development of the national economy, taking into account the achievements of science and technology, with the conduct of a single centralized policy in developing major branches of the national economy and, on this basis, with ensuring correct distribution of the country's production forces and balanced development of all branches of the national economy, and also with working out plans for the material and technical supply of the national economy and with ensuring control over strict observance of state discipline in providing supplies for industrial production.

In this connection, to abolish the USSR Council of Ministers' State Economic Commission for Current Planning of the National Economy, inasmuch as its functions will be carried out by the USSR State Planning Committee and the Union-republic state planning commissions.

ARTICLE 19. To set up a State Scientific and Technical Committee under the USSR Council of Ministers, entrusting it with the study of the achievements of Soviet and foreign science and technology and of advanced production experience, with wide-scale propaganda of these achievements, with the publication of scientific and technical literature and with control over the development and introduction of new machinery in the national economy.

In this connection, to abolish the USSR Council of Ministers' State Committee on New Technology.

To consider it expedient to set up scientific and technical committees under the union-republic Councils of Ministers and, when necessary, under the economic councils of the economic administrative regions.

ARTICLE 20. To add to the composition of the USSR Council of Ministers the chairmen of the union-republic Councils of Ministers, the chairman of the USSR Council of Ministers' State Scientific and Technical Committee and the head of the USSR Council of Ministers' Central Statistical Administration.

To establish that vice-chairmen of the USSR State Planning Committee and the heads of the major departments of the USSR State Planning Committee, on the recommendation of the chairman of the USSR Council of Ministers to the USSR Supreme Soviet, may be appointed USSR Ministers and included in the USSR Council of Ministers.

ARTICLE 21. To instruct the USSR Council of Ministers to work out and approve Statutes on the Economic Councils of Economic Administrative Regions, on the USSR Council of Ministers' State Planning Committee, on the USSR Council of Ministers' State Scientific and Technical Committee and on the USSR Council of Ministers' Central Statistical Administration.

ARTICLE 22. To establish that reorganization of the management of industry and construction, provided for by this law, must be carried out by 1 July 1957.

D. KOROTCHENKO, Chairman of the Presidium, USSR Supreme Soviet.

M. GEORGADZE, Secretary of the Presidium.

The Kremlin, Moscow, 10 May 1957.

Source: V. N. Malin, i drugie, *Spravochnik partiinogo rabotnika* (Moscow, 1957), p. 227.
Translation: Current Digest of the Soviet Press, ed. Leo Gruliow (published by the American Association for the Advancement of Slavic Studies, Ohio State University, Columbus, Ohio 43210), Vol. IX, No. 20, p. 14.
This publication is hereafter referred to as *CDSP*.

18. The Restrictions on the Publication of Supreme Soviet Legislation

19 June 1958

One characteristic of the Soviet regime is its failure to publish all-important laws passed by the central authorities. A series of laws published in the mid-'twenties legalized this form of state secrecy, though it was occasionally criticized by Soviet writers. The edict reproduced below was an attempt to clarify the position at a time when a great deal of Stalinist legislation was being revised. To this extent it was a step forward : but it will be noted that the Supreme Soviet, with which it was specifically concerned, retained considerable freedom to restrict publication of its decisions. In the late 'sixties only a small fraction of all the decrees of the Council of Ministers of the USSR and RSFSR were in fact being made known to the public, though the most important of them were probably in this category.[1] The Party presumably has its own set of regulations on the publication of party decrees, but this is certainly even more restrictive.

18. On the Method of Publishing and Implementing Laws of the USSR, Decrees of the Supreme Soviet of the USSR, Edicts and Decrees of the Presidium of the Supreme Soviet of the USSR

Edict of 19 June 1958

With the aim of regularizing the publication of laws of the USSR and edicts of the Presidium of the Supreme Soviet of the USSR, and fixing the terms for bringing them into force, the Presidium of the Supreme Soviet of the USSR *decrees* that

1. The laws of the USSR, decrees and other acts of the Supreme Soviet of the USSR, edicts and decrees of the Presidium of the Supreme Soviet of the USSR, are subject to publication in the *Vedomosti Verkhovnogo Soveta SSSR* in the languages of the union republics not later than seven days after they have been approved.[2]

2. The most important of the acts indicated in Article 1, which are subject to widespread and immediate promulgation, are published in the *Izvestia sovetov deputatov trudyashchikhsya SSSR.*

When necessary these acts may also be promulgated by radio or transmitted by telegraph.

[1] D. A. Loeber, 'Legal Rules "For Internal Use Only" ', in *The International and Comparative Law Quarterly*, January 1970.

[2] Article 1 of this Edict is presented in the form in which it functioned up until April 1960, and after September 1965. (Ed.)

3. The edicts and decrees of the Presidium of the Supreme Soviet of the USSR which are not of general significance or do not bear a normative character are sent out to the corresponding administrations and institutions and brought by them to the notice of persons whom the measures affect. These acts may remain unpublished at the decision of the Presidium of the Supreme Soviet of the USSR.

4. Contracts, agreements, and conventions, concluded by the USSR with foreign states and ratified in the accepted manner, and the corresponding Edicts, are published on ratification in the *Vedomosti* at the representation of the Ministry of Foreign Affairs of the USSR to the Presidium of the Supreme Soviet of the USSR.

5. Laws of the USSR, decrees and other acts of the Supreme Soviet of the USSR, and edicts and decrees of the Supreme Soviet of the USSR bearing a general normative character come into force throughout the territory of the USSR simultaneously, on the expiry of ten days after they have been published in the *Izvestia* or the *Vedomosti*, unless some other term for their implementation has been indicated in the acts themselves; but acts published in accordance with Article 2 of this edict in the *Izvestia* before being published in the *Vedomosti* come into force on the expiry of ten days after being published in the *Izvestia*.

All other acts which do not have a general normative character come into force from the moment they are approved, unless another term is indicated in them for implementation.

6. Edicts and Decrees of the Presidium of the Supreme Soviet of the USSR which according to Article 3 of this Edict are not published come into force from the moment they have been received by the corresponding administrations and institutions unless some other term for implementing them has been indicated.

7. In connection with the publication of this Edict:
(a) the following are annulled:

The Decree of the TsIK and the SNK of the USSR of the 22 August 1924, 'On the Method of Publishing Laws and Instructions of the Government of the USSR' (SZ SSSR, 1924, No. 7, art. 71) with the changes of 14 August 1925, (SZ SSSR, 1925, No. 53, art. 401) and of 10 September 1926 (SZ SSSR, 1926, No. 61, art. 454);

The decree of the TsIK and the SNK of the USSR of 7 December 1933, 'On the Method of Publishing Decrees of the Government of the USSR and Information of its Decisions and Work' (SZ SSSR, 1934, No. 45, art. 351);

The decree of the TsIK and SNK of the USSR of 6 February 1925 'On the Time of Entry into Force of Laws and Instructions of the Government of the USSR, and also of Instructions of Administrations of the USSR' (SZ SSSR, 1925, No. 8, art. 75) with additions of 1 June 1927

(SZ SSSR, 1927, No. 32, art. 326) and of 6 March 1929 (SZ SSSR, 1929, No. 20, art. 171);

(b) the Council of Ministers of the USSR is entrusted with establishing a method for publishing and implementing decrees and instructions of the Council of Ministers of the USSR.

8. This Edict is to be presented for confirmation by the Supreme Soviet of the USSR.

Source: V. I. Vasiliev, i drugie, *Sbornik Zakonov SSSR*, Vol. 1 (Moscow, 1968), p. 261. Editor's translation.

19. Brezhnev's Criticism of Local Government under Khrushchev

16 *November* 1972

This decree refers to the local soviets of a single oblast, *but like so many other documents of this nature it is important for its general validity. It would not otherwise have been published prominently in the journal* Party Life *and in at least two handbooks. Although it reflects the Brezhnev leadership's sombre view of local government under Khrushchev, it virtually duplicates criticisms contained in the decree of 22 January* 1957, *and reiterates all the old frictions. There is no evidence that it led to any significant improvements.*

19. On the Work of the Soviets of Workers' Deputies of the Poltava Oblast

Decree of the Central Committee of the CPSU, 16 *November* 1965

The Central Committee of the CPSU heard a report on this question by comrade S. K. Boiko, chairman of the executive committee of the [Poltava] *oblast* soviet of workers' deputies, and passed a decree on it. In this it is pointed out that since the October 1964 Plenum of the CC CPSU and the re-establishment of unified party and soviet organs the local soviets have become more active. They show more initiative, and pay more attention to questions of economic and cultural construction and the communist education of the working people ... The soviet organs take an active part in carrying out the decisions of the March and September (1965) decisions of the Central Committee of the CPSU. They have begun to play a greater part in the development of agricultural and industrial production, the construction of houses, roads, cultural and service institutions, the improvement of amenities in towns and settlements. The network of public-service enterprises, trade and catering has been extended.

The party and soviet organs of the *oblast* have improved the quality of the official staff in the soviet. The most active members receive systematic instruction and exchange views on their work, and this helps to perfect the style and methods of work of the executive committees of the soviets and their departments. The majority of the executive committees of urban and *raion* soviets regularly report at meetings of deputies, and it is also the practice for executive committees, and the heads of departments and of communal and public-service enterprises to make reports to the public.

At the same time, the CC CPSU has noted that there are serious short-comings in the work of the local soviets of the Poltava *oblast*, especially at *raion*, settlement and village level. The soviets do not by any means use the rights granted them by the constitution and the statutes of local soviets. Many of them have still not defined very exactly their role in the solution of problems of economic construction, they do not exercise proper control over the fulfilment of production and finance plans by each collective and state farm, and are timid about inquiring into how the latter are being run. The majority of executive committees of village and *raion* soviets and the permanent commissions on agriculture have not been participating in compiling the collective and state farms' output plans on the basis of the state purchase plans for 1966–70.

The executive committees of *oblast*, *raion* and village soviets do not heed numerous instances of violation of the democratic basis of the collective-farm system, or the Statute of the Agricultural Artel,[1] they ignore unauthorized use of collective-farm land, and do not struggle earnestly enough against damage to agricultural land by cattle. Frequently the soviets put up with cases of infringement of citizens' rights and the violation of socialist legality... they do not halt in good time the execution of those decisions of collective-farm boards which contradict the Statute of the Agricultural Artel. Illegal decisions are annulled by the *raion* executive committees only after procurators have protested them.

Many executive committees of town, *raion*, village and settlement soviets do not show the necessary concern for satisfying the everyday requirements of the people. Persons living in settled districts are quite often deprived of the minimal cultural and public services. Frequently manufactured goods and foodstuffs which are available at *raion* or *oblast* warehouses are absent from the shops. On some farms catering services for people working in the field are badly organized.

The soviet organs of the *oblast* do not pay sufficient attention to the construction of dwelling houses, social and cultural amenities, and the completion plans for these remain unfulfilled year after year. The nine-month plan of the current year for the completion of living space has been fulfilled by only 87 per cent, the plan for general schools by 64 per cent and that for pre-school institutions by 59 per cent. And of the hospital buildings due for completion none have been brought into use. The majority of village soviets do not exercise control over the planning or construction of villages, or over the organization of amenities for them. The allocation of plots for the construction of dwelling houses and cultural or public-amenity buildings is as a rule carried out by collective-farm boards and the state-farm managements without the participation of the executive committees of the soviets. By no means all the opportunities for the production of household goods or local building materials are taken.

These shortcomings are mainly due to the fact that in their organizational work the soviets are not up to the tasks facing them. They frequently conduct their work apart from the masses, they do not combat bureaucracy sufficiently,

[1] i.e. the Collective Farm Statute.

and spend too much time at meetings. Questions which should be dealt with by organizations subordinate to the executive committees are frequently included in the agenda of executive committee meetings. A large proportion of the decisions arrived at remain on paper. The sessions of soviets are not carefully prepared, and are often conducted as a mere formality. They do not consider information on the fulfilment of the soviet's decisions, nor on the steps taken to meet delegates' criticism. They fail to discuss the basic questions of the work of their executive committees and the deputies' questions. The executive committees do not give the permanent commissions enough guidance in their work, and sometimes just issue orders to them. The commissions of a number of soviets do not use the powers granted them to the full. Work with deputies is badly conducted; some of the deputies themselves are not active enough and do not meet their constituents regularly.

The party organs of the *oblast* do not guide the activities of the local soviets enough, nor help them to improve their style and methods of work. Occasionally they interfere in the administrative and directive work of soviet organs, and take over the handling of economic and other questions. The practice of taking joint party–soviet decisions has become widespread. This happens even with questions which lie entirely in the competence of the soviets, so that their initiative is fettered, their responsibility reduced, and harm done to the matter in hand. At the same time the *oblast*, town and *raion* committees of the Party do not trouble themselves enough to improve the work of primary party organizations of the apparatus, or the departments of soviet organs. The majority of party groups in the soviets fulfil their functions, as set out in the CPSU statutes, unsatisfactorily.

The managers of some collective and state farms, enterprises and institutions do not implement the decisions and commissions of rural, settlement, *raion* or urban soviets; they do not appear at meetings or sessions of the executive committees, and retain deputies at work, thereby preventing them from participating in the meetings of the soviets. The executive committees of local soviets put up with actions of this kind. The town and *raion* committees of the Party do not provide the necessary help in consolidating the authority of the local soviets as organs of state power.

The CC CPSU has suggested to the Poltava *oblast* committee of the Communist Party of the Ukraine and the Communists of the executive committee of the *oblast* soviet of workers' deputies that they should ensure the removal of these serious shortcomings from the work of the local soviets of the *oblast*, as indicated in this resolution.

The local soviets and their executive committees, in realizing the rights and duties envisaged by the constitution and statutes of local soviets, are obliged:

To increase their influence over the development of industry and agricultural production, to offer the necessary aid to enterprises, collective farms, state farms, and economic organizations in their work. The local soviets should carry out their functions with regard to economic organs not by administrative order or through interference in their production and economic activities, but by means of daily control over the observance of state order in the enterprises' use of natural and labour resources, of legislation, and of the Statute of the Agricultural Artel; by control over the correct use of land and holdings, the preservation of machinery, the timely fulfilment by collective and state farms of their production plans and obligations to the state;

To develop local industry to the greatest possible extent, to influence the work of enterprises not subordinate to them with the object of seeking out ways of increasing the production of consumer goods and improving social and cultural services for the public;

To effect control over the observance of socialist legality and order, the preservation of public and personal property, the defence of citizens' rights, and the struggle with crime;

To devote more attention to the provision of amenities in towns and settlements, the organization of housing, cultural, communal and road construction, and to ensure that all the necessary public services for the population are available on the territory of each town, *raion*, village, or settlement soviet; to use more fully the powers of the soviet for setting aside and using land, and ensuring the observance of rules for the construction of settlements and villages;

To bring about an improvement in the work of schools, hospitals, childrens' institutions, shops, dining rooms, clubs, libraries, and other enterprises and institutions which serve the public; to check up on the correct use of money from the cultural funds of enterprises, collective farms, state farms, which are situated on the territory of the soviet.

The decree emphasizes the necessity of ensuring an improvement in the organizational and mass work of the soviet organs; of bringing forward for discussion at sessions of the soviet topical questions relating to the development of the economy, culture, and services for the population; of systematically informing deputies about the execution of decisions which they have taken, the demands of the electors, and the examination of citizens' proposals and complaints; of activating the work of the permanent commissions, achieving their direct participation in the preparation of questions put forward for discussion at the soviet, in checking the work of enterprises, organizations, and institutions, in coming to decisions and controlling their implementation.

Party and soviet organs are obliged to support the initiative of their deputies, increase their feeling of responsibility to the people for carrying out public demands and proposals. A deputy must meet his electors systematically, inform them of the decisions taken by the soviets and their executive committees, and regularly, not less than twice a year, give reports on his work. It is necessary to organize instruction for deputies (so that they may study Soviet law, and their rights and duties), and also to arrange exchanges of opinion between them about their work.

Executive committees, their departments and administrations must report regularly to the public, and inform workers of decisions taken by meetings of the soviet. They must discuss at general meetings questions of housing, communal construction and public amenities, the reports of the managers of enterprises and the organizations which serve the public, and develop further the voluntary element in the work of the soviets. The editorial offices of newspapers, radio and television stations should be recommended to propagate the positive work-practices of the soviets more widely, and illuminate topical questions of soviet construction.

The attention of the Poltava *obkom* of the Communist Party of the Ukraine, and of the town and the *raion* committees of the Party is directed to the need for a marked improvement in party guidance of the soviets, an increase in their role in carrying out the tasks of communist construction. It is necessary to ensure the soviets use their rights to the full, but this without permitting any petty tutelage or unwarranted interference in the work of the soviets. They should be provided with the opportunity to decide independently all those questions which are within their competence. The effectiveness of decisions taken by the soviets and their executive committees must be raised, and the responsibility of all Communists for carrying them out increased.

The work of party organizations of the apparatus and departments of the soviet organs must be improved, and their active influence ensured in perfecting the work of the apparatus and educating officials in a spirit of lofty responsibility for the work entrusted to them. The work of party groups in the soviets and executive committees must also be activated.

Source: K. U. Chernenko, i drugie, *Spravochnik partiinogo rabotnika vypusk 6* (Moscow, 1966), p. 392, published in condensed form.
Editor's translation.

20. New Commissions formed in the Supreme Soviet

3 August 1966

At the Twenty-third Party Congress held in March 1966, L. I. Brezhnev called for an activation of the Supreme Soviet of the USSR and the Supreme Soviets of the union republics. The establishment of permanent commissions in the Soviet of the Union and the Soviet of Nationalities was directed to this end. The proposal was made officially by the President, N. V. Podgorny, at the first session of the seventh convocation of the Supreme Soviet, in August 1966. Prior to this each chamber had three commissions for handling legislative proposals, budgets, and foreign affairs, while the Soviet of Nationalities also had a commission for economic affairs. On 19 December 1969, Commissions for Youth Affairs were set up in each chamber. Like so many other alterations to the Supreme Soviets, this change was principally of propaganda significance.

20. On the Formation of Permanent Commissions of the Soviet of the Union

Decree of the Soviet of the Union, 3 August 1966

After hearing the report of N. V. Podgorny, Chairman of the Presidium of the Supreme Soviet of the USSR, on the formation of permanent commissions of the Soviet of the Union and the Soviet of Nationalities, the Soviet of the Union decrees that

1. Permanent commissions of the Soviet of the Union be formed to suit the basic trends in state, economic, social and cultural construction, and also for certain matters connected with the work of the Supreme Soviet of the USSR.
2. It be recognized as expedient to have the following permanent commissions in the Soviet of the Union.

A Planning and Budget Commission
A Commission for Transport and Communications
A Commission for Construction and the Construction
  Materials Industry
A Commission for Agriculture
A Commission for Health and Social Insurance
A Commission for Education, Science and Culture
A Commission for Trade and Public Services
A Commission for Legislative Proposals
A Commission for Foreign Affairs
A Mandate Commission.

3. Approval should be given to the proposal of the Council of Nationalities that the Presidium of the Supreme Soviet of the USSR and the chairmen of

the Soviet of the Union and the Soviet of Nationalities should work out, in conjunction with the permanent commissions of each chamber, and submit for examination by the Supreme Soviet of the USSR, a draft set of statutes for permanent commissions in the Soviet of the Union and the Soviet of Nationalities.

Source: Vedomosti Verkhovnogo Soveta SSSR, 1966, No. 32, statya 711.
Editor's translation.

21. A Set of Results of Elections to Republican Supreme Soviets

20 June 1971

The results of elections held under the terms of the 1936 constitution have always been statistically impressive. In 1937 nearly 97 per cent of the eligible population were already participating; since 1950 the figure has apparently never fallen below 99 per cent. In recent elections less than one per cent of the voters appear to have opposed the candidates. In absolute terms, however, a significant number of people—perhaps a quarter of a million or more—express opposition by absence from the polling booths or by recording a negative vote. In a tiny percentage of the cases candidates fail to obtain the 50 per cent vote needed for election. The distribution of this protest in 1971 may be seen from published returns reproduced below.

21. Report on Results of Elections to Union-Republic and Autonomous-Republic Supreme Soviets and Local Soviets

Data on election results published from materials received from the Presidiums of the Union-Republic Supreme Soviets, 20 June 1971

Regular elections to the Supreme Soviets of the union and autonomous republics and the territory, province, autonomous-province, national-region, district, city, borough, rural and settlement Soviets were held in all the union and autonomous republics on 13 June, 1971.

The elections took place in an atmosphere of high political and labour activeness on the part of the population, under the banner of the struggle for the implementation of the decisions of the Twenty-fourth CPSU Congress and the mobilization of the working people's efforts for the successful fulfilment of the assignments of the Ninth Five-Year Plan for the Development of the USSR National Economy.

A total of 2,232,808 election commissions, in whose work 9,057,074 people participated, were formed to conduct the elections. The commissions were made up of 5,521,084 workers and collective farmers, or 60·9 per cent of the total; 4,157,436 women, or 45·9 per cent; 3,130,506 Party members and candidate members, or 34·6 per cent; and 5,926,568 non-Party persons, or 65·4 per cent. Soviet young people took an active part in the work of the commissions. The membership of the commissions included 2,044,814 people under 30 years of age, or 22·6 per cent of the total; this included 1,158,870 members of the Young Communist League, or 12·8 per cent.

The number of registered voters for the country as a whole was

154,018,436, of which 153,958,004, or 99·96 per cent, took part in the elections.

The total number of voters and the number of ballots cast in the elections by union republics are characterized by the following data:

Union republic	Voters registered	Ballots cast	% of voters
Russian	85,153,877	85,105,630	99·94
Ukraine	32,729,395	32,726,360	99·99
Belorussian	5,875,569	5,874,561	99·98
Uzbek	5,656,373	5,655,992	99·99
Kazakh	7,177,170	7,176,651	99·99
Georgian	2,821,739	2,821,713	99·99
Azerbaijan	2,485,278	2,484,815	99·98
Lithuanian	2,060,249	2,058,522	99·92
Moldavian	2,208,479	2,206,199	99·90
Latvian	1,711,537	1,711,172	99·98
Kirgiz	1,498,505	1,498,399	99·99
Tadzhik	1,366,488	1,366,397	99·99
Armenian	1,272,757	1,272,626	99·99
Turkmenian	1,041,459	1,041,153	99·97
Estonain	959,561	957,854	99·82

Results of Elections to the Union-Republic Supreme Soviets

A total of 5,879 election districts were formed to conduct the elections to the union-republic Supreme Soviets, or 49 districts more than in the 1967 Supreme Soviet elections.

A total of 153,782,814 voters, or 99·89 per cent of all those voting, cast ballots for candidates for deputy to the union-republic Supreme Soviets. A total of 174,796 persons voted against them. A total of 434 ballots were declared invalid.

In all 15 union republics, the candidates on the ballot for deputy to the union-republic Supreme Soviets received an absolute majority of the votes and were elected deputies.

The results of the voting in the elections to the union-republic Supreme Soviets is shown on page 121.

A total of 5,879 deputies were elected to the Supreme Soviets of all the union republics; of this number, 3,834 were men, or 65·2 per cent; 2,045 were women, or 34·8 per cent; 3,974 were CPSU members or candidate members, or 67·6 per cent; 1,905 were non-party persons, or 32·4 per cent; 1,742 were workers, or 29·6 per cent; and 1,221 were collective farmers, or 20·8 per cent. A total of 1,012 deputies under the age of 30, or 17·2 per cent of the total, were elected to the Supreme Soviets; of this number, 529, or 9·0 per cent, were YCL members.

Union republic	Ballots cast for candidates	% of vote	Deputies elected
Russian	84,971,410	99·84	894
Ukraine	32,713,782	99·96	484
Belorussian	5,871,319	99·94	425
Uzbek	5,651,756	99·93	452
Kazakh	7,165,523	99·85	482
Georgian	2,821,523	99·99	400
Azerbaijan	2,484,291	99·98	385
Lithuanian	2,058,072	99·98	300
Moldavian	2,205,383	99·96	315
Latvian	1,710,439	99·96	310
Kirgiz	1,495,536	99·81	339
Tadzhik	1,365,386	99·93	315
Armenian	1,272,124	99·96	310
Turkmenian	1,040,513	99·94	285
Estonian	955,757	99·78	183

Results of Elections to the Autonomus-Republic Supreme Soviets

A total of 2,994 election districts were formed to conduct the elections to the Supreme Soviets of the 20 autonomous republics, or 9 districts more than at the last elections.

A total of 11,543,183 voters, or 99·97 per cent of all voters, took part in the elections to the autonomous-republic Supreme Soviets.

A total of 11,519,165 persons, or 99·79 per cent, voted for the candidates for deputy to the autonomous-republic Supreme Soviets. A total of 24,008 persons voted against them. Ten ballots were declared invalid.

In all the election districts, the candidates on the ballot for deputy to the autonomous-republic Supreme Soviets received an absolute majority of the votes and were elected deputies.

Data on the results of the voting in the elections to the Supreme Soviet of each autonomous republic are given on page 122.

A total of 2,994 deputies were elected to the Supreme Soviets of all the autonomous republics; of this number, 1,857 were men, or 62·0 per cent of the total; 1,137 were women, or 38·0 per cent; 1,902 were CPSU members or candidate members, or 63·5 per cent; 1,092 were non-Party persons, or 36·5 per cent; 945 were workers, or 31·6 per cent; and 489 were collective farmers, or 16·3 per cent. A total of 554 persons under the age of 30 were elected deputies, or 18·5 per cent of the total; of these 326, or 10·9 per cent, were YCL members.

Results of Elections to the Local Soviets

Elections were conducted for 49,817 local soviets, including 6 territory soviets, 108 province soviets, 8 autonomous-province soviets, 10 national-region soviets, 2,926 district, 1,933 city, 452 borough, 40,907 rural and 3,467 settlement soviets. In view of the fact that province soviets were elected in the newly formed Issyk-Kul and Naryn Provinces of the Kirgiz Republic, in Leninabad Province of the Tadzhik Republic and in Mary, Tashauz and

Autonomous republic	Ballots cast for candidates	% of vote	Deputies elected
Abkhaz	286,738	99·99	130
Adzhar	179,476	99·99	90
Bashkir	2,146,011	99·80	254
Buryat	485,355	99·77	137
Dagestan	700,665	99·92	181
Kabardino-Balkar	343,455	99·82	142
Kalmyk	142,250	99·56	118
Kara-Kalpak	322,785	99·97	164
Karelian	442,565	99·67	133
Komi	531,787	99·77	156
Mari	411,731	99·87	120
Mordvinian	615,682	99·97	146
Nakhichevan	92,770	99·99	80
North Ossetian	334,147	99·80	133
Tatar	1,909,600	99·74	207
Tuva	120,446	99·79	120
Udmurt	835,322	99·88	178
Chechen-Ingush	542,421	99·64	149
Chuvash	700,880	99·58	153
Yakut	375,079	99·67	203

Chardzhou Provinces of the Turkmenian Republic in February, 1971, no elections were held there on 13 June.

A total of 2,165,168 election districts were formed for elections to all local soviets, including:

Soviets	Number of election districts
Territory	1,901
Province	23,137
Autonomous-province	1,158
National-region	969
District	229,600
City	252,116
Borough	95,867
Rural	1,356,986
Settlement	203,434

Voter participation in the elections of deputies to the local bodies of state authority is characterized by the following data:

Soviets	Ballots cast	% of voters
Territory	10,350,750	99·90
Province	104,693,053	99·96
Autonomous-province	1,125,376	99·96
National-region	592,821	99·98
District	77,299,710	99·98
City	85,206,982	99·95
Borough	39,712,203	99·94
Rural	61,539,982	99·97
Settlement	13,469,818	99·95

The results of the elections to the local soviets were as follows:

Soviets	Ballots cast for candidates	% of vote	Ballots cast against candidates	Ballots declared invalid
Territory	10,336,770	99·87	13,965	15
Province	104,539,202	99·85	153,489	362
Autonomous-province	1,123,419	99·83	1,955	2
National-region	591,011	99·69	1,810	—
District	77,192,988	99·86	106,670	52
City	85,043,251	99·81	163,553	178
Borough	39,627,517	99·79	84,607	79
Rural	61,436,616	99·83	103,291	75
Settlement	13,439,634	99·78	30,180	4

A total of 2,165,037 deputies to local soviets were elected. Of this number, 1,900 are deputies to territory soviets, 23,137 are deputies to province soviets, 1,158 are deputies to autonomous-province soviets, 969 are deputies to national-region soviets, 229,594 are deputies to district soviets, 252,111 are deputies to city soviets, 95,866 are deputies to borough soviets, 1,356,878 are deputies to rural soviets and 203,424 are deputies to settlement soviets.

The deputies to the local soviets include 1,172,401 men, or 54·2 per cent of the total; 992,636 women, or 45·8 per cent; 963,173 CPSU members and candidate members, or 44·5 per cent; 1,201,864 non-Party persons, or 55·5 per cent; 790,340 workers, or 36·5 per cent; and 623,405 collective farmers, or 28·8 per cent. A total of 557,015 deputies to the local soviets, or 25·7 per cent of the total, are under 30 years old; of this number, 319,916 are YCL members, or 14·8 per cent.

In 95 election districts (89 for election to rural soviets, 4 for election to settlement soviets and 2 for election to district soviets) the candidates on the ballot did not receive an absolute majority of the votes and were not elected deputies.

Elections were not held in 30 election districts because of the withdrawal of the candidates.

In six election districts, the elections were declared invalid because of violations of the Statute on Elections.

New elections will be conducted in all these districts.

The composition of the deputies elected to the local soviets is characterized by the following data, by union republics:

	Total deputies elected	Were not deputies to the preceding soviet	% of total
Total	2,165,037	1,083,702	50·1
Republics:			
Russian	1,092,653	567,937	52·0
Ukraine	513,899	239,204	46·6
Belorussian	80,648	39,120	48·5
Uzbek	83,282	37,938	45·6
Kazakh	111,756	63,738	57·0
Georgian	48,887	26,110	53·4
Azerbaijan	45,657	23,639	51·8
Lithuanian	29,314	12,694	43·3
Moldavian	33,477	15,353	45·9
Latvian	23,986	11,514	48·0
Kirgiz	24,595	11,236	45·7
Tadzhik	21,150	9,705	45·9
Armenian	25,459	13,260	52·1
Turkmenian	18,995	7,112	37·4
Estonian	11,279	5,142	45·6

	No. of women	% of total
Total	992,636	45·8
Republics:		
Russian	515,631	47·2
Ukraine	222,500	43·3
Belorussian	36,259	45·0
Uzbek	38,466	46·2
Kazakh	50,284	45·0
Georgian	22,623	46·3
Azerbaijan	20,426	44·7
Lithuanian	13,069	44·6
Moldavian	15,961	47·7
Latvian	11,566	48·2
Kirgiz	11,020	44·8
Tadzhik	9,531	45·1
Armenian	11,804	46·4
Turkmenian	8,064	42·5
Estonian	5,432	48·2

	CPSU members and candidate members	% of total	Non-party persons	% of total
Total	963,173	44·5	1,201,864	55·5
Republics:				
Russian	473,512	43·3	619,141	56·7
Ukraine	241,578	47·0	272,321	53·0
Belorussian	35,372	43·9	45,276	56·1
Uzbek	37,943	45·6	45,339	54·4
Kazakh	46,738	41·8	65,018	58·2
Georgian	21,933	44·9	26,954	55·1
Azerbaijan	21,236	46·5	24,421	53·5
Lithuanian	12,960	44·2	16,354	55·8

table continued on next page

Republics:	CPSU members and candidate members	% of total	Non-party persons	% of total
Moldavian	15,913	47·5	17,564	52·5
Latvian	10,973	45·7	13,013	54·3
Kirgiz	10,904	44·3	13,691	55·7
Tadzhik	9,501	44·9	11,649	55·1
Armenian	11,809	46·4	13,650	53·6
Turkmenian	8,148	42·9	10,847	57·1
Estonain	4,653	41·3	6,626	58·7

	YCL members	% of total	Under 30 years old	% of total
Total	319,916	14·8	557,015	25·7
Republics:				
Russian	164,458	15·1	275,154	25·2
Ukraine	75,048	14·6	133,875	26·1
Belorussian	12,192	15·1	20,502	25·4
Uzbek	10,369	12·5	24,124	29·0
Kazakh	17,655	15·8	31,633	28·3
Georgian	7,284	14·9	11,158	22·8
Azerbaijan	5,778	12·7	8,905	19·5
Lithuanian	3,820	13·0	7,554	25·8
Moldavian	5,996	17·9	11,328	33·8
Latvian	3,396	14·2	6,027	25·1
Kirgiz	3,552	14·4	6,747	27·4
Tadzhik	2,987	14·1	5,764	27·3
Armenian	3,043	12·0	5,601	22·0
Turkmenian	2,949	15·5	6,145	32·4
Estonian	1,389	12·3	2,498	22·1

	Workers	% of total	Collective farmers	% of total
Total	790,340	36·5	623,405	28·8
Republics:				
Russian	444,227	40·7	234,208	21·4
Ukraine	152,248	29·6	217,574	42·3
Belorussian	24,793	30·7	26,204	32·5
Uzbek	23,979	28·8	31,779	38·2
Kazakh	61,659	55·2	11,167	10·0
Georgian	12,978	26·5	18,946	38·8
Azerbaijan	13,729	30·1	16,216	35·5
Lithuanian	9,067	30·9	9,321	31·8
Moldavian	8,220	24·6	13,780	41·2
Latvian	8,011	33·4	7,631	31·8
Kirgiz	8,273	33·6	8,395	34·1
Tadzhik	5,206	24·6	9,164	43·3
Armenian	8,821	34·6	8,350	32·8
Turkmenian	4,606	24·2	8,243	43·4
Estonian	4,523	40·1	2,427	21·5

Soviets	Total deputies elected	Were not deputies to the preceding soviet	% of total
Territory	1,900	1,206	63·5
Province	23,137	13,201	57·1
Autonomous-province	1,158	686	59·2
National-region	969	562	58·0
District	229,594	124,759	54·3
City	252,111	142,776	56·6
Borough	95,866	57,189	59·7
Rural	1,356,878	634,435	46·8
Settlement	203,424	108,888	53·5

Soviets	Women	% of total
Territory	880	46·3
Province	10,296	44·5
Autonomous-province	505	43·6
National-region	444	45·8
District	104,235	45·4
City	115,495	45·8
Borough	43,839	45·7
Rural	623,532	46·0
Settlement	93,410	45·9

Soviets	CPSU members and candidate members	% of total	Non-party persons	% of total
Territory	1,027	54·1	873	45·9
Province	13,041	56·4	10,096	43·6
Autonomous-province	640	55·3	518	44·7
National-region	497	51·3	472	48·7
District	116,795	50·9	112,799	49·1
City	120,844	47·9	131,267	52·1
Borough	47,592	49·6	48,274	50·4
Rural	574,387	42·3	782,491	57·7
Settlement	88,350	43·4	115,074	56·6

Soviets	YCL members	% of total	Under 30 years old	% of total
Territory	366	19·3	543	28·6
Province	3,810	16·5	6,060	26·2
Autonomous-province	191	16·5	290	25·0
National-region	184	19·0	260	26·8
District	36,131	15·7	61,031	26·6
City	42,422	16·8	69,232	27·5
Borough	15,561	16·2	25,623	26·7
Rural	191,385	14·1	342,329	25·2
Settlement	29,866	14·7	51,647	25·4

Soviets	Workers	% of total	Collective farmers	% of total
Territory	800	42·1	262	13·8
Province	8,871	38·3	3,790	16·4
Autonomous-province	435	37·6	192	16·6
National-region	405	41·8	127	13·1
District	71,932	31·3	64,745	28·2
City	142,074	56·4	3,106	1·2
Borough	53,722	56·0	31	0·0
Rural	400,883	29·5	538,546	39·7
Settlement	111,218	54·7	12,606	6·2

Source: Pravda, Izvestia, 20 June 1971.
Translation: CDSP, Vol. XXIII, No. 25, p. 5.

Part II

The Party

22. The Problem of Centralized Control
23 March 1919

23. The First Post-Revolutionary Party Statute
4 December 1919

The decree 'On the Organizational Question' dealt with some exceedingly important matters. Among other things it established the central party bodies which were to become characteristic of Bolshevik power—the Politburo, Orgburo, and Secretariat. Their membership was interlocking from the first. Ia. M. Sverdlov, who had handled the most important organizational matters in the Party after the Bolshevik coup, died on the eve of the Eighth Congress and this, together with the difficulty of calling the whole Central Committee together in the Civil War, accentuated the need for a more formal structure. The subordination of the state organs to the Party was formally noted, though the relationship between them was never to be satisfactorily solved. At the same time it was explicitly stated that Central Committee controlled local party organizations everywhere.

These changes were incorporated in the greatly expanded statute passed at the Eighth Conference. These regulations were the first to be approved by the Party as a ruling power, replacing the rudimentary set adopted by the Sixth Congress in August 1917. *The new version contained details of the new party administrative network in the localities and more rigorous conditions of party membership.*

22. On the Organizational Question
Decree of the Eighth Congress of the RKP(B), 18–23 March 1919

After discussing the matter of the reforms needed in the sphere of: (1) *party* construction, (2) *Soviet* construction and (3) the relationship between the Party and the Soviets, the Eighth Congress of the RKP decrees as follows:

A. Party Construction

I. THE GROWTH OF THE PARTY

The numerical growth of the Party is only progressive in so far as healthy proletarian elements of town and country flow into the party ranks. The doors of the Party should be opened wide to workers and to working and peasant youth. But the Party must keep a constant and attentive watch over the changes which take place in its social composition. All party organizations are obliged to keep an accurate record of their composition and inform the

Central Committee of the Party about it periodically. The growth in the size of party organizations must not in any circumstances be bought at the cost of a deterioration in their quality. The admission of non-working and non-peasant elements into the Party must be dealt with very selectively.

The Congress decrees that a general registration of all party members should be conducted throughout Russia by the 1st of May. The Central Committee is charged with publishing, not later than the 10th of April, a detailed instruction on the conduct of this re-registration, so that special verification measures may be applied to those members of the Party who entered its ranks after October 1917.

2. THE LINK WITH THE MASSES

The Russian Communist Party which is in power and which holds the whole Soviet apparatus in its hands, has naturally had to give up hundreds of thousands of its members for the cause of administering the country. One of the most important tasks of the Party at this moment is to include thousands of its best workers in the network of state management (railways, food production, verification, army, courts, etc.).

A serious danger has, however, arisen in connection with the fulfilment of this vital task. Many members of the Party who have been put on such state work to a significant extent divorce themselves from the masses, and become infected with bureaucratism; this may also be said very often of many workers who are members of soviets. It is essential to begin a most resolute struggle against this evil immediately. Communists and members of soviets must at all costs be obliged to make reports to their electors at least once a fortnight. Workers who have been engaged in purely soviet work continuously for more than three months should be sent back to their factories for a month at least. All soviet officials who are members of the Party are obliged to conduct some kind of party work in their district. All Communists are obliged to be members of their trade union and attend its general meetings.

3. THE CENTRAL COMMITTEE AND THE LOCAL ORGANIZATIONS

The Central Committee consists of nineteen members (eight candidate members). The CC summons a party conference of representatives of *gubernia* and capital committees of the Party at least once every three months. At these conferences the most important current questions facing the Party are discussed.

At least once a month the CC sends out to *gubernia* and capital committees of the Party a written account of its work. Items subject to wide publicity are printed in the newspapers, if possible, every two weeks. A special travelling collegium of party instructors made up of responsible leading party workers should be attached to the CC.

Local organizations are obliged to present, at least once every two months, written reports on their work: the *uezd* committees, to the *gubernia* committee; and *gubernia* committees, to the Central Committee of the Party.

It is essential to start a section entitled 'From Party Life' in all party and soviet organs of the press.

The Central Committee of the Party is charged with taking energetic measures to supply all party organizations with adequate funds for essential party work.

4. THE INTERNAL STRUCTURE OF THE CENTRAL COMMITTEE

The Central Committee has not less than two plenary sessions a month on days fixed beforehand. All the most important political and organizational matters which do not need to be dealt with very urgently are discussed at these plenary meetings of the Central Committee.

The Central Committee organizes, firstly, a *political bureau*, secondly, an *organizational bureau*, and thirdly, a *secretariat*.

The political bureau [Politburo] consists of five members of the Central Committee. All the other members of the Central Committee, who have the opportunity to participate at any given session of the Politburo, have the right to a deliberate vote at that session. The political bureau makes decisions on urgent matters, and submits a report on all its work over the two weeks to the regular plenary meeting of the Central Committee.

The organizational bureau [Orgburo] consists of five members of the Central Committee. Each of the members of the organizational bureau heads a corresponding department of work. The organizational bureau meets at least three times a week. The organizational bureau directs all the organizational work of the party. The organizational bureau reports to the Plenum of the Central Committee every two weeks.

The Secretariat of the CC consists of one responsible secretary, a member of the organizational bureau of the CC, and five technical secretaries chosen from among experienced party workers. The Secretariat organizes a number of departments. The Secretariat reports to the Plenum of the CC every two weeks.

5. NATIONAL ORGANIZATIONS

At the present time the Ukraine, Latvia, Lithuania, and Belorussia exist as separate Soviet republics. The problem of the form of their *state* existence has been solved in this way for the moment.

But that does not at all mean that the RKP should in turn organize itself on the basis of a federation of independent Communist parties.

The Eighth Congress of the RKP decrees that the existence of a *single* centralized Communist Party, with a single CC directing all the work of the Party in all parts of the RSFSR, is essential. All the decisions of the RKP and its leading institutions are unconditionally obligatory for all parts of the Party, regardless of their national composition. The Central Committees of the Ukrainian, Latvian and Lithuanian Communists have the rights of *oblast* committees of the Party and are completely subordinate to the Central Committee of the RKP.

6. THE EXISTENCE OF SPECIAL ORGANIZATIONS

The existence of special party organizations such as the railway, post and telegraph, or military organizations, etc., is superfluous and the Central Committee must therefore, with the agreement of the local organizations, gradually disband such organizations, dissolving them in the general Communist organization.

7. CENTRALISM AND DISCIPLINE

The Party finds itself in a situation in which the strictest centralism and most severe discipline are an absolute necessity. All decisions of a higher body are absolutely obligatory for lower ones. Every decree must first be implemented, and appeal to the corresponding party organ is admissible only after this has been done. In this sense outright military discipline is needed in the Party in the present epoch. All party enterprises which are suitable for centralization (publishing, propaganda, etc.), must be centralized for the good of the cause.

All conflicts are decided by the corresponding higher party body.

8. THE DISTRIBUTION OF PARTY FORCES

The correct distribution of party forces at the present time is our main guarantee of success, and one of our most important tasks. The whole business of distributing party workers is in the hands of the Central Committee of the Party. The decision of the CC is obligatory for everyone. In each *gubernia* the *gubernia* forces are distributed by the *gubernia* committee of the Party; in the capitals they are distributed by the city committees, under the general guidance of the Central Committee. The Central Committee is charged with conducting a most resolute struggle against separatism and parochialism of all kinds in these matters.

The Central Committee is charged with shifting party workers from one branch of work to another and from one *raion* to another so that they may be used most productively.

9. THE TRAINING OF PARTY WORKERS

The Central Committee of the Party is charged with: (1) organizing a higher party school attached to the Central Committee; (2) working out a general curriculum and work-plan for local party schools; (3) helping local party schools by sending them suitable lecturers.

10. THE 'IZVESTIA' OF THE CENTRAL COMMITTEE

The Central Committee is charged with arranging the weekly publication of the *Izvestia of the Central Committee*, which is devoted entirely to party life.

The Congress entrusts the Central Committee with outlining, on the basis of materials which have come in from the localities, a number of necessary changes to the statute. These changes must be approved at the next party conference which is convened by the Central Committee.

All the materials of an organizational character which have been received in the organizational section are likewise handed over to be worked through in the Central Committee.

B. Relations between the Party and the Soviets

The soviets are state organizations of the working class and poorest peasantry which implement the dictatorship of the proletariat until such time as every state existing withers away.

The soviets unite in their ranks tens of millions of toilers; they must strive to unite in their ranks the whole working class and all the poorest and middle peasantry.

The Communist Party is an organization which unites in its ranks only the *avant-garde* of the proletariat and the poorest peasantry, i.e. the part of these classes which consciously strives to realize the Communist programme.

The Communist Party has taken upon itself the task of winning a decisive influence in and complete management of all of the toilers' organizations: the trade unions, co-operatives, rural communes, etc. The Communist Party in particular endeavours to get its programme carried out and effect complete control of modern state organizations such as the soviets.

It is absolutely essential to set up, in Soviet organizations, party factions which are very strictly subordinate to party discipline. All members of the RKP who are working in the given Soviet organization must be members of the faction.

The RKP must, by its practical, day-to-day, selfless work in the soviets, and by promoting its most reliable and devoted members to all soviet posts, win for itself undivided political rule in the soviets and real control over all their work.

The functions of the party collectives must not in any circumstances be mixed up with the functions of state organs such as the soviets. This would bring disastrous results, particularly in military matters. The Party must ensure that its decisions are implemented through the Soviet organs, *within the framework of the Soviet constitution*. The Party endeavours *to guide*[1] the work of the soviets but not to replace them ...

Source: KPSS v rezolyutsiyakh, chast' I (Moscow, 1954), p. 441.
Editor's translation, extracts.

[1] Here *rukovodit*. (Ed.)

23. Statute of the Russian Communist Party (Bolsheviks)

(Eighth Conference of the RKP(B), Moscow, 2–4 December 1919)

Section I—On Party Membership

1. Any person who accepts the programme of the Party and works in one of its organizations, who submits to the decrees of the Party and pays membership dues, is considered to be a member of the Party.

2. New members are accepted by local party committees from among candidate members, and are confirmed by the following general meeting of the organization.

> NOTE. It is permitted, in exceptional cases, on the recommendation of two members of the Party admitted before October 1917, to accept new members from among those who are not candidates. The same exception may be allowed in the course of a Party Week, in accordance with the instructions of the Central Committee.

3. Any member of one organization is accepted by another organization with the agreement of the first when he moves to the area in which the latter is operating.

4. The question of exclusion from the Party is determined by the general meeting of the organization of which the person concerned is a member. The decree on his exclusion comes into force only after it has been confirmed by the *gubernia* committee, though the person concerned is removed from party work until confirmation of his exclusion. Notice of exclusion of party members is published in the party press together with an indication of the reason for it.

Section II—On Candidate Members of the Party

5. All persons wishing to become party members have to go through a candidate stage, the aim of which is to acquaint that person thoroughly with the programme and tactics of the Party and verify his personal qualities.

6. New members are accepted as candidates on the recommendations of two members of the Party who have a six-month term of membership behind them, and after these recommendations have been checked by the local party committee.

7. Workers and peasants must spend not less than two months as candidates, other persons not less than six months.

8. Candidates are allowed to attend open general meetings of the party organization with a deliberative vote.

9. Candidates pay the usual membership dues to the accounts office of the local party committee.

Section III—On the Organizational Structure of the Party

10. The guiding principle of the organizational structure of the Party is democratic centralism.

11. The Party is constructed on the basis of democratic centralism on a territorial principle: the organization which serves any *raion* is considered to be higher than organizations serving part of that *raion*.

12. All party organizations are autonomous in deciding local questions.

13. The guiding organ of each organization is the general meeting, conference, or congress.

14. The general meeting, conference or congress elects a committee, which is its executive organ and which guides all the day-to-day work of the local organization.

15. The scheme of party organizations is as follows:

(a) for the territory of the RSFSR—the All-Russian Congress and Central Committee;
(b) for the *oblasti* and soviet republics which form part of the RSFSR—*oblast* conferences and *oblast* committees;
(c) for *gubernia*—conferences of *gubernii*, and *gubernia* committees;
(d) for *uezdy*—*uezd* conferences and *uezd* committees;
(e) for *volosti*—*volost* meetings and *volost* committees;
(f) for enterprises, settlements, Red Army units, institutions—general meetings of cells and cell bureaux.

16. The scheme of subordination and responsibility, and the manner of handling or questioning all party decisions (from the highest level to the lowest) is as follows: The All-Russian Congress, the Central Committee, the *oblast* conference, the *oblast* committee, the *gubernia* conference and so on.

17. Special departments are set up for special kinds of party work (nationality work, work among women or among young people, etc.). These departments exist alongside the committees and are directly subordinate to them. The method for organizing departments is fixed by special instructions approved by the Central Committee.

18. All the lower organizations right up to the *uezd* level are confirmed by the *uezd* committees with the sanction of the *gubernia* committee; the *uezd* committees are confirmed by the *gubernia* committees with the sanction of the *oblast* committee, and in its absence by the Central Committee; the *gubernia* committees are confirmed by the *oblast* committee with the sanction of the Central Committee, and in the absence of the *oblast* committee, directly by the Central Committee itself.

19. After it has been finally confirmed, each organization has the right to acquire its own seal, but only with the sanction of the corresponding higher party body.

Section IV—On the Central Institutions of the Party

20. The supreme organ of the Party is the Congress. Ordinary congresses are convened every year. Extraordinary congresses are convened by the Central Committee on its own initiative, or at the request of not less than one-third of the total number of members represented at the last party congress.

The convening of a party congress and its agenda are made public not less than a month and a half before the congress. An extraordinary congress may be called after an interval of two months. The congress is valid if not less than half of all the party members represented at the last ordinary congress are represented at it.

The norms of representation at the party congress are fixed by the Central Committee and the ordinary pre-congress conference.

21. If an extraordinary congress is not convened by the Central Committee in the period indicated in Point One,[1] the organizations which demanded it have the right to form an organization committee which shall enjoy all the rights of the Central Committee in convening a Congress.

22. The Congress:

(a) hears and approves reports of the Central Committee, the revision commission and other central institutions;
(b) reviews and alters the programme of the Party;
(c) determines the tactical line of the Party in current matters;
(d) chooses a Central Committee and a revision commission, etc.

23. The Central Committee is composed of nineteen elected members and twelve candidates. When members of the Central Committee drop out their numbers are made up from among the candidates who were chosen by the Congress, in an order fixed by the Congress.

24. The Central Committee represents the Party in relations with other parties and institutions, organizes the various institutions of the Party and guides their work, nominates the editorial boards of the central organs which work under its control, organizes and directs enterprises which are of general importance to the Party, distributes the forces and funds of the Party, and manages the central accounts office. The Central Committee directs the work of Soviet and public organizations through the party factions in them. The Central Committee holds not less than two plenary sessions a month on days fixed beforehand.

25. The Central Committee sets up a political bureau for its political work, an organizational bureau for its organizational work, and a secretariat headed by a secretary who is a member of the organizational bureau of the Central Committee.

26. Once every three months the Central Committee convenes a party conference of representatives from *gubernia* and capital party committees.

[1] Evidently point 20, the first in the section. (Ed.)

27. Once a month the Central Committee sends out to *gubernia* and capital party committees a written report on its work.

28. The revision commission is composed of three persons who systematically inspect the accounts office and all the Central Committee enterprises, and present a report thereon to the following Party Congress.

Section V—On Oblast Organizations

29. Party organizations, with the permission of the Central Committee, may unite by *oblast*. The *oblast* committee is elected at the *oblast* conference. The boundaries of the *oblast* are fixed by the *oblast* conference and approved by the Central Committee.

30. Party organizations which serve the territories of the federal parts of the RSFSR are equal in all respects to *oblast* party organizations, i.e., they are totally subordinate to the Central Committee of the Russian Communist Party (Bolsheviks).

31. An ordinary *oblast* conference is called by the *oblast* committee every six months, while an extraordinary conference is called on the decision of the *oblast* committee, or that of one-half of the total membership of the organizations in the *oblast*. The representational norm for the *oblast* conference is fixed by the *oblast* committee with the agreement of the *gubernia* committees in that *oblast*.

The *oblast* conference hears and approves the report of the *oblast* committee, the revision commission and other *oblast* institutions, and elects a committee and a revision commission.

32. The *oblast* committee is elected at an ordinary conference. The *oblast* committee elects, for its day-to-day work, a presidium composed of not less than three persons. The *oblast* committee organizes various party institutions in the *oblast*, guides their work, nominates the editorial board of the *oblast* party organ, which works under its control, organizes and directs enterprises which are of general importance for the *oblast*, distributes the forces and funds of the Party within the confines of the *oblast* and manages the *oblast* accounts office. The *oblast* committee directs the activities of the executive organs of the soviets through the party factions and presents a detailed report of its activities to the Central Committee of the Russian Communist Party every three months.

The *oblast* committee meets twice a month on a fixed day.

Section VI—On Gubernia Organizations

33. The ordinary *gubernia* party conference is convened by the *gubernia* committee once in three months, while an urgent conference is convened on the decision of the *gubernia* committee or one-third of the total membership of the organizations in the *gubernia*.

The *gubernia* conference hears and approves the report of the *gubernia* committee, the revision commission and other *gubernia* institutions, and elects a committee and revision commission.

34. The *gubernia* committee is elected by a conference, and must include officials of both the *gubernia* and other important workers' centres of the given *gubernia*. The *gubernia* committee meets twice a month on a fixed day. The *gubernia* committee designates a presidium of at least five of its members for day-to-day work.

35. The *gubernia* committee approves the *uezd* or *raion* organizations of the *gubernia* with the sanction of the *oblast* committee or the Central Committee, organizes various party institutions in the confines of the *gubernia*, guides their work, nominates the editorial board of the *gubernia* party organ, which works under its control, organizes all enterprises which are important for the *gubernia*, distributes the forces and funds of the Party within the confines of the *gubernia* and manages the *gubernia* accounts office. The *gubernia* committee directs the activity of the soviet, the trade-unions, and the co-operative organizations through the corresponding party factions. Every month the *gubernia* committee presents a detailed report of its work and of the work of the *uezd* committees to the Central Committee.

36. The *gubernia* committees, in the intervals between the conferences, periodically make information reports to the general meeting or conference of the town organization, besides which the *gubernia* committee convenes *gubernia* meetings of representatives of the *uezd* and town organizations every month.

37. In the *gubernia* towns, town committees which are subordinate to the *gubernia* committees can be set up only with the permission of the *gubernia* committees and the sanction of the Central Committee.

NOTE. In Petersburg and Moscow the town committees are in all respects equal to *gubernia* committees.

Section VII—On the Uezd Organizations

38. The *uezd* conference hears and approves the report of the *uezd* committee, and the *uezd* revision commission; it elects a committee and revision commission. The conference meets not less than once every three months.

39. The *uezd* committee, composed of five to nine persons, is elected at *uezd* conferences.

The *uezd* committee designates from its ranks a presidium of three persons, of whom the secretary must be free from all work except party work.

40. The *uezd* committee approves the *volost* organizations and cells in the *uezd* with the sanction of the *gubernia* committee; it organizes various party institutions within the confines of the *uezd*, guides their work, organizes all enterprises which are of importance for the *uezd*, arranges meetings of

representatives of the *volost* cells and manages the *uezd* party accounts office.

NOTE. The right to publish a party organ and party literature in the *uezd* belongs solely to the *uezd* committee.

41. The *uezd* committee directs, through the party faction, the work of the *uezd* executive committee, the soviet and all *volost* soviets, and also of professional organizations, co-operative and other groupings within the confines of the *uezd*.

Section VIII—On the Volost Organizations

42. The supreme organ of the *volost* is the general meeting of members of the Party in the given *volost*.

NOTE. In large *volosti*, where it is difficult to convene a general meeting, this may be replaced by a *volost* conference.

43. The general meeting of the *volost* takes place not less than once a month. The general meeting: (a) admits and excludes members of the Party; (b) elects the *volost* committee and revision commission; (c) discusses and confirms the reports of the *volost* committee and the revision commission; (d) elects delegates to the *gubernia*, *uezd* and other conferences; (e) discusses and approves the report of the [party] faction in the *volost* executive committee.

44. The *volost* committee is elected at the general meeting (or conference), consisting of three or five members, for three months.

45. The *volost* committee directs and guides the work of all organizations in the *volost*, conducts the registration of all members of the Party, organizes the distribution of literature, arranges meetings, lectures, etc., organizes new cells and presents them for approval by the *uezd* committee, manages the *volost* party accounts office, sends a report of its work once a month to the *uezd*, *gubernia*, *oblast* and Central Committees, directs the work of the *volost* soviet, and the executive committee through the party faction in it.

46. The revision commission checks up on the *volost* accounts office once a month.

Section IX—On Party Cells

47. The basis of the party organization is the party cell. The cell is approved by the *uezd*, town or *raion* committee and is composed of not less than three members.

NOTE. A cell which reaches considerable size may, with the permission of the corresponding committee, be split up into several cells, which together make up a sub-*raion*.

48. The cell is an organization which links the working and peasant masses with the guiding organ of the Party in a given locality. The task of the cell is to:

(a) bring party slogans and decisions to the notice of the masses;
(b) attract new members;
(c) co-operate with the local committee in its organizational and agitational work;
(d) take an active part as a party organ in the economic and political work of the country.

49. The cell elects a bureau of three members for one month to conduct its day-to-day work.

Section X—On Party Discipline

50. The strictest party discipline is the primary duty of all members of the Party and all party organizations. The decrees of party centres must be executed quickly and exactly. At the same time, inside the Party the discussion of all contentious questions of party life is completely free up until the moment when a decision is taken.
51. Failure to execute the decrees of higher organizations, or other misdemeanours that are recognized as criminal by public opinion in the Party, entails: for an organization—censure, nomination of a temporary committee from above, and a general re-registration (dissolution of the organization); for individual members of the Party—party censure, public censure, temporary removal from responsible party and soviet work, temporary removal from any party and soviet work, exclusion from the Party, and exclusion from the Party with notice of the misdemeanour given to the administrative and judicial authorities.
52. Each committee has the right, for the examination of any kind of disciplinary misdemeanour, to nominate specially the days when it will meet, and to form special committees, but without turning these in any respect into permanent party courts.
53. Disciplinary misdemeanours are examined by committees and general meetings in the normal way and through the established channels.

Section XI—On the Finances of the Party

54. The finances of [party] organizations are composed of membership dues, subsidies from higher party organizations, and other income.
55. Membership dues are fixed at not less than one-half of 1 per cent of the member's wage. Four categories of membership due are established, depending on the size of the salary. The first category pays one-half of 1 per cent,

the second 1 per cent, the third 2 per cent, and the fourth 3 per cent. The absolute figures for salaries so covered are fixed by instruction.

56. New members pay an entrance fee of five roubles.

57. Membership dues for persons who do not receive a fixed wage, for example peasants, are established by the local *gubernia* committee with regard to general norms.

58. Members of the Party who have not paid their membership dues without good reason for three months are considered to have left the organization, and the general meeting is informed of this.

59. All local organs set aside for the Central Committee 10 per cent of all the membership dues and other money income which does not have a special use. The *volost* organizations pay 60 per cent to the *uezd* committee accounts office, including 10 per cent for the Central Committee, while the *uezd* committee pays 30 per cent to the accounts office of the *gubernia* committee.

10 per cent of all income is sent by the *gubernia* committee to the Central Committee accounts office.

Section XII—On Factions in Non-Party Institutions and Organizations

60. In all non-party congresses, conferences, institutions and organizations (soviets, executive committees, trade unions, communes, etc.) where there are not less than three members of the Party, factions are organized whose task it is to increase party influence in every direction, carry out party policies in non-party milieux, and effect party control over the work of all the institutions and organizations indicated.

61. When questions concerning a faction are being discussed in a committee, the faction sends its representative to the plenary session of that committee with a deliberative vote. Factions may elect a bureau for day-to-day work.

62. Factions, regardless of their significance, are completely subordinated to the Party. In all matters on which a legal decision of the corresponding party organization exists, the faction must observe these decisions strictly and unswervingly. The committee has the right to include any member in the faction or remove him, but is obliged to inform the faction without fail of the reasons for this measure. The faction is independent (autonomous) in questions concerning its internal life and day-to-day work. In the event of a serious disagreement between the party committee and the faction in any question which is within its competence, the committee is obliged to examine this question a second time with the representatives of the faction and come to a final decision, which is subject to immediate execution by the faction.

63. Candidates for all the most important posts in the institution or organization that the faction works are nominated by the faction together with the corresponding party organization. Transfer from one post to another is conducted in the same manner.

64. All questions which are of political significance and are subject to discussion by the faction must be discussed in the presence of representatives of the committee. Committees are obliged to delegate their representatives when the faction makes its first application.

65. Every question which is to be decided by that non-party organization in which the faction works must be discussed beforehand at a general meeting or in the bureau of the faction.

66. All members of the faction of a non-party organization at the general meeting of that organization are obliged to vote unanimously on any question already decided upon by the faction. Persons who infringe this rule are subject to the usual disciplinary measures.

(The statute was passed unanimously.)

Source: KPSS v rezolyutsiyakh, chast' I (Moscow, 1954), p. 461.
Editor's translation.

24. Party Control of Staffing

5 *April* 1920

In the first years after the Revolution the size and distribution of the Party, which was but a tiny majority in an indifferent or hostile society, was of crucial concern to the leadership. Purges of suspect members in the spring and summer of 1919 were followed by a new recruiting drive. This resolution throws an interesting light on the placement and promotion of existing members and shows how the party organs were encouraged to supervise all promotions.

24. On the Organizational Question

Resolution of the Ninth Congress of the VKP(B), 29 March–5 April 1920

1. The immediate organizational problems of our party are always closely connected with the immediate tasks of a general political, social and economic character. At the present moment our party is faced with a special organizational task in connection with economic problems. The Party will have to co-ordinate its work in accordance with the new economic problems, reconstruct its ranks and carry out a radical redistribution of its forces ...
3. The chief organizational problem of the Party is correctly to distribute the party work amongst every one of the six hundred thousand members. The general rule is that the local organizations send each of their members to work at his trade or speciality. The regrouping of party forces in every town, province and factory must be carried out from the point of view of their use in the various processes of production; the most important concerns should be first supplied with communist workers, whilst these Communists are to be distributed in them in such a way that every workshop possesses a communist nucleus capable of independent intitiative. This is the point of view which guides the Central Committee in redistributing party forces on a national scale.
4. To carry out successfully the task indicated in paragraph 3, the registration of party members must be organized in a competent manner. The basis of this registration must be the system of a single party ticket. In the registration of the members of the Party both local organizations and the Central Committee should pay particular attention to the member's trade, to his economic and organizing qualifications and to the part which he can play in the economic revival of the country.
5. The exact registration of party members should be utilized in the interests of introducing a systematic distribution of the party forces, and also gradually promoting more and more members from limited or less responsible work

to work of a more responsible and wider nature. For the purpose of realizing this principal task the Congress recommends the following measures:

(a) Every lower group (collective) transfers once in every one or two months a list of names to the corresponding higher organized group; this list is to be composed of 5–10 per cent of the staff of the lower group, pointing out their work in the past and indicating the particular kind of work for which the group considers the comrades named best suitable. Similar lists are periodically supplied by the factory and works communist groups or sections to the district committees and by the latter to the Central Committee. At the same time the groups (collectives) are recommended to compile the said lists with the greatest care and attention in view of the fact that the members of the group bear full responsibility for the comrades whom they recommend.

(b) To speed up and successfully raise the level of the work of party workers in the economic sphere, all party organizations should pay the most serious attention to the Communist factions which are to be found in non-party organizations, i.e., to Communist factions in trade unions, soviets and so forth. These factions are to be requested to introduce the same form of lists as has been indicated above for party groups (collectives).

(c) The party organizations are to pursue a similar policy in the organization of non-party conferences. The party organization should have a group of comrades present at every non-party conference, to examine the persons making up the conference for the purpose of selecting suitable Soviet workers who could be entrusted with responsible work. For this purpose it is necessary to organize extensive non-party conferences, which are to be carefully prepared and devoted to practical questions of economic construction not only in large provincial cities and towns generally, but also in villages, in the Red Army, the militia and especially amongst women and young workers, boys and girls.

(d) Local party organizations should adopt all other possible measures which are likely to lead to the desired aim ...

Source: KPSS v rezolyutsiyakh, chast' I (Moscow, 1954), p. 497.
Translation: Resolutions and Regulations of the IXth Congress (Moscow, 1920), p. 33. Some terms modified by the editor.

25. The Demands of the Kronstadt Insurgents

28 February 1921

The demands of the Kronstadt insurgents are perhaps the most vivid expression of opposition to Lenin's policies from erstwhile supporters.[1] *Kronstadt, a military fortress with some 15,000 men under arms, had initially been a centre of Bolshevik support. Disillusioned with the new government, the insurgents remained true to many current socialist ideals, as is evident from the document translated here. The uprising was nevertheless suppressed with considerable bloodshed on 17 March. Fear of such events was undoubtedly one of the factors which prompted Lenin to switch abruptly to the New Economic Policy.*

25. Demands of the Kronstadt Insurgents, Expressed in the Resolution of the General Meeting of the Crews of the Ships of the Line

Kronstadt, 28 *February* 1921

Having heard the report of the representatives of the crews despatched by the General Meeting of the crews from the ships to Petrograd in order to learn the state of affairs in Petrograd, we decided:

1. In view of the fact that the present soviets do not represent the will of the workers and peasants, to re-elect the soviets immediately by secret voting, with free canvassing among all workers and peasants before the elections.
2. Freedom of speech and press for workers, peasants, Anarchists and Left Socialist Parties.
3. Freedom of meetings, trade unions and peasant associations.
4. To convene, not later than 1 March 1921, a non-party conference of workers, soldiers and sailors of Petrograd City, Kronstadt and Petrograd Province.
5. To liberate all political prisoners of Socialist Parties, and also all workers, peasants, soldiers and sailors who have been imprisoned in connection with working-class and peasant movements.
6. To elect a commission to review the cases of those who are imprisoned in jails and concentration camps.
7. To abolish all Political Departments, because no single party may enjoy privileges in the propagation of its ideas and receive funds from the state for this purpose. Instead of these Departments, locally elected cultural-educational commissions must be established and supported by the state.

[1] This is the reason for the inclusion of this document in a collection otherwise devoted entirely to official publications.

8. All 'cordon detachments'[1] are to be abolished immediately.

9. To equalize rations for all workers, harmful sectors being excepted.

10. To abolish all Communist fighting detachments in all military units, and also the various Communist guards at factories. If such detachments and guards are needed they may be chosen from the companies in military units and in the factories according to the judgment of the workers.

11. To grant the peasant full right to do what he sees fit with his land and also to possess cattle, which he must maintain and manage with his own strength, but without employing hired labour.

12. To ask all military units and also our comrades, the military cadets, to associate themselves with our resolutions.

13. We demand that all resolutions be widely published in the press.

14. To appoint a travelling bureau for control.

15. To permit free artisan production with individual labour.

The resolutions were adopted by the meeting unanimously, with two abstentions.

President of the Meeting, PETRICHENKO.

Secretary, PEREPELKIN.

Source: Pravda o Kronshtadte (Prague, 1921), pp. 46-7.

Translation: W. H. Chamberlin, The Russian Revolution (The Macmillan Company, New York, 1965), Vol. II, p. 495. Some terms modified by the editor.

[1] Requisitioning detachments which searched railway passengers for food.

26. Lenin Demands Unity in the Party
16 *March* 1921

27. Lenin Outlaws the Party Opposition
16 *March* 1921

These decrees were of lasting importance for the development of intra-party relations. Lenin had always been impatient with colleagues whose ideas differed from his own, but their basic adherence to the Bolshevik faction ensured for them (in the first years of Soviet power at least) some freedom of manoeuvre. The resolution on party unity formally banned any instances of factionalism in the leadership itself: the doctrine of democratic centralism was thus taken to its logical conclusion. The resolution on 'syndicalism' and 'anarchism' was Lenin's way of suppressing several Bolshevik opposition groups which had become very vocal. It seems that Lenin expected vigorous opposition to both these resolutions, because he brought them forward only on the last day of the Congress. The last clause of the resolution on party unity in any case remained secret until January 1924 (see the Soviet editorial note), when Stalin used it against Trotsky and the 'Left Opposition'.

26. On the Unity of the Party
Decree of the Tenth Congress of the RKP(B), 8–16 March 1921

1. The Congress directs the attention of all members of the Party to the fact that the unity and solidarity of its ranks, guaranteeing complete confidence between members of the Party and work that is really enthusiastic, work that genuinely embodies the unified will of the vanguard of the proletariat, is especially necessary at the present moment, when a number of circumstances increase the waverings among the petty-bourgeois population of the country.
2. On the other hand, even before the general party discussion about the trade unions, some signs of factionalism were manifested in the Party. Groups grew up with special platforms and with a desire to maintain to a certain degree a separate existence and to create their own group discipline.

All class-conscious workers must clearly recognize the harm and impermissibility of any kind of factionalism, which inevitably leads in fact to a weakening of amicable work and a strengthening of the repeated attempts of enemies who have crept into the governing Party to deepen any difference and to exploit it for counter-revolutionary purposes.

The ability of the enemies of the proletariat to exploit any departures from a strictly maintained Communist line was most clearly revealed at the time of the Kronstadt mutiny, when the bourgeois counter-revolution and the

White Guards in all countries of the world showed their readiness even to accept the slogans of the Soviet regime in order to overthrow the dictatorship of the proletariat in Russia, when the Socialist Revolutionaries and the bourgeois counter-revolution in general exploited in Kronstadt the slogans of uprising, as it were, for the sake of the Soviet regime against the Soviet Government in Russia. Such facts furnish clear proof that the White Guards attempt and are able to assume the colouring of Communists and even to pose as more 'left' than the Communists, only in order to weaken and overthrow the bulwark of the proletarian revolution in Russia. The Menshevik pamphlets in Petrograd on the eve of the Kronstadt mutiny show in equal measure how the Menshevik exploited the differences within the Russian Communist Party in order actually to encourage and support the Kronstadt mutineers, Socialist Revolutionaries and White Guards, representing themselves, in words, as opponents of rebellions and adherents of the Soviet regime, though with, as it were, some few corrections.

3. Propaganda in this question must consist, on one hand, in a detailed explanation of the harm and danger of factionalism from the standpoint of party unity and that of implementing the unified will of the vanguard of the proletariat, as a fundamental condition for the success of the proletarian dictatorship; it must also consist, on the other hand, in an exposition of the peculiarities of the latest tactical devices of the enemies of the Soviet regime. These enemies, convinced of the hopelessness of counter-revolution under an openly White Guard banner, now bend all their energies, exploiting the differences within the Russian Communist Party, to promote counter-revolution by transferring power to the political groupings which are superficially closest to recognizing the Soviet regime.

Propaganda must also set forth the experience of preceding revolutions, when counter-revolution supported the petty-bourgeois groupings which were closest to the extreme revolutionary party, in order to shake and overthrow the revolutionary dictatorship, thereby opening up the road for the further complete victory of the counter-revolution, the capitalists and landlords.

4. Every party organization must very strictly see to it that the absolutely necessary criticism of the failings of the Party, that any analysis of the general policy of the Party or appraisal of its practical experience, examination of the fulfilment of its decisions and of means to correct mistakes, etc., should be submitted not for the consideration of groups which have formed on the basis of some 'platform' or other, etc., but for the consideration of all the members of the Party. For this purpose the Congress gives instructions to publish the 'Discussion Pamphlet' more regularly and to publish special collections of material. Anyone who voices criticism must take account of the position of the Party among the enemies who surround it; they must also attempt to correct in practice the mistakes of the Party by participating directly in soviet and party work.

5. In commissioning the Central Committee to abolish any kind of factionalism, the Congress states at the same time that on questions which attract the special attention of members of the Party,—purging non-proletarian and unreliable elements from the Party, the struggle with bureaucratism, development of democracy and of the workers' initiative, etc.—any practical proposals must be considered with the greatest attention and tested in practical work. All members of the Party must know that, as regards these problems, the Party doesn't take all the necessary measures because it encounters many varied obstacles, and that, in decisively rejecting impractical and factional criticism, the Party will continue to test new methods and fight with all means against bureaucratism, for the extension of democratism and initiative, for the discovery, exposure and expulsion of hangers-on, etc.

6. The Congress gives instructions that all groups which have been organized on the basis of any platform whatever should be immediately dissolved and commissions all organizations to watch out very closely, so that no factional demonstrations may be permitted. Nonfulfilment of this decision of the Congress must incur unconditional and immediate expulsion from the Party.

7. [1] In order to bring about strict discipline in the Party and in all soviet work, and to achieve the greatest possible unity by removing all factionalism, the Congress empowers the CC to apply, in the case (or cases) of violation of party discipline or reappearance of, or connivance at, factionalism, all measures of party punishment right up to expulsion and, with regard to members of the CC, their transfer to candidate status and even, as an extreme measure, expulsion from the Party. The summoning of a plenum of the CC, together with an invitation to all candidate members of the CC and all members of the Control Commission to attend, must be a condition of the application (to members of the CC, candidate members of the CC and members of the Control Commission) of this extreme measure. If such a general meeting of the most responsible leaders of the Party considers it necessary, by a two-thirds vote, to transfer the member of the CC to candidate status or expel him from the Party, then this measure must be carried out immediately.

Source: KPSS v rezolyutsiyakh, chast' I (Moscow, 1954), p. 527.
Translation: W. H. Chamberlin, op cit. (see document 25), Vol. II, p. 499. Some terms modified by the editor, who also translated paragraph 7.

[1] Point 7 of the resolution was, in accordance with the decision of the Congress, not published, and was first referred to in I. V. Stalin's report to the Thirteenth Party Conference. [Editorial note to text in KPSS v resolyutsiyakh, chast' I (Moscow, 1954), p. 530.]

27. On the Syndicalist and Anarchist Deviation in our Party

Decree of the Tenth Congress of the Russian Communist Party, circa 16 *March* 1921

1. A syndicalist and anarchist deviation has been definitely revealed in our Party in the past few months. It calls for the most resolute measures of ideological struggle and also for purging the Party and restoring its health.
2. The said deviation is due partly to the influx into the Party of elements who have not yet fully assimilated the communist world outlook. Mainly, however, this deviation is due to the influence exercised upon the proletariat and on the Russian Communist Party by the petty-bourgeois element, which is exceptionally strong in our country, and which inevitably engenders vacillation towards anarchism, particularly at a time when the condition of the masses has greatly deteriorated as a consequence of the crop failure and the devastating effects of war, and when the demobilization of the army numbering millions sets loose hundreds and hundreds of thousands of peasants and workers unable immediately to find regular means of livelihood.
3. One of the most theoretically complete and clearly defined expressions of this deviation are the theses and other literary productions of the so-called Workers' Opposition group. Sufficiently illustrative of this is, for example, the following thesis propounded by this group: 'The organization of the management of the national economy is the function of an All-Russia Congress of Producers organized in industrial unions which shall elect a central body to run the whole of the national economy of the Republic.'

The ideas at the bottom of this and numerous similar statements are radically wrong in theory, and represent a complete break with Marxism and communism, with the practical experience of all semi-proletarian revolutions and of the present proletarian revolution.

First, the concept 'producer' combines proletarians with semi-proletarians and small commodity producers, thus radically departing from the fundamental concept of the class struggle and from the fundamental demand that a precise distinction be drawn between classes.

Secondly, the incorrect framing of the question of the relationship between the Party and the broad non-party masses, which leads to the subordination of the Party to a non-party milieu, as given in this thesis, is an equally radical departure from Marxism.

Marxism teaches—and this tenet has not only been formally endorsed by the whole of the Communist International in the decisions of the Second (1920) Congress of the Comintern on the role of the political party of the proletariat, but has also been confirmed in practice by our revolution—that only the political party of the working class, i.e., the Communist Party, is capable of uniting, training and organizing a vanguard of the proletariat and of the whole mass of the working people that alone will be capable of withstanding the inevitable petty-bourgeois vacillations of this mass and the inevitable traditions and relapses of narrow craft unionism or craft prejudices among the proletariat, and of guiding all aspects of the proletarian movement, which means of all the working masses. Without this the dictatorship of the proletariat is impossible.

The wrong understanding of the role of the Communist Party in its relation to the non-party working masses on the one hand, and an equally wrong understanding of the role of the working class in its relationship to the whole mass of the toilers on the other, are a radical theoretical departure from communism and a deviation towards syndicalism and anarchism, and this deviation permeates all the views of the Workers' Opposition group.

4. The Tenth Congress of the Russian Communist Party declares that it also regards as radically wrong all attempts on the part of the said group and of other persons to defend their fallacious views by referring to Paragraph 5 of the economic section of the Programme of the Russian Communist Party, which deals with the role of the trade unions. This paragraph says that 'the trade unions should eventually arrive at a *de facto* concentration in their hands of the whole administration of the whole national economy as a single economic entity' and that they will 'ensure in this way indissoluble ties between the central state administration, the national economy and the broad masses of working people', 'drawing' these masses 'into direct economic management'.

This paragraph in the Programme of the Russian Communist Party also says that a prerequisite for the state at which the trade unions 'should eventually arrive' is the process whereby they increasingly 'divest themselves of the narrow craft-union spirit' and embrace the majority 'and eventually all' of the working people.

Lastly, this paragraph in the Programme of the Russian Communist Party emphasizes that 'on the strength of the laws of the RSFSR, and established practice, the trade unions participate in all the local and central organs of industrial management'.

Instead of studying the practical experience of participation in administration, and instead of developing this experience further, strictly in conformity with successes achieved and mistakes rectified, the syndicalists and anarchists advance as an immediate slogan 'congresses or a congress of producers' 'to elect' the organs of economic management. Thus, the leading, educational and organizing role of the Party in relation to the trade unions of the proletariat, and of the latter to the semi-petty-bourgeois and even wholly petty-bourgeois masses of working people, is completely evaded and eliminated, and instead of continuing and correcting the practical work of building new forms of economy already begun by the Soviet state, we get petty-bourgeois–anarchist disruption of this work, which can only lead to the triumph of the bourgeois counter-revolution.

5. In addition to the theoretical fallacies and a radically wrong attitude

towards the practical experience of economic organization already begun by the Soviet government, the Congress of the Russian Communist Party discerns in the views of this and similar groups and persons a gross political mistake and a direct political danger to the very existence of the dictatorship of the proletariat.

In a country like Russia, the overwhelming preponderance of the petty-bourgeois element and the devastation, impoverishment, epidemics, crop failures, extreme want and hardship inevitably resulting from the war, engender particularly sharp vacillations in the temper of the petty-bourgeois and semi-proletarian masses. First they incline towards a strengthening of the alliance between these masses and the proletariat, and then towards bourgeois restoration. The experience of all revolutions in the eighteenth, nineteenth, and twentieth centuries shows most clearly and convincingly that the only possible result of these vacillations—if the unity, strength and influence of the revolutionary vanguard of the proletariat is weakened in the slightest degree—will be the restoration of the power and property of the capitalists and landowners.

Hence, the views of the Workers' Opposition and of like-minded elements are not only wrong in theory, but are an expression of petty-bourgeois and anarchist wavering in practice, and actually weaken the consistency of the leading line of the Communist Party and help the class enemies of the proletarian revolution.

6. In view of all this, the Congress of the RCP, emphatically rejecting the said ideas, as being expressive of a syndicalist and anarchist deviation, decrees that:

First, it be considered necessary to wage an unswerving and systematic struggle against these ideas;

Secondly, the congress recognizes the propaganda of these ideas as being incompatible with membership of the Russian Communist Party.

Instructing the CC of the Party strictly to enforce these decisions, the Congress at the same time points out that special publications, symposiums, etc., can and should provide space for a most comprehensive exchange of opinion between Party members on all the questions herein indicated.

Source: KPSS v rezolyutsiakh, chast' I (Moscow, 1954), p. 530.
Translation: Taken from the almost identical draft text in V. I. Lenin, *Collected Works*, Vol. 32 (Moscow, London, Lawrence and Wishart, 1965), p. 245, amended by the editor so as to correspond with the final decree.

28. Lenin's Testament

23 December 1922–4 January 1923

This remarkable document was composed by Lenin after he had suffered his third stroke in December 1922. It may well be that he never saw any of his close political associates again. The 'testament' afforded some praise to Trotsky, Bukharin and Pyatakov, mentioned Zinoviev and Kamenev slightingly, but condemned Stalin directly. The 'triumvirate', as the last three came to be called, had an interest in suppressing these comments at the Thirteenth Congress in May 1924, after Lenin died; they apparently obtained approval for this action at a meeting of senior Central Committee members prior to the Congress. Trotsky, who had most to gain from the disclosure, was present, but he remained silent. A translation of the testament was published by Max Eastman in the New York Times on 18 October 1926, though at one time Trotsky himself found it expedient to deny its authenticity. It was published in the USSR for the first time in June 1956, as part of the 'de-Stalinization' campaign.

28. Letter to the Congress ('Lenin's Testament')

Dictated 23 December 1922–4 January 1923

I

I recommend very much that at this Congress a number of changes be undertaken in our political system.

I wish to share with you the considerations which I regard as the most important.

I give first place to increasing the number of members of the Central Committee to several dozen or even to a hundred. It seems to me that our Central Committee would be threatened with great dangers if the trend of events were to be not completely favourable to us (and we cannot count on this), if we did not undertake this reform.

Next, I am thinking of inviting the attention of the Congress to the idea of imparting a legislative character to the decisions of the State Planning Commission on certain conditions, in this respect moving toward Comrade Trotsky's views to a certain extent and under certain conditions.

As regards the first item, that is, increasing the number of members of the Central Committee, I think that such a thing is necessary for raising the authority of the Central Committee, for serious work to improve our apparatus, and for averting a situation in which conflicts among small sections of the Central Committee might become of inordinate significance for all the destinies of the Party.

It seems to me that our party has the right to demand 50–100 Central Committee members from the working class and can obtain them without excessive strain upon it [the working class].

Such a reform would considerably increase the stability of our party and lighten for it the struggle among hostile states which, in my opinion, can and must grow much sharper in the next few years. It seems to me that the stability of our party, thanks to this measure, would gain a thousandfold. — LENIN.

23/XII/22. Dictated to M.V.

II

Continuation of Notes.

24 December 1922.

By the stability of the Central Committee, to which I referred above, I mean measures against a split, insofar as such measures can be taken in general. For, of course, the White Guard in *Russkaya mysl* [Russian Thought] (S. F. Oldenburg, I think it was) was right when, firstly, in their game against Soviet Russia he banked on a split in our party and when, secondly, he banked for this split on extremely serious dissensions within the Party.

Our party rests on two classes, and therefore its instability is possible, and its collapse is inevitable if there could not be agreement between these two classes. In that event it would be useless to take any measures or in general to discuss the stability of our Central Committee. In that case no measures would prove capable of preventing a split. But I trust that this is too remote in the future and is too improbable an event to talk about.

I have in mind stability as a guarantee against a split in the near future and I intend to examine here a number of considerations of a purely personal nature.

I think that fundamental in the question of stability from this point of view are such members of the Central Committee as Stalin and Trotsky. The relations between them constitute, in my opinion, a good half of the danger of a split which could be avoided and the avoidance of which, in my opinion, should be furthered by, among other things, raising the number of members of the Central Committee to 50 or 100.

Having become General Secretary, Comrade Stalin has acquired immense power, and I am not sure that he will always know how to use this power with sufficient caution. On the other hand, Comrade Trotsky, as already shown by his struggle against the Central Committee over the question of the People's Commissariat of Railroads, is distinguished not only by outstanding abilities. Personally, he is no doubt the most able man in the present Central Committee, but he is also possessed by excessive self-confidence and overly attracted by the purely administrative side of matters.

These two qualities in the two outstanding leaders of the present Central

Committee may inadvertently lead to a split and, unless our party takes measures to prevent it, the split may occur unexpectedly.

I shall not go on to characterize the other members of the Central Committee as to personal traits. I shall recall only that the October episode of Zinoviev and Kamenev[1] was not, of course, fortuitous, but that it ought as little to be held against him[2] personally as the non-Bolshevism of Trotsky.

Of the young members of the Central Committee I wish to say a few words about Bukharin and Pyatakov. These are in my opinion the most outstanding forces (among the youngest) and the following should be borne in mind in regard to them: Bukharin is not only a most valuable and most eminent Party theoretician, he is also rightly considered the favourite of the whole Party, but it is very doubtful whether his theoretical views can be classified as fully Marxist, because there is something pedantic in them (he never studied and, I think, never fully understood dialectics).

25/XII—Next, Pyatakov, a man of undoubtedly outstanding will and outstanding ability, but too much given to administration and the administrative aspect of matters to be relied on in a serious political issue.

Of course, I make both comments only as regards the present, on the assumption that both these outstanding and devoted workers may find occasion to increase their knowledge and correct their one-sidedness.— LENIN.

25/XII/22. Dictated to M.V.

POSTSCRIPT TO LETTER OF 24 DECEMBER 1922

Stalin is too rude,[3] and this failing, which is quite tolerable in our midst and in relations among us Communists, becomes intolerable in the office of General Secretary. Therefore, I propose to the comrades that they think of a way of removing Stalin from this post and appointing to it another person who in all other respects differs from Comrade Stalin in one advantage alone, namely, that he be more tolerant, more loyal, more courteous and more considerate to comrades, less capricious, etc. This circumstance may seem an insignificant trifle. But I think that from the point of view of averting a

---

[1] The reference is to the capitulationist behaviour of Zinoviev and Kamenev at the sessions of the Party Central Committee of 10 (23) and 16 (29) October 1917, when they spoke and voted against Lenin's resolution for immediate preparation of an armed uprising. After being firmly rebuffed at both sessions of the Central Committee, Kamenev and Zinoviev on 18 October published a declaration in the Menshevist newspaper Novaya zhizn [New Life], mentioning the preparation of an uprising by the Bolsheviks and saying that they considered the uprising a reckless venture. Thereby they disclosed to Rodzyanko and Kerensky the Party's greatest secret—the Central Committee decision to organize an uprising in the immediate future. On the same day Lenin, in 'Letter to Members of the Bolshevik Party', condemned this act, calling it unheard-of strikebreaking. [Sov. Ed.]

[2] Evidently an error of transcription: Instead of 'him', the sense here requires 'them'. [Sov. Ed.]

[3] [The word gruby, used here, may be translated as 'crude', 'heavy-handed', 'rough', 'tough'.—Trans.]

split and from the point of view of the mutual relations between Stalin and Trotsky, of which I wrote above, it is not a trifle, or it is such a trifle as may acquire decisive importance. —LENIN.
Dictated to L. F.
4 January 1923.

III

Continuation of Notes.
26 December 1922.

Increasing the membership of the Central Committee to 50 or even 100 should, in my opinion, serve a double or even triple purpose. The more members there are in the Central Committee, the more training there will be in Central Committee work, and the less danger of a split due to any carelessness. The enlistment of many workers in the Central Committee will help the workers to improve our apparatus, which is terribly bad. Essentially we inherited it from the old regime, since it was quite impossible to refashion it in such a short period, particularly during the war, the famine, etc. Therefore, to those 'critics' who sneeringly or maliciously point out to us the defects in our apparatus, we can reply calmly that these people have no understanding whatsoever of the conditions of the contemporary revolution. In five years it is altogether impossible to refashion the apparatus adequately, in particular under the conditions in which the revolution took place in our country. It is enough if in five years we have created a new type of state, in which the workers march ahead of the peasants against the bourgeoisie, and this, in the face of the hostile international atmosphere, constitutes a huge task. But awareness of this must in no way conceal from us that essentially we took the old apparatus from the Tsar and the bourgeoisie, and that now, with the advent of peace and the ensuring of minimum requirements against famine, all work must be directed toward improving the apparatus.

The way I see things is that a few dozen workers, joining the Central Committee, can, better than anyone else, conduct a checkup, improvement and reorganization of our apparatus. The Workers' and Peasants' Inspection, which originally had this function, has proved incapable of coping with it and can be used only as an 'accessory' or as an aid, in certain conditions, to these members of the Central Committee. The workers entering the Central Committee should, in my opinion, be for the most part not from among those workers who have behind them a long record of service in the Soviets (everywhere in this part of my letter I include peasants with the workers), because in these workers there have already arisen certain traditions and certain prejudices which it is desirable to combat.

The workers joining the Central Committee should include for the most part workers who stand below the stratum that has risen in our country in five years to be Soviet office employees, and who are closer to rank-and-file workers and peasants, not falling, however, into the category of direct or indirect exploiters. I think that such workers, attending all meetings of the Central Committee and the Politburo and reading all documents of the Central Committee, can constitute a cadre of devoted supporters of the Soviet regime capable, first, of giving stability to the Central Committee itself and, secondly, of really working to renew and improve the apparatus. — LENIN.

Dictated to L. F.

26/XII/22.

Source: Kommunist, No. 9, June 1956.

Translation: C. Saikowsky and L. Gruliow (eds.) *Current Soviet Policies*, Vol. IV, 1962, p. 210.

29. Stalin Condemns the Trotsky Opposition

19 December 1927

Stalin uttered the criticisms of the 'Left Opposition' contained in this document on earlier occasions, but this particular expression of them marked his victory over the group as a real political force.

Trotsky and Zinoviev were expelled from the Party altogether in November 1927, while Kamenev lost his membership during the Fifteenth Party Congress. Kamenev and Zinoviev were readmitted later, only to be involved in the first 'show trial' of August 1936. The 1927 expulsions were accompanied by a purge of seventy-four other members of the Left Opposition and eighteen 'Democratic Centralists'.

29. On the Opposition

Decree of the Fifteenth Congress of the VKP(B), 2–19 December 1927

The Fifteenth Congress, having heard the report of the Commission which made a careful study of all material concerning the Opposition, records the following.

1. In the ideological sphere the Opposition has gone over from differences of a tactical character to differences of a programmatic character, revising Lenin's ideas and descending to the standpoint of Menshevism. The denial of the possibility of the victorious building up of Socialism in the USSR and the consequent denial of the Socialist character of our revolution; the denial of the Socialist character of our State industry; the denial of the Socialist path of rural development under the conditions of proletarian dictatorship, and the policy of alliance of the proletariat with the basic masses of the proletariat on the basis of Socialist construction; and, finally, the actual denial of the proletarian dictatorship of the USSR ('Thermidor') and the capitulation and defeatism connected with it—this whole ideological orientation transformed the Trotskyist Opposition into a tool of petty-bourgeois democracy within the USSR and an accessory detachment of international Social Democracy abroad.

2. In the tactical sphere, the Opposition, by intensifying and accentuating its work against the Party, passed the boundary not only of the Party Statutes, but also of Soviet law (illegal meetings, illegal printing establishments, illegal organs of the Press, violent seizure of premises, etc.). The transition to an open struggle against the regime of the proletarian dictatorship, the organization of street demonstrations against the Party and the Soviet Government on 7 November 1927, marked the climax of this anti-Soviet tactic. The anti-Soviet tactic of the Opposition, also employed abroad in

connection with the propagation of slanderous attacks on the USSR, has actually placed the Opposition on a level with the avowed enemies of the country of proletarian dictatorship.

3. In the organizational sphere the Opposition, basing itself on a revision of Lenin's views, has passed over from factionalism to the establishment of its own Trotskyist Party. The commission established beyond doubt that the Opposition has its own central, regional, provincial, town and district committees, a technical apparatus, membership dues, press, organs, etc., etc. Abroad, the Trotskyist Opposition established connections not only with factional groups of anti-Leninist tendencies existing within the Parties of the Comintern, but also with organizations, groups and individuals who never belonged to the Communist International, as well as enemies and traitors of the Communist movement (Maslow, Ruth Fischer, Korsch, Souvarine, Rosmer, Roland Holst, Liebers, etc., etc.) who were expelled from the Communist International. Such an organizational practice on the part of the Opposition resulted in the fact that within the USSR it established connections with non-Party bourgeois intellectuals (Shcherbakov and Co.), who were in turn connected with avowed counter-revolutionaries; abroad it became the object of extensive support on the part of the bourgeoisie of all countries.

Based on the above, the Fifteenth Congress holds that the CC and CCC were right in expelling Trotsky and Zinoviev on 14 November 1927 from the ranks of the CPSU, and the other Opposition members of the CC and CCC from these bodies, and in bringing up the Opposition question as a whole for the consideration of the Congress.

In its resolution on the report of the CC the Congress declared that membership of the Trotskyist Opposition and the propagation of its views are incompatible with membership of the CPSU. The Congress holds in this connection that the Opposition must disarm both ideologically and organizationally, emphatically condemn its views outlined above as anti-Leninist and Menshevik, and take upon itself the obligation to defend the opinions and decisions of the Party, its Congresses, its conferences, and its CC.

However, the Opposition rejected this demand of the Party. In the Opposition documents of 3 December 1927, signed by 121 active members of the Opposition, the latter not only do not renounce, but, on the contrary, insist on the propagation of their Menshevik views.

After the Congress adopted the resolution on the report of the CC, the Commission received two new Opposition documents on 10 December 1927, one of which (signed Rakovsky, Muralov, and Radek) insists not only on the necessity of preserving these Menshevik views, but also on the necessity of advocating them, and the other (signed Kamenev, Bakayev, Yevdokimov, and Avdeyev) insists on the preservation of the Menshevik views of the Opposition, but renouncing their propagation, which does not meet the demands of ideological capitulation and is tantamount to a refusal to defend the decisions of the Party.

Recording the obvious difference of opinion between the two Opposition groups, the Congress nevertheless holds that both Opposition statements are absolutely unsatisfactory.

Based on the aforegoing, and taking into consideration the twofold violation by the Opposition of its solemn pledges renouncing factionalism, the Congress resolves:

1. To expel from the Party the following active members of the Trotskyist Opposition. [75 names]
2. To expel from the Party, as obviously anti-revolutionary, the Sapronov group: [23 names]
3. To authorize the CC and CCC to take all measures for ideological persuasion of the rank and file members of the Trotskyist Opposition with the object of convincing them, and simultaneously purging the Party of all the obviously incorrigible elements of the Trotskyist Opposition.

Source: KPSS v resolyutziyakh, chast' II (Moscow, 1954), p. 488.
Translation: Report of the Fifteenth Congress of the All-Union Communist Party (Bolsheviks) (Moscow, 1928), p. 404. Some terms slightly modified by the editor.

30. Stalin on Bukharin and the Right Deviation (extracts)

9 *February* 1929

Stalin's drive against the 'Right Opposition' culminated in a summons to the leaders, Bukharin, Rykov and Tomsky, to a meeting of the Central Control Commission in February 1929, *ostensibly to explain their attempt to co-ordinate their activities with Kamenev. This joint CC–CCC decree, which contained a detailed attack on them, was not made public immediately, although the breach between them and Stalin was common knowledge. Stalin made a show of trying to retain their services as members of the Politburo for reasons of party unity, but by the end of the following year all three had lost their positions in that body. Tomsky committed suicide after Vyshinski had threatened an investigation of the 'rightists' during the show trial of August* 1936, *while Bukharin and Rykov were apparently arrested early in* 1937.

30. Resolution of the Joint Meeting of the Politburo of the Central Committee and the Presidium of the Central Control Commission on Intra-Party Affairs, 9 February 1929

Approved by the joint plenary session of the Central Committee and the Central Control Commission of the All-Union Communist Party (*Bolsheviks*), 23 *April* 1929

The joint session of the Politburo of the CC and the Presidium of the CCC, after perusal of the documents and consideration of the opinions exchanged at a joint session of the Politburo of the Central Committee and the Presidium of the Central Control Commission on 30 January 1929 ... find that:

1. Bukharin's utterly incorrect criticism of the activity of the CC, which has found expression in such documents as Kamenev's 'record', the article 'Notes of an Economist', and Bukharin's declaration of 30 January 1929, is aimed at discrediting CC policy, both in the sphere of internal party policy and Comintern policy.
2. Bukharin, by discrediting the Central Committee line and using all manner of gossip about the CC to this end, is clearly edging towards the formation of a 'new' line which is different from that of the Party, and which cannot be anything but a reconciliation with Frumkin's[1] line (in the sphere of internal policy), aimed at unleashing capitalist elements; it cannot be anything but a

---

[1] M. I. Frumkin—an Old Bolshevik who held responsible office in the People's Commissariat of Foreign Trade. He proposed a milder policy towards the peasantry and more moderate plans for economic growth.

repetition of Humbert-Droz's[1] line (in the sphere of Comintern policy), directed towards a diplomatic defence of right-wing elements in the Comintern;

3. Bukharin's leanings towards a 'new' line may increase in the immediate future, because of difficulties which face the Party and because of the political unsteadiness which Bukharin has, not for the first time, betrayed in the history of our party, unless the Party takes all the measures it can to keep Bukharin in its ranks. Lenin was right when he said of Bukharin, in his letter addressed to Shlyapnikov in 1916: 'Nikolai Ivanovich is a practising economist, and we have always supported him in this. But he is (1) gullible to rumours and (2) devilishly unsteady in politics';[2]

4. Bukharin's waverings may be given fresh impetus if the Party sanctions his and Tomsky's resignation.

Proceeding from this, and with a view to preserving party unity at all costs, the joint session of the Politburo of the Central Committee and the Presidium of the Central Control Commission decrees as follows:

(a) to recognize Bukharin's criticism of the CC's activity as absolutely without substance;
(b) to propose to Bukharin that he should dissociate himself decisively from Frumkin's line in internal policy, and from Humbert-Droz's line in Comintern policy;
(c) to refuse to allow Bukharin and Tomsky to resign;
(d) to order Bukharin and Tomsky loyally to fulfil all decisions of the ECCI, the Party, and its Central Committee.

III. An Appeal to the Plenum of the Central Committee and the Central Control Commission

The disagreements with Bukharin first became evident at the CC's July plenary session in 1928. The disagreements involved three questions: the question of the split with the peasantry (Bukharin maintained that this split had already come about); the question of the limits of freedom of trade (Bukharin spoke out in favour of complete freedom of trade, unregulated by the organs of state); and the question of the collective farm movement (the importance of which Bukharin underestimated). No disagreements arose on the question of abolishing extreme measures. But these disagreements had been exhausted by debate and finally dispelled when a unanimous resolution on grain-procurements was passed. The passing of a unanimous resolution at that time provided an opportunity for making a declaration to

[1] Jules Humbert-Droz, Swiss Comintern Secretary. He favoured a rapprochement with social democratic parties against fascism.
[2] Lenin's works, 4th edn., Vol. 35, p. 168 [Soviet editor's note].

the Council of Elders of the Sixth Congress on the absence of disagreement in the Politburo. This explains why the Politburo of the CC and the Presidium of the CCC did not deem it necessary to report to the plenum of the CC on disagreements which had already been settled. It is understandable that the Politburo and the Presidium could not have known of Bukharin's secret talks with Kamenev during the July plenum of the CC.

Disagreements with Bukharin were disclosed a second time just before the November plenum, when Bukharin, Tomsky and Rykov submitted to the Politburo a statement of their resignation. The disagreements then chiefly involved three questions: the question of assessing the agricultural situation (whether agriculture was declining or developing); the question of whether to continue individual taxation of the most wealthy kulaks; and the question of the sharpening of the class struggle in our country. But these disagreements were covered by the passing of a unanimous resolution on the control figures for the economy in 1928–1929, and the retraction of their resignation by these three members. This circumstance made it possible for all the Politburo members to declare, both in their speeches at the plenum and outside, that there was an absence of dissension within the Politburo, as was in fact done by Rykov and Comrade Stalin. This explains why the Politburo and the Presidium did not find it necessary to report on these disagreements, which were already resolved by the plenum of the CC. Understandably, the Politburo and the Presidium could have no knowledge of the fact that Bukharin, Rykov and Tomsky were keeping to their own opinions and that two of them were about to hand in their resignations again.

The publication by the Trotskyites of Kamenev's 'record' of Bukharin and Sokolnikov's under-cover activity directed at organizing a factionary bloc with Kamenev has changed the situation substantially. It is now clear to all that Bukharin and his followers did not renounce their disagreement with the Party's Central Committee which had come to light even before the July 1928 plenum. It is now clear to all that these disagreements continue to exist even at the present time. This is now confirmed not only by Bukharin's statement of 30 January 1929, but also by his policy of resignation and by the speeches and declarations made by Bukharin, Tomsky and Rykov at the joint session of the Politburo of the CC and the Presidium of the CCC on 30 January 1929.

In view of this the joint session of the Politburo of the CC and the Presidium of the CCC considers it a duty to place at the disposal of the joint plenum of the CC and the CCC all the material available on this matter, including a verbatim report of speeches made at the joint session of the Politburo of the CC and the Presidium of the CCC on 30 January 1929.

The Politburo of the CC and the Presidium of the CCC jointly request the joint plenum of the CC and CCC to confirm this decree.

The joint session of the Politburo of the CC and the Presidium of the CCC expresses the firm belief that the plenum can ensure in the party ranks that iron unity which is so essential to us, especially in the present difficult circumstances.

Source: KPSS v rezolyutsiyakh, chast' II (Moscow, 1954), p. 556.
Editor's translation.

31. The Party Prepares for a Purge

28 *April* 1933

This decree announced yet another purge of party membership. The measure was, however, of particular significance, since it in fact heralded a period of mass repression. The vague categorization of undesirable members which it contained greatly simplified the process of arrest, and allowed all kinds of abuses. At the Seventeenth Congress, which took place in January–February 1934, *comparable provisions were inserted into the party statute.*

31. On Party Purges

Resolution of the CC and of the CCC of the VKP(B), 28 April 1933

I. The Necessity of the Purge

The fulfilment of the Five Year Plan in four years, the victory of the industrialization in the USSR, the success of the *kolkhoz* movement and the colossal numerical growth of the proletariat have resulted in a fresh impetus to political activity of the proletariat and peasantry.

On the basis of this impetus the Party, during the last two-and-a-half years, has increased its strength by 1,400,000; the total membership now being 3,600,000 (2,400,000 members and 1,200,000 candidates).

But under the conditions of mass recruiting which, very often, was carried out by local organizations in a wholesale manner, without carefully ascertaining the quality of the recruits, some alien elements have wormed their way into the ranks of the Party, and have made use of their membership for careerist and selfish purposes; there are also many double-faced persons who swear true allegiance to the Party but, actually, try to undermine its policy.

On the other hand, owing to the unsatisfactory state of Marxist-Leninist education of the Party members, there is a considerable number of comrades who, though honest and ready to defend the Soviet Government, are either not sufficiently stable and not enough versed in the spirit and requirements of the Party discipline, or politically poorly educated, ignorant of the programme, statutes and principal decisions of the Party and, consequently, incapable of pursuing the policy of the Party actively.

Having these circumstances in view, the joint plenary session of the Central Committee and of the Central Control Commission of the All-Union Communist Party (Bolsheviki) held in January last, resolved to arrange for the purging of the Party in 1933 and 'to organize the business of the purging in such manner as to secure iron proletarian discipline in the Party and to expel from the Party all unreliable, unstable and selfish elements.'

In passing this decision, the Party was guided by the resolution of the Communist International of 30 July 1920, according to which 'the Communist Parties of all countries where the Communists conduct their work openly, must make periodical purges (re-registrations) of the personnel of the party organizations, in order systematically to purge the Party of petty-bourgeois elements which inevitably worm their way into a Communist Party.'

Following the directions of the Communist International, our Party has arranged a re-registration of Party membership in 1920, a Party purge in 1921, a purging of non-industrial cells in 1924, a re-registration of members in the village cells in 1925, and a purge of the Party in 1929–1930. These purges and re-registrations, as everybody knows, resulted in strengthening the ranks of our Party, in raising its fighting spirit, in a growing sense of the responsibility of every Party member for the work done by the Party.

II. Aims and Purposes of the Purge

The purpose of the Party purge is to achieve a higher ideological standard of Party members, to strengthen the Party organization politically, to secure further confidence in the Party on the part of millions of non-party men and women.

This purpose will be attained, during the purge, in the following manner: (a) by carrying out open and honest self-criticism of the party members and party organizations; (b) by checking the activities of each party cell from the point of view of the execution of the decisions and directions of the Party; (c) by participation in the party purge of the toiling non-party masses; and (d) by expulsion from the Party of such persons as are not worthy of the highly honourable rank of a party member.

The following elements must be expelled: (1) Alien and hostile elements which have won their way into the Party by fraudulent means and which remain there in order to corrupt members of the Party; (2) underhanded persons who live by deceiving the Party, concealing their real desires under a false oath of loyalty, and who thus in practice undermine party policy; (3) open and secret breakers of the iron discipline of the Party who do not carry out the decisions of the Party and of the Government, who express doubts in the wisdom of the Party decisions and the plans marked out by the Party, who discredit these decisions and plans by empty talk about their 'impossibility' and 'futility'; (4) degenerate persons who fall under the influence of capitalist elements, who do not wish to fight class enemies, who do not fight the kulaks, unscrupulous egotists, loafers, thieves and pilferers of public property; (5) careerist, selfish and bureaucratic elements which make use of their membership and their positions in the Soviet administration for their own selfish interests, which have broken away from the masses, which neglect the needs and requirements of the workers and peasants; (6) persons who are morally degenerate, who by their improper conduct lower the dignity of the Party and soil its banner.

III. Methods of the Purge

The purge is a manifestation of the Bolshevist self-criticism of our Party. It must be carried out without any favouritism, and be guided by the following considerations: the fulfilment of the most important party decisions by members and candidates, their participation in socialist competition and shock-brigades, active efforts for the fulfilment of the financial and industrial programmes and of other important economic tasks, combating absenteeism from work, combating the pilfering of Socialist property.

The purging commissions must request that every member should know the party programme, its statutes and its most important decisions ... But the purging commissions must not, while examining the political knowledge of members, put complicated, 'catchy' and litigious questions. They must take into account the general cultural standard of the members examined and not put outside the party pale such comrades as have proved their unconditional allegiance to the Party and their zeal in socialist construction, but who could not attain the necessary standard of political education. This especially refers to industrial workers and to members of *kolkhozy* ...

The purge must be carried out at open meetings of the cells with the participation of non-party men and women ... All members and candidates must go through the purge with the exception of members and candidates of the Central Committee and of the Central Control Commission and members of the Committee of Inspection of the Central Committee, as having been elected by the Party Congress, and also the chiefs of the Political Departments of the Machine-and-Tractor Stations and of the *sovkhozy*, because these men have already been examined by the Party at the time of their appointment to their posts. But if a detailed application should be made by a party meeting or by a group of party members requesting the examination of [these officials, they] must also be subjected to the purge.

IV. Direction of the Purge

The general direction of the purge in the whole of the USSR is to be in the hands of the Central Purging Commission composed of the following comrades: Rudzutak (Chairman), Kaganovich, Kirov, Yaroslavsky, Shkiryatov, Yezhov, Stasova and Pyatnitsky.

The Central Purging Commission appoints corresponding purging commissions for the direction of the purge in provincial and republican organizations. The provincial and republican commissions organize district purging commissions.

... Any cell may, at its general meeting, criticize any decision of a purging commission and lodge an appeal against such decisions, but may not cancel them. The members of the purging commissions must remember that they themselves are liable to prosecution for any infringement of party democracy, for rudeness and tactlessness during the purge, as persons who compromise the purge.

The purge must be begun as from 1 June, in Moscow, Leningrad, the Urals, Donetsk, Odessa, Kiev, Vinnitsa, Eastern Siberia, the Far East and White Russia, and completed not later than by the end of November of the current year.

The Central Committee of the All-Union Communist Party (Bolsheviks).
The Central Control Commission of the All-Union Communist Party (Bolsheviks).

Source: Izvestia, 29 April 1933.
Translation: Slavonic and East European Review, Vol. XII, No. 34, July 1933, p. 212, abridged.

32. The End of the Purges Announced

19 January 1938

For most people the end of the 'Great Purge' was heralded by the publication of this document. Stalin adopted his usual tactic of blaming low-grade officialdom for 'excesses', and claiming that he had warned against such dangers before. Although he then confused the issue by emphasizing their continued existence, the main drift of the decree was clear. In July L. P. Beria was made deputy to N. I. Ezhov, who had been responsible for the purge since his nomination as head of the NKVD in September 1936. The purge then virtually came to a stop. Ezhov himself was replaced by Beria on 8 December 1938.

The decree was extremely detailed and repetitive, and for this reason is presented here in extract form.

32. On the Mistakes of Party Organizations in Excluding Communists from the Party, on the Formal and Bureaucratic Attitude to the Appeals of Persons excluded from the VKP(B) and on Measures for Removing these Shortcomings

Decree of the Plenum of the CC of the VKP(B), Pravda, 19 *January* 1938

The plenum of the Central Committee of the VKP(B) considers it necessary to draw the attention of party organizations and their heads to the fact that while doing much to clear the Trotskyist and rightist agents of fascism from their ranks, they commit, in the course of this work, serious mistakes and distortions which hinder the removal of double-dealers, spies and wreckers from the Party. Despite numerous instructions and warnings from the Central Committee of the VKP(B), party organizations in many instances approach the exclusion of Communists from the Party in a completely incorrect and criminally irresponsible manner.

The Central Committee of the VKP(B) has more than once demanded of party organizations and their heads an attentive, individual approach to members of the Party when exclusion from the Party or the readmittance of those incorrectly excluded from the VKP(B) is being decided.

In its decision of 5 March 1937 on Comrade Stalin's report 'On shortcomings in party work and measures for liquidating Trotskyist and other double-dealers' the plenum of the Central Committee of the VKP(B) indicated that:

> Certain of our party leaders lack the care needed to deal with people, members of the Party, and officials. Moreover they do not study these officials, they do not know what interests them or how they are developing,

they do not know their staff at all. It is precisely on account of this that they do not have an individual approach to members of the Party or party officials. But an individual approach is the main thing in our organizational work. And it is precisely because they do not have an individual approach in evaluating members of the Party and party officials that they usually act haphazardly; either they praise them immoderately and indiscriminately, or they assault them immoderately and indiscriminately, and exclude them from the Party in thousands and tens of thousands. Some of our party leaders try in general to think in tens of thousands, without worrying about 'individuals', separate members of the Party, or their fate. They consider the exclusion of thousands or tens of thousands from the Party as a trifling matter, and console themselves with the thought that our party is large, and tens of thousands of exclusions cannot do anything to change its standing. But only people who are in essence profoundly anti-party can approach members of the Party in this way.

As a result of this heartless attitude towards people, towards members of the Party and party officials, dissatisfaction and spite are being artificially engendered among some members.

Understandably, the Trotskyist double-dealers nimbly ensnare such embittered comrades and skilfully drag them into the bog of Trotskyist wrecking activities.

In the same decision of the plenum of the Central Committee of the VKP(B) it is stated:

The prevalence of a formal, heartless, and bureaucratic attitude in the matter of the fate of individual members of the Party, exclusions of members of the Party from party ranks, or the readmittance of excluded party members, is to be condemned.

Party organizations are obliged to show maximum caution and comradely concern when deciding the matter of exclusion from or readmittance to the Party.

In its letter of 24 June 1936 'On mistakes in examining the appeals of people excluded from the Party during the verification and exchange of party documents' the Central Committee of the VKP(B) noted the superficial, and in many cases heartless and bureaucratic attitude of party organs to the examination of appeals of those excluded:

Despite the instructions of the Central Committee—it was stated in that letter—the appeals of persons excluded from the Party are examined extremely slowly. Many of these people spend months getting the appeals they have submitted examined. A large number of their appeals have been examined in their absence, without any check-up on the appellants' declarations, and without giving appellants the opportunity to provide a detailed explanation of the reasons for their exclusion from the Party.

In many regional party organizations a totally intolerable arbitrariness has been permitted against persons excluded from the Party. Those excluded for concealing their social origins and for passivity, rather than for motives of hostile activity against the Party or Soviet power, have been automatically removed from their work, deprived of their homes, etc.

In this way party leaders of these party organizations who have failed to master properly the instructions of the Party on Bolshevik vigilance have, by their formal and bureaucratic attitude to the examination of the appeals of people excluded from the Party through the verification of party documents, played into the hands of the Party's enemies.

As may be seen, warning instructions were indeed given to local party organizations.

Nevertheless, despite this, many party organizations and their heads continue to regard the fate of individual members of the Party formally, and in a heartless and a bureaucratic manner.

There are many known instances of party organizations, without any verification and consequently without proper grounds, having excluded Communists from the Party, and deprived them of their work; such organizations have frequently even declared them without basis to be enemies of the people, and have acted illegally and arbitrarily towards members of the Party ...

[*A series of examples follows*]

The plenum of the Central Committee of the VKP(B) considers that all these, and similar facts, are widespread in party organizations mainly because there exist among the Communists, as yet concealed and unmasked, *certain Communist-careerists who try to distinguish themselves and get promotion through exclusions from the Party, through repressions against party members. Such people try to ensure themselves against possible accusations of a lack of vigilance by applying mass repressions against party members ...*

Party organizations and their leaders, instead of tearing the mask of false vigilance from such 'Communists' and bringing them out into the open, themselves frequently create for them the halo of vigilant fighters for the purity of the party ranks.

It is time to unmask such so-called Communists and brand them as careerists who are trying to advance themselves by bringing about exclusions from the Party, and who are trying to re-insure themselves with the help of repressions against party members.

Furthermore there are many known instances of hidden enemies of the people, wreckers and double-dealers organizing, for provocative purposes, the submission of slanderous statements against party members, and bringing about, under the guise of 'spreading vigilance', the exclusion of honest and devoted Communists from the ranks of the VKP(B). By so doing they avert the blow against themselves and remain in the party ranks ...

In many *oblast* and *krai* organizations a large quantity of unexamined appeals lies without any movement whatever. In the Rostov Oblast more than 2,500 appeals have not been examined, there are 2,000 in the Krasnodar Krai, 2,300 in the Smolensk Oblast, 1,200 in the Voronezh Oblast, 500 in the Saratov Oblast, and so on.

Obkomy, *kraikomy*, and the Central Committees of national Communist parties which have refused to examine the appeals of persons excluded from the Party have, despite the statutes of the Party, transformed the decisions of *raikomy* and *gorkomy* of the VKP(B) on this question into final decisions not open to appeal.

All this means that the *obkomy*, *kraikomy*, and Central Committees of national Communist parties have in fact divorced themselves from the management of the work of local party organizations in this most important and acute question, which concerns the fate of members of the Party; they have left this matter to take its own course, and sometimes to arbitrary decision.

The *obkomy*, *kraikomy*, and Central Committees of national Communist parties themselves encourage the practice of mass exclusions from the Party by leaving unpunished those party leaders who permit arbitrary action against Communists ...

The plenum of the Central Committee of the VKP(B) demands of all party organizations and their heads the greatest possible improvement in Bolshevik vigilance in the party masses, the unmasking and final uprooting of all willing or unwilling enemies of the Party.

The plenum of the Central Committee of the VKP(B) considers that a most important condition for the successful solution of this task is the complete liquidation of the anti-party practice of dealing with people and members of the Party in a mass, impersonal or undifferentiated manner.

The plenum of the Central Committee of the VKP(B) decrees that:

1. *Obkomy*, *kraikomy*, the Central Committees of national Communist parties and all party organizations should resolutely put an end to mass, indiscriminate exclusions from the Party and really adopt an individual, differentiated approach when deciding questions of exclusion from the Party or readmitting excluded members.

2. *Obkomy*, *kraikomy*, and the Central Committees of national Communist parties should remove from party posts and call to account before the Party those party leaders who do not fulfil the directives of the Central Committee of the VKP(B), who exclude members and candidates from the Party without

a detailed check-up on all relevant materials, and who make arbitrary decisions with regard to party members.

3. It be suggested to *obkomy*, *kraikomy*, and the Central Committees of the national Communist parties and party collegiums of the KPK attached to the Central Committee of the VKP(B), that they complete, in the course of three months, their examination of the appeals of all persons excluded from the Party.

4. All party committees should be obliged to set out clearly and exactly in their decrees on the exclusion of Communists from the Party the motives which served as the basis for the exclusion, so that higher party organs have the opportunity to check up on the correctness of these decrees. The *raikom*, *gorkom*, *obkom* and Central Committee of a national Communist party must be obliged to publish every decree of this kind in the press.

5. To establish that party organs, when readmitting members incorrectly excluded by local party organizations, are obliged to indicate in their decrees exactly which *raikom* or *gorkom* of the VKP(B) must issue party documents to the person readmitted to the Party.

6. *Raikomy* and *gorkomy* of the Party must issue party documents immediately to persons readmitted to the Party, involve them in party work, and explain to all members of primary party organizations that they are responsible for the Bolshevik education of persons readmitted to the ranks of the VKP(B).

7. Party organizations must arraign before the Party persons guilty of slandering party members, rehabilitate these party members, and publish the decrees in those cases when material discrediting the member of the Party had already appeared in the press.

8. Party organizations are forbidden to enter on the Communist's party card the fact of his exclusion from the Party before his appeal has been investigated and a final decision on exclusion reached.

9. The incorrect and harmful practice of immediately removing persons excluded from the VKP(B) from their job is forbidden.

In all instances when it proves necessary to release an official from his job in connection with his exclusion from the VKP(B), this release must be effected only after he has been given other work.

10. *Obkomy*, *kraikomy*, and the Central Committees of national Communist parties are obliged to ensure, not later than 15 February 1938, through the corresponding Soviet and economic organs, that persons excluded from the VKP(B) are given employment, and that persons excluded from the VKP(B) should not henceforth be left without work.

Source: *KPSS v rezolyutsiyakh*, chast' III (Moscow, 1954), p. 306.
Editor's translation: extracts.

33. The Announcement of Stalin's Death

6 *March* 1953

From Central Committee of Communist Party of the Soviet Union, USSR Supreme Soviet

To all Members of the Party, to all the Working People of the Soviet Union, 6 *March* 1953

Dear Comrades and Friends: The Central Committee of the Communist Party of the Soviet Union, the USSR Council of Ministers and the Presidium of the USSR Supreme Soviet announce with profound sorrow to the Party and all working people of the Soviet Union that at 9.50 p.m. 5 March, Joseph Vissarionovich STALIN, Chairman of the USSR Council of Ministers and Secretary of the Central Committee of the Communist Party of the Soviet Union, died after a grave illness.

The heart of Lenin's comrade-in-arms and the inspired continuer of Lenin's cause, the wise leader and teacher of the Communist Party and the Soviet people—Joseph Vissarionovich STALIN—has stopped beating.

STALIN's name is boundlessly dear to our party, to the Soviet people, to the working people of the world. Together with Lenin, Comrade STALIN created the mighty party of Communists, reared and forged that party; together with Lenin, Comrade STALIN was the inspirer and leader of the great October socialist revolution, founder of the world's first socialist state. Continuing Lenin's immortal cause, Comrade STALIN led the Soviet people to the world-historic triumph of socialism in our land. Comrade Stalin led our country to victory over fascism in the second world war, which wrought a radical change in the entire international situation. Comrade STALIN armed the Party and the entire people with a great and clear programme of building communism in the USSR.

The death of Comrade STALIN, who devoted all his life to the great cause of communism, constitutes a great loss to the Party and to the working people of the Soviet land and of the whole world.

The news of Comrade STALIN's death will bring profound pain to the hearts of the workers, collective farmers, intelligentsia and all the working people of our motherland, to the hearts of the warriors of our glorious army and navy, to the hearts of millions of working people in all countries of the world.

In these sorrowful days all the peoples of our country are rallying closer in a great fraternal family under the tested leadership of the Communist Party, created and reared by Lenin and STALIN.

The Soviet people have boundless faith in and are imbued with deep love for their Communist Party, for they know that the supreme law governing all the activity of the Party is to serve the interests of the people.

The workers, collective farmers, Soviet intelligentsia and all the working people of our country steadfastly follow the policy mapped out by our party, which is in conformity with the vital interests of the working people and pursues the continued consolidation of the might of our socialist motherland. The correctness of this policy of the Communist Party has been proved by decades of struggle. It has led the working people of the Soviet country to the historic victories of socialism. Inspired by this policy, the peoples of the Soviet Union, under the leadership of the Party, advance confidently toward fresh successes of communist construction in our land.

The working people of our country know that the further improvement of the material well-being of all strata of the population—workers, collective farmers, intelligentsia—maximum satisfaction of constantly growing material and cultural needs of the entire society has always been and is the subject of the particular concern of the Communist Party and the Soviet government.

The Soviet people know that the defence capacity and might of the Soviet state are growing and strengthening, that the Party is in every way strengthening the Soviet Army, Navy and intelligence agencies with a view to constantly raising our preparedness to rebuff decisively any aggressor.

The foreign policy of the Communist Party and the government of the Soviet Union has always been and is a policy of maintaining and strengthening peace, of struggle against the preparation for and the unleashing of another war, a policy of international co-operation and development of business relations with all countries.

The peoples of the Soviet Union, true to the banner of proletarian internationalism, are strengthening and developing fraternal friendship with the great Chinese people, with the working people of all the people's democracies, friendly relations with the working people of capitalist and colonial countries who are fighting for the cause of peace, democracy and socialism.

Dear Comrades and friends!

The great directing and guiding force of the Soviet people in the struggle for the building of communism is our Communist Party. The steel-like and monolithic unity of the ranks of the Party constitutes the main condition for its strength and might. Our task is to guard the unity of the Party as the apple of our eye, to educate Communists as active political fighters for carrying out the policy and decisions of the Party, to strengthen even more the Party's ties with all the working people, the collective farmers and the intelligentsia—for in this indissoluble link with the people lies the strength and invincibility of our party.

The Party regards as one of its most essential tasks the education of all Communists and working people in high political vigilance, irreconcilability and stalwartness in the struggle against internal and external foes.

The Central Committee of the Communist Party of the Soviet Union, the

USSR Council of Ministers and the Presidium of the USSR Supreme Soviet, appealing in these sorrowful days to the Party and the people, express their firm conviction that the Party and all the working people of our motherland will rally closer around the Central Committee and the Soviet government, will mobilize all their forces and creative energy in the great cause of building communism in our land.

The immortal name of STALIN will live for ever in the hearts of the Soviet people and all progressive mankind.

Long live the great and all-conquering teachings of Marx, Engels, Lenin and Stalin!

Long live our mighty socialist motherland!

Long live our heroic Soviet people!

Long live the great Communist Party of Soviet Union!

> CENTRAL COMMITTEE OF COMMUNIST PARTY OF
> THE SOVIET UNION.
> USSR COUNCIL OF MINISTERS.
> PRESIDIUM OF USSR SUPREME SOVIET.

5 March 1953.

Source: Pravda, 6 March 1953.
Translation: CDSP, Vol. V, No. 6, p. 5.

34. The Denunciation of Beria

10 *July* 1953

This Pravda *criticism of Beria was a landmark in the post-Stalin demotion of the KGB apparatus, though some of the references in it still puzzle Western observers. Beria's arrest (which had probably taken place about two weeks before) was no doubt primarily due to the danger he presented to other members of the leadership, but the timing may have been linked with the June uprising in East Berlin. He had evidently been dabbling in German–Soviet relations, and may have been regarded as a suitable scapegoat. Beria was shot in December. His arrest heralded a nationwide purge of the secret police.*

34. The Indestructible Unity of the Party, Government and Soviet People

Pravda, 10 *July* 1953

The Presidium of the Supreme Soviet of the USSR, after examining a report of the Council of Ministers of the USSR on this question, decrees that:

1. L. I. Beria should be removed from the post of First Deputy Chairman of the Council of Ministers of the USSR and from the post of Minister of Internal Affairs of the USSR.

2. The case of L. I. Beria's criminal acts should be handed over to the Supreme Court of the USSR for examination.

Beria, now exposed as an enemy of the people, wormed his way into confidence and climbed to leadership by various careerist machinations. While his criminal anti-Party and anti-state activity had been deeply concealed and disguised in the past, Beria more recently grew bold and unbridled and began to display his true countenance—that of a bitter enemy of the Party and the Soviet people. This activization of Beria's criminal work was due to the general intensification of subversive anti-Soviet efforts by the international reactionary forces which are hostile to our state. [When] international imperialism grows more active, its agents grow more active.

Beria's evil scheming to seize power began with trying to set the Ministry of Internal Affairs [MVD] above the Party and government and to employ the agencies of the MVD, both in the centre and locally, against the Party and its leadership, against the government of the USSR; he promoted officials in the Ministry of Internal Affairs on the basis of their personal loyalty to him.

It has now been established that Beria, under various fictitious excuses, hindered in every way the solution of very important, urgent problems in the sphere of agriculture. This was done to undermine the collective farms and to create difficulties in the country's food supply.

By various cunning methods Beria sought to undermine the friendship of peoples of the USSR—the absolute foundation of the multinational socialist state and the chief requirement for all the successes of the fraternal Soviet republics; to sow friction among the peoples of the USSR and to activize bourgeois-nationalist elements in the union republics.

Obliged to carry out direct instructions of the Party Central Committee and of the Soviet government to strengthen observance of Soviet law and to liquidate certain cases of illegality and high-handedness, Beria deliberately hindered the application of these instructions and in many cases tried to distort them.

Indisputable facts show that Beria lost the character of a Communist and turned into a bourgeois degenerate, in actuality becoming an agent of international imperialism. This adventurer and hireling of foreign imperialist forces nurtured plans for seizing leadership of the Party and country for the purpose of factually destroying our Communist Party and changing the policy worked out by the Party over many years into a policy of capitulation which would have led in the long run to the restoration of capitalism.

Thanks to the timely and firm measures taken by the Presidium of the Central Committee of the CPSU and unanimously and completely approved by a plenary session of the Central Committee of the Party, Beria's criminal anti-Party and anti-state designs have been exposed. The liquidation of Beria's criminal venture shows over and over that any anti-Soviet plans of foreign imperialist forces have come to grief and will come to grief on the indestructible might and great unity of the Party, the government and the Soviet people.

At the same time, political lessons and the necessary conclusions must be drawn from the Beria case.

The strength of our leadership is in its collective nature, its unity and monolithic character. Collective leadership is the supreme principle of leadership in our party. This principle completely corresponds to Marx's well-known proposition on the harm and impermissibility of the cult of the individual figure. 'Out of dislike for any cult of the individual figure,' wrote Marx, 'during the existence of the International I never allowed to be made public the numerous declarations of recognition of my services, declarations with which I was plagued from all countries—I never even answered them, except sometimes to acknowledge their receipt. Engels and I entered the secret society of Communists on condition that everything which might foster superstitious worship of authorities would be deleted from the charter.' Only the collective political experience and collective wisdom of the Central

Committee, resting on the scientific basis of Marxist-Leninist theory, assures correct leadership of the Party and country, assures firm unity and closeness of ranks of the Party and success in building communism in our country.

Translation: Provisions from the decree of the Presidium—the editor. Remainder of text—*CDSP*, Vol. V, No. 24, p. 9.

35. Khrushchev Expels the 'Anti-Party Group'
29 June 1957

This resolution is in effect the official statement on the opposition which Khrush-chev's policies met from most other members of the Presidium. The so-called Anti-Party Group was not a cohesive group at all, but an association of individuals with independent and sometimes conflicting ideas which did not accord with Khrushchev's.

It appears that the Soviet leader's policies had only two supporters (Mikoyan and Kirichenko) out of a Presidium of eleven full members, while one, Suslov, remained neutral. The Soviet leader was out of Moscow when the Presidium met but he returned as soon as he learned about it, and hurriedly summoned a full meeting of the Central Committee, where he was able to engineer an overwhelming majority. The public announcement of the dispute and its resolution came on 4 July. In the following months Khrushchev succeeded in removing from the Presidium virtually all of those who had come out against him.

35. On the Anti-Party Group of G. M. Malenkov, L. M. Kaganovich, and V. M. Molotov
Decree of the Plenum of the CC CPSU, 22–29 June 1957

At its meetings of 22 June to 29 June 1957, the plenary session of the Party Central Committee considered the question of the anti-party group of Malenkov, Kaganovich and Molotov which had formed within the Presidium of the Party Central Committee.

At a time when the Party, led by the Central Committee and supported by the people as a whole, is doing tremendous work to carry out the historic decisions of the Twentieth Congress—intended to develop the national economy further and steadily raise the living standard of the Soviet people, to re-establish Leninist norms of inner-party life, to eliminate violations of revolutionary legality, to expand the Party's ties with the masses, to develop Soviet socialist democracy, to strengthen the friendship of the Soviet peoples, to pursue a correct nationality policy and, in the sphere of foreign policy, to relax international tension in order to secure a lasting peace—and when notable progress, well known to every Soviet citizen, has been made in all these fields, the anti-party group of Malenkov, Kaganovich and Molotov came out against the Party line.

Seeking to change the Party's political line, this group used anti-party, factional methods in an attempt to change the composition of the Party's leading bodies, elected by the plenary session of the Party Central Committee.

This was not accidental.

In the past three or four years, during which the Party has been steering a resolute course toward rectifying the errors and shortcomings engendered by the personality cult and waging a successful struggle against revisionists of Marxism-Leninism, both in the international arena and inside the country— years during which the Party has done appreciable work to rectify past distortions of Leninist nationality policy—the members of the anti-party group, now laid bare and fully exposed, have been offering constant opposition, direct or indirect, to this course approved by the Twentieth Party Congress. This group attempted, in effect, to oppose the Leninist course towards peaceful coexistence among states with different social systems, to oppose the relaxing of international tension and the establishment of friendly relations between the USSR and all the peoples of the world.

They were against enlarging the powers of the union republics in the sphere of economic and cultural development and in the sphere of legislation and also against enhancing the role of the local Soviets in carrying out these tasks. Thereby, the anti-party group opposed the Party's firm course toward more rapid development of the economy and culture in the national republics —a course assuring further strengthening of Leninist friendship among all the peoples of our country. Not only did the anti-party group fail to understand the Party's measures aimed at combating bureaucracy and reducing the inflated state apparatus, it opposed them. On all these points, it came out against the Leninist principle of democratic centralism implemented by the Party.

This group persistently opposed and sought to frustrate so vastly important a measure as the reorganization of industrial management and the setting up of economic councils in the economic regions, a measure approved by the entire Party and the people. They refused to understand that at the present stage, when progress in socialist industry has assumed a tremendous scale and continues to grow rapidly, with the development of heavy industry receiving priority, it was essential to find new, more perfect forms of industrial management which would uncover great reserves and assure an even more powerful rise in Soviet industry. This group went so far as to continue its struggle against the reorganization of industrial management, even after the approval of these measures in the course of the nationwide discussion and the subsequent adoption of the law at a session of the USSR Supreme Soviet.

With regard to agricultural questions, the members of this group failed to understand the new and vital tasks. They did not acknowledge the need to increase material incentives for the collective farm peasantry in increasing the output of agricultural products. They opposed abolition of the old bureaucratic system of planning on the collective farms and the introduction of the new system of planning which unleashes the initiative of the collective farms in managing their own affairs—a measure which has already yielded positive results. They have become so divorced from life that they cannot understand the real opportunity which makes it possible to abolish obligatory deliveries of farm products from collective farm households at the end of this year. Implementation of this measure, which is of vital importance for the millions of working people of the land of the Soviets, has been made possible by substantial progress in communal animal husbandry on the collective farms and by the development of the state farms. Instead of supporting this pressing measure, the members of the anti-party group opposed it.

They waged an entirely unwarranted struggle against the Party's appeal— actively supported by the collective farms, provinces and republics—to overtake the USA in per capita output of milk, butter and meat in the next few years. Thereby the members of the anti-party group demonstrated lordly indifference to the vital life-interests of the broad masses of the people and lack of faith in the enormous potentialities inherent in the socialist economy, in the nationwide movement now going on for a faster increase in milk and meat production.

It cannot be considered accidental that Comrade Molotov, a participant in the anti-party group, manifesting conservatism and a stagnant attitude, not only failed to realize the need for developing the virgin lands but even opposed the ploughing up of 35,000,000 hectares of virgin land, which has been of such tremendous importance in our country's economy.

Comrades Malenkov, Kaganovich and Molotov stubbornly opposed those measures which the Central Committee and our entire party carried out to eliminate the consequences of the cult of the individual leader, to eliminate the violations of revolutionary law which had occurred and to create conditions which would preclude their recurrence.

Whereas the workers, collective farmers, our glorious youth, our engineers and technicians, scientists, writers, the entire intelligentsia, unanimously supported the measures promulgated by the Party in accordance with the decisions of the Twentieth Party Congress, whereas the entire Soviet people joined the active struggle to carry out these measures, and whereas our country is experiencing a mighty increase in the active part played by the people and a fresh surge of new creative forces, the participants in the anti-party group remained deaf to this creative movement of the masses.

In the sphere of foreign policy, this group, in particular Comrade Molotov, were sluggish, and hampered in every way implementation of new and pressing measures intended to alleviate international tension and strengthen world peace. As Minister of Foreign Affairs, Comrade Molotov for a long time not only failed to take any measures through the Ministry of Foreign Affairs to improve relations between the USSR and Yugoslavia but repeatedly came out against those measures which the Presidium of the Central Committee carried out to improve relations with Yugoslavia. Comrade Molotov's erroneous stand on the Yugoslav question was unanimously condemned by the July 1955 plenary session of the Party Central Committee as 'not corresponding to the interests of the Soviet state and the socialist camp and not conforming to the principles of Leninist policy.'

Comrade Molotov raised obstacles to the conclusion of the state treaty with Austria and the improvement of relations with this state in the centre of Europe. The conclusion of the treaty with Austria was of great importance in lessening general international tension. He was also against normalizing relations with Japan, whereas this normalization has played an important part in relaxing international tension in the Far East. He opposed the fundamental propositions worked out by the Party on the possibility of preventing wars under present conditions, on the possibility of different ways of transition to socialism in different countries, on the necessity of strengthening contacts between the Communist Party of the Soviet Union and the progressive parties of foreign countries.

Comrade Molotov repeatedly opposed the Soviet government's necessary new steps in defence of peace and the security of peoples. In particular he denied the advisability of establishing personal contacts between leaders of the USSR and the statesmen of other countries, which is essential in the interests of achieving mutual understanding and improving international relations.

On many of the above questions Comrade Molotov's opinion was supported by Comrade Kaganovich and in a number of cases by Comrade Malenkov. The Presidium of the Central Committee and the Central Committee as a whole patiently corrected them and combated their errors, assuming that they would learn from their errors, that they would not persist in them and would fall into step with the entire guiding collective of the Party. However, they continued to hold their erroneous un-Leninist positions.

What underlies the position of Comrades Malenkov, Kaganovich and Molotov—which is at variance with the party line—is the fact that they were and still are shackled by old notions and methods, that they have become divorced from the life of the Party and country and fail to see the new conditions, the new situation, that they take a conservative attitude and cling stubbornly to obsolete forms and methods of work that are no longer in keeping with the interests of the movement toward communism, rejecting what is engendered by life and arises from the interests of the development of Soviet society, from the interests of the entire socialist camp.

Both in domestic questions and in questions of foreign policy they are sectarian and dogmatic and they use a scholastic, inert approach to Marxism-Leninism. They fail to realize that under present conditions living Marxism-Leninism in action and the struggle for communism manifest themselves in implementation of the decisions of the Twentieth Party Congress, in persistent pursuit of the policy of peaceful coexistence, the struggle for friendship among peoples and the policy of thorough consolidation of the socialist camp, in improved industrial management, in the struggle for an over-all advance in agriculture, for an abundance of food products, for large-scale housing construction, for enlargement of the powers of the union republics, for the flourishing of national cultures, for general development of the initiative of the masses.

Seeing that their erroneous statements and actions were constantly rebuffed in the Presidium of the Central Committee, which has been consistently carrying out the line of the Twentieth Party Congress, Comrades Molotov, Kaganovich and Malenkov embarked on a group struggle against the party leadership. Reaching agreement among themselves on an anti-party basis, they set out to change the policy of the Party, to return the Party to those erroneous methods of leadership which were condemned by the Twentieth Party Congress. They resorted to methods of intrigue and reached a secret agreement against the Central Committee. The facts revealed at the plenary session of the Central Committee show that Comrades Malenkov, Kaganovich and Molotov, as well as Comrade Shepilov, who joined them, having embarked on the path of factional struggle, violated the Party Statutes and the 'On Party Unity' decision of the Tenth Party Congress, drafted by Lenin, which states:

In order to effect strict discipline within the Party and in all Soviet work and to achieve maximum unity in eliminating all factional activity, the Congress empowers the Central Committee to apply in cases of breach of discipline or of a revival or occurrence of factional activity, all measures of party punishment, including expulsion from the Party, and in respect to members of the Central Committee, their reduction to the status of candidates for membership or even, as an extreme measure, their expulsion from the Party. The condition for application of this extreme measure to members of the Central Committee and members of the Control Commission shall be the convening of a plenary session of the Central Committee to which all candidates for membership in the Control Commission shall be invited. If such a general meeting of the most responsible party leaders recognizes by a two-thirds vote the necessity of reducing a member of the Central Committee to the status of a candidate for membership or his expulsion from the Party, then this measure shall be carried out immediately.

This Leninist resolution makes it obligatory for the Central Committee and all party organizations constantly to strengthen party unity, resolutely to rebuff any manifestation of factional or group activity, to assure truly integrated work which really expresses the unity of will and action of the vanguard of the working class, the Communist Party.

The plenary session of the Central Committee notes with great satisfaction the monolithic unity and solidarity of all the members of and candidates for membership in the Central Committee and the members of the Central

Inspection Commission of the Communist Party, who unanimously condemned the anti-party group. Not a single member of the plenary session of the Central Committee supported the group.

Faced with unanimous condemnation of the anti-party activity of the group by the plenary session of the Central Committee, in a situation where the members of the plenary session of the Central Committee unanimously demanded the removal of the members of the group from the Central Committee and their expulsion from the Party, they admitted the existence of collusion and the harmful nature of their anti-party activity and bound themselves to comply with the Party's decisions. On the basis of the above and guided by the interests of comprehensively strengthening the Leninist unity of the Party, the plenary session of the Party Central Committee resolves:

1. To condemn as incompatible with the Leninist principles of our party the factional activities of the anti-party group of Malenkov, Kaganovich and Molotov, and of Shepilov, who joined them.

2. To exclude Comrades Malenkov, Kaganovich and Molotov from membership in the Presidium of the Central Committee and from the Central Committee; to remove Comrade Shepilov from the post of Secretary of the Central Committee and to exclude him from the list of candidates for membership in the Presidium of the Central Committee and from membership in the Central Committee.

The unanimous condemnation of the factional activity of the anti-party group of Comrades Malenkov, Kaganovich and Molotov by the Party Central Committee will serve to strengthen further the unity of the ranks of our Leninist party, to strengthen its leadership, to promote the struggle for the general line of the Party.

The Party Central Committee calls on all Communists to rally still more closely around the invincible banner of Marxism-Leninism, to direct all their powers toward success in solving the tasks of communist construction.

(Adopted on 29 June 1957, by unanimous vote of all the members of the Central Committee, candidates for membership in the Central Committee and members of the Central Inspection Commission, with one abstention in the person of Comrade Molotov.)

Source: KPSS v rezolyutsiyakh, chast' IV (Moscow, 1960), p. 271.
Translation: CDSP, Vol. IX, No. 23, p. 6.

36. Khrushchev's Party Statute

31 October 1961

This statute was approved when Khrushchev was arguably at the height of his power. The draft was published on 31 July 1961 and accepted, virtually without amendment, at the Twenty-second Party Congress in October. There were many textual changes vis-à-vis the 1952 and (slightly amended) 1956 versions, but the most noteworthy change was a provision for a turnover of elected officials (Article 25). It is not clear whether Khrushchev genuinely desired more flexibility of appointment in the party bureaucracy, or whether he was moved by some more sinister motives. In any case the reference to the possibility of retaining experienced leaders meant that well-proven individuals could when necessary be kept in office for several successive terms. This article, not unexpectedly, met with a great deal of opposition, and was removed at the Twenty-third Congress (see document 40).

36. The Statute of the CPSU

Approved at the Twenty-second Congress of the CPSU, 17–31 October 1961

The Communist Party of the Soviet Union is the militant, tested vanguard of the Soviet people, uniting on a voluntary basis the advanced, most socially conscious part of the working class, collective-farm peasantry and intelligentsia of the USSR.

Founded by V. I. Lenin, the Communist Party, the vanguard of the working class, has traversed a glorious path of struggle and has led the working class and working peasants to the victory of the Great October Socialist Revolution, to the establishment of the dictatorship of the proletariat in the USSR. Under Communist Party leadership the exploiting classes were eliminated in the Soviet Union and the moral and political unity of Soviet society has taken shape and grown in strength. Socialism has triumphed completely and finally. The Communist Party, the party of the working class, has now become the party of the entire Soviet people.

The Party exists for the people and serves the people. It is the highest form of socio-political organization, the leading and guiding force of Soviet society. The Party directs the great creative activity of the Soviet people and imparts an organized, planned and scientific character to their struggle to achieve the ultimate goal, the victory of communism.

The CPSU organizes its work on the basis of unswerving observance of the Leninist norms of party life—the principle of collectivity of leadership, the comprehensive development of inner-party democracy, the activeness and initiative of Communists, and criticism and self-criticism.

Ideological and organizational unity, monolithic solidarity of its ranks and conscious discipline on the part of all Communists are the inviolable law of the life of the CPSU. Any manifestation of factionalism or clique activity is incompatible with Marxist-Leninist party principles and with party membership.

In all its activity the CPSU is guided by the Marxist-Leninist teaching and the Programme based on it, which defines the Party's fundamental tasks for the period of the construction of communist society.

The CPSU, creatively developing Marxism-Leninism, resolutely combats any manifestations of revisionism and dogmatism, which are profoundly alien to revolutionary theory.

The Communist Party of the Soviet Union is an inseparable part of the international Communist and workers' movement. It firmly adheres to the tested Marxist-Leninist principles of proletarian internationalism, actively promotes strengthening of the unity of the entire international Communist *and workers'* movement and fraternal ties with the great army of Communists of all countries.

I. Party Members, their Duties and Rights

1. Any citizen of the Soviet Union who accepts the Party Programme and Statutes, takes an active part in communist construction, works in one of the party organizations, carries out party decisions and pays membership dues may be a member of the CPSU.
2. It is the duty of a party member:

    (a) to fight for the creation of the material and technical base of communism, to set an example of the communist attitude toward labour, to raise labour productivity, to take the initiative in all that is new and progressive, to support and propagate advanced experience, to master technology, to improve his qualifications, to safeguard and increase public, socialist property—the foundation of the might and prosperity of the Soviet homeland;

    (b) to carry out party decisions firmly and undeviatingly, to explain the policy of the Party to the masses, to help strengthen and broaden the Party's ties with the people, to be considerate and attentive toward people, to respond promptly to the wants and needs of the working people;

    (c) to take an active part in the political life of the country, in the management of state affairs and in economic and cultural construction, to set an example in the fulfilment of public duty, to help develop and strengthen communist social relations;

(d) to master Marxist-Leninist theory, to raise his ideological level and to contribute to the moulding and rearing of the man of communist society. To combat *resolutely* any manifestations of bourgeois ideology, remnants of a private-property psychology, *religious prejudices* and other survivals of the past, to observe the *principles* [rules] of communist morality and to place public interests above personal ones;

(e) to be an active proponent of the ideas of socialist internationalism and Soviet patriotism among the masses of the working people, to combat survivals of nationalism and chauvinism, to contribute by word and deed to strengthening the friendship of peoples of the USSR and the fraternal ties of the Soviet people with the peoples of the socialist countries and the proletarians and working people of all countries;

(f) to *strengthen* [guard] the ideological and organizational unity of the Party in every way, to safeguard the Party against the infiltration of persons unworthy of the lofty title of Communist, to be truthful and honest with the Party *and people*, to display vigilance, to preserve party and state secrets;

(g) to develop criticism and self-criticism, to boldly disclose shortcomings and strive for their removal, to combat ostentation, conceit, complacency and localism, to rebuff firmly any attempts to suppress criticism, to resist any actions detrimental to the Party and the state and to report them to party bodies, up to and including the Central Committee of the CPSU;

(h) to carry out unswervingly the party line in the selection of cadres according to their political and work qualifications. To be uncompromising in all cases of violation of the Leninist principles of the selection and training of cadres;

(i) to observe party and state discipline, which is equally binding on all party members. The Party has a single discipline, one law for all Communists, regardless of their services or the positions they hold;

(j) *to help in every way to strengthen the defence might of the USSR, to wage a tireless struggle for peace and friendship among peoples.*

3. A party member has the right:

(a) to elect and be elected to party bodies;

(b) to discuss freely questions of the Party's policies and practical activities at party meetings, conferences and Congresses, at the meetings of party committees and in the party press; to introduce motions; openly to express and uphold his opinion until the organization has adopted a decision;

(c) to criticize any Communist, regardless of the position he holds, at party meetings, conferences and Congresses and at plenary meetings of party committees. Persons guilty of suppressing criticism or persecuting anyone for criticism must be held to strict party responsibility, up to and including expulsion from the ranks of the CPSU;

(d) to participate in person at party meetings and bureau and committee meetings at which his activity or conduct is discussed;

(e) to address questions, statements or proposals to party bodies at any level up to and including the Central Committee of the CPSU and to demand an answer on the substance of his address.

4. Admission to membership in the Party is exclusively on an individual basis. Membership in the Party is open to socially conscious and active *workers, peasants and representatives of the intelligentsia, devoted to the cause of communism* [working people, devoted to the cause of communism, from among the workers, peasants and intelligentsia]. New members are admitted from among the candidate members who have completed their period as candidates.

Persons may join the Party on attaining the age of eighteen. Young persons up to twenty years of age inclusive may join the Party only via the Young Communist League.

The procedure for the admission of candidate members to full Party membership is as follows:

(a) Applicants for party membership shall submit recommendations from three party members who have a party standing of not less than three years and who know the applicant from having worked with him on the job and in volunteer work for not less than one year;

NOTE 1. In admitting members of the YCL to membership in the Party, the recommendation of the YCL district *or city* committee is equal to the recommendation of one party member.
NOTE 2. Members and candidate members of the Central Committee of the CPSU shall refrain from giving recommendations.

(b) The question of admission to the Party is discussed and decided by a general meeting of the primary party organization; the decision comes into force upon ratification by the district party committee or, in cities where there is no district subdivision, upon ratification by the city party committee.
The presence of the persons recommending admission is not essential at the discussion of the application.

(c) Citizens of the USSR who formerly belonged to the Communist or Workers' Party of another country are admitted to membership in the Communist Party of the Soviet Union on the basis of rules established by the Central Committee of the CPSU.
Persons who had formerly belonged to other parties are admitted to membership in the CPSU in conformity with the regular procedure, but only if their admission is approved by a province or territory party

committee or the Central Committee of a union-republic Communist Party.

5. Those who recommend applicants are responsible to the party organizations for the objectivity of their description of the applicant's *political, work and moral* [work and political] qualifications.

6. Tenure of membership dates from the adoption, by a general meeting of the primary party organization, of a resolution to admit the candidate to party membership.

7. The procedure for registering members and candidate members in the party organization and for transferring them to another party organization is determined in accordance with instructions of the Central Committee of the CPSU.

8. If a party member or candidate member has without valid reason failed to pay membership dues for three months, the matter shall be discussed in the primary party organization. Should it turn out that the party member or candidate member has in effect lost contact with the party organization, he shall be considered to have dropped out of the Party; the primary party organization shall adopt a decision to this effect and shall submit it to the district or city party committee for ratification.

9. A party member *or candidate member* who fails to perform the duties set forth in the statutes or commits other offences shall be called to responsibility and may be punished by admonition, by reprimand (or severe reprimand), or by reprimand (or severe reprimand) with a note to this effect in his registration card. The highest party penalty is expulsion from the Party.

When it is necessary as a party penalty, a party organization may transfer a member of the Party to the status of candidate member for a period of up to one year. The decision of a primary party organization to return a party member to candidate status is *ratified* [subject to ratification] by the district or city party committee. On expiration of the established period the person who has been returned to candidate status is admitted to party membership on the regular basis and retains his former tenure of party membership.

For minor offences measures of party education and influence, in the form of comradely criticism, party censure, warnings or reproof, should be taken.

When deciding the question of expulsion from the Party, the maximum [prudence and] thoughtfulness must be exercised and a thorough examination must be made of whether the accusation against the party member is justified.

10. The question of expelling a Communist from the Party is decided by a general meeting of the primary party organization. The decision of the primary party organization on expulsion from the Party is considered adopted if no less than two-thirds of the party members at the meeting vote for it, and it *is ratified by the district or city party committee. The decision of a district or city party committee on expulsion from the Party* comes into force

after it is ratified by a province or territory party committee or the Central Committee of a union-republic Communist Party.

Until the province or territory party committee or union-republic Communist Party Central Committee ratifies the resolution expelling the Communist from the Party, his party card *or candidate's card* remains in his hands and he has the right to attend closed party meetings.

A person expelled from the Party retains the right to submit an appeal within two months to superior party bodies, up to and including the Central Committee of the CPSU.

11. Questions of party penalty for a member or candidate member of the Central Committee of a union-republic Communist Party or of a territory, province, region, city or district party committee, and also of a member of an inspection commission, shall be discussed in the primary party organizations.

Decisions of party organizations on penalties for members and candidate members of these party committees and members of inspection commissions shall be adopted by the regular procedure.

The proposals of the party organizations regarding expulsion from the Party shall be reported to the party committee of which the given Communist is a member. A decision to expel a member or candidate member of the Central Committee of a union-republic Communist Party or of a territory, province, region, city or district party committee or a member of an inspection commission shall be adopted at a plenary session of the respective committee by a two-thirds majority vote of its members.

The question of expelling from the Party a member or candidate member of the Central Committee of the CPSU or a member of the Central Inspection Commission shall be decided by a Party Congress or, in the interval between Party Congresses, at a plenary session of the Central Committee members.

12. If a party member has committed an offence punishable under criminal procedure, he is expelled from the Party and held liable under the law.

13. Appeals by those expelled from the Party or subjected to penalties, as well as decisions of party organizations to expel members from the Party, shall be reviewed by the party bodies concerned within a period of not more than one month from the day of their receipt.

II. Candidates for Party Membership

14. [All persons] *Those* entering the Party pass through a candidate stage, which is essential in order that the candidate may acquaint himself with the Programme and Statutes and prepare for admission to the Party. The party organization must help the candidate to prepare for admission to the Party and must verify his personal qualifications.

The period of candidacy is set at one year.

15. The procedure for admitting candidates (individual admission,

presentation of recommendations, the resolution of the primary party organization on admission and its ratification) is identical with that for admission to party membership.

16. Upon expiration of the candidature, the primary party organization takes up and decides the question of admitting the candidate to membership in the Party. If during his candidature the candidate has not proved himself and because of his personal qualifications *cannot be admitted* [has turned out to be unworthy of admission] to party membership, the party organization adopts a resolution to refuse him admission to party membership, and after ratification of this resolution by the district or city party committee, he is considered dropped from candidature for party membership.

17. Candidates for party membership take part in the entire activity of the party organization and enjoy the right to a consultative vote at party meetings. Candidates for party membership may not be elected to executive party bodies or as delegates to party conferences and congresses.

18. Candidates for Party membership pay the same party dues as party members.

III. Organizational Structure of the Party. Inner-Party Democracy.

19. The guiding principle of the organizational structure of the Party is democratic centralism, meaning:

- (a) election of all party executive bodies from bottom to top;
- (b) periodic accountability of party bodies to their party organizations and to higher bodies;
- (c) strict party discipline and subordination of the minority to the majority;
- (d) the unconditionally binding nature of the decisions of higher bodies upon lower ones.

20. The Party rests on a territorial-production basis. The primary organizations are created at the Communists' places of work and are territorially united in district organizations, city organizations, etc. The organization serving a given area is superior to all party organizations serving parts of this area.

21. All party organizations are autonomous in deciding local questions, provided that the decisions are not contrary to the Party's policy.

22. The highest executive body of a party organization is the general meeting (for primary organizations), the conference (for district, city, region, province and territory organizations) and the Congress (for the Communist Parties of union republics and the Communist Party of the Soviet Union).

23. The general meeting, conference or congress elects a bureau or committee, which is the executive body and directs the entire current work of the party organization.

24. Elections of party bodies are held by closed (secret) ballot. In elections

all party members have the unrestricted right to challenge candidates and to criticize them. Voting must be on individual candidates. Candidates who receive more than one-half of the votes of the participants in the meeting, conference or congress are considered elected.

25. The principle of systematic turnover of the membership of party bodies and of continuity of leadership is observed in elections of party bodies.

At all regular elections of the Central Committee of the CPSU and its Presidium, not less than one-fourth of the membership shall be newly elected. Presidium members shall as a rule be elected for not more than three successive terms. Particular party workers may, by virtue of their recognized authority and high political, organizational or other abilities, be successively elected to executive bodies for a longer period. In such cases, election requires a majority of at least three-fourths of the votes cast by closed (secret) ballot.

At least one-third of the members of the Central Committees of the union-republic Communist Parties and of territory and province committees chosen at each regular election, and one-half of the members of region, city and district party committees and the committees and bureaux of primary party organizations, shall be new members. Furthermore, members of these executive party bodies may be elected for not more than three successive terms. The secretaries of primary party organizations may be elected for not more than two successive terms.

A *meeting, conference or congress* [party organization] may, in consideration of the political and work qualities of an individual, elect him to an executive body for a longer period. In such cases election requires that not less than three-fourths of the Communists participating in the voting cast their ballots for him.

Party members who are not re-elected to an executive party body on the expiration of their terms may be re-elected in subsequent elections.

26. A member or candidate member of the Central Committee of the CPSU must by his entire activity justify the high trust placed in him by the Party. If a member or candidate member of the Central Committee of the CPSU has sullied his honour and dignity, he cannot remain a member of the Central Committee. The question of removing a member or a candidate member of the Central Committee of the CPSU from membership in the Central Committee is decided at a plenary session of the Central Committee by closed (secret) ballot. The decision is regarded as adopted if at least two-thirds of all the members of the Central Committee of the CPSU vote for it.

The question of removing a member or candidate member of the Central Committee of a union-republic Communist Party committee from the given party body is decided at a plenary session of the given committee. A decision is considered adopted if at least two-thirds of all the members of the committee vote for it by closed (secret) ballot.

If a member of the Central Inspection Commission does not justify the high trust placed in him by the Party, he must be removed from the

Commission. This question is decided at a meeting of the Central Inspection Commission. A decision is considered adopted if at least two-thirds of all the members of the Central Inspection Commission vote for removal of a given member of the Central Inspection Commission from that body by closed (secret) ballot.

The question of removing members of inspection commissions of republic, territory, province, region, city and district party organizations from these commissions is decided at meetings of the given commissions under the procedure established for members and candidate members of the party committees.

27. The free and businesslike discussion of questions of party policy in individual party organizations or in the Party as a whole is an inalienable right of the party member and an important principle of inner-party democracy. Only on the basis of inner-party democracy can criticism and self-criticism be developed and party discipline, which must be conscious and not mechanical, be strengthened.

Discussions on disputed or insufficiently clear questions are possible within the framework of individual organizations or of the Party as a whole.

General party discussion is necessary if:

(a) this need is recognized by several party organizations at the province or republic level;
(b) if within the Central Committee there does not exist a sufficiently firm majority on major questions of party policy;
(c) if the Central Committee of the CPSU considers it essential to consult with the entire Party on given questions of policy.

Broad discussion, especially discussion on an all-union scale, of questions of party policy must be carried out in such a way as to ensure the free expression of the views of Party members and to prevent the possibility of attempts to form factional groupings destructive to party unity or of attempts to split the Party.

28. The highest principle of party leadership is collectivity *of leadership* — the indispensable condition of the normal functioning of party organizations, the correct rearing of cadres and the development of the activeness and initiative of Communists. The cult of the individual and the violations of inner-party democracy connected with it cannot be tolerated in the Party; they are incompatible with the Leninist principles of party life.

Collective leadership does not absolve officials of individual responsibility for matters entrusted to them.

29. *In the period between Congresses and conferences the* [The] Central Committees of the union-republic Communist Parties and the territory, province, region, city and district party committees shall keep party organizations periodically informed about their work.

30. Meetings of the *aktiv* of district, city, region, province and territory

party organizations and of the union-republic Communist Parties are called to discuss major party decisions and to work out [practical] measures for implementing them, and also to consider questions of local life.

IV. The Supreme Bodies of the Party

31. The highest body of the Communist Party of the Soviet Union is the Party Congress. Regular congresses are convened *by the Central Committee* not less often than once every four years. Convocation of a Party Congress and the agenda are announced at least one-and-a-half months before the congress. Extraordinary Congresses are convened by the Party Central Committee on its own initiative or on the demand of not less than one-third of the total party membership represented at the preceding Party Congress. Extraordinary congresses are convened on two months' notice. A congress is considered valid if no less than one-half of the total party membership is represented at it.

The norms of representation at the Party Congress are fixed by the Central Committee.

32. If no extraordinary congress is convened by the Party Central Committee within the term indicated in Article 31, the organizations demanding the convocation of an extraordinary Congress have the right to form an organizational committee possessing the rights of the Party Central Committee to convene an extraordinary congress.

33. The Congress:

(a) hears and approves reports of the Central Committee, the Central Inspection Commission and other central organizations;
(b) reviews, amends and approves the Programme and Statutes of the Party;
(c) determines the line of the Party on questions of domestic and foreign policy and considers and decides major questions of communist construction;
(d) elects the Central Committee and the Central Inspection Commission.

34. The number of members of the Central Committee and the Central Inspection Commission is determined and their members are elected by the Congress. In the event of vacancies in the membership of the Central Committee, they are filled from among the candidate members of the Central Committee of the CPSU elected by the Congress.

35. In the intervals between congresses the Central Committee of the Communist Party of the Soviet Union directs the entire work of the Party and local party bodies; selects and places executive cadres; directs the work of central state organizations and public organizations of the working people through the party groups within them; creates various agencies, institutions and enterprises of the Party and directs their work; appoints the editorial

boards of central newspapers and magazines that function under its control; and distributes the funds of the party budget and supervises its implementation.

The Central Committee represents the CPSU in its relations with other parties.

36. The Central Committee of the CPSU keeps party organizations regularly informed about its work.

37. The Central Inspection Commission checks on the promptness of the conduct of affairs in central bodies of the Party and audits the treasury and undertakings of the Central Committee of the CPSU.

38. The Central Committee of the CPSU holds not less than one plenary session every six months. Candidate members of the Central Committee attend plenary sessions of the Central Committee with the right to a consultative vote.

39. The Central Committee of the Communist Party of the Soviet Union elects a Presidium to direct the work of the Central Committee between plenary sessions and a Secretariat to direct current work, chiefly in the selection of cadres and organization of checkup on fulfilment; it creates a Bureau of the CPSU Central Committee for the Russian Republic.

40. The Central Committee of the Communist Party of the Soviet Union organizes a Party Control Committee under the Central Committee.

The Party Control Committee under the Party Central Committee:

(a) verifies the observance of party discipline by members and candidate members of the CPSU; calls to account Communists guilty of violating the Party Programme and Statutes or party and state discipline, as well as violators of party ethics;

(b) examines appeals against decisions of the Central Committees of the union-republic Communist Parties and of territory and province party committees concerning expulsion from the Party and party penalties.

V. The Republic, Territory, Province, Region, City and District Organizations of the Party

41. The republic, territory, province, region, city and district party organizations and their committees are guided in their work by the Programme and Statutes of the CPSU; carry out within the limits of the republic, territory, province, region, city or district the entire work of implementing party policy; and organize execution of the directives of the Central Committee of the CPSU.

42. The chief duties of republic, territory, province, region, city and district party organizations and their executive bodies are:

(a) political and organizational work among the masses and their mobilization for accomplishment of the tasks of communist construction, for all-round development of industrial and agricultural production and for the fulfilment and overfulfilment of state plans; concern for a steady rise in the living standard and cultural level of the working people;

(b) organization of ideological work; propaganda of Marxism-Leninism; increasing the communist awareness of the working people; guidance of the local press, radio and television; supervision of the work of cultural-enlightenment institutions;

(c) guidance of the soviets, trade unions, the Young Communist League, co-operative enterprises and other public organizations through the party groups within them; the ever broader enlistment of the working people in the work of these organizations; development of the initiative and activeness of the masses as a necessary condition for the gradual transition from a socialist state system to communist public self-government.

Party organizations do not supplant soviet, trade-union, co-operative and other public organizations of the working people and must not permit a merging of the functions of Party and other agencies or un-necessary parallelism in work;

(d) selection and placement of executive cadres and the rearing of them in a spirit of communist ideology, honesty and truthfulness and a high sense of responsibility to the Party and the people for the work en-trusted to them;

(e) broad enlistment of Communists in the conduct of party work as unsalaried workers, as a form of public activity;

(f) organization of various institutions and enterprises of the Party within the bounds of their republic, territory, province, region, city or district and guidance of their work; distribution of party funds within their organizations; systematic reporting to the higher party body and accountability to it for their work.

THE EXECUTIVE BODIES OF REPUBLIC, TERRITORY AND PROVINCE PARTY ORGANIZATIONS

43. The highest body of the province, territory or republic party organiza-tion is the province or territory party conference or the Congress of the union-republic Communist Party, and in the intervals between them the province committee, the territory committee or the Central Committee of the union-republic Communist Party.

44. A regular province or territory conference or regular Congress of a union-republic Communist Party is convened by the province or territory committee or the Central Committee of the union-republic Communist Party once every two years, and extraordinary sessions by decision of the province or territory committee or the Central Committee of the union-republic Communist Party or upon the demand of one-third of the total

number of members of the organizations belonging to the province, territory or republic party organization. Congresses of the Communist Parties of the union republics having province divisions (the Ukraine, Belorussia, Kazakhstan and Uzbekistan) may be held once in four years.

The norms of representation at the province or territory conference or Congress of a union-republic Communist Party are fixed by the given party committee.

The province or territory conference or Congress of a union-republic Communist Party hears the reports of the province or territory committee or the Central Committee of the union-republic Communist Party and of the inspection commission; discusses at its own discretion other questions of party, economic and cultural work; and elects the province or territory committee or Central Committee of the union-republic Communist Party, the inspection commission and delegates to the Congress of the CPSU.

45. Each province and territory committee and Central Committee of a union-republic Communist Party elects a bureau, which includes the secretaries of the committee. Party membership of not less than five years is compulsory for secretaries. The plenary sessions of the committees also approve the chairmen of party commissions, the heads of the departments of these committees and the editors of party newspapers and magazines.

Secretariats may be set up in the province and territory committees and Central Committees of the union-republic Communist Parties to handle current questions and check on fulfilment.

46. The plenary session of the province committee, territory committee or Central Committee of the union-republic Communist Party is convened not less than once in four months.

47. The province committees, territory committees and Central Committees of the union-republic Communist Parties direct the region, city and district party organizations, check on their work and periodically hear the reports of the region, city and district party committees.

The party organizations of the autonomous republics as well as of autonomous and other provinces within territories and union republics work under the direction of the territory committees or the Central Committees of the union-republic Communist Parties.

THE EXECUTIVE BODIES OF THE REGION, CITY AND DISTRICT
(RURAL AND URBAN) PARTY ORGANIZATIONS

48. The highest body of the region, city or district party organization is the region, city or district party conference or the general meeting of Communists convened by the region, city or district committee not less than once in two years, and the extraordinary conference convened by decision of the committee or on demand of one-third of the total number of members of the Party in the given party organization.

The region, city or district conference (meeting) hears the reports of the committee and the inspection commission; discusses at its own discretion other questions of party, economic and cultural work; and elects the region, city or district committee, the inspection commission and the delegates to the province or territory conference or Congress of the union-republic Communist Party.

The norms of representation at the region, city or district conference are fixed by the given party committee.

49. Each region, city or district committee elects a bureau, which includes the secretaries of the committee, and also approves the heads of the departments of the committee and the editors of newspapers. Party membership of at least three years is compulsory for secretaries of a region, city or district committee. The secretaries of the committees are approved by the province committee, territory committee or Central Committee of the union-republic Communist Party.

50. The region, city and district committees organize and approve the primary party organizations, direct their work, periodically hear reports on the work of the party organizations and keep the records of the Communists.

51. The plenary session of the region, city or district committee is convened not less than once in three months.

52. The region, city or district committee has unsalaried instructors, sets up permanent or temporary commissions for various questions of party work and employs other forms of enlisting Communists in the work of the party committee as a public duty.

VI. Primary Organizations of the Party

53. The primary organizations are the foundations of the Party.

The primary party organizations are set up at the places of work of party members—at plants, factories, state farms and other enterprises, collective farms, units of the Soviet Army, offices, educational institutions, etc., wherever there are no fewer than three party members. Primary party organizations may also be set up on a territorial basis at the places of residence of Communists in villages or in apartment-house administrations.

54. At enterprises, collective farms and offices where there are more than fifty party members and candidate members, party organizations may be set up within the over-all primary party organization in workshops, sectors, livestock sections, brigades, departments, etc., with the authorization of the district, city or region party committee.

Party groups by brigades and other production units may be set up within shop organizations, sector organizations, etc., and also within primary party organizations with fewer than fifty members and candidate members.

55. The highest body of the primary party organization is the party meeting, which is held not less than once a month.

In large party organizations with more than 300 Communists, the general party meeting is convened when necessary at times fixed by the party committee or on the demand of several shop party organizations.

56. The primary or shop party organization elects a bureau for a term of one year to conduct current work; the number of its members is fixed by the party meeting. Primary and shop party organizations with fewer than fifteen party members elect a secretary and an assistant secretary of the party organization instead of a bureau.

At least one year's membership in the Party is compulsory for secretaries of primary and shop party organizations.

Full-time paid party posts are as a rule not set up in primary party organizations embracing fewer than 150 party members.

57. In large enterprises and institutions with more than 300 party members and candidate members, and also in organizations with more than 100 Communists in cases where special production conditions or geographical dispersion make it necessary, party committees may be set up, with the authorization of the province or territory party committee or the Central Committee of the union-republic Communist Party; the shop party organizations of these enterprises and institutions are granted the rights of primary party organizations.

The party organizations of collective farms that have fifty Communists may set up party committees.

The party committee is elected for a term of one year, and the number of its members is fixed by the general party meeting or conference.

58. The primary party organization is guided in its work by the Programme and Statutes of the CPSU. It conducts work directly among the working people, rallies them around the Communist Party of the Soviet Union and organizes the masses for carrying out the Party's policy and for the struggle to build communism.

The primary party organization:

(a) admits new members to the CPSU;
(b) rears Communists in a spirit of devotion to the cause of the Party, ideological conviction and communist ethics;
(c) organizes the study by Communists of Marxist-Leninist theory in close connection with the practice of communist construction and opposes any attempts at revisionist distortions of Marxism-Leninism and at its dogmatic interpretation;
(d) concerns itself with enhancing the vanguard role of Communists in labour and in the socio-political and economic life of the enterprise, collective farm, office, educational institution, etc.;
(e) acts as the organizer of the working people in carrying out routine tasks of communist construction; heads socialist competition for the fulfilment of state plans and pledges *of the working people*; mobilizes the masses for disclosing and making better use of the internal reserves

of enterprises and collective farms and for widely introducing in production the achievements of science, technology and the experience of leading workers; works for the strengthening of labour discipline and for a steady rise in labour productivity and an improvement of quality of output; shows concern for protecting and increasing public wealth at enterprises and state and collective farms;

(f) conducts mass agitation and propaganda work; rears the masses in the spirit of communism; helps the working people to develop skills in administering state and public affairs;

(g) on the basis of broad development of criticism and self-criticism, combats manifestations of bureaucracy, localism and violations of state discipline; thwarts attempts to deceive the state; takes measures against laxity, mismanagement and waste at enterprises, collective farms and institutions;

(h) assists the region, city and district party committees in all their activity and accounts to them for its work.

The party organization must see to it that every Communist observes in his own life and inculcates in the working people the moral principles set forth in the Programme of the CPSU, *in the moral code of the builder of communism*:

devotion to the cause of communism, love of the socialist homeland, of the socialist countries;

conscientious labour for the good of society: he who does not work, neither shall he eat;

concern on the part of everyone for the preservation and growth of public wealth;

a high sense of public duty, intolerance of violations of the public interest;

collectivism and comradely mutual assistance: one for all and all for one;

humane relations and mutual respect among people: man is to man a friend, comrade and brother;

honesty and truthfulness, moral purity, guilelessness and modesty in public and private life;

mutual respect in the family and concern for the upbringing of children;

an uncompromising attitude to injustice, parasitism, dishonesty, careerism *and money-grubbing*;

friendship and brotherhood of all peoples of the USSR, intolerance of national and racial animosity;

an uncompromising attitude to the enemies of communism, peace and the freedom of peoples;

fraternal solidarity with the working people of all countries and with all peoples.

59. Primary party organizations of production and trade enterprises, state and collective farms, and planning organizations, design bureaux and

research institutes directly connected with production have the right to supervise the work of the administration.

The Party organizations of ministries, state committees, economic councils and other central and local Soviet and economic institutions and agencies, which do not have the function of supervising the work of the administration, must actively promote improvement of the work of the apparatus, foster among the personnel a high sense of responsibility for the work entrusted to them, take measures to strengthen state discipline and improve services to the public, vigorously combat bureaucracy and red tape, and inform the proper party bodies in good time about shortcomings in the work of the institutions as well as of individuals, regardless of the posts they occupy.

VII. The Party and the Young Communist League

60. The All-Union Leninist Young Communist League is an independent public organization of young people, an active assistant and reserve of the Party. The Young Communist League helps the Party to rear young people in the spirit of communism, to enlist them in the practical work of building a new society and to train a generation of harmoniously developed people who will live, work and direct public affairs under communism.

61. Young Communist League organizations enjoy the right of broad initiative in discussing and submitting to the appropriate party organizations questions of the work of an enterprise, collective farm or institution. They must be really active champions of party directives in all spheres of communist construction, especially where there are no primary party organizations.

62. The YCL *works* [conducts its work] under the guidance of the Communist Party of the Soviet Union. The work of local YCL organizations is directed and supervised by the appropriate republic, territory, province, region, city and district party organizations.

In their work in the communist education of young people, local party bodies and primary party organizations rely on Young Communist League organizations and support and disseminate their useful undertakings.

63. YCL members who *are admitted to* [become members or candidate members of] the Party leave the Young Communist League from the moment they join the Party, unless they occupy executive posts in Young Communist League organizations.

VIII. Party Organizations in the Soviet Army

64. Party organizations in the Soviet Army are guided in their activity by the Programme and Statutes of the CPSU and function on the basis of instructions approved by the Central Committee.

The party organizations of the Soviet Army ensure the implementation of party policy in the armed forces; rally their personnel around the Communist

Party; educate servicemen in the spirit of the ideas of Marxism-Leninism and selfless devotion to the socialist homeland; actively help to strengthen the unity of the army and the people; show concern for strengthening military discipline; and mobilize personnel for fulfilling the tasks of combat and political training, mastering new equipment and weapons and irreproachably carrying out their military duty and the orders and instructions of the command.

65. The guidance of party work in the armed forces is exercised by the Central Committee of the CPSU through the Chief Political Administration of the Soviet Army and Navy, which functions with the powers of a department of the Central Committee of the CPSU.

Party membership of five years is compulsory for the heads of the political administrations of military districts and fleets and the heads of the political departments of armies, and Party membership of three years for the heads of the political departments of military units.

66. The party organizations and political bodies of the Soviet Army support close contact with local party committees and keep them periodically informed about political work in the military units. The secretaries of military party organizations and the heads of political bodies participate in the work of the local party committees.

IX. Party Groups in Non-Party Organizations

67. Party groups are organized at congresses, conferences and meetings convened by soviet, trade-union, co-operative and other mass organizations of the working people as well as in the elective bodies of these organizations where there are at least three party members. The tasks of these groups is to strengthen the influence of the Party in every way and to carry out its policy among non-party people, to strengthen party and state discipline, to combat bureaucracy and to check on the fulfilment of party and Soviet directives.

68. Party groups are subordinate to the appropriate party bodies: the Central Committee of the Communist Party of the Soviet Union, the Central Committee of the union-republic Communist Party or the territory, province, region, city or district party committee.

In all matters the party groups must be guided strictly and undeviatingly by the decisions of the executive party bodies.

X. Party Funds

69. The financial resources of the Party and its organizations consist of membership dues, revenue from party undertakings and other revenue.

70. The monthly membership dues for party members and candidate members are established as follows:

MONTHLY EARNINGS	DUES
up to 50 roubles	10 kopeks
from 51 to 100 roubles	0·5% of monthly earnings
from 101 to 150 roubles	1·0% ”
from 151 to 200 roubles	1·5% ”
from 201 to 250 roubles	*2·0%* ”
from 251 to 300 roubles	*2·5%* ”
[from 201 to 300 roubles	2·0% ”]
over 300 roubles	3·0% ”

71. An initiation fee in the amount of 2 per cent of monthly earnings is assessed upon admission as a candidate member of the Party.

Source: XXII S'ezd KPSS, tenografichesky otchet, Vol. III (Moscow, 1962), p. 337.
Translation: L. Gruliow, *Current Soviet Policies, IV*, p. 34. The variations between the published draft (in square brackets) and the final version (in italics), as indicated by the translator, have been retained.

37. On Elections Inside the Party

29 March 1962

This instruction is a detailed explanation of how Articles 24 and 25 of the Party Statute (1961 version) were to be applied.

The party leadership has always shown a curious sensitivity about voting procedures, partly, no doubt, because of the dichotomy between democratic appearances and the standard practice of nomination from above. This document shows that contrary to Article 24 of the new statute the more important elections at each level had to be made by open voting—obviously so that it could be better controlled. Some attempt was made to preserve an element of democracy, in that extra candidates' names could be written on the ballot papers, and the number of elective positions changed. However, an additional element of control could be provided by the presence of officials from higher party bodies. Significantly, the instruction does not cover elections to the All-Union Central Committee.

37. Instructions on Conducting the Elections of Leading Party Organs

Approved by the CC of the CPSU, 29 March 1962

1. In accordance with the Statutes of the CPSU, elections to the leading party organs are held:

in primary and workshop party organizations, and in party groups—once a year;
in *raion*, city, *okrug*, *oblast* and *krai* party organizations, and in the Communist Parties of the union republics—once in two years.

Communist Parties of the union republics which have *oblast* sub-divisions (Ukraine, Belorussia, Kazakhstan, Uzbekistan) may hold elections to their central party organs once in four years.

2. Report and election meetings of primary party organizations, city and *raion* party conferences (or *raion* party meetings) usually take place outside working hours.

3. In primary party organizations, the elections of party committees and bureaux, and where there are no bureaux, those of secretaries and deputy secretaries, are made at the general party meeting. In certain cases, with the permission of the *oblast* party committee, the *krai* party committee, or the Central Committee of the Communist Party of the union republic, primary party organizations which have more than 500 members can elect their party committees at party conferences. The representational norms at the

conferences are fixed by the party committee in agreement with the *raion* party committee or the city party committee.

Elections of *raion*, city, *okrug*, *oblast* and *krai* committees of the Party are held at the corresponding party conferences, and those of the Central Committees of the Communist Parties of the union republics are held at the congresses of the Communist parties of the union republics. The auditing commissions are elected simultaneously with the party committees. The representational norms at the conferences and the congresses are fixed by the corresponding party committees.

4. Delegates to *raion*, city and *okrug* party conferences are elected at general meetings (conferences) of the primary party organizations.

In cities which are divided into *raiony*, delegates to the city party conferences may be chosen at the *raion* party conferences.

Delegates to *oblast* and *krai* party conferences, and to congresses of the Communist Parties of the union republics are elected at the *raion*, city and *okrug* party conferences. Delegates to congresses of the Communist Parties of the union republics can be elected at *oblast* party conferences.

In the party organizations of cities with *raion* sub-divisions the election of delegates to *oblast* and *krai* party conferences and to congresses of the Communist Parties of the union republics can, on the decision of the *oblast* or *krai* party committees, or the Central Committees of the Communist Parties of union republics, be held directly at *raion* party conferences.

5. Reports of the party organs are discussed and approved at plenums of the corresponding committees, and in primary party organizations—at meetings of the party committees and bureaux of these organizations. Reports of the auditing commissions are discussed and approved at meetings of these commissions.

Preliminary discussion of these reports does not deprive members of the party organs of the right to criticize the leadership of the party organization in their speeches at party meetings, conferences and congresses.

6. Members and candidate members of the Party who are on the temporary register of the primary party organization take part, like everyone else, in the report and election meetings of these party organizations.

7. For the guiding[1] of party meetings, conferences and congresses the following are elected by open vote:

at report and election meetings in primary and workshop party organizations—a presidium, or a chairman and secretary;
at conferences and congresses—a presidium and other leading organs.

The size of these leading organs is determined by the meeting itself, the conference or the congress.

Delegates with the right to a consultative vote and also representatives of

[1] Here *rukovodstvo*. (Ed.)

higher party committees may be elected to the leading organs of the conferences and congresses.

The Procedure for the Turnover of the Membership of Party Organs

8. In electing party organs the principle of a systematic turnover of their membership, with the transference of leadership, is observed. In accordance with paragraph 25 of the Statute of the CPSU not less than one-third of the membership of the Central Committees of the Communist Parties of the union republics, of the *krai* committees, and of the *oblast* committees of the Party must be replaced at every election. One half of the membership of the *okrug*, city and *raion* party committees, and of party committees and bureaux of primary party organizations, must similarly be replaced.

At the same time, members of these leading organs cannot be elected for more than three terms of office in succession.

Secretaries of primary party organizations cannot be elected for more than two successive convocations.

The rates of membership turnover in the auditing commissions are the same as in the corresponding party committees. The rate of turnover of the membership of party committees must be applied separately to members and candidate members of these organs.

9. A meeting, conference or congress may elect certain party workers to their leading organs for longer periods on the basis of their political and professional qualities. A majority of three-quarters of the Communists participating in the voting is required for election in these cases.

If a Communist is elected to an analogous organ of another party organization, the length of time for which he served on the previous committee is not taken into account.

10. Members of the Party who have left leading Party organs because the period of their eligibility for election has expired can be elected again at the following elections.

When a Communist is elected to full membership of a committee, the period of his candidate membership of the same committee or of the auditing commission is not taken into account. Members of party committees cannot be elected as candidate members of these committees, or as members of the auditing commissions, immediately after the expiry of their term of office on these committees, as envisaged in paragraph 25 of the Statute of the CPSU.

Nomination and Discussion of Candidates for Party Organs

11. Elections of leading party organs are held after the meeting, conference or congress has heard and discussed the report of the corresponding party organ, and the report of the auditing commission, and has passed the

necessary resolutions on them. Before the elections are held the party meeting, conference or congress determines by open vote the size of the party organ to be elected.

12. Candidates for election to the new party organs are nominated by participants of the party meetings, and by delegates to the conferences or congresses, at party meetings and at sessions of conferences and congresses. Candidates for full or candidate membership of the party committee, and for membership of the auditing commission, are nominated separately.

Delegates to the conference or congress with the right to a consultative vote, and party members who are not delegates to the given party conference or congress, may be nominated as candidates for membership of the party organs which are being elected.

If a proposal is made to close the nomination of candidates, the presidium of the meeting, conference or congress puts this proposal to the meeting, conference or congress, which will decide by an open vote whether the registration of new candidates should be continued or stopped.

13. At *raion*, town, *okrug*, *oblast* and *krai* party conferences, and congresses of the Communist Parties of the union republics, the presidium of the conferences or congresses can convoke a gathering of representatives of delegations to make a preliminary selection of candidates for membership to the party organ. For the same purpose gatherings of representatives of workshop party organizations can be called at meetings (conferences) of primary party organizations—should the meetings (conferences) so decide.

Candidates who are selected by these gatherings are nominated in the name of the gathering at the session of the party conference or congress.

The preliminary nomination of candidates for membership to party organs at these caucuses does not limit the right of delegates to nominate and discuss candidates at the conference or congress itself.

14. Before candidates are nominated at meetings, conferences or congresses, those present are informed which members and candidate members of the party organs have reached the expiry of their term of office in these organs.

15. Participants at the meeting and delegates to the conference or congress discuss all nominated candidates personally at their sessions in the order in which they appear on the list. Every participant at a meeting or delegate to a conference or congress has the unlimited right to reject or criticize candidates during elections.

If there is a proposal to halt discussion of a candidate, the meeting, conference or congress decides by an open vote whether to halt the discussion or continue it.

16. After candidates against whom there have been objections have been discussed, there must in each case be an open vote to decide whether the candidate should or should not be included in the list for secret voting.

Candidates against whom there have been no objections are included, without open vote, in the list for election by closed (secret) voting.

17. Delegates to party conferences and congresses who have only a consultative vote (candidate members of the CPSU at meetings of primary party organizations) take part in the discussion of candidates for membership of the party organ with the right to a deliberative vote.

Voting Procedure

18. The following are elected by closed (secret) voting:

(a) members of party committees, bureaux, and, where there are no bureaux, secretaries and deputy secretaries of primary and workshop party organizations; members and candidate members of *raion*, city, *okrug*, *oblast* and *krai* party committees; members and candidate members of the Central Committees of the Communist Parties of the union republics; and members of the auditing commissions;

NOTE: Elections of the organizers of party groups can be held by open vote if the Communists of the party group do not insist on conducting the election with closed (secret) voting.

(b) delegates to the conferences of primary party organizations, to *raion*, city, *okrug*, *oblast* and *krai* party conferences, and to congresses of the Communist Parties of the union republics.

19. The following are elected by open vote:

(a) secretaries and deputy secretaries of party committees, secretaries and deputy secretaries of bureaux of primary and workshop party organizations—at meetings of party committees and at meetings of bureaux of primary and workshop party organizations;

(b) secretaries and members (including candidate members) of bureaux of the *raion*, city, *okrug*, *oblast* and *krai* party committees, and of the Central Committees of the Communist Parties of the union republics —at plenums of the corresponding committees;

(c) chairmen of the auditing commissions—at meetings of the commissions.

20. A counting commission is chosen by an open vote of the party meeting, conference or congress to conduct the closed (secret) elections and count the results. The size of this commission is decided by the meeting, conference or congress. The commission chooses a chairman and a secretary.

Before the voting takes place the chairman of the counting commission explains the procedure for closed (secret) voting to the participants of the meeting or to the delegates of the conference or the congress.

Before the closed voting, the counting commission prepares the voting papers (lists) for secret voting, and seals the ballot boxes.

In primary party organizations with less than ten party members counting commissions are not chosen. The party meeting charges the chairman of the meeting or one of the members of the given party organization with calculating the election results. The results of the voting are entered into the protocol of the meeting.

21. [A paragraph on party organizations for shift workers is here excluded.]

22. Secret voting for the election of party organs is held at closed meetings, or at closed sessions of conferences or congresses, at which only members of the CPSU or delegates with a full vote are present.

Representatives of higher party organs have the right to be present at both open and closed sessions.

23. Every participant at a meeting and every conference delegate who has a full vote receives one copy of the voting paper (list) containing the candidates nominated for membership by the meeting, conference or congress, and (separately) the names of candidates for candidate membership of the party organs being elected. When the voting paper is given out a note is made in the credentials of the delegate to the conference or congress, or in the list of members of the CPSU who attend the meeting, that the given party member has taken part in the voting.

24. During a closed (secret) election every participant at a meeting, and every delegate to a conference or congress has the right to cross off the names of candidates from the voting paper or to add new ones, irrespective of the number of members decided on beforehand for election to the party organ in question.

25. After the voting has taken place the counting commission, without leaving the building where the meeting, conference or congress is held, opens the electoral boxes and works out the results of the voting for members and candidate members of the party organ separately. During the count the commission draws up a protocol of the proceedings and enters the results of the voting into it, showing the number of votes for and against each candidate. The protocol is signed by all members of the commission.

No one except the members of the counting commission has the right to be in the room where the count takes place.

26. The commission informs the meeting, conference or congress of the results of the voting for each candidate separately. Candidates are elected if they receive more than half the votes of the CPSU members who take part in the meeting, or of the conference or congress delegates with a full vote.

Communists who are nominated for membership of party organs for periods exceeding those laid down in paragraph 25 of the Statutes of the CPSU are elected if no less than three-quarters of the participants voted for them.

27. The report of the counting commission on the results of the elections is approved by the meeting, conference or congress.

If, as a result of secret voting, rather more or fewer members (candidate members) are elected to the party organs than was decided beforehand, the meeting, conference or congress can decide by an open vote to approve the new size of the party organ, in accordance with the [secret] vote. If the majority of participants of the meeting, conference or congress vote to retain the party organ at the size which was originally decided upon, nominated candidates must be discussed again and a second closed (secret) election held. 28. All the materials of the closed (secret) election are kept as secret documents in the party organs until the next election, after which they are by order destroyed.

Source: V. N. Malin, i drugie, *Spravochnik partiinogo rabotnika, vypusk* 4 (Moscow, 1963), p. 482.
Editor's translation, slightly abbreviated.

38. Khrushchev Splits the Party Apparatus
23 *November* 1962

39. The Party Apparatus Reunified
16 *November* 1964

Khrushchev introduced many changes into party organization during his tenure of office. Perhaps the most drastic was the splitting of the party hierarchy into industrial and agricultural sectors from the republican level down, together with the establishment of a series of bureaux in the Central Committee. Some four-fifths of all oblast, *or* oblast-*type organizations were split. Intended primarily as an attempt to increase the power of the Party vis-à-vis the state apparatus, and overcome growing economic difficulties, the move was generally unpopular. It not only antagonized non-party officials, but tended to weaken the cohesion of the party apparatus itself. One of the first measures of the post-Khrushchev leadership was to rescind it. A parallel reorganization of the Soviet and Komsomol structures was also quickly abandoned.*

38. On the Development of the USSR Economy and Reorganization of Party Guidance of the National Economy
Decree of the plenary session of the CC CPSU, 23 November 1962

The plenary session of the CPSU Central Committee notes that in the year that has elapsed since the Twenty-second Party Congress our country has achieved major successes both in its internal life and in the international arena. The decisions of the Congress and the new Party Programme constituted a powerful accelerator of social development and activated the struggle of the working masses for peace, democracy and socialism.

The historic decisions of the Twenty-second Party Congress called forth a new surge of creative activeness on the part of the Soviet people. In implementing these decisions, the Party achieved a further elevation of the Communists' vanguard role, expanded and strengthened its ties with the working people and was enriched with new experience in the political guidance of the masses.

Workers, collective farmers and the Soviet intelligentsia through their labour are multiplying the wealth of our homeland, strengthening its economic might and defence capability and actively fighting for fulfilment of the seven-year plan.

The Soviet Union's industry fulfilled the gross output plan for the first four years of the seven-year plan by 104·5 per cent. The growth in the output of industry for the period 1959–1962 amounts to 45 per cent, instead of the 39 per cent called for in the control figures. The industrial output produced will exceed the assignments by 28,000,000,000 roubles.

Capital construction has gained momentum along a broad front. The total volume of state capital investments in the years 1959–1962 will reach 107,000,000,000 roubles and will be almost 6,000,000,000 roubles higher than provided for in the seven-year plan for these years.

Major measures for the further advance of agricultural production have been taken in recent years. Despite unfavourable climatic conditions in a number of areas of the country, 9,000,000,000 poods of grain was produced in 1962. Procurements of grain exceed 3,400,000,000 poods, which is 270,000,000 poods more than in 1961.

As before, the Party has paid much attention to improving the working people's well-being. The output of consumer goods has increased and the trade turnover plan has been overfulfilled. Housing construction is proceeding on a large scale. Apartment houses with a total space of 325,000,000 square metres, or 8,800,000 new apartments, have been opened for tenancy in cities and workers' settlements during the first four years of the seven-year plan, and 2,400,000 dwellings have been built in rural localities.

In the recent period, especially since the Twentieth Party Congress, the Party has done extensive work in removing shortcomings in the guidance of the economy and in perfecting the management of the national economy on the basis of Leninist principles.

Life has fully confirmed the correctness of the Leninist course taken by the Party and its Central Committee. The economic councils and the collective-farm–state-farm production administrations are forms of economic guidance that correspond to the present-day level of socialist economics.

The measures taken by the Party for improving the guidance of the national economy are having a positive effect on the successful fulfilment of the seven-year plan.

The Twenty-second Party Congress set forth the further improvement of guidance of the national economy as one of the primary and most important of the Party's tasks. It is now necessary also to bring party guidance of industry, construction and agriculture into line with the demands of the time. In conditions of full-scale communist construction, when the Party's role is growing immeasurably, the organizational restructuring of the guidance of the national economy has great political significance.

In our time what is required of the Party is the ability not only to issue the proper slogan at the proper time but also to give knowledgeable day-by-day, concrete guidance to production, to the development of industry, agriculture and all branches of the economy.

The rate of the development of the country's national economy depends chiefly on the labour efforts of the millions and on an ability to organize the implementation of party policy and of plans for economic construction.

However, the organizational forms of guidance of the national economy that took shape earlier, and that played in their time a positive role, now are preventing a more closely planned and concrete treatment of all branches of industry and agriculture and the taking of timely, effective measures to remove existing shortcomings, are engendering the guidance of the economy by proclamation and in 'campaign style', and are preventing the proper placement of party cadres and the better employment of their knowledge and experience.

To overcome the above-mentioned shortcomings and to improve the guidance of the national economy, *it is necessary to shift to the production principle in the structure of the guiding party agencies from bottom to top.*

The organization of party agencies according to the production principle will present an opportunity to ensure more concrete and closely planned guidance of industry, construction and agriculture and to concentrate the principal attention on production questions. Such a reorganization will stimulate all aspects of the Party's activity and will link organizational and ideological work still more closely to the tasks of creating the material and technical base for communism and of rearing the new man.

The creation of the material and technical base for communism requires acceleration of the rate of technical progress. At present the guidance of a large part of the research and design organizations is dispersed among economic councils, ministries and departments, which hampers the pursuit of a unified technical policy in the branches of the national economy and slows down the introduction of new technology.

The plenary session of the CPSU Central Committee deems it necessary to reorganize the guidance of research and design organizations, to eliminate parallelism and lack of co-ordination in their activity and to carry out measures for the centralization of the guidance of technical policy.

The plenary session of the CPSU Central Committee calls the attention of party, Soviet and economic agencies to the shortcomings that exist in the organization of industrial, housing and cultural and service construction. Certain economic councils, union-republic State Planning Committees and local party agencies frequently undertake the construction of new projects without considering general state interests and without taking into account the possibilities for providing their projects with designs, materials, manpower and equipment, and they scatter funds among a multitude of construction projects.

Excesses are permitted in designing and construction, and modern standard designs are introduced extremely slowly. The activity of construction design organizations is not properly steered and co-ordinated. Many design institutes work in isolation, maintaining poor contact with other design organizations and research institutes. The USSR State Construction

Committee is not taking a leading position in organizing construction design.

To remove these major shortcomings it is necessary to set the designing of construction in order, to improve the guidance of the affairs of capital construction on the part of the party organizations.

The five years' experience of the activity of the economic councils has shown that large economic councils manage the branches of industry more skilfully, have more opportunities for manoeuvring material and technical resources and enjoy better conditions for concentration, specialization and co-operation of production. It is necessary now to take a new stride in amalgamating economic councils in order to make fuller use of the possibilities and advantages of the socialist system.

The expanded scale of the national economy and the rapid progress of science and technology demand a still greater rise in the scientific level of planning. However, in many respects the work of the State Planning Committee, the State Scientific-Economic Council and other planning agencies does not meet the demands of the present stage in the development of our country's economy. Economic plans are not always based on the most careful economic calculations and research, the rates of development of individual branches and economic regions are determined by the proportions that have become established, and the necessity for accelerating the development of the most promising branches of industry — for example, chemistry and electronics — is not taken into account.

In accordance with the requirements of the CPSU Programme, it is necessary to improve the business of planning the national economy and to complete the reorganization of the work of planning agencies that was started earlier.

The plenary session of the CPSU Central Committee calls the attention of all party organizations, all state and economic agencies, the trade unions, the Young Communist League and other public organizations to the necessity for the further development of democratic principles of participation by the working people in the management of production and the correct combination of one-man command with the broad enlistment of the masses in the management of enterprises and construction projects.

In the period of full-scale construction of communist society, the role and significance of party, state and public control grow immeasurably. The measures taken by the Party in recent years for the liquidation of the consequences of the cult of the individual have made it possible to improve somewhat the work of control agencies. However, the organizational structure of party and state control in the Leninist sense has not yet been fully restored.

Major shortcomings in the organization of control are seriously reflected in the course of our economic and cultural construction. The state control agencies are still weak in checking on the fulfilment of the most important party and government directives and wage a poor fight against hoodwinking, embezzlement, bribery, bureaucratism, red tape and other negative phenomena alien to the nature of the socialist system.

The plenary session of the CPSU Central Committee believes that the implementation of new measures for improving party guidance of the national economy, perfecting the economic management of industry and construction and creating a single party–state control in the country will play an important role in the advance of the national economy, in the solution of the Party's chief task—further improvement of the people's well-being and satisfaction of the material and spiritual requirements of the working people of the Soviet Union.

Proceeding from the Party's general line of reducing the administrative apparatus and improving its activity, the plenary session of the CPSU Central Committee stresses that the implementation of the radical reorganization of the work of party, Soviet and economic agencies not only will not increase the number of officials of the apparatus but, on the contrary, will lead to a decrease in their number and to a reduction of expenditures for maintaining the apparatus.

The Soviet people, to whom has fallen the honour of being the first to blaze the trail toward communism, have accumulated great experience in economic construction. In implementing the reorganization of the guidance of the national economy, the Communist Party is proceeding from Lenin's teachings about the necessity for constant improvement of the forms of organization of the new society and of the management of the socialist economy.

The plenary session of the Central Committee of the Communist Party of the Soviet Union resolves:

I. In the Sphere of Party Guidance of the National Economy

1. To approve the measures for the reorganization of party guidance of the national economy worked out by the Presidium of the CPSU Central Committee and set forth in Comrade N. S. Khrushchev's report at the present plenary session.

2. To recognize it as necessary to reorganize the leading party agencies from bottom to top on the basis of the production principle, and thereby to ensure more concrete guidance of industrial and agricultural production.

To form within the limits of the existing territories and provinces, as a rule, two independent party organizations:

—a territory or province party organization uniting Communists who work in industry, construction and transport, in educational institutions and research institutes, and in design organizations and other institutions that serve industrial production and construction;
—a territory or province party organization uniting Communists who work

on collective and state farms, at experimental stations, in agricultural educational institutions and research institutes, at enterprises that process agricultural raw materials, and in procurement and other institutions and organizations connected with agricultural production.

In the territory and province party organizations to have, correspondingly:

—a territory or province party committee for guiding industrial production;
—a territory or province party committee for guiding agricultural production.

3. For purposes of improving the guidance of the national economy, to recognize as expedient the formation in the CPSU Central Committee and the Central Committees of the union-republic Communist Parties of Central Committee Bureaux for Guiding Industrial Production and Central Committee Bureaux for Guiding Agricultural Production.

To elect a Presidium of the Central Committee in the Central Committees of the union-republic Communist Parties for deciding questions of republic-wide significance and for co-ordination of the activities of the Bureaux.

4. To consider it expedient to have collective-farm–state-farm production administrations formed on the basis of the merger of now-existing rural districts and to create party committees of the production administrations in lieu of the rural district party committees.

For the guidance of the party organizations of enterprises and construction projects situated on the territory of newly formed rural production administrations where no city party committees exist, to have zonal (group) industrial production party committees.

5. To establish that the newly created party agencies for guiding industrial production and agricultural production are governed in all their activity by the appropriate provisions of the CPSU Statutes on territory and province party organizations, and the party committees of the collective-farm–state-farm production administrations by the provisions of the CPSU Statutes on city and district party organizations.

6. To conduct conferences of the party organizations of the collective-farm–state-farm production administrations, and also city, borough, province and territory conferences of industrial and agricultural party organizations, in December 1962, and January 1963, for electing the new guiding party agencies.

II. In the Sphere of the Economic Management of Industry, Construction and Planning

1. For purposes of carrying out a single technical policy in the national economy, to recognize it as expedient to reorganize the guidance of research and design organizations. To this end:

(a) to transfer leading scientific and design institutes and the design bureaux of plants with testing and experimental bases to the jurisdiction of the USSR Council of Ministers' State Committees for the branches of industry;

(b) to invest in the State Committees the responsibility for the introduction of new machinery and technology in production, for the technical level of development of the given branch and the specialization of industrial production;

(c) to charge the State Committees for the branches of industry with specializing research and design organizations in the creation of definite types of machines and equipment with the maximum standardization of assemblies and parts;

(d) taking into account the scope of capital construction in the country and the necessity for radical improvement of the guidance of this matter and for more rapid transition to construction according to standard designs, to reorganize the USSR State Construction Committee into a union-republic agency, to subordinate to it the design and research organizations in the field of construction, except for the design organizations of the Ministries of Power and Electrification and of Transport Construction, and to vest in the State Construction Committee the responsibility for the conduct of technical policy in the field of capital construction and for confirming title lists.

2. To deem it advisable to withdraw the construction organizations from the jurisdiction of the economic councils. To create independent construction organizations or associations in the republics and economic regions, leaving the economic councils with the functions of clients.

3. To charge the USSR Council of Ministers' State Committee for Co-ordinating Scientific Research and the Presidium of the USSR Academy of Sciences, jointly with the union-republic Councils of Ministers, with working out proposals for improving the activity of the USSR Academy of Sciences and the union-republic Academies of Sciences, with a view to concentrating scientific forces on the solution of fundamental tasks directly linked with the development of production.

4. To approve the measures set forth in Comrade N. S. Khrushchev's report for the further amalgamation of economic councils with consideration for community of economic interests among individual areas.

5. In connection with the merger of economic councils and enterprises, to charge the USSR Council of Ministers with

(a) revising the legal basis of the economic councils, making provisions so that the economic councils are endowed with broad powers, are free of petty tutelage and able to display extensive independence in deciding economic questions and in utilizing reserves for increasing industrial production;

(b) working out and presenting for confirmation by the USSR Supreme Soviet a draft Law on the Socialist Enterprise, keeping in mind the further expansion of the powers of enterprise directors and the managers of construction organizations and the more active participation of the working people in the management of production.

6. In the interests of improving long-range planning of the development of the country's national economy and the guidance of realization of annual plans, it is necessary to draw a more precise distinction between the functions of the central planning agencies.

For these purposes, to transfer the functions of the USSR State Planning Committee, which now implements the realization of the annual provisions of the long-range plan, to a new agency—the USSR Council of the National Economy—assigning to the latter the necessary administrative functions. To reorganize the State Scientific-Economic Council as the USSR State Planning Committee, entrusting long-range planning to it.

III. In the Sphere of Party–State Control

1. To reorganize the system of control in the country, and to make its basis Lenin's teaching on the unity of party and state control, the creation of a system of unified and constant control with the participation of broad masses of the working people.
2. To form a unified agency of party and state control—the Party–State Control Committee of the CPSU Central Committee and the USSR Council of Ministers—and corresponding agencies in the localities.

To consider a highly important task of party–state control agencies the rendering of assistance to the Party and the state in the fulfilment of the CPSU Programme, in organizing a systematic check on the execution of party and government directives, in the further improvement of the guidance of communist construction and in the observance of party and state discipline and socialist legality.
3. To transform the present Party Control Committees under the CPSU Central Committee into a Party Commission under the CPSU Central Committee, entrusting to it the responsiblity for considering appeals on decisions of the Central Committees of the union-republic Communist Parties on expulsion from the CPSU and on party penalties.
4. To consider inexpedient the future retention of the USSR Council of Ministers' State Control Commission and its agencies in the localities.

The plenary session of the CPSU Central Committee stresses that the reorganization of party guidance of the national economy on the production principle will create favourable conditions for the swiftest possible implementation of the decisions of the Twenty-second Party Congress on the development of industry, construction, transport and agriculture and on improving the people's living standard.

Our homeland now finds itself on the threshold of the fifth year of the seven-year plan, in which it remains for the Soviet people to seize new outposts in industry and agriculture, in all branches of the economy. The Central Committee of the CPSU calls upon workers, collective farmers, engineers and technicians, all working people, Communists and non-party people, to ensure by their selfless labour the fulfilment of the national economic plan for 1963 and thereby to take a major new stride on the path of communist construction.

The Party Central Committee expresses its certainty that the implementation of the reorganization of party guidance of industry, construction and agriculture will meet with the full support and approval of the entire Party and all the people and will be an important weapon in ensuring the successful fulfilment of the great Programme for communist construction adopted by the Twenty-second Congress of the Communist Party of the Soviet Union.

Source: Pravda, 24 November 1962.
Translation: CDSP, Vol. XIV, No. 48, p. 12.

39. On Uniting Industrial and Agricultural *Oblast* and *Krai* Party Organizations
Decree of the Plenum of the CC of the CPSU, 16 November 1964

1. With the aim of strengthening the leading role of the Party and its local organs in communist construction, and solving more successfully the tasks of economic and cultural development of each *oblast*, *krai* and republic, it is considered necessary to revert to the principle of structuring party organizations and their leading organs on the territorial-production basis, which was a very important component of the Statute of the CPSU approved at the Twenty-second Congress of the Party.
2. In *oblasti* and *kraiya*, where party organizations were divided into industrial and agricultural, single *oblast* or *krai* party organizations uniting all the Communists of the *oblast* or *krai*, who work in both industry and agriculture, are to be re-established.

In *krai* and *oblast* party organizations there must be a single *krai* or *oblast* committee of the Party.
3. The necessity must be recognized of reorganizing party committees of the production collective- and state-farm administrations into *raion* committees of the Party, and concentrating in these the leadership of all party organizations, including those of industrial enterprises and building sites situated on the territory of the given *raion*.

The industrial-production (zonal) party committees which were created earlier on the territory of rural *raiony* and in *oblast* and republican centres are to be dissolved.

4. In December 1964, party conferences for the election of the corresponding party organs are to be held in all *kraiya* and *oblasti* where single *kraikomy* and *obkomy* of the Party are being re-established.

5. The proposals worked out by the Presidium of the Central Committee or the CPSU on the means of uniting the *krai* and *oblast* industrial and rural party organizations are to be approved. The Presidium of the Central Committee is to be entrusted with examining and deciding all organizational matters linked with the creation of single party organizations and their leading organs in the *kraiya* and *oblasti*, and also with matters relating to the re-establishment of single Soviet organs.

Source: K. U. Chernenko, i drugie, *Spravochnik partiinogo rabotnika, vypusk* 6 (Moscow, 1966), p. 101.
Editor's translation.

40. The 1966 Revisions of the Party Statute

8 April 1966

41. The 1971 Revisions of the Party Statute

9 April 1971

The first post-Khrushchev Congress saw the removal from the party statutes of Khrushchev's provisions for a turnover of officials. Brezhnev's reintroduction of the title of General Secretary, the renaming of the Presidium as the Politburo, and introduction of stricter rules for entry to the Party were indications of a return to more Stalinist concepts. The slowdown in the frequency of party meetings approved by the Twenty-fourth Congress only reflected post-Khrushchev practice, while the slight upgrading of some primary organizations may have been necessitated by the growth of party membership and the desire to improve control over non-party organizations.

40. Decree of the Twenty-Third Congress of the CPSU on Partial Changes in the Statute of the CPSU

8 April 1966

The Twenty-third Congress of the Communist Party of the Soviet Union resolves to make the following changes in the CPSU Statutes:

1. For the purpose of further improving the qualitative composition of those admitted to the CPSU and raising the responsibility of party organizations for the admission into the Party of new members, to establish that:

(a) young persons up to twenty-three years of age inclusive may join the Party only via the Young Communist League. YCL members entering the CPSU shall submit a recommendation from a district or city YCL committee, which is equal to the recommendation of one party member;

(b) persons recommending applicants for admission to the Party must have a party standing of not less than five years;

(c) a decision of a primary party organization on admission to the Party shall be considered adopted if no fewer than two-thirds of the Party members present at the meeting vote for it.

2. Proceeding from the tasks of further strengthening party discipline and raising the responsibility of Communists for the fulfilment of statutory obligations:

(a) to supplement the introductory section of the Statutes with a provision that the Party rids itself of persons who violate the CPSU Programme and Statutes and who by their behaviour compromise the lofty title of Communist;

(b) to establish that a decision of a primary party organization on the expulsion of a Communist from the Party becomes valid once it has been approved by a district or city party committee;

(c) to abolish the transfer of a party member to the status of a candidate member as a party penalty.

3. In view of the proposals of many party bodies and Communists, and taking into consideration that in party elections the membership of party committees is regularly renewed, depending on specific local conditions and also upon the work and political qualities of the officials, and that the regulations on these questions have not justified themselves in practice, it is considered inexpedient to retain in the CPSU Statutes the provisions determining the norms of renewal and turnover of the composition of party bodies and the secretaries of party organizations. In this connection, paragraph 25 of the Statutes is cancelled. Paragraph 24 is supplemented with the provision that in elections to all party bodies, from the primary organizations to the CPSU Central Committee, the principle of systematic renewal of their composition and of the continuity of leadership is observed.

4. The section of the Statutes on the primary party organizations is supplemented with a new paragraph stipulating that the party committees of primary party organizations numbering more than 1,000 Communists may, with the permission of the Central Committee of the Communist Party of the union republic, be granted the rights of a district party committee on questions concerning admission to the CPSU, registration of party members and candidate members, and review of the personal affairs of Communists. Within these organizations, in the necessary cases, party committees may be created in the shops, while the party organizations of production sectors may be granted the rights of a primary organization. Party committees that are granted the rights of a district party committee are elected for a period of two years.

5. Paragraph 57 of the Statutes is supplemented with a provision that party committees may be set up on state farms if there are fifty Communists present.

6. Taking into consideration the proposals of party organizations that the CPSU Statutes should provide for greater differentiation in the holding of meetings in the primary organizations, depending on the conditions of their work, structure and size, it is established that in primary party organizations that number up to 300 Communists and have shop organizations, a general party meeting is to be held at least once every two months.

7. It is stipulated in the Statutes that Congresses of the Communist

Parties of all the union republics are to be held at least once every four years.

8. It is provided in the Statutes that in the period between Party Congresses the Central Committee may as necessary convene an All-Union Party Conference to discuss urgent questions of party policy, and the Central Committees of the Communist Parties of the union republics may call republic party conferences.

The procedure for holding an All-Union Party Conference is determined by the CPSU Central Committee and for holding republic party conferences by the Central Committees of the Communist Parties of the union republics.

9. It is stipulated in the Statutes that the Central Committee of the Communist Party of the Soviet Union elects a Politburo to guide the work of the Party between plenary sessions of the Central Committee; and a Secretariat to guide current work, chiefly the selection of cadres and the organization of checkups on fulfilment. The Central Committee elects a General Secretary of the CPSU Central Committee.

The provision in paragraph 39 of the Statutes that the Central Committee creates a Bureau of the CPSU Central Committee for the Russian Republic is deleted.

10. The reference to economic councils in paragraph 59 of the Statutes is deleted.

Source: *XXIII S'ezd KPSS, stenograficheskey otchet,* Vol. II (Moscow, 1966), p. 318.
Translation: *CDSP,* Vol. XVIII, No. 15, p. 9.

41. Decree of the Twenty-Fourth Congress of the CPSU on Partial Changes in the Statute of the CPSU

9 *April* 1971

The Twenty-fourth Congress of the Communist Party of the Soviet Union resolves:

1. To establish that:

   (a) regular Congresses of the Communist Party of the Soviet Union are to be convened by the Central Committee at least once every five years;
   (b) regular congresses of the union-republic Communist Parties are to be convened by the Communist Party Central Committees at least once every five years;
   (c) regular territory, province, regional, city and district party conferences are to be convened by the respective party committees twice during the five-year period between CPSU Congresses, i.e., every two or three years;

(d) report-and-election meetings (conferences) in primary party organizations having party committees are to be held once every two or three
years, in accordance with the time periods of the convocation of
district and city party conferences. In other primary party organizations and in shop party organizations, report-and-election meetings
are to be held every year.

2. For the purpose of further increasing the responsibility and activeness of
the primary party organizations in the implementation of the Party's policy
and intensifying their organizational and educative work in the collectives
of working people:

(a) to extend the clause of the CPSU Statutes on the right of control over
the activity of administration to the primary party organizations of all
design organizations, design bureaux, research institutes, educational
establishments, cultural-enlightenment, medical and other institutions
and organizations the functions of whose administration do not extend
beyond their collectives.

With respect to the party organizations of ministries, state committees and other central and local Soviet and economic institutions
and departments, it is determined that they exercise control over the
work of the apparatus in fulfilling the directives of the Party and the
government and in the observance of Soviet laws;

(b) to establish that when necessary and with the permission of the
province or territory party committee or the union-republic Communist
Party Central Committee, primary party organizations can be created
within the framework of several enterprises that form a production
association and are located, as a rule, on the territory of one borough
of a single city;

(c) to permit province and territory party committees and union-republic
Communist Party Central Committees to form, in individual cases in
party organizations with more than 500 Communists, party committees
in large shops, and to grant the rights of primary party organizations to
the party organizations of production sectors.

3. To make partial changes in the text of the present Party Statutes in
accordance with this resolution.

Source: Pravda, 10 April 1971.
Translation: CDSP, Vol. XXIII, No. 17, p. 29.

Part III

Legality, the Courts and the Police

42. The Establishment of the People's Courts
22 November 1917, *OS*

43. The Revolutionary Tribunal and its Function
19 December 1917, *OS*

The decree on People's Courts was extremely important in that it abolished all existing laws which contradicted those of the new regime, and established a new court system. Lenin regarded any court system as a tool of the ruling class, and the destruction of the tsarist judicial organs was for him essential. The People's Court was initially established to deal with less important cases, while the so-called Revolutionary Tribunals handled serious criminal offences and crimes against the state. In fact the Tribunals quickly became closely associated with the Cheka, or secret police, and were granted the right to pass the death sentence by an instruction of 16 June 1918. They were reduced in number in 1921, and some of their functions transferred to the People's Courts, which were by then better organized. The latter substantially assumed their present-day form in 1922. The Revolutionary Tribunals were then transformed into military and military-transport courts.

42. The Decree of the People's Commissars on the Court
22 November 1917, *OS*

The Council of People's Commissars resolves:

1. To abolish all existing general legal institutions, such as *okrug* courts, courts of appeal, and the governing Senate with all its departments, military and naval courts of all grades, as well as commercial courts, and to replace all these institutions with courts established on the basis of democratic elections.

A special decree will be issued on further procedures and the continuation of unfinished cases.

Beginning from 25 October of this year, the passage of legal time limits is stopped until the issuance of a special decree.

2. To abolish the existing institution of justices of the peace, and to replace the justices of the peace elected up to the present by indirect vote, by local courts consisting of a permanent local judge and two assessors in turn, the latter being summoned to each session from judges' special lists. Local judges are henceforth to be elected on the basis of direct democratic vote, and, until the time of such elections, are to be chosen by *raion* and *volost*

soviets or, where there are none, by *uezd*, city, and *gubernia* soviets of workers', soldiers', and peasants' deputies.

The same soviets make up the lists of alternating assessors and determine the order of their attendance at the session.

The former justices of the peace are not deprived of the right to be elected as local judges, either temporarily by the soviets or finally by democratic election, if they express their consent thereto.

Local judges try all civil cases involving amounts not exceeding 3,000 roubles, and criminal cases if the accused is liable to a penalty of not more than two years' deprivation of freedom. The verdicts and rulings of the local courts are final and no appeal can be made against them. In cases in which the sentence involves recovery of over 100 roubles in money or deprivation of freedom for more than seven days a request for appeal is allowed. The court of appeal is the *uezd* session, and in the capitals the metropolitan session, of local judges.

For the trial of criminal cases at the fronts, local judges are elected by regimental soviets in the same manner, and where there are none, by regimental committees.

A special decree will be issued on procedure in other legal cases.

3. To abolish all existing institutions of judicial investigators, the procurator's office, and also the institutions of counsellor-at-law and private attorney.

Until the reformation of the entire system of legal procedure, the preliminary investigation in criminal cases is to be made by the local judges singly, but their orders on personal detention and commission to trial must be confirmed by a decision of the entire local court.

The functions of prosecutors and counsels for the defence, whose presence is allowed even at the stage of preliminary investigation, and, in civil cases, the functions of solicitors, may be performed by all citizens of moral integrity and of either sex who enjoy civil rights.

4. For the acceptance and hearing of cases, and proceedings of legal bodies, as well as of officials engaged in preliminary investigations or working in the procurator's office, and also of the counsels of barristers, the respective local soviets elect special commissars who take charge of the archives and the properties of those bodies.[1]

All low-grade and clerical personnel of institutions which have been abolished are ordered to stay at work and to perform, under the general direction of the commissar, all duties necessary to dispose of unfinished cases, and also to give information, on appointed days, to interested persons regarding the state of their cases.

5. Local judges try cases in the name of the Russian Republic, and are guided in their rulings and verdicts by the laws of the governments which have been overthrown only in so far as those laws have not been annulled by the

[1] The Russian wording of this paragraph is somewhat obscure. (Ed.)

revolution, and do not contradict the revolutionary conscience and revolutionary conception of what is right.

NOTE. All those laws which contradict decrees of the Central Executive Committee of the Soviets of Workers', Soldiers', and Peasants' Deputies and the Workers' and Peasants' Government, including the minimum programmes of the Russian Social-Democratic Labour Party and the party of Socialist-Revolutionaries, are annulled.

6. In all civil as well as criminal cases the parties may resort to the arbitration court. The organization of the arbitration court will be determined by a special decree.

7. The right of pardon and restoration of rights of persons convicted in criminal cases belongs henceforth to the legal authorities.

8. For the struggle against the counter-revolutionary forces through protecting the revolution and its achievements from them and also for deciding cases involving the struggle against profiteering, speculation, sabotage, and other misdeeds of merchants, manufacturers, officials, and other persons, workers' and peasants' revolutionary tribunals are established, consisting of a chairman and six assessors who serve in turn, and are elected by *gubernia* or city soviets of workers', soldiers', and peasants' deputies.

Special investigating commissions are formed under the above soviets for the conduct of the preliminary investigation in such cases.

All investigating commissions existing up to the present are abolished, and their cases and proceedings are transferred to the newly formed investigating commissions.

V. ULIANOV (LENIN), President of the Sovnarkom.

A. SHLIKHTER, L. TROTSKY, A. SHLIAPNIKOV, I. DZHU-GASHVILI (STALIN), N. AVILOV (GLEBOV), P. STUCHKA, Commissars.

Source: G. D. Obichkin, i drugie, *Dekrety sovetskoi vlasti*, Vol. I (Moscow, 1957), p. 124. *Translation*: *International Conciliation*, No. 136, March 1919, pp. 24–6, with the editor's modifications.

43. Instruction on the Revolutionary Tribunal

Instruction of I. Z. Shteinberg, People's Commissar of Justice, 19 December 1917, OS.

1. The Revolutionary Tribunal has jurisdiction in cases of persons (a) who organize uprisings against the authority of the Workers' and Peasants' Government, actively oppose the latter or do not obey it, or call upon other persons to oppose or disobey it; (b) who utilize their position in the state or public service to disturb or hamper the regular progress of work in the

institution or enterprise in which they are or have been serving (by sabotage, concealing or destroying documents or property, etc.); (c) who stop or reduce production of consumer goods without there being any actual necessity for so doing; (d) who violate the decrees, orders, binding ordinances and other published acts of the organs of the Workers' and Peasants' Government, if such acts stipulate a trial by the Revolutionary Tribunal for their violation; (e) who, taking advantage of their social or administrative position, misuse the authority given them by the revolutionary people; (f) crimes committed against the people by means of the press come under the jurisdiction of a specially instituted Revolutionary Tribunal of the press.

2. The Revolutionary Tribunal, for offences indicated in Article 1, imposes upon the guilty the following penalties: (1) a fine, (2) deprivation of freedom, (3) exile from the capitals, from particular localities, or from the territory of the Russian Republic, (4) public censure, (5) declaration of the offender to be a public enemy, (6) deprivation of all or some political rights, (7) sequestration or confiscation, partial or general, of property, (8) a sentence to perform compulsory public work.

The Revolutionary Tribunal, guided by the circumstances of the case and dictates of the revolutionary conscience, fixes the penalty.

3. (a) The Revolutionary Tribunal is elected by the soviets of workers', soldiers' and peasants' deputies, and consists of one permanent chairman, two permanent substitutes, one permanent secretary and two substitutes, and forty assessors. All persons, except the assessors, are elected for three months and may be recalled by the soviets before the expiration of that term.

(b) The assessors are selected for one month from a general list of assessors by the Executive Committees of the soviets of workers', soldiers' and peasants' deputies by drawing lots. The lists of assessors, to the number of six, with one or two extra as a reserve, are made up for each session of the tribunal.

(c) The session of each successive assessor of the Revolutionary Tribunal lasts not longer than one week.

(d) A stenographic record is kept of the entire proceedings of the Revolutionary Tribunal.

(e) The grounds for instituting proceedings are: reports of legal and administrative institutions and officials, public, trade, and party organizations, and private persons.

(f) For the conduct of the preliminary investigation in such cases an investigating commission is created under the Revolutionary Tribunal, consisting of six members elected by the soviets of workers', soldiers' and peasants' deputies.

(g) Upon receiving information or a complaint, the investigating commission makes an examination and, within forty-eight hours, either orders the dismissal of the case, if it does not find that a crime has been committed, or transfers it to the proper jurisdiction, or brings it up for trial at a session of the Revolutionary Tribunal.

(h) The orders of the investigating commission regarding arrests, searches, removal of papers, and releases of detained persons are valid if issued jointly by three members. In cases which do not permit of delay such orders may be issued by any member of the investigating commission singly, on the condition that within twelve hours the measure shall be approved by the investigating commission.

(i) The order of the investigating commission is carried out by the Red Guard, the militia, the troops, and the executive organs of the Republic.

(j) Complaints against the decisions of the investigating commission are submitted to the Revolutionary Tribunal through its president, and are considered at executive sessions of the Revolutionary Tribunal.

(k) The investigating commission has the right: (a) to demand of all departments and officials, as well as of all local self-governing bodies, legal institutions and authorities, public notaries, social and trade organizations, commercial and industrial enterprises, and governmental, public and private credit institutions, the submission of necessary documents and information, and of unfinished cases; (b) to examine, through its members or special representatives, the transactions of all institutions and officials enumerated above in order to secure necessary information.

4. The sessions of the Revolutionary Tribunal are public.

5. The verdicts of the Revolutionary Tribunal are reached by a majority of votes of the members of the Tribunal.

6. The legal investigation is made with the participation of the prosecution and the defence.

7. (a) Citizens of either sex who enjoy political rights are admitted at the will of the parties as prosecutors and counsels for the defence, with the right to participate in the case.

(b) A collegium of persons who devote themselves to the service of the law, both for public prosecution and public defence, is established under the Revolutionary Tribunal.

(c) The above-mentioned collegium is formed by the free registration of all persons who desire to render aid to revolutionary justice, and who present recommendations from the soviets of workers', soldiers' and peasants' deputies.

8. The Revolutionary Tribunal may invite a public prosecutor from the membership of the above-named collegium for each case.

9. If the accused does not for some reason use his right to invite a counsel for the defence, the Revolutionary Tribunal may, at his request, appoint a member of the collegium for his defence.

10. Besides the above-mentioned prosecutors and defence counsels, one prosecutor and one counsel for defence drawn from the public present at the

session may take part in the court's proceedings.

11. The verdicts of the Revolutionary Tribunal are final. In case of violation of the procedure established by these instructions, or the discovery of indications of obvious injustice in the verdict, the People's Commissary of Justice has the right to request the Central Executive Committee of the Soviets of Workers', Soldiers' and Peasants' Deputies to order a second and last trial of the case.

12. The maintenance of the Revolutionary Tribunal is charged to the State account. The amount of compensation and the daily fees are fixed by the soviets of workers', soldiers' and peasants' deputies. The assessors receive the difference between the daily fees and their daily earnings, if the latter are less than the daily fees; at the same time the assessors may not be deprived of their jobs during the session.

People's Commissar of Justice,
I. Z. SHTEINBERG.

Source: Sobranie uzakonenii i rasporyazhenii rabochego i krestyanskogo pravitelstva, 1917, No. 12, pp. 179–81.
Translation: International Conciliation, No. 136, March 1919, pp. 27–30, with the editor's modifications.

44. The Secret Police (Cheka) Appears

7 *December* 1917, *OS*

The Cheka (or, to give it its full name, the 'All-Russian Extraordinary Commission for Combating Counter-Revolution, Sabotage and Speculation') was the political police organization which was to develop into a central feature of the Bolshevik regime. The foundation document on which its existence depended was not, however, the decree one might expect, but merely a set of hasty protocol notes of the Council of People's Commissars. The Cheka was directly subordinate to this body, and its chairman, Feliks Dzerzhinsky, was also a member of the collegium of the People's Commissariat of Internal Affairs. The Cheka had its own local organs throughout Bolshevik Russia. They were used to conduct a ruthless drive against real and supposed opponents of the regime, and promote the 'Red Terror'. The Cheka quickly acquired its own powers of execution. It served as a basis for the establishment, in February 1922, of the infamous State Political Administration (GPU).

44. From the Protocol of the Council of People's Commissars, No. 21, on the Creation of the All-Russian Extraordinary Commission

7 *December* 1917, *OS*

... The Commissars heard

9. Dzerzhinski's report on the organization and composition of the commission for the struggle with sabotage ...

They decreed that ...

The commission should be named the All-Russian Extraordinary Commission attached to the Council of People's Commissars for the struggle with counter-revolution and sabotage, and its existence confirmed. (To be published.)

The composition of the commission (as yet incomplete): Ksenofontov, Zhedilev, Averin, Peterson, Peters, Evseev, Trifonov, V., Dzerzhinski, Sergo,[1] Vagilevski.[1]

The tasks of the commission: (1) to stop and liquidate all attempts at, and acts of counter-revolution and sabotage throughout Russia on the part of any person whatsoever; (2) to bring before the court of the revolutionary tribunal all saboteurs and counter-revolutionaries, and to work out measures for the struggle against them; (3) the commission conducts only the preliminary investigation, in so far as that is needed to stop such acts; (4) the

[1] *Soviet editor's note:* A question mark stands against these surnames.

commission is divided into the following departments: 1. information, 2. organization department (for the organization of the struggle with counter-revolution throughout Russia and branch departments), 3. the fighting department.

The commission will be formed finally tomorrow. At present the liquidation commission of the Military-Revolutionary Committee is functioning.

The commission is to turn its attention in the first instance to the press, sabotage, etc., of the right-wing SRs, saboteurs and strikers.

Measures to be taken—confiscation, eviction, deprivation of ration cards, publication of lists of enemies of the people, etc.

Source: G. A. Belov, i drugie, *Iz istorii vserossiiskoi chrezvychainoi kommissii, 1917–1921* (Moscow, 1958), p. 78. (Taken from the archives of the Institute of Marxism-Leninism attached to the CC CPSU.)

Editor's translation. This document appears in the source with numerous abbreviations, completed by the Soviet editors by means of square brackets, suggesting that it was never fully drawn up.

45. The First Soviet Criminal Code (extracts)

1 *June* 1922

This was in effect the first complete criminal code to be drafted after the Revolution: it was intended to unify criminal law (as the Bolsheviks understood it) and replace the unco-ordinated practices of the Cheka and the Revolutionary Tribunals. Yet it was in some ways a retrograde measure: in particular, crimes against the state were given special prominence. This section, and the articles most relevant to Soviet polity, have been selected for presentation here.

After the establishment of the USSR, the RSFSR Code was closely copied by the other union republics, federal principles being approved post factum *in* 1924. *A revised and harsher version of the* 1924 *Code was published in November* 1926, *and this, with numerous modifications, remained the basis of criminal law until the* 1958 *and later revisions.*

45. The Criminal Code of the RSFSR, 1922

Introduced on 1 *June* 1922 *by a decree of the All-Russian Central Executive Committee*

General Section

II. GENERAL PRINCIPLES GOVERNING THE APPLICATION OF PUNISHMENT

5. The Criminal Code of the Russian Socialist Federative Soviet Republic has as its object the legal protection of the Workers' State from crimes and from socially dangerous elements, and achieves this object by applying punishments or other means of social protection against violators of the revolutionary system of law.

6. A crime is any socially dangerous act or omission which threatens the foundations of the Soviet structure and that system of law which has been established by the Workers' and Peasants' Government for the period of transition to a Communist structure.

7. A person is dangerous if he commits acts which are injurious to the community, or if his actions present a serious menace to the established laws of the community.

8. Punishment and other measures of social protection are applied for the following purposes: (a) generally to prevent the commission of further offences, both by the particular offender and by other unstable elements of the community; (b) to adapt the offender to the conditions of social life by subjecting him to the influence of corrective labour; (c) to deprive the offender of the possibility of committing further offences.

9. Punishment is to be determined by the judicial bodies in accordance with their socialistic conception of law, and in conformity with the Articles and fundamental principles of the present Code.

10. In cases where the Criminal Code makes no direct reference to particular forms of crime, punishment or other measures of social protection are applied in accordance with those Articles of the Criminal Code which deal with crimes most closely approximating, in gravity and in kind, to the crimes actually committed, and in conformity with the regulations laid down in the General Section of the Present Code ...

IV. CLASSIFICATION AND FORMS OF PUNISHMENT AND OF OTHER MEASURES OF SOCIAL PROTECTION

32. The punishments which may be applied under the provisions of the Criminal Code are: (a) temporary or permanent banishment from the territories of the RSFSR; (b) imprisonment with or without strict isolation; (c) compulsory labour without custody; (d) conditional conviction; (e) confiscation of property in whole or in part; (f) fine; (g) forfeiture of rights; (h) dismissal from office; (i) public censure; (j) the imposition of an obligation to make good the harm done.

33. In cases examined by the revolutionary tribunals, until abolition by the All-Russian Central Executive Committee, whenever the supreme penalty is specified by articles of this Code, execution takes place by shooting ...

46. Among other measures of social protection which may, by sentence of the Court, be substituted for the punishment imposed, or may succeed it, are the following:

(a) Internment in an institution for the mentally or morally defective.
(b) Compulsory medical treatment.
(c) Prohibition from holding a particular office, or from engaging in a particular occupation or craft;
(d) Removal from a specified locality ...

Special Section

CHAPTER I. STATE CRIMES

(1) Of Counter-revolutionary Crimes

57. The term counter-revolutionary is applied to any act committed with the intention of overthrowing, undermining or weakening the authority of the Workers' and Peasants' Soviets, and of the Workers' and Peasants' Government founded on the constitution of the Russian Socialist Federative Soviet Republic, and also to any acts calculated to assist that portion of the international *bourgeoisie* which does not recognize the rights of the communistic system of ownership which is replacing capitalism, and which strives to

overthrow that system by means of intervention or blockade, espionage, press subsidies, etc.

An act is also to be counter-revolutionary which, though not directly aimed at attaining the above objects, nevertheless, to the knowledge of the person committing it, endangers the fundamental political or economic conquests of the proletarian revolution.

58. The organization, with counter-revolutionary intentions, of armed risings, or of the invasion of Soviet territory by armed detachments or bands; likewise participation in any attempt, made with such intentions, to seize power at the metropolis or in the provinces, or forcibly to detach from the Russian Socialist Federative Soviet Republic any portion of its territory, or to subvert any treaties concluded by it, is punishable with—

the supreme penalty and confiscation of all property. This punishment may, however, in extenuating circumstances, be reduced to imprisonment for not less than five years with strict isolation, and confiscation of all property.

Where the Court is satisfied that a participator was ignorant of the ultimate purpose of the crime described in the present Article, such participation is punishable with imprisonment for not less than three years.

59. Communication with foreign Governments or with their individual representatives with the object of inducing their armed interference in the affairs of the Republic or a declaration of war on it, or the organization of a military expedition; likewise the rendering of assistance, in any shape or form, to foreign Governments after war has been declared on them or after the despatch of an expedition, is punishable with—

the penalties prescribed in the first part of Article 58 of the Criminal Code.

60. Participation in an organization aiming at the commission of the crimes specified in Articles 57–59 of the Criminal Code, is punishable with—

the penalties prescribed in the first and second parts of Article 58.

61. Participation or co-operation in an organization aiming at assisting the international *bourgeoisie* as specified in Article 57 of the Criminal Code, is punishable with—

the same penalties.

62. Participation in an organization aiming at the objects specified in Article 57 of the Criminal Code, by inciting the populace to mass disturbances, non-payment of taxes, non-fulfilment of obligations, or by any other means, to the manifest detriment of the dictatorship of the working class and the proletarian revolution, even in cases where an armed rising or armed invasion was not the primary object of such organization, is punishable with—

the same penalties.

63. Participation in an organization which, for counter-revolutionary ends, operates against the normal working of Soviet institutions or enterprises, or which uses such institutions or enterprises for the same ends, is punishable with—

the same penalties.

64. The organization, with counter-revolutionary intent, of terroristic acts directed against representatives of the Soviet Government or against officials of the revolutionary Workers' and Peasants' organizations; likewise participation in the performance of such acts, even if the participator did not belong to a counter-revolutionary organization, is punishable with—

the penalties prescribed in the first part of Article 58.

65. The organization, with counter-revolutionary intent, of the destruction or injury—by explosion, by fire or by any other means—of railways or other routes and their equipment, the public postal, telegraphic and telephone services, aqueducts, public depots and other buildings or structures; likewise participation in the commission of the aforesaid crimes, is punishable with—

the penalties prescribed in the first and second parts of Article 58.

66. Participation in any form of espionage, involving the delivery or communication or abstraction or collection—with counter-revolutionary intent or for a reward—of information bearing the character of State secrets, and in particular of military information, to or for foreign Powers or counter-revolutionary organizations, is punishable with—

the penalties prescribed in the first part of Article 58.

The publication of such information, in the absence of counter-revolutionary or venal intentions and in ignorance of the possible consequences of such acts, is punishable with—

the penalties prescribed in the second part of Article 58.

67. Active participation in the struggle against the labouring class and the revolutionary movement by persons who were in responsible positions in the tsarist regime is punishable with—

the penalties prescribed in the first part of Article 58.

68. The concealment or aiding of any of the forms of crime described in Articles 57-67, in the absence of direct participation in the performance of such crimes or in ignorance of the ultimate purposes of such crimes, is punishable with—

imprisonment for a period of not less than one year.

69. Propaganda and agitation in the form of a call to overthrow the Soviet power by means of acts of violence or treachery, or by active or passive opposition to the Workers' and Peasants' Government, or by mass non-fulfilment of the obligations imposed on citizens in the matter of military service or taxation, is punishable with—

imprisonment for a period of not less than three years, with strict isolation.

The punishment for these crimes, if committed in time of war or popular disturbance, is the supreme penalty.
In cases where counter-revolutionary intent is not proven, summons to non-fulfilment of, or opposition to, orders of the central or local authorities is punishable with—

the penalties prescribed in Article 83 of the Criminal Code.

70. Propaganda and agitation intended to assist the international *bourgeoisie* specified in Article 57 is punishable with—

banishment from the territory of the Russian Socialist Federative Soviet Republic, or imprisonment for a period of not less than three years.

71. Unauthorized return to the territory of the Russian Socialist Federative Soviet Republic after the application of punishment under paragraph (a) of Article 32 is punishable with—

the supreme penalty.

72. The distribution of agitation literature of a counter-revolutionary character and the preparation or storage of such literature for the purposes of distribution is punishable with—

imprisonment for a period of not less than one year.

73. The invention and diffusion, with counter-revolutionary intent, of false rumours or unconfirmed news which may create a panic among the public or provoke lack of confidence in the authorities or discredit them, is punishable with—

imprisonment for a period of not less than six months.

In cases where counter-revolutionary intent is not proven, the penalty may be reduced to compulsory labour for a period of three months ...

(2) *Crimes against Public Administration*
84. The distribution of literary productions inciting to the commission of the criminal acts specified in Articles 75–81 of the Criminal Code, and the preparation or storage of such productions for the purpose of such distribution, is punishable with—

imprisonment for a period of not less than six months;

but in the aggravating circumstances described in the second part of Article 83 —

imprisonment for a period of not less than one year ...

87. The insulting expression of disrespect towards the Russian Socialist Federative Soviet Republic, in the form of reviling the emblem or flag of the State, or a memorial of the revolution, is punishable with —

imprisonment for a period not less than six months ...

Source: *Sobranie uzakonenii i rasporyazhenii rabochego i krestyanskogo pravitelstva*, 1922, No. 15, statya 153.
Translation: O. T. Rayner, *The Criminal Code of the RSFSR* (HMSO, London, 1925), Articles 33, 46, 63, 67 have been amended by the editor to correspond with the 1922 version.

46. The 'Unified State Political Administration' (OGPU) Established

25 November 1923

*The establishment of the OGPU (the 'Unified State Political Administration')
corresponded with the formation of the USSR. Unlike the GPU, which was
merely part of the NKVD, the OGPU was attached directly to the Sovnarkom
of the USSR. It co-operated closely with the Party's Central Control Commission, and played a major role in suppressing small traders and 'NEP-men'.
Stalin used it ruthlessly to back the collectivization and industrialization drives.
It gradually assumed immense administrative power, including control of the
militia, border guards, censorship, forced-labour camps, and the internal passport system.*

46. On Organizing the Unified State Political Administration of the USSR

*Decree of the Presidium of the Central Executive Committee, 25 November
1923*

1. In conformity with Article 61 of the constitution of the USSR, in order to
consolidate the revolutionary efforts of the republics in their struggle against
political and economic counter-revolution, espionage, and banditism, the
OGPU shall be created and attached to the Sovnarkom of the USSR.
2. The president of the OGPU and his deputy are appointed by the presidium of the TsIK of the USSR. The President and his deputy are members
of the Sovnarkom of the USSR with the right of a deliberate vote.
3. The president of the OGPU of the USSR is assisted by a collegium,
whose members are appointed with the consent of the Sovnarkom of the
USSR and have all rights of the members of the collegia of people's commissariats of the USSR.
4. The following fall within the jurisdiction of the OGPU:

(a) The direction of the activity of all state political administrations of the
    union republics and special departments of the military circuits sub-
    ordinate to them as well as of the activity of all organs of transportation
    of the state political administrations on the rail and waterways through-
    out the corresponding union republics.
(b) The immediate direction of, and supervision over, the special depart-
    ments of the frontiers and armies.
(c) The organization of the protection of the boundaries of the USSR.
(d) Immediate operative work on an all-union scale.

5. The OGPU and its local organs have the rights of active units of the Red Army in all matters relating to the use of rail, water and airways, as well as of the state means of communication (telephone, mail, telegraph, etc.); and also in matters relating to the equipment of these special departments, frontier branches, and of the personnel of the OGPU with supplies and clothing.

6. The agents of the OGPU and its local organs have a status similar to persons in active military service with regard to their rights and duties and in all other aspects.

7. The OGPU has its own separate budget, approved by the Sovnarkom and included in the budget of the USSR. In the budget of the OGPU there are included the budgets of the special branches engaged on the fronts and in the armies, as well as the budgets of the state political administrations of the union republics, including the budgets of all special branches in the military circuits and of the organs of transportation subordinate to them.

8. At the immediate disposal of the OGPU are special military units whose number shall be determined by the STO; they are subordinate in all respects to the president of the OGPU or his deputy.

9. The OGPU directs the activity of the local organs of the state political administrations through its plenipotentiaries accredited to the Sovnarkom of the union republics and acting in conformity with special statutes ratified in a legislative manner.

10. The OGPU, state political administrations of the union republics, special units, the frontier organs, as well as all organs of transportation act in conformity with the decisions of the VTsIK, dated 6 February 1922, 16 October 1922, and 22 March 1922, as well as of the central executive committees of the union republics, and in conformity with the decision of the presidium of the TsIK of the USSR on 2 November 1923.

11. The OGPU has its representative in the supreme court of the USSR, subject to the consent of the Presidium of the TsIK of the USSR as provided for in Article 45 of the Constitution of the USSR.

12. Supervision over the legality of the actions of the OGPU of the USSR lies within the jurisdiction of the prosecutor of the supreme court of the USSR in an order and within the limits determined by the statute of the supreme court of the USSR ratified at the third session of the TsIK of the USSR, and in special decisions of the presidium of the TsIK of the USSR.

Source: Sistematickeskoe sobranie deisvuyushchikh zakonov SSR, 1926, pp. 194–5.
Translation: W. R. Batsell, Soviet Rule in Russia (Macmillan, New York, 1929), p. 609. Some terms modernized by the editor.

47. Pre-Purge Legislation on the Labour Camps (extracts)

1 *August* 1933

The first labour correction code of the RSFSR was published in 1924. The more elaborate 1933 version placed a new emphasis on mass labour camps (or 'corrective colonies' as they were called) for all types of offenders: the old tsarist practice of giving favoured treatment to 'politicals' had by then been completely abandoned. The camps served as the institutional basis for the widespread arrests of the 'thirties and 'forties. The articles chosen here illustrate all forms of detention then at the disposal of the authorities.

The system remained virtually unchanged until the mid-'fifties, when, it is said, improvements were made in prisoners' living conditions, and there was an increase in supervision from outside. A new set of all-union Corrective Labour Principles, promulgated in July 1970, retained the basic characteristics of this document.

47. The Corrective Labour Code of the RSFSR

Approved by the decree of the All-Union Central Executive Committee and the Council of People's Commissars of the RSFSR, 1 August 1933

Part II: Deprivation of Freedom

CHAPTER I: PLACES OF DETENTION

28. Places of detention are

(a) Isolators for persons under investigation.
(b) Deportation prisons.
(c) Corrective colonies; factory colonies, agricultural colonies, mass labour colonies and penalty colonies.
(d) Institutions for applying measures of a medical nature to those deprived of freedom (institutes of psychiatric examination, colonies for tubercular and other patients).
(e) Institutions for minors (persons under age) deprived of freedom (factory schools of the industrial and agricultural types).

A. Isolators for Persons Under Investigation

29. Isolators for persons under investigation are intended only for those who are under investigation or on trial, and are organized as independent places of detention or as departments at other places of detention.

The above-mentioned persons are detained in isolators only until the sentence of the court or a resolution of some other competent organ comes into force.

The rules and regime of confinement and internal order in isolators are framed accordingly.

B. Deportation Prisons (Forwarding Prisons)

30. Deportation prisons are organized either as independent institutions or as departments at other places of detention.

31. Persons under investigation are placed in deportation prisons separately from convicts.

32. All deported prisoners (prisoners *en route* to their place of exile), if they are still under investigation, are subject to all the regulations of the system established for persons under investigation; persons who have been already sentenced are subject to all the regulations of the system established for the prisons in which such convicts were confined before they were moved.

C. Corrective Colonies

33. Factory colonies are organized for the purpose of inculcating labour habits in the prisoners and raising their labour qualification; in order to bring political, educational and disciplinary influences to bear on them; and to secure their adaptation to life and work in an organized collective based on industrial labour.

Agricultural colonies are organized for the same purpose on the basis of agricultural labour.

Prisoners of working-class origin are sent to the various colonies according to their labour habits.

The produce of agricultural colonies is used for the needs of the system of corrective institutions. Any surplus of goods is delivered to trading organizations.

34. Prisoners who belong to class-hostile elements, and also prisoners who are toilers but who are especially class-dangerous by the nature of the crime committed by them (necessitating the application of a more severe regime), are sent to mass labour colonies which are situated in district localities. Both the above-mentioned categories of prisoners and also toilers who have committed crimes which are not of an especially class-dangerous nature can be sent to other mass labour colonies; the regime to which this latter category of prisoners is subject is the same as that established for prisoners in agricultural colonies.

Penalty Corrective Colonies

35. Those prisoners who previously were confined in other colonies and who have shown systematic insubordination to the established regime or labour discipline, are sent to penalty corrective colonies.

36. Transfer to penalty colonies is effected as a disciplinary measure ex-

clusively by order of the Chief Department of Corrective Institutions for those republics, both on the initiative of these institutions and on the initiative of Inspection Commissions.

37. The regime in penalty colonies is framed on the basis of strict isolation of the prisoners within the limits established by the present Code.

Prisoners who are sent to penalty colonies for the purpose of household service in them are subject to the regime established for factory colonies.

D. Medical-Sanitary Institutions and Institutions for Medical Examination

38. The method of confinement of prisoners in institutions for medical examination by experts, in colonies for sick convicts, and in medical institutions at prisons and quarantines is determined by Instructions issued by the Chief Department of Corrective Institutions by agreement with corresponding departments of the Commissariat of Health of the RSFSR.

E. Institutions for Minors

39. For violators of law who are under age, there are organized schools of a special factory type. The task of these is to train juvenile delinquents as skilled workers for industry and agriculture, and give them, on the basis of communist education, the knowledge necessary for active participation in socialist construction.

40. Persons aged from fifteen to eighteen are sent to the schools mentioned in Article 39, on the basis

(a) of court sentences,
(b) of resolutions of special commissions on cases of minors and of other competent organs.

41. An Educational Council may annul the record of conviction in respect of those who have finished these schools. Such Councils are formed at each school.

42. If a minor's sentence expires before his school education is finished and there is no possibility of ensuring his further education, the Educational Council may fix an obligatory period of education, regardless of the term of sentence or resolution, provided, however, that the period of such education should not exceed three years.

43. Regulations with respect to the schools mentioned in Article 39 are issued by the Commissariat of Justice of the RSFSR in agreement with the Commissariat of Education of the RSFSR ...

Part III: Exile Combined with Corrective Labour

100. The serving of a sentence of exile combined with corrective labour is organized in a place of exile by departments of corrective institutions of the *krai*, *oblast*, autonomous republic or autonomous *oblast*.

101. Persons sentenced to exile with corrective labour work

(a) as hired workers in state, co-operative and social institutions and enterprises, on contracts entered into by these enterprises and institutions with corrective institutions;
(b) in industrial enterprises especially organized for this purpose by corrective institutions;
(c) on mass projects organized by contracts between corrective institutions and government and co-operative organs;
(d) in mass labour colonies.

102. Persons who are serving a term of exile with corrective labour cannot leave the boundaries of the locality intended for residence without the permission of corrective organs, but within the boundaries of this locality they are not limited in the choice of place where they and their families may reside.

Persons who are serving a sentence of exile with corrective labour in mass labour colonies are not subject to any restrictions such as are established for prisoners.

103. Persons who are serving a term of exile with corrective labour are placed on the same basis in respect of conditions and payment of labour as workers of corresponding qualification working on labour contracts, with a deduction of 15 to 5 per cent from their basic earnings in order to cover the organizational expenses of the corrective organs (depending on the time passed in exile) ...

107. Should the person who is serving a term of exile with corrective labour lose his working capacity, the Inspection Commission, on the basis of conclusions of medical experts, files a petition to the nearest People's Court to replace the remaining term of exile by other measures of social protection.

108. The following disciplinary measures are applied to those who are serving a term of exile with corrective labour and violate the established order and labour discipline:

(a) remark,
(b) reprimand,
(c) arrest for up to twenty days,
(d) transfer to a more distant place of exile.

109. In case of wilful avoidance of work the corrective institution raises with the People's Court at the place where the sentence is being served the question of replacing exile by confinement in prison.

Source: Sobranie zakonov RSFSR, 1933, No. 48, statya 208.

Translation: Hsinwoo Chao, The Labour Correction Code of the RSFSR (Sweet and Maxwell Ltd, London, 1936), extracts. Some terms modernized by the editor.

48. The Concept of Treason Extended

8 *June* 1934

49. The Decree Following S. Kirov's Murder

1 *December* 1934

These two decrees illustrate the marked worsening of the political atmosphere which took place in 1934. *The first of them reintroduced the old Russian concept of treason,* izmena rodine, *into the all-union Principles of Criminal Law, and extended it to cover flight abroad; the relatives of the person concerned now became subject to prosecution for his actions.*

The second was the so-called 'Kirov decree', issued immediately after the murder of S. Kirov, first secretary of the Leningrad party organization, and one of Stalin's possible rivals. The incident was used, with the help of this document, to initiate a massive purge of so-called 'terrorists'.

48. Supplement to the Statute on Crimes Against the State by Articles on Treason

Decree of the Central Executive Committee of the USSR, 8 *June* 1934

The Central Executive Committee of the USSR decrees:

The statute regarding crimes against the state (counter-revolutionary crimes and crimes against the administration which are particularly dangerous to the USSR) shall be supplemented by Articles 1 (1)–(4) composed as follows:[1]

1 (1). Treason to the fatherland, i.e., any act committed by a Soviet citizen to the prejudice of the military strength of the USSR, its independence as a state, or of the inviolability of its territory, e.g., espionage, the betrayal of any military or state secret, passing over to the enemy, or taking flight across the frontier by air or otherwise, is punishable by the supreme measure of criminal punishment—death by shooting and confiscation of the whole of the offender's property; or, where there are extenuating circumstances, by deprivation of liberty for ten years and confiscation of the whole of the offender's property.

(2). Any such crime, if committed by a person in military service, is punishable by the supreme measure of criminal punishment—death by shooting and confiscation of the whole of the offender's property.

[1] This corresponded to Article 57 of the 1922 RSFSR Criminal Code; *see* p. 240.

(3). If a person in military service takes flight across the frontier by air or otherwise, any member of his family who is of full age and who assists him in preparations for or in committing such treason, or who, having knowledge of it, fails to bring it to the knowledge of the authorities, is liable to deprivation of liberty for a period of from five to ten years and confiscation of the whole of his property.

Any other member of the traitor's family who is of full age and was living with or dependent on him at the time when the crime was committed is liable to deprivation of electoral rights and exile to a remote region of Siberia for five years.

(4). Failure by any person in military service to reveal information regarding any act of treason which is in preparation or has been committed, entails deprivation of liberty for ten years.

Failure by any other citizen (i.e., any person not in military service) to reveal such information shall be prosecuted in accordance with Article 12[1] of the present statute.

Source: Sobranie uzakonenii i rasporyazhenii raboche-krestyanskogo pravitelstva, 1934, No. 36, statya 283.

Translation: The Penal Code of the RSFSR (U.K. Foreign Office, London, 1934), Appendix III.

49. On the Amendment of the Criminal Procedural Codes of the Union Republics (*the 'Kirov Decree'*)

Decree of the Central Executive Committee of the USSR, 1 December 1934

The Central Executive Committee of the USSR decrees that the following amendments on the investigation and consideration of cases relating to terrorist organizations and terrorist acts against agents of the Soviet Government shall be introduced into the existing criminal codes of the union republics.

1. The investigation of such cases must be terminated during a period of not more than ten days.

2. The indictments should be presented to the accused twenty-four hours before the hearing of the case in court.

3. The cases must be heard without participation of a defence counsel.

4. Appeal against the sentences and also petitions for pardon are not to be admitted.

5. Sentence to the highest degree of punishment must be carried out immediately after the passing of the sentence.

President of the Central Executive Committee of the USSR,
M. KALININ.
Secretary of the Central Executive Committee of the USSR,
A. YENUKIDZE.

[1] I.e. deprivation of liberty with solitary confinement for at least six months.

Source: Sobranie zakonov i rasporyazhenii raboche-krestyanskogo pravitelstva *USSR*, No. 64, 1934, statya 459.

Translation: Slavonic and East European Review, Vol. XIII, No. 38, January 1935, p. 453. Some terms modified by the editor.

50. The People's Commissariat for Internal Affairs (NKVD) Upgraded

10 *July* 1934

The NKVD, established in November 1917, had existed since December 1922 on a union-republican basis. This decree raised it to all-union status, which meant that the local administrations were now directly subordinated to Moscow. The OGPU became a 'Main Administration' in this framework and G. Yagoda, the OGPU head, took over the whole Commissariat until he was replaced by N. I. Yezhov in September 1936. The infamous 'special board' whch wielded extra-legal powers of arrest and imprisonment was mentioned in Article 8 : it was to be disbanded only in September 1953.

The NKVD continued to grow throughout the 'thirties and absorbed many state economic functions. The old OGPU came back into existence as a People's Commissariat (Ministry) for State Security for a few months in 1941 and from 1943–1953. The present equivalent—the KGB (Committee for State Security)—was established on 13 March 1954.

50. On the Organization of the All-Union People's Commissariat of Internal Affairs

Decree of the Central Executive Committee of the USSR, 10 July 1934

The Central Executive Committee of the USSR decrees:

1. To establish the All-Union People's Commissariat for Internal Affairs and to include in it the United Main Political Administration (OGPU).
2. The People's Commissariat for Internal Affairs is to be charged with the following duties:

(a) Ensuring revolutionary order and security of the State.
(b) Safeguarding public (socialist) property.
(c) The registration of civil acts (registration of births, deaths, marriages and divorces).
(d) Guarding frontiers.

3. To form the following departments in the People's Commissariat for Internal Affairs:

(a) Department of Security of the State.
(b) Department of Workers' and Peasants' Police.
(c) Department of Security of frontiers and of order in the country.

(d) Department of Fire Defence.

(e) Department of Corrective and Labour Camps and Labour Settlements.

(f) Department of Civil Acts.

(g) Administrative and Economic Department.

4. To organize, in the union republics, republican People's Commissariats for Internal Affairs which are to function on the basis of the same Regulations as the All-Union People's Commissariat for Internal Affairs, and to establish in the Russian Soviet Federal Socialist Republic, instead of the republican People's Commissariat for Internal Affairs, the office of Plenipotentiary Representative of the People's Commissariat for Internal Affairs of the USSR. To organize in autonomous republics, provinces and regions, local departments of the People's Commissariat for Affairs of the allied republics.

5. To abolish the judicial commission of the OGPU.

6. The People's Commissariat for Internal Affairs and its local departments are to hand over the papers regarding criminal offences which are investigated by them, after the investigation has been completed, to the courts in accordance with their jurisdiction and with regard for the existing legal procedure.

7. Documents relating to cases investigated by the Department of Security of the State in the People's Commissariat for Affairs, are to be handed over to the Supreme Court of the USSR, and the papers relating to such crimes as treason, espionage and the like, are to be handed over to the Military Collegium of the Supreme Court of the USSR or to the Military Tribunals according to their jurisdiction.

8. To form a special board attached to the People's Commissariat for Internal Affairs of the USSR which, in accordance with its Statute, shall have power to issue orders regarding administrative deportation, exile, imprisonment in correctional and labour camps for a term not exceeding five years and deportation outside the confines of the USSR.

9. To instruct the People's Commissariat for Internal Affairs of the USSR to present the Statute of the All-Union People's Commissariat for Internal Affairs to the Council of People's Commissars of the USSR for confirmation.

> President of the Central Executive Committee of the USSR,
> M. KALININ.
> Secretary of the Central Executive Committee of the USSR,
> A. YENUKIDZE.

Source: *Sobranie zakonov i rasporyazhenii raboche-krestyanskogo pravitelstva,* 1934, No. 36, statya 283.

Translation: *The Slavonic and East European Review,* Vol. XIII, No. 38, January 1935, p. 436. Some terms slightly modified by the editor.

51. The First Post-Stalin Amnesty

27 *March* 1953

*Amnesty has a strong tradition in the Soviet Union, perhaps because imprison-
ment has been so common. The first post-Stalin amnesty was, however, particularly significant because it marked the virtual rejection by the new leadership of
a large proportion of the accusations made against Soviet citizens in the preceding decades. It was followed by a number of other amnesties, of which the most
important was that of 17 September 1955, freeing Soviet citizens who had
supposedly collaborated with the Germans during the Nazi occupation. Moscow
officials are said to have declared privately that by May 1957 the post-Stalin
amnesties had resulted in the freeing of 70 per cent of the country's prisoners.*

51. On the Amnesty

Edict of 27 March 1953

As a result of the strengthening of the Soviet social and state systems, the
rise in the well-being and cultural level of the population, the growth of
consciousness of the citizens, and their honest attitude towards the fulfilment
of their social duty, legality and socialist law and order have been consolidated,
while crime has been significantly reduced.

The Presidium of the Supreme Soviet of the USSR considers that in these
circumstances it is no longer necessary to detain further in places of confinement persons who have committed crimes which do not represent a great
danger to the State, and who have, by a conscientious attitude towards their
work, proved that they can return to an honest life of labour and become
useful members of society.

The Presidium of the Supreme Soviet of the USSR decrees that:

1. Persons who were sentenced to up to five years inclusive are to be released
from their places of detention and from other measures of punishment connected with deprivation of freedom.
2. Persons convicted of official or economic crimes, and also of military
crimes covered by Articles 139 (4 paragraph 'a'), 193 (7), 193 (8), 193 (10),
193 (10a), 193 (14), 193 (15), 193 (16), and 193 (17 paragraph 'A') of the
criminal code of the RSFSR and by the corresponding articles of the criminal
codes of other union republics, are to be released from places of detention,
regardless of their terms of imprisonment.
3. Women convicts who have children under 10 years of age, or who are
pregnant; juveniles up to 18 years of age; men over 55 years of age and
women over 50 years of age, and also convicts who suffer from severe

incurable illness, are to be released from places of detention regardless of their term of punishment.

4. The term of punishment of those convicted to deprivation of freedom for a period of more than five years is to be shortened by one-half.

5. The conduct of all investigations and cases of crimes committed before the publication of this law but not yet examined by courts is to cease if

- (a) they entail in law a punishment of deprivation of freedom up to five years, or other measures of punishment not connected with detention in places of confinement;
- (b) they are official, economic or military crimes, listed in Article 2 of this law;
- (c) they were committed by persons indicated in Article 3 of this law.

In other cases of crimes committed before the publication of this law, which in law entail deprivation of freedom for a term of over five years, the court may, if it considers it necessary to choose punishment in the form of deprivation of freedom for not more than five years, release the accused from his punishment; but if the court considers it necessary to choose a measure of punishment of deprivation of freedom of more than five years, it may reduce the term by half.

6. The convictions and loss of election rights of citizens who were formerly sentenced and have served their term, or who were freed beforehand on the basis of this law, is to be annulled.

7. This amnesty is not to apply to persons who were sentenced to a period of more than five years for counter-revolutionary crimes, massive theft of socialist property, banditry, or premeditated murder.

8. It is considered necessary to revise the criminal legislation of the USSR and union republics, with a view to replacing criminal responsibility for certain official, economic, social and other less dangerous crimes by measures of an administrative or disciplinary character, and also to lessen criminal responsibility for certain crimes.

The Ministry of Justice of the USSR is entrusted with working out, within a month, suitable proposals, and bringing them forward for examination by the Council of Ministers of the USSR, so that they may be presented to the Presidium of the Supreme Soviet of the USSR.

Source: V. I. Vasiliev, i drugie, *Sbornik Zakonov SSSR*, 1938–1967 (Moscow, 1968), Vol. 2, p. 627.
Editor's translation.

52. The Procuracy Revitalized

24 *May* 1955

One of the more significant judicial changes to follow Stalin's death was the re-organization of the procuracy, the centralized office charged with ensuring the strict observance of law by courts, organizations and citizens alike (see Articles 113–17 of the 1936 constitution). The 1955 statute replaced one which dated from the early 'thirties: the new document was much more detailed, and afforded the procurator's office more power, including the right to supervise the actions of the KGB, and administrative practices in places of confinement. This change corresponded with the post-Stalin demotion of the secret police, but it is doubtful whether it was of any long-term value.

52. Statute on the Supervisory Powers of the Procurator's Office in the USSR

Approved by a decree of the Presidium of the Supreme Soviet of the USSR of 24 May 1955

CHAPTER I: GENERAL PROVISIONS

ARTICLE 1. In accordance with Article 113 of the Constitution of the USSR, supreme supervisory power to ensure the strict observance of the law by all Ministries and institutions subordinated to them, as well as by officials and citizens of the USSR generally, is vested in the Procurator-General of the USSR.

ARTICLE 2. The purpose of supreme supervisory power over the strict observance of the law is to strengthen socialist legality in the USSR and safeguard from any encroachments:

(1) the social and state system of the USSR legislatively embodied in the constitution of the USSR and the constitutions of the union and autonomous republics, the socialist system of economy and socialist property;

(2) the political, labour, housing and other personal and property rights and law-protected interests of the Soviet citizens guaranteed by the constitution of the USSR and the constitutions of the union and autonomous republics;

(3) the rights and law-protected interests of state institutions, collective farms, co-operative and other public organizations.

The Procurator-General of the USSR and the procurators subordinated to him shall watch over the correct and uniform application of the laws of the USSR and of the union and autonomous republics, irrespective of all local differences and notwithstanding any local influences.

Article 3. The Procurator-General of the USSR and the procurators subordinated to him shall discharge the duties entrusted to them by:

(1) supervising the strict application of the law by all Ministries and departments and all institutions and enterprises under their jurisdiction, by executive and administrative organs of local soviets of working people's deputies, co-operative and other public organizations, and also supervising the strict observance of the law by all officials and citizens;

(2) instituting criminal proceedings against persons who committed offences;

(3) supervising the observance of legality in the actions of organs of inquiry and preliminary investigation;

(4) supervising the legality and validity of sentences, judgements and decisions of judicial bodies;

(5) supervising the legality of the execution of court sentences;

(6) supervising the observance of legality in the treatment of convicts in places of confinement.

Article 4. Exercising in the name of the state supervision over legality, the Procurator-General of the USSR and the procurators subordinated to him shall take timely measures to eliminate any violations of the law, irrespective of who has committed such violations.

Article 5. The organs of the Procurator's Office in the USSR constitute a single centralized system which is headed by the Procurator-General of the USSR and is based on the principle of subordination of the lower organs to the higher ones.

Article 6. According to Article 117 of the constitution of the USSR, the organs of the Procurator's Office perform their functions independently of any local bodies whatsoever, being subordinate solely to the Procurator-General of the USSR.

Article 7. The Procurator-General of the USSR is responsible and accountable to the Supreme Soviet of the USSR, and in the intervals between sessions of the Supreme Soviet of the USSR, to the Presidium of the Supreme Soviet of the USSR.

Article 8. On the basis of the laws in operation and in pursuance of them, the Procurator-General of the USSR issues orders and instructions which are binding on all organs of the Procurator's Office.

The orders and instructions of the Procurator-General of the USSR may be annulled by the Presidium of the Supreme Soviet of the USSR if they do not conform to the law.

Article 9. The Procurator-General of the USSR may make representations to the Presidium of the Supreme Soviet of the USSR on matters which are to be settled legislatively or require interpretation of the law in accordance with point C, Article 49, of the constitution of the USSR.

CHAPTER II: SUPERVISION OVER THE OBSERVANCE OF THE LAW
BY INSTITUTIONS, ORGANIZATIONS, OFFICIALS AND CITIZENS
OF THE USSR

ARTICLE 10. The Procurator-General of the USSR and the procurators subordinated to him supervise, within the limits of their authority:

(1) the strict conformity of all documents issued by ministries and departments, institutions and enterprises under their jurisdiction, and also by executive and administrative organs of local soviets of working people's deputies, co-operative and other public organizations—to the constitution and laws of the USSR, the constitutions and laws of the union and autonomous republics, decisions of the Council of Ministers of the USSR, and Councils of Ministers of the union and autonomous republics;

(2) the strict observance of the laws by officials and citizens of the USSR.

ARTICLE 11. The Procurator-General of the USSR, the procurators of the union and autonomous republics, territories, regions, autonomous regions, national areas, districts and towns, and also military and transport procurators have the right, within the limits of their authority:

(1) to demand and obtain orders, instructions, decisions, rules, regulations and other documents issued by Ministries and departments, institutions and enterprises under their jurisdiction, and also by executive and administrative organs of local soviets of working people's deputies, co-operative and other public organizations and officials—for the purpose of verifying the conformity of these documents to the law;

(2) to demand from the heads of ministries, departments, institutions, enterprises, executive and administrative organs of local soviets of working people's deputies, co-operative and other public organizations and officials that they present all the necessary documents and information;

(3) to check on the spot the observance of the laws in connection with statements, complaints, or other information concerning breaches of the law;

(4) in connection with available information concerning breaches of the law, to demand from the heads of ministries, departments, institutions, enterprises, executive and administrative organs of local soviets of working people's deputies, co-operative and other public organizations, and officials that they arrange a check-up and auditing of the activities of institutions, enterprises and organizations under their jurisdiction and also of officials subordinated to them;

(5) to demand from officials and citizens personal explanations concerning breaches of the law.

ARTICLE 12. The ministries, departments, institutions, enterprises, executive and administrative bodies of local soviets of working people's deputies, co-operative and other public organizations, and officials shall submit to a procurator, at his request, orders, instructions, decisions, rules, regulations and other documents, and also all the necessary information and explanations.

ARTICLE 13. The Procurator-General of the USSR and the procurators subordinated to him shall lodge protests against any orders, instructions, decisions, rules, regulations and other documents not conforming to the law either with the organ which issued the document, or with an organ of higher jurisdiction.

A procurator's protest shall be taken up within ten days. The procurator who made the protest shall be informed of the decision taken on the protest.

The lodging of a protest by a procurator against a decision of a duly authorized body to take administrative action against a certain person stays the application of the administrative penalty, pending the consideration of the protest by the body concerned.

ARTICLE 14. A procurator shall receive and examine statements and complaints of citizens concerning breaches of the law, shall check these statements and complaints within the time stipulated by law and adopt measures aimed at restoring the violated rights and protecting the lawful interests of the citizens.

ARTICLE 15. As regards officials or citizens who have violated the law, the procurator, depending on the nature of the violation, either institutes criminal proceedings against the guilty persons or takes measures to make them answerable in an administrative or disciplinary way.

In necessary cases the procurator takes measures to ensure the compensation of the material damage caused by the violation of the law.

ARTICLE 16. The Procurator-General of the USSR and the procurators subordinated to him have the right to make representations to corresponding state bodies and public organizations concerning the elimination of breaches of the law and the causes conducive to such breaches.

A state body or public organization shall within one month consider the representation of a procurator and take the necessary measures to eliminate the breaches of the law and the causes conducive to such breaches.

CHAPTER III: SUPERVISION OVER THE OBSERVANCE OF THE LAW
IN THE ACTIVITIES OF ORGANS OF INQUIRY AND PRELIMINARY
INVESTIGATION

ARTICLE 17. Exercising supervision over the strict observance of the law in the activities of organs of inquiry and preliminary investigation, the Procurator-General of the USSR and the procurators subordinated to him shall:

(1) institute criminal proceedings against persons who committed offences and adopt measures so that not a single crime should remain unsolved and not a single criminal should escape responsibility;

(2) closely watch that no citizen should be subjected to unlawful and ungrounded criminal prosecution, or to any other unlawful restriction of rights;

(3) to watch over the strict observance by organs of inquiry and preliminary investigation of the crime investigating procedure established by law.

ARTICLE 18. A procurator shall see to it that no person is arrested except by court order or with the sanction of a procurator.

In deciding the question of sanctioning an arrest, a procurator shall thoroughly examine all the evidence substantiating the necessity of arrest and, in case of need, personally interrogate the citizen whose arrest is being demanded.

ARTICLE 19. In supervising the investigation of criminal offences, a procurator has the right:

(1) to give the organs of inquiry and preliminary investigation instructions on the investigation of criminal offences, on the choice, change and cancellation of restrictive measures with regard to the accused and also on the search for criminals in hiding;

(2) to demand from organs of inquiry and preliminary investigation that they submit for verification purposes records of criminal cases, documents, materials and other information on offences committed;

(3) to take part in the preliminary investigation of, and inquiry into, criminal offences and, whenever necessary, personally to investigate certain cases;

(4) to return criminal cases to organs of inquiry and preliminary investigation with instructions to make an additional investigation;

(5) to annul unlawful and ungrounded decisions taken by organs of inquiry and preliminary investigation;

(6) to remove an investigator or any other person handling a case from further investigation or inquiry, if in the course of the investigation of the case they have violated the law;

(7) to withdraw any case from an inquiry organ and turn it over to an organ of preliminary investigation and also to transfer a case from one

preliminary investigation organ to another to ensure the fullest and most objective investigation;

(8) to instruct organs of inquiry to perform certain investigatory actions in cases handled by investigators of the organs of the Procurator's Office, particularly, in cases concerning detention, arrest of the accused, the making of a search, seizure of relevant materials and search for criminals in hiding;

(9) to nol-pros criminal cases on grounds provided for by the law.

ARTICLE 20. Instructions, given by a procurator in accordance with the procedural law to the organs of inquiry and preliminary investigation in connection with the investigation of criminal offences are binding upon these organs.

ARTICLE 21. A procurator shall consider, within the time stipulated by law, all complaints, addressed to him or otherwise received by him, concerning the actions of organs of inquiry and preliminary investigation, and inform the complainants of the decisions taken on their complaints.

CHAPTER IV: SUPERVISION OVER THE LEGALITY AND VALIDITY OF SENTENCES, JUDGEMENTS AND DECISIONS OF JUDICIAL BODIES

ARTICLE 22. The Procurator-General of the USSR and all procurators subordinated to him shall supervise the legality and validity of the sentences, judgements and decisions of judicial bodies.

ARTICLE 23. The Procurator-General and the procurators subordinated to him:

(1) participate in the preparatory sittings of the court;

(2) participate in court hearings of criminal and civil cases and submit conclusions on questions arising during trials;

(3) act as state prosecutor in court during the trial of criminal cases;

(4) institute law-suits in civil cases and civil actions in criminal cases and support them in court if it is necessary to protect the state or public interests or the rights and lawful interests of citizens;

(5) lodge, in accordance with the procedure established by law, protests against unlawful and ungrounded sentences, judgements and decisions of judicial bodies;

(6) submit conclusions on criminal and civil cases tried by a court of higher jurisdiction in connection with an appeal or protest;

(7) supervise the execution of court sentences.

ARTICLE 24. The Procurator-General of the USSR and all procurators subordinated to him have the right, within the limits of their authority, to demand from judicial bodies the record of any civil or criminal case for verification by way of supervision.

ARTICLE 25. The right to protest against court sentences, judgements and decisions which have come into force, belongs:

to the Procurator-General of the USSR and his Deputy—with regard to sentences, judgements and decisions of any court of the USSR, and of the union and autonomous republics;

to the procurator of a union republic and his deputies—with regard to sentences, judgements and decisions of the courts of a union republic and of the autonomous republics within a union republic, except decisions of the Presidium of the Supreme Court of a union republic;

to the procurator of an autonomous republic—with regard to sentences, judgements and decisions of the People's Courts of an autonomous republic and decisions of the collegiums of the Supreme Court of an autonomous republic acting as courts of second instance;

to the procurator of a territory, region or autonomous region—with regard to sentences, judgements and decisions of People's Courts, and also decisions of the judicial collegiums of the respective courts of territories, regions and autonomous regions, acting as courts of second instance;

to the Chief Military Procurator and the Chief Transport Procurator—with regard to sentences and decisions of any military tribunal or transport court respectively;

to the military procurator of a military district (fleet)—with regard to sentences and decisions of lower military tribunals.

ARTICLE 26. A protest against a sentence, judgement or decision of a court can be withdrawn by the procurator who has made the given protest, or by a superior procurator, prior to the consideration of the protest by the court.

ARTICLE 27. The Procurator-General of the USSR and his deputies have the right to stay the execution of a protested sentence, judgement and decision of any court of the USSR and of a union and autonomous republic pending a decision on the question by way of supervision.

The procurator of a union republic has the right to stay the execution of a protested sentence, judgement and decision of any court of a union republic and of autonomous republics which are part of it pending decision of the question by way of supervision.

ARTICLE 28. The participation of the Procurator-General of the USSR in plenary sessions of the Supreme Court of the USSR is obligatory.

ARTICLE 29. If the Procurator-General of the USSR finds that a decision adopted by the Plenary Session of the Supreme Court of the USSR does not conform to the law, he is in duty bound to make a representation on this matter to the Presidium of the Supreme Court of the USSR.

ARTICLE 30. The Procurator-General of the USSR has the right to submit for the consideration of the Plenary Session of the Supreme Court of the USSR representations concerning the issuance of guiding instructions to judicial bodies on matters of judicial practices.

ARTICLE 31. The procurators of the union and autonomous republics, territories, regions and autonomous regions participate in the hearing of criminal and civil cases by the Presidiums of the Supreme Courts of the union and autonomous republics, and courts of territories, regions and autonomous regions.

CHAPTER V: SUPERVISION OVER THE OBSERVANCE OF LEGALITY IN PLACES OF CONFINEMENT

ARTICLE 32. The Procurator-General of the USSR and the procurators subordinated to him, within the limits of their authority, shall exercise supervision to ensure that only persons placed under arrest with the sanction of a procurator or by court decision are kept in places of confinement, and that the rules established by law for the treatment of convicts are observed.

The organs of the Procurator's Office are responsible for the observance of socialist legality in the places of confinement.

ARTICLE 33. A procurator shall regularly visit the places of confinement, directly acquaint himself with the activities of their administration, stay the execution of any orders and instructions issued by the administration of a place of confinement if they run counter to the law, lodge protests against such orders and instructions in accordance with the established procedure, and institute criminal or disciplinary proceedings against persons guilty of violating legality in places of confinement.

ARTICLE 34. A procurator shall immediately release from custody any person unlawfully placed under arrest or unlawfully kept in custody in places of confinement.

ARTICLE 35. In supervising the observance of legality in the treatment of convicts in places of confinement, the Procurator-General and the procurators subordinated to him have the right, within the limits of their authority:

(1) to visit any place of confinement at any time, with free access to all of its premises, to check the observance of the rules of treating convicts in custody, established by law;

(2) to study the documents on the basis of which the given persons have been deprived of their liberty;

(3) personally to question the convicts;

(4) to check whether the orders and instructions of the administration of places of confinement regulating the conditions and system of treating the convicts conform to the law;

(5) to demand from representatives of the administration of places of confinement personal explanations concerning violations of legality in the treatment of convicts.

ARTICLE 36. The administration of a place of confinement shall forward to a procurator, not later than within twenty-four hours, any complaint or application addressed by a convict to a procurator.

On receiving the convict's complaint or application a procurator shall consider it within the time established by law, take corresponding measures and inform the complainant of his decision.

A procurator shall see to it that the complaints and applications of convicts should be forwarded without delay by the administration of the place of confinement to the organs or officials to whom they are addressed.

ARTICLE 37. The administration of a place of confinement shall fulfil a procurator's instructions concerning the observance of the rules for the treatment of convicts in custody, established by law.

CHAPTER VI: STRUCTURE OF THE ORGANS OF THE PROCURATOR'S OFFICE; PROCEDURE OF APPOINTMENT AND SERVICE OF OFFICIALS OF THE PROCURATOR'S OFFICE

ARTICLE 38. The Procurator's Office of the USSR is headed by the Procurator-General of the USSR.

In accordance with Article 114 of the constitution of the USSR, the Procurator-General of the USSR is appointed by the Supreme Soviet of the USSR for a term of seven years.

ARTICLE 39. The Procurator-General of the USSR directs the activities of the organs of the Procurator's Office and controls the work of the procurators subordinated to him.

ARTICLE 40. The Procurator-General of the USSR has deputies, appointed on his representation by the Presidium of the Supreme Soviet of the USSR.

ARTICLE 41. A number of administrations and departments and also the Chief Military Procurator's Office and the Chief Transport Procurator's Office are formed within the Procurator's Office of the USSR.

The administrations and departments of the Procurator's Office of the USSR are headed by senior assistants and assistants of the Procurator-General of the USSR.

The administrations and departments have on their staffs procurators of administrations and departments respectively.

The Chief Military Procurator's Office is headed by the Chief Military Procurator. The Chief Transport Procurator's Office is headed by the Chief Transport Procurator.

The Chief Military Procurator's Office and the Chief Transport Procurator's Office may form their own departments.

ARTICLE 42. The structure of the central apparatus of the Procurator's Office of the USSR is endorsed by the Presidium of the Supreme Soviet of the USSR.

ARTICLE 43. Procurator's offices are set up in the union republics, autonomous republics, territories, regions, autonomous regions, national areas, towns under republican, territorial and regional jurisdiction, and districts.

By decision of the Procurator-General of the USSR, one procurator's office may be set up for several administrative districts.

ARTICLE 44. Military procurator's offices of military districts, fleets, formations and garrisons are set up in the Soviet Army and Navy.

ARTICLE 45. Transport procurator's offices of districts, railways, waterways and sections are set up in the railway and waterway systems.

ARTICLE 46. The procurator's offices of the union republics are headed by the procurators of the union republics.

The procurators of the union republics are appointed by the Procurator-General of the USSR for a term of five years.

The procurators of the union republics have deputies, senior assistants and assistants.

The procurator's offices of the union republics set up departments which are headed by the senior assistants and assistants of the procurators of the union republics.

ARTICLE 47. The procurator's offices of the autonomous republics are headed by the procurators of the autonomous republics.

The procurators of the autonomous republics are appointed by the Procurator-General of the USSR for a term of five years.

The procurators of the autonomous republics have deputies, senior assistants and assistants.

The procurator's offices of the autonomous republics may set up departments headed by the senior assistants and assistants of the procurators of the autonomous republics.

ARTICLE 48. The procurator's offices of territories, regions and autonomous regions are headed by the procurators of territories, regions and autonomous regions.

The procurators of territories, regions and autonomous regions are appointed by the Procurator-General of the USSR for a term of five years.

The procurators of territories, regions and autonomous regions have deputies, senior assistants and assistants.

The procurator's offices of territories and regions may set up departments headed by the senior assistants and assistants of the procurators of territories, regions and autonomous regions.

ARTICLE 49. The procurator's offices of areas, districts and towns are headed by area, district and town procurators.

The area, district and town procurators are appointed by the procurators of the union republics, subject to the approval of the Procurator-General of the USSR, for a term of five years.

Area, district and town procurators have deputies and assistants.

ARTICLE 50. The Procurator-General of the USSR and the procurators of the union republics have on their staff investigators of specially important cases.

The procurator's offices of autonomous republics, territories, regions and autonomous regions have senior investigators.

The procurator's offices of areas, towns and districts have senior investigators and investigators.

ARTICLE 51. The structure and staffs of the organs of the Procurator's Office are established by the Procurator-General of the USSR within the limits of the approved number of personnel and wage fund.

ARTICLE 52. The posts of procurators and investigators are filled by persons having a higher legal education.

Persons having no higher legal education may in certain cases be appointed to the posts of procurators and investigators only with the authorization of the Procurator-General of the USSR.

Persons who graduated from higher law schools may be appointed to the posts of procurators and investigators only after having worked for a year as investigators of district (town) procurator's offices or assistants of district (town) procurators.

Service in the organs of the Procurator's Office cannot be combined with work in other institutions, except scientific and pedagogical work.

ARTICLE 53. The posts of procurators of territories, regions, autonomous regions, areas, towns and districts, and also the posts of military and transport procurators may be filled by persons who have reached the age of twenty-five.

ARTICLE 54. The procedure of appointing officials to the posts of procurators and investigators, and also of releasing them from these posts, except officials whose procedure of appointment is set forth in Articles 40, 46, 47, 48 and 49, is determined by the Procurator-General of the USSR.

ARTICLE 55. The procedure of disciplinary responsibility of procurators and investigators is determined by the Presidium of the Supreme Soviet of the USSR on the representation of the Procurator-General of the USSR.

ARTICLE 56. Officials of the organs of the Procurator's Office of the USSR are given ranks in conformity with their posts.

The rank of High State Councillor of Justice is conferred by the Presidium of the Supreme Soviet of the USSR.

The ranks of State Councillor of Justice of First, Second and Third Classes, are conferred by the Presidium of the Supreme Soviet of the USSR on the presentation of the Procurator-General of the USSR.

Other ranks are conferred by order of the Procurator-General of the USSR.

ARTICLE 57. Procurators and investigators having ranks shall wear their uniform and insignia when on duty.

Source: V. I. Vasiliev, i drugie, Sbornik Zakonov SSSR, 1938–1967 (Moscow, 1968), Vol. 2, p. 573.
Translation: S. Belsky and M. Saifulin, in A. Denisov and M. Kirichenko, Soviet State Law (Moscow, 1960), p. 444.

53. Khrushchev's All-Union Criminal Legislation

25 December 1958

This code was presented for approval by the Supreme Soviet in December 1958, along with the laws on criminal responsibility for state crimes and military crimes. It was a central element in Khrushchev's reform of Soviet law, and was followed by new codes at the union-republic level.

The all-union code has been described as an attempt to define more exactly the concept of a criminal act. It contained such 'liberal' elements as the exclusion of the old concepts of 'enemy of the people' and guilt by analogy, the stipulation that sentences could only be passed by judges, the raising of the age of responsibility, and the reduction of normal prison sentences from a maximum of twenty-five to ten years.

At the same time the code was a disappointment to many. It retained the totalitarian character of earlier legislation and afforded no specific presumption of innocence for the accused. A reform of Soviet criminal procedure which was launched at the same time was also very restricted.

53. Principles of Criminal Legislation of the USSR and the Union Republics

Approved by the law of the Supreme Soviet, 25 December 1958

I. General Provisions

ARTICLE 1. *Aims of Soviet Criminal Legislation.* The aim of the criminal legislation of the USSR and the union republics is to protect the Soviet social and state system, socialist property, the persons and rights of citizens and the entire socialist legal system from criminal encroachments.

In order to carry out this aim, the criminal legislation of the USSR and the union republics determines what socially dangerous acts are criminal and establishes measures of punishment to be applied to persons who have committed a crime.

ARTICLE 2. *Criminal Legislation of the USSR and the Union Republics.* The criminal legislation of the USSR and the union republics consists of the present Principles, which determine the bases and establish the general provisions of the criminal legislation of the USSR and the union republics; all-union laws determining responsibility for specific crimes; and the criminal codes of the union republics.

Responsibility for state and military crimes and, where necessary, for other crimes directed against the interests of the USSR, is determined by all-union criminal laws.

ARTICLE 3. *Basis of Criminal Responsibility.* Only persons who are guilty of a crime—that is, who have, deliberately or through negligence, committed a socially dangerous act specified by criminal law—may be held criminally liable and subject to punishment.

Criminal punishment may be applied only upon sentence of the court.

ARTICLE 4. *Operation of Criminal Laws of the USSR and the Union Republics With Respect to Acts Committed on the Territory of the USSR.* All persons who have committed a crime on the territory of the USSR are liable under the criminal laws in effect in the place where the crime was committed.

The question of the criminal responsibility of diplomatic representatives of foreign states and other citizens who under existing laws and international agreements are not subject in criminal cases to the jurisdiction of Soviet court institutions shall, in the event that such a person commits a crime on the territory of the USSR, be settled by diplomatic means.

ARTICLE 5. *Operation of Criminal Laws of the USSR and the Union Republics With Respect to Acts Committed Outside the USSR.* A citizen of the USSR who has committed a crime abroad is criminally liable under the criminal laws in effect in the union republic in which he is held criminally liable or brought to trial.

A person without citizenship living in the USSR who has committed a crime outside the USSR is liable on this same basis.

If such persons have been punished abroad for a crime, the court may accordingly reduce their sentences or completely release them from serving sentence.

Foreigners who have committed a crime outside the USSR are liable under Soviet criminal laws in cases stipulated in international agreements.

ARTICLE 6. *Operation of Criminal Law in Time.* A crime and punishability for an act are determined by the law operating at the time the crime was committed.

A law that eliminates punishability for an act or reduces punishment is retroactive, that is, it applies to acts committed before it was promulgated.

A law that establishes punishability for an act or increases punishment is not retroactive.

II. Crimes

ARTICLE 7. *Concept of a Crime.* A crime is recognized to be a socially dangerous act (of commission or omission) specified by criminal law which violates the Soviet social or state system, the socialist system of economy, socialist property or the person or political, labour, property or other rights of citizens, or any other socially dangerous act specified by criminal law which violates the socialist legal system.

An act of commission or omission which possesses the formal attributes of an act stipulated in criminal law but which is too insignificant to be socially dangerous is not a crime.

ARTICLE 8. *Deliberate Commission of a Crime.* A crime is considered committed deliberately if the person who committed it realized the socially dangerous nature of his act of commission or omission, foresaw its socially dangerous consequences and desired these consequences or consciously brought them about.

ARTICLE 9. *Commission of a Crime Through Negligence.* A crime is considered committed through negligence if the person who committed it foresaw the possible socially dangerous consequences of his act of commission or omission but thoughtlessly counted on averting them or failed to foresee the possibility of such consequences even though he should and could have foreseen them.

ARTICLE 10. *Responsibility of Minors.* Persons who have reached the age of sixteen at the time of committing a crime are criminally liable.

Persons who commit a crime between the ages of fourteen and sixteen are criminally liable only for murder, deliberate bodily injury causing impairment of health, rape, armed robbery, theft, malicious hooliganism, or deliberate destruction or damage with grave consequences of state or public property or the personal property of citizens, and also for deliberate acts that could result in a train wreck.

If the court finds that it is possible, without applying criminal penalty, to reform a person who under the age of eighteen committed a crime not representing great social danger, it may apply to this person coercive measures of an educational nature that are not criminal punishment.

The types of educational coercive measures and the procedure for applying them are established by the legislation of the union republics.

ARTICLE 11. *Irresponsibility.* A person who was in an irresponsible state while committing a socially dangerous act, that is, could not account for his actions or control them because of chronic mental illness, temporary derangement of mental activity, imbecility or other state of illness, is not criminally liable. Coercive measures of a medical nature, established by the legislation of the union republics, may be applied to such a person.

A person who was in a responsible state while committing a crime but who before the court passes sentence becomes mentally ill and is thus unable to account for or control his actions is also not subject to punishment. In the case of such a person the court may apply coercive measures of a medical nature, and after the person has been restored to health he may be subject to punishment.

ARTICLE 12. *Responsibility for a Crime Committed While Intoxicated.* A person who commits a crime while intoxicated is not released from criminal liability.

ARTICLE 13. *Necessary Defence.* An act which has the attributes of an act stipulated in criminal law but which was committed in the course of necessary defence, that is, while defending the interests of the Soviet state, public interests or the person or rights of the defender or of another person from a socially dangerous violation by causing injury to the violator, is not a crime if the limits of necessary defence were not exceeded.

A clear discrepancy between the defence and the nature and danger of the violation is considered to be exceeding the limits of necessary defence.

ARTICLE 14. *Extreme Necessity.* An act which has the attributes of an act stipulated in criminal law but which was committed in extreme necessity, that is, for the purpose of averting a danger threatening the interests of the Soviet state, public interests or the person or rights of the given individual or of other citizens, is not a crime if under the given circumstances this danger could not be averted by other means and if the harm done is less than the harm averted.

ARTICLE 15. *Liability for Preparing a Crime and for Attempting to Commit a Crime.* The procuring or adaptation of means or weapons or other deliberate creation of conditions for commiting a crime is considered to be preparation for a crime.

A deliberate act directly aimed at the commission of a crime is considered to be an attempt to commit a crime if the crime was not fully carried out for reasons not dependent on the will of the guilty person.

Punishment for preparing to commit a crime or for attempting to commit a crime is prescribed by the law stipulating responsibility for the given crime. In setting penalty, the court considers the nature and extent of the social danger of the acts committed by the guilty person, the extent to which the criminal intent was carried out and the reasons why the crime was not carried out.

ARTICLE 16. *Voluntary Refusal to Commit a Crime.* A person who has voluntarily refused to carry out a crime fully is criminally liable only if the act actually committed by him contains the elements of another crime.

ARTICLE 17. *Complicity.* Deliberate joint participation of two or more persons in the commission of a crime is considered complicity.

The organizers, instigators and accomplices, along with the executors, are considered accessories to a crime.

A person who directly commits a crime is considered the executor.

A person who organizes or directs the commission of a crime is considered the organizer.

A person who incites the commission of a crime is considered the instigator.

A person who aids in the commission of a crime by advice, instructions, the provision of means or the elimination of obstacles or a person who promises in advance to hide the criminal, weapon or means of commission of a crime, the traces of a crime or objects obtained by criminal means is considered an accomplice.

The extent and nature of the participation by each of the accessories to a crime should be taken into account by the court in setting penalty.

ARTICLE 18. *Concealment.* Concealment not promised in advance of a criminal or of weapons and means of commission of a crime, the traces of a crime or objects obtained by criminal means entails liability only in cases specially stipulated by criminal law.

ARTICLE 19. *Failure to Report.* Failure to report a crime reliably known to be under preparation or to have been committed entails criminal liability only in cases specially stipulated by criminal law.

III. Punishment

ARTICLE 20. *Purposes of Punishment.* A penalty is not only punishment for a crime committed. It also has the aim of reforming and re-educating those convicted in an honest attitude toward work and strict observance of laws and respect for the rules of socialist society, as well as averting the commission of new crimes both by convicted persons and by others.

Punishment does not pursue the aim of causing physical suffering or belittling human dignity.

ARTICLE 21. *Forms of Punishment.* The following basic forms of punishment may be applied to persons who have committed a crime:

(1) deprivation of freedom; (2) exile; (3) banishment; (4) corrective labour without deprivation of freedom; (5) deprivation of the right to occupy certain posts or to engage in a certain activity; (6) fine; (7) public censure.

Punishment in the form of service in a disciplinary battalion may also be applied to servicemen during their period of draft service.

In addition to the principal forms of punishment, the following additional penalties may be applied to convicted persons: confiscation of property; revocation of a military or special title.

Banishment, exile, deprivation of the right to hold certain posts or to engage in a certain activity, and fines may be imposed not only as basic but also as additional penalties.

The legislation of the union republics may establish other forms of punishment, in addition to the penalties specified in this article, in accordance with the bases and general provisions of these Principles.

ARTICLE 22. *Extraordinary Penalty — Capital Punishment.* Capital punishment, by shooting, may be applied as an extraordinary penalty, pending its abolition, in cases of high treason, espionage, sabotage, terrorist acts, banditry and premeditated murder under aggravated circumstances stipulated in articles of the criminal laws of the USSR and the union republics, and also, in wartime or under combat conditions, for other especially serious crimes in cases specially stipulated in the legislation of the USSR.

Persons who were under eighteen years of age at the time of commission of a crime and women who were pregnant during the commission of a crime or are pregnant at the time of sentencing may not be sentenced to death. Capital punishment may not be applied to women who are pregnant at the time the sentence is to be carried out.

ARTICLE 23. *Deprivation of Freedom.* Deprivation of freedom is established for periods of not more than ten years, or for not more than fifteen years in the case of especially grave crimes or for especially dangerous habitual offenders in cases stipulated in the legislation of the USSR and the union republics.

A person who had not reached the age of eighteen at the time of committing a crime may not be sentenced to more than ten years' deprivation of freedom.

Persons sentenced to deprivation of freedom serve their terms in a corrective-labour colony or a prison, and minors serve their terms in a labour colony for minors.

Persons who have committed grave crimes and especially dangerous habitual offenders may be sentenced by a court to deprivation of freedom in the form of imprisonment for the entire term of sentence or for part of the term.

In the case of persons who have served at least half their prison terms and have displayed exemplary conduct, a court may substitute detention in a colony for imprisonment.

In the case of persons who maliciously violate the regimen established in a corrective-labour colony, the serving of the sentence in the colony may be changed by decision of the court to imprisonment for not more than three years, with the remaining term of the sentence to be served out in the corrective-labour colony.

ARTICLE 24. *Exile and Banishment.* Exile consists of removing the convicted person from his place of residence with obligatory settlement in a definite locality.

Banishment consists of removing the convicted person from his place of residence and forbidding him to live in certain localities.

Exile and banishment, both as basic and as additional penalties, may be established for periods of not more than five years.

Exile and banishment may be applied as additional penalties only in cases specially stipulated in the law.

Exile and banishment may not be applied to persons who were under the age of eighteen at the time of commission of a crime. Exile may also not be applied to pregnant women or to women on whom children under the age of eighteen are dependent.

The procedure, places and conditions for serving out exile, as well as the procedure and conditions for banishment, are established by legislation of the USSR and the union republics.

ARTICLE 25. *Corrective Labour Without Deprivation of Freedom.* Corrective labour without deprivation of freedom may be set for a period of up to one year and is carried out either at the place of work of the convicted person or in other places in the area in which he lives. A deduction from the earnings of the person sentenced to corrective labour without deprivation of freedom, in an amount set by the court but not exceeding 20 per cent, is paid over to the state.

The procedure for carrying out corrective labour without deprivation of freedom is established by legislation of the union republics.

ARTICLE 26. *Deprivation of the Right to Hold Certain Posts or to Engage in a Certain Activity*. Deprivation of the right to hold certain posts or to engage in a certain activity may be set by a court for a period of up to five years, as a basic or an additional penalty.

This penalty may be applied in cases in which the court considers it impossible, because of the nature of the crimes committed by the guilty person in his official capacity or while engaged in a certain activity, to let the person retain the right to hold certain posts or to engage in a certain activity.

ARTICLE 27. *Fine*. A fine is a monetary sum exacted by the court in cases and within limits established by law.

The size of a fine is determined on the basis of the gravity of the crime, with consideration of the property status of the guilty person.

Deprivation of freedom may not be substituted for a fine or a fine for deprivation of freedom.

ARTICLE 28. *Public Censure*. Public censure consists of the open censure of the guilty person by a court; in the necessary cases, public censure may be brought to the attention of the public through the press or by other means.

ARTICLE 29. *Placing Servicemen Who Have Committed a Crime in a Disciplinary Battalion and Substituting Detention in a Guardhouse for Corrective Labour*. Conscripted servicemen who have committed a crime may be sentenced to serve in a disciplinary battalion for a period of from three months to two years in cases provided by law and also in cases in which the court, in view of the circumstances of the case and the personality of the individual convicted, finds it expedient, instead of deprivation of freedom for a period of up to two years, to hand down a sentence of service in a disciplinary battalion for the same period.

For servicemen, dentention in a guardhouse for a period of up to two months is substituted for corrective labour without deprivation of freedom.

ARTICLE 30. *Confiscation of Property*. Confiscation of property consists of the compulsory transfer to the state, without indemnity, of all or part of the convicted person's personal property.

Confiscation of property may be set by a court only for state and serious mercenary crimes in cases stipulated in the law.

The procedure for applying confiscation of property; a list of articles needed by the convicted person himself and by persons dependent on him for support, and not subject to confiscation; and the conditions and procedure for meeting the convicted person's obligations out of the confiscated property are established by legislation of the union republics.

ARTICLE 31. *Revocation of Military and Other Titles and of Orders, Medals and Honorary Titles*. On being convicted of a serious crime, a person who has a military or special title may have this title revoked by sentence of the court.

In convicting of a serious crime a person who holds an Order, medal or honorary title conferred by the Presidium of the USSR Supreme Soviet or the Presidium of a union- or autonomous-republic Supreme Soviet or a military or other title conferred by the Presidium of the USSR Supreme Soviet or the USSR Council of Ministers, the court, in handing down sentence, decides upon the advisability of submitting a recommendation to the agency that awarded the convicted person the Order or medal or conferred the title upon him to divest him of the Order or medal or the honorary, military or other title.

IV. On Passing Sentence and on Release from Sentence

ARTICLE 32. *General Bases of Sentencing.* A court passes sentence within the limits established by articles of the law providing for responsibility for commission of a crime and in strict accordance with the provisions of these Principles and the criminal code of the union republic. In passing sentence a court, guided by socialist legal consciousness, considers the nature and extent of the social danger of the crime, the personality of the guilty person and the circumstances of the case that mitigate or aggravate responsibility.

ARTICLE 33. *Circumstances Mitigating Responsibility.* In passing sentence, the following are considered circumstances mitigating responsibility:

(1) prevention by the guilty person of the harmful consequence of the crime, or voluntary compensation for the injury done, or elimination of the harm caused;

(2) commission of a crime as the result of difficult personal or family circumstances;

(3) commission of a crime under the influence of threat or coercion or because of material or other dependence;

(4) commission of a crime under the influence of strong emotional disturbance caused by unlawful actions of the injured party;

(5) commission of a crime in the course of defence against a socially dangerous violation, even though exceeding the limits of necessary defence;

(6) commission of a crime by a minor;

(7) commission of a crime by a pregnant woman;

(8) sincere repentance or voluntary surrender and admission of guilt.

The union-republic criminal codes may also stipulate other circumstances mitigating responsibility.

In passing sentence, a court may also take into account mitigating circumstances not stipulated in the law.

ARTICLE 34. *Circumstances Aggravating Responsibility*. In passing sentence, the following are considered circumstances aggravating responsibility:

(1) commission of a crime by a person who has previously committed a crime.

The court has the right, depending on the nature of the earlier crime, not to give it the significance of an aggravating circumstance.

(2) commission of a crime by an organized group;

(3) commission of a crime with mercenary or other base motives;

(4) serious consequences arising from the crime;

(5) commission of a crime against a child, an aged person or a helpless person;

(6) instigation of minors to commit a crime or enlistment of minors in participation in a crime;

(7) commission of a crime with particular cruelty toward the victim or mockery of him;

(8) commission of a crime by taking advantage of a public disaster;

(9) commission of a crime by a method that constitutes a general danger.

The union-republic criminal codes may stipulate circumstances aggravating the responsibility of a guilty person in addition to those specified in this article.

ARTICLE 35. *Passing Sentence for the Commission of Several Crimes*. If a person has been found guilty of committing two or more crimes stipulated in various articles of the criminal law and has not been convicted of any of them, the court, after setting a separate penalty for each crime, sets the final and total penalty by including the lighter penalty within the heavier penalty or by adding up the penalties in full or in part within the limits set by the articles of the law providing for more severe penalty.

Any of the additional penalties stipulated in articles of the law establishing responsibility for the crimes of which a person was found guilty may be added to the basic penalty.

The same rules apply in the setting of a penalty if it is established after a sentence has been handed down that the convicted person is guilty of still another crime committed before the passing of sentence in the first case. In such an event, the term of punishment includes the time served in full or in part under the first sentence.

ARTICLE 36. *Passing Sentence in the Case of Several Sentences*. If after the passing of a sentence, but before the sentence has been fully served, the convicted person commits another crime, the court adds the unserved term of the sentence for the first crime either in full or in part to the penalty set by the new sentence.

In adding the penalties under the procedure set forth by this article, the total sentence must not exceed the maximum term established by the law for the given form of punishment. In adding penalties in the form of deprivation of freedom, the total term of punishment must not exceed ten years, or fifteen years in the case of crimes which under the law are punishable by deprivation of freedom for periods of more than ten years.

ARTICLE 37. *Setting a Lighter Penalty than Provided by Law.* A court, considering the exceptional circumstances of a case and the personality of the guilty person and recognizing the necessity of setting a lighter sentence than the minimum provided by the law for the given crime or changing to another, less severe form of punishment, may so reduce the sentence; in doing so, it must stipulate its reasons.

ARTICLE 38. *Suspended Sentence.* If in setting a penalty in the form of deprivation of freedom or corrective labour the court, considering the circumstances of the case and the personality of the guilty person, is convinced that it is inadvisable for the guilty person to serve the sentence, it may order a suspended sentence; in doing so, the court must stipulate in the sentence its reasons for the suspension. In such cases the court orders that the sentence shall not be put into effect if the person does not commit another similar or no less serious crime within the probationary period set by the court.

If in the course of the probationary period the convicted person who has received a suspended sentence commits another similar or no less serious crime, the court sets a penalty for him under the rules stipulated in Article 36 of these Principles.

In suspending sentence, additional penalties, with the exception of a fine, may not be set.

The length of the probationary period and the procedure for supervising a convicted person with a suspended sentence and conducting educational work with him are established by the legislation of the union republics.

Considering the circumstances of a case, the personality of the guilty person and petitions from public organizations or a group of workers, employees or collective farmers at the guilty person's place of work regarding suspension of his sentence, a court may charge such organizations or groups with re-educating and reforming a convicted person who receives a suspended sentence.

ARTICLE 39. *Deferment of Execution of Sentence for a Serviceman or Reservist During Wartime.* During wartime, execution of a sentence of deprivation of freedom applied to a serviceman or a reservist subject to call or mobilization may be deferred by the court until the termination of military action; the guilty person will be assigned to active army duty. In such cases, the court may also defer the execution of additional penalties.

If the convicted person assigned to active army duty proves to be a staunch defender of the socialist homeland, the court may, upon the petition of the appropriate military command, release him from punishment or substitute another, more lenient penalty.

If a person whose sentence has been deferred commits another crime, the court adds to the new penalty the earlier penalty under the rules stipulated in Article 36 of these Principles.

ARTICLE 40. *Allowance for Pre-Trial Detention.* In sentences involving deprivation of freedom or assignment to a disciplinary battalion, the court subtracts one day for every day of pre-trial detention, and in sentences involving corrective labour, exile or banishment, it subtracts three days for every day of pre-trial detention.

ARTICLE 41. *Statutes of Limitations in Holding a Person Criminally Liable.* A person may not be held criminally liable if the following periods of time have elapsed since the day he committed the crime:

(1) three years from the day of the commission of a crime which by law is punishable by deprivation of freedom for a period of not more than two years or by a penalty not involving deprivation;

(2) five years from the day of the commission of a crime which by law is punishable by deprivation of freedom for a period of not more than five years;

(3) ten years from the day of the commission of a crime which by law is punishable by a more severe penalty than deprivation of freedom for a period of five years.

Briefer statutory limits may be established for specific crimes by the legislation of the union republics.

The statutory limit is interrupted if prior to the expiration of the period specified in the law a person commits another crime which by law is punishable by deprivation of freedom for a period of more than two years. The limit in such a case is calculated from the moment of commission of the second crime.

The statutory limit is suspended if the person who committed a crime hides from the investigation or the court. In such cases the statutory limit is resumed from the moment the person is arrested or gives himself up. A person may not be held criminally liable if fifteen years have elapsed since the commission of a crime and the statutory limit has not been interrupted by the commission of another crime.

The question of applying the statute of limitations to a person who has committed a crime which by law is punishable by death is decided by the court. If the court does not find it possible to apply the statute of limitations, the death penalty may not be set and a sentence involving deprivation of freedom is imposed instead.

ARTICLE 42. *Statutes of Limitations in the Execution of a Sentence.* A sentence is not to be carried out if it has not been carried out within the following periods from the day the sentence takes legal force:

(1) three years in the case of sentences involving deprivation of freedom for a period of not more than two years or of sentences not involving deprivation of freedom;

(2) five years in the case of sentences involving deprivation of freedom for a period of not more than five years;

(3) ten years in the case of sentences involving a heavier penalty than deprivation of freedom for a period of five years.

Briefer statutory limits may be established for specific crimes by the legislation of the union republics.

The statutory limit is interrupted if the convicted person evades serving a sentence or if prior to the expiration of the above periods he commits another crime for which the court imposes a penalty of deprivation of freedom for a period of not less than one year or of exile or banishment for a period of at least three years. The statutory limit in the case of the commission of another crime is calculated from the moment that crime is committed, and in the case of evasion of serving a sentence it is calculated from the moment the convicted person in hiding gives himself up to serve his sentence or from the moment he is arrested. A sentence may not be carried out if fifteen years have elapsed since it was passed and the statutory limit has not been interrupted by the commission of another crime.

The question of applying the statute of limitations to a person sentenced to death is decided by the court. If the court does not find it possible to apply the statute of limitations, the death penalty is replaced by a sentence of deprivation of freedom.

ARTICLE 43. *Release From Criminal Liability and Punishment.* A person who has committed a crime may be released from criminal liability if it is recognized that, as a result of a change in the circumstances, the act committed by the guilty person is no longer socially dangerous or that the person has ceased to be socially dangerous by the time of the investigation or trial of the case.

A person who has committed a crime may be released from punishment if it is recognized that, by virtue of his subsequent irreproachable conduct and honest attitude toward work, he cannot be considered socially dangerous by the time the case comes to trial.

ARTICLE 44. *Parole and Commutation of Sentence.* If a person sentenced to deprivation of freedom, corrective labour, exile or banishment or assigned to a disciplinary battalion has shown by his exemplary conduct and honest attitude toward work that he has reformed, the court may parole him or commute the unserved part of his sentence, provided he has actually served at least half of his term. The convicted person may also be released from additional penalties in the form of exile, banishment or deprivation of the right to hold certain posts or to engage in certain activities.

In the case of persons convicted for especially dangerous state crimes, or for other grave crimes in cases stipulated in the legislation of the union republics, parole or commutation of a sentence may be applied after a person has actually served at least two-thirds of his term.

If a person who has been paroled commits another similar or no less serious crime during the unserved part of his sentence, the court sets a penalty for him in accordance with the rules stipulated in Article 36 of these Principles.

Parole and commutation of the unserved part of a sentence are not applied to especially dangerous habitual offenders.

ARTICLE 45. *Release From Serving Out a Sentence and Commutation in the Case of Persons Who Committed a Crime Under the Age of Eighteen.* If a person sentenced to deprivation of freedom or to corrective labour for a crime committed under the age of eighteen has shown by his exemplary conduct and honest attitude toward work that he has reformed, the court may, after he has actually served at least one-third of his sentence, apply to him one of the following:

(1) parole, where release from serving out a sentence is applied when the convicted person has reached the age of eighteen, or
(2) release from serving out the remainder of a sentence, where such release is applied before the convicted person has reached the age of eighteen, or
(3) commutation of sentence.

ARTICLE 46. *Release From Serving Out a Sentence.* Release of a convicted person from serving out a sentence and commutation of sentence, except release from serving out a sentence or commutation of sentence by amnesty or pardon, may be applied by the court in cases and under a procedure stipulated in the law.

ARTICLE 47. *Cancellation of a Criminal Record.* The following are considered not to have a criminal record:

(1) persons who have served a sentence in a disciplinary battalion or who have been released before expiration of their sentence, and also servicemen who have served a sentence in the form of detention in a guardhouse instead of corrective labour;
(2) persons who have received suspended sentences, provided they do not commit another crime during the probationary period;
(3) persons who have received a sentence of public censure, fine, deprivation of the right to hold certain posts or to engage in a certain activity, or corrective labour, provided they do not commit another crime within a year from the last served day of the sentence;
(4) persons sentenced to deprivation of freedom for a period of not more than three years, or to exile or banishment, provided they do not commit another crime within three years from the last served day of the sentence (basic and additional);
(5) persons sentenced to deprivation of freedom for a period of more than three years but not more than six years, provided they do not commit

another crime within eight years from the last served day of the sentence (basic and additional);

(6) persons sentenced to deprivation of freedom for a period of more than six years but not more than ten years, provided they do not commit another crime within eight years from the last served day of the sentence (basic and additional);

(7) persons sentenced to deprivation of freedom for a period of more than ten years, provided they do not commit another crime within eight years from the last served day of the sentence (basic and additional) and provided the court establishes that the convicted person has reformed and there is no need to regard him as having a criminal record.

If a person sentenced to deprivation of freedom has shown by his exemplary conduct and honest attitude toward work after serving his sentence that he has reformed, the court may, upon the petition of public organizations, cancel his criminal record prior to the expiration of the periods stipulated in this article.

Source: V. I. Vasiliev, i drugie, *Sbornik Zakonov SSSR*, 1938–1967 (Moscow, 1968), Vol. 2, p. 428.
Translation: CDSP, Vol. XI, No. 4, p. 5.

54. All-Union Legislation on State Crimes
25 *December* 1958

55. RSFSR Supplement
16 *September* 1966

The continuing sensitivity of the Soviet leadership to anything smacking of opposition to the regime is perhaps most clearly reflected in the current legislation on state crimes.

This document replaced the all-union principles of October 1924 and a tangle of legislation which had been introduced in the 'thirties and 'forties. Its provisions were later incorporated in the union-republican criminal codes. Of particular note is the article on anti-Soviet agitation and propaganda, which has been used extensively for the suppression of oppositionist tendencies in the field of culture and religion. The relevant additions to the RSFSR criminal code of September 1966 (articles 190 (1), (2), (3)) are given immediately afterwards.

54. On Criminal Liability for State Crimes
Approved by the law of the Supreme Soviet, 25 December 1958

I. Especially Dangerous State Crimes

ARTICLE 1. *High Treason.* High treason, that is, an act committed deliberately by a citizen of the USSR to the detriment of the state independence, territorial inviolability or military might of the USSR: defection to the side of the enemy, espionage, handing over a state or military secret to a foreign state, fleeing abroad or refusal to return to the USSR from abroad, helping a foreign state to carry on hostile activity against the USSR, or conspiracy for the purpose of seizing power—

is punished by deprivation of freedom for a period of ten to fifteen years with confiscation of property or by death with confiscation of property.

ARTICLE 2. *Espionage.* The transmission of information constituting a state or military secret to a foreign state or foreign organization or its agents or the theft or gathering of such information for this purpose or the transmission or gathering on assignment from a foreign intelligence service of other information to be used to the detriment of the interests of the USSR, if the espionage is committed by a foreigner or a person without citizenship—

is punished by deprivation of freedom for a period of seven to fifteen years with confiscation of property or by death with confiscation of property.

ARTICLE 3. *Terrorist Acts.* Murder of a state or public figure or a government representative committed in connection with his state or public activity for the purpose of undermining or weakening Soviet rule —

is punished by deprivation of freedom for a period of ten to fifteen years with confiscation of property or by death with confiscation of property.

Severe bodily injury inflicted on a state or public figure or a government representative in connection with his state or public activity for this same purpose —

is punished by deprivation of freedom for a period of eight to fifteen years with confiscation of property.

ARTICLE 4. *Terrorist Acts Against a Representative of a Foreign State.* Murder of a representative of a foreign state for the purpose of provoking war or international complications —

is punished by deprivation of freedom for a period of ten to fifteen years with confiscation of property or by death with confiscation of property.

Severe bodily injury inflicted on such a person for this same purpose —

is punished by deprivation of freedom for a period of eight to fifteen years with confiscation of property.

ARTICLE 5. *Sabotage.* Destruction or damage by explosion, arson or other means of an enterprise, installation, ways or means of transportation, means of communication or other state or public property, or mass poisoning or spread of an epidemic or an epizootic for the purpose of weakening the Soviet state —

is punished by deprivation of freedom for a period of eight to fifteen years with confiscation of property or by death with confiscation of property.

ARTICLE 6. *Wrecking.* An act of commission or omission aimed at undermining industry, transport, agriculture, the monetary system, trade, or some other branch of the national economy, of the activity of a state agency or public organization for the purpose of weakening the Soviet state, if such act is committed by utilizing a state or public institution, enterprise or organization or by hindering its normal work —

is punished by deprivation of freedom for a period of eight to fifteen years with confiscation of property.

ARTICLE 7. *Anti-Soviet Agitation and Propaganda.* Agitation or propaganda carried out for the purpose of undermining or weakening Soviet rule or of committing especially dangerous state crimes, the dissemination for this same purpose of slanderous fabrications defaming the Soviet state and social system, or the dissemination, production or keeping of literature of such content for this same purpose —

is punished by deprivation of freedom for a period of six months to seven years or by exile for a period of two to five years.

These same acts committed by a person previously convicted for especially dangerous state crimes, or committed during wartime —

are punished by deprivation of freedom for a period of three to ten years.

ARTICLE 8. *War Propaganda.* War propaganda, regardless of the form in which it is conducted —

is punished by deprivation of freedom for a period of three to eight years.

ARTICLE 9. *Organizational Activity Directed at the Commission of Especially Dangerous State Crimes and Participation in an Anti-Soviet Organization.* Organizational activity directed at the preparation or commission of especially dangerous state crimes or at the establishment of an organization having the aim of committing such crimes, or participation in an anti-Soviet organization —

is punished in accordance with Articles 1 to 8 of this law.

ARTICLE 10. *Especially Dangerous State Crimes Committed Against Another Working People's State.* In view of the international solidarity of the working people, especially dangerous state crimes committed against another working people's state —

are punished in accordance with Articles 1 to 9 of this law.

OTHER STATE CRIMES

ARTICLE 11. *Violation of National and Racial Equality of Rights.* Propaganda or agitation for the purpose of arousing racial or national enmity or dissension and direct or indirect limitation of the rights of citizens or establishment of direct or indirect advantages for citizens on the basis of their race or nationality —

is punished by deprivation of freedom for a period of six months to three years or by exile for a period of two to five years.

ARTICLE 12. *Divulging a State Secret.* Divulging of information constituting a state secret by a person who was entrusted with this information or who gained it in his official capacity or work, and given the absence of indications of high treason or espionage —

is punished by deprivation of freedom for a period of two to five years.

This same act, if it has grave consequences —

is punished by deprivation of freedom for a period of five to eight years.

285

ARTICLE 13. *Loss of Documents Containing a State Secret.* Loss of documents containing a state secret, or of articles information about which constitutes a state secret, by a person entrusted with them, if the loss was the result of a violation of the established regulations for handling these documents or articles —

is punished by deprivation of freedom for a period of one to three years.

This same act, if it has grave consequences —

is punished by deprivation of freedom for a period of three to eight years.

ARTICLE 14. *Banditry.* The organization of armed bands for the purpose of attacking state or public institutions or enterprises or individual persons, or participation in such bands and in the attacks committed by them —

is punished by deprivation of freedom for a period of three to fifteen years with confiscation of property or by death with confiscation of property.

ARTICLE 15. *Contraband.* Contraband, that is, the unlawful transfer of goods or other valuables across the USSR state border with concealment of the objects in special repositories or with fraudulent use of customs or other documents, or in large quantities, or by a group of persons who have organized themselves for contraband activity or by an official who utilizes his official position, or contraband in explosives, narcotics, virulent or poisonous substances, weapons or military equipment —

is punished by deprivation of freedom for a period of three to ten years with confiscation of property.

ARTICLE 16. *Mass Disorders.* The organization of mass disorders accompanied by pogroms, destruction, arson or other such actions, or the direct commission of the above crimes by the participants in such disorders, or armed resistance to the regime by them —

is punished by deprivation of freedom for a period of two to fifteen years.

ARTICLE 17. *Evasion of Regular Call to Active Military Service.* Evasion of a regular call to active military service —

is punished by deprivation of freedom for a period of one to three years.

This same act committed by causing oneself bodily injury or feigning illness, by forging documents or by other deceit, or committed under other aggravating circumstances —

is punished by deprivation of freedom for a period of one to five years.

ARTICLE 18. *Evasion of a Mobilization Call.* Evasion of a call for mobilization in the ranks of the USSR Armed Forces —

is punished by deprivation of freedom for a period of three to ten years.

This same act, as well as evasion of subsequent calls for recruitment in the USSR Armed Forces, committed in war-time—

is punished by deprivation of freedom for a period of five to ten years or by death.

ARTICLE 19. *Evasion of Performance of Duties or Payment of Taxes in War-time.* Evasion of labour mobilization or performance of other duties or evasion of the payment of taxes in wartime—

is punished by deprivation of freedom for a period of one to five years or by corrective labour for a period of six months to one year.

ARTICLE 20. *Unlawful Departure Abroad and Unlawful Entry Into the USSR.* Departure abroad, entry into the USSR or the crossing of the border without the prescribed passport or the permission of the proper authorities—

is punished by deprivation of freedom for a period of one to three years.

This article does not apply to cases of a stay in the USSR by a foreign citizen or to cases of authorization to use the right of sanctuary granted by the USSR constitution.

ARTICLE 21. *Violation of the Rules of International Flights.* Flight into or out of the USSR without the prescribed authorization, failure to observe the routes, landing places, air gates or flight altitudes specified in the authorization, or other violation of the rules of international flights—

is punished by deprivation of freedom for a period of one to ten years or by a fine of up to 10,000 roubles, with or without confiscation of the aircraft.

ARTICLE 22. *Violation of the Regulations on Traffic Safety and the Use of Transport.* A violation by a worker in railroad, water or air transport of the regulations on traffic safety, or the use of transport resulting in an accident involving individuals, or a wreck or crash or having other grave consequences, or poor repair of a means or way of transportation or means of signalling or communication having the same consequences—

is punished by deprivation of freedom for a period of three to fifteen years.

These same acts, if they did not have these consequences but by intent created the danger of these consequences—

are punished by deprivation of freedom for a period of one to three years or by corrective labour for a period of up to one year.

ARTICLE 23. *Damage of the Ways or Means of Transportation.* Deliberate destruction or damage of a way of transportation, an installation on it, rolling stock, ship, or means of communication or signalling that results or might have resulted in a train wreck, ship disaster or disruption of the normal work of transport or communications —

is punished by deprivation of freedom for a period of three to fifteen years.

ARTICLE 24. *Making or Uttering Counterfeit Money or Securities.* The making for the purpose of uttering, or the uttering, of counterfeit state treasury notes, notes of the USSR State Bank, coins, state securities or foreign currency —

is punished by deprivation of freedom for a period of three to fifteen years with confiscation of property.

ARTICLE 25. *Violation of the Regulations on Currency Transactions.* Violations of the regulations on currency transactions and speculation in currencies or securities —

are punished by deprivation of freedom for a period of three to eight years with confiscation of the currencies or securities.

ARTICLE 26. *Failure to Report State Crimes.* Failure to report state crimes specified in Articles 1-6, 9, 14 and 24 of this law known to have been under preparation or to have been committed —

is punished by deprivation of freedom for a period of one to three years or by corrective labour for a period of six months to one year.

> K. VOROSHILOV, Chairman of the Presidium, USSR Supreme Soviet.
> M. GEORGADZE, Secretary of the Presidium.

The Kremlin, Moscow, 25 December 1958.

Source: V. I. Vasiliev, i drugie, *Sbornik Zakonov SSSR*, 1938-1967, Vol. 2 (Moscow, 1968), p. 450.
Translation: CDSP, Vol. XI, No. 4, p. 9.

55. Supplement to the Criminal Code of the RSFSR

Edict of the Presidium of the Supreme Soviet, RSFSR, 16 September 1966

The Presidium of the Supreme Soviet of the RSFSR decrees that

Chapter nine, entitled 'Crimes against Public Administration' of the Criminal Code of the RSFSR, be supplemented by articles 190(1), 190(2), 190(3), as follows:

ARTICLE 190(1). The dissemination of deliberate fabrications which defame the Soviet state and social system.

The systematic dissemination in oral form of deliberate fabrications which defame the Soviet state and social system, and similarly the preparation or dissemination in written, printed or any other form of works of like content —

is punished by deprivation of freedom for a term of up to three years, or corrective labour for a term of up to one year, or a fine of up to one hundred roubles.

ARTICLE 190(2). The vilification of the state emblem or flag.

The vilification of the state emblem or flag of the USSR, RSFSR, or any other union republic —

is punished by deprivation of freedom for a term of up to two years, or corrective labour for a term of up to one year, or a fine of up to fifty roubles.

ARTICLE 190(3). The organization of, or active participation in, group activities which violate public order.

The organization of, and similarly active participation in, group activities which seriously violate public order, or which are linked with an obvious refusal to obey the lawful demands of representatives of the authorities, or which cause a breakdown in the work of transport, state and social organizations or enterprises —

are punished by deprivation of freedom for a term of up to three years, or corrective labour for a term of up to one year, or a fine of up to one hundred roubles.

> A. KHAKHALOV, Deputy Chairman of the Presidium of the Supreme Soviet of the RSFSR.
> S. ORLOV, Secretary of the Presidium of the Supreme Soviet of the RSFSR.

Moscow, 16 September 1966

Sources: Vedomosti Verkhovnogo Soveta RSFSR 1966, No. 38, statya 1038.
Editor's translation.

56. All-Union Legislation on the Court System
25 *December* 1958

The Khrushchev law reform naturally involved a redrafting of the all-union law on the court system. No substantive changes were made in the structure which had crystallized in the 'twenties. A modification of the republican codes which followed did, however, cause a sharp reduction in the number of people's courts at the raion *level. This presumably meant a better status for the remaining institutions.*

56. Principles of Legislation on the Judicial System of the USSR and the Union and Autonomous Republics
Approved by the law of the Supreme Soviet, 25 *December* 1958

ARTICLE 1. *The Court System.* In accordance with Article 102 of the USSR constitution, justice is administered in the USSR by a USSR Supreme Court, union-republic Supreme Courts, autonomous-republic Supreme Courts, province, territory and city courts, courts of the autonomous provinces and national regions, district and urban people's courts and military tribunals.

ARTICLE 2. *The Aims of Justice.* It is the function of justice in the USSR to protect the following from all encroachments:

- (a) the public and state system of the USSR laid down in the USSR constitution and the union- and autonomous-republic constitutions, the socialist system of economy and socialist property;
- (b) the political, labour, housing and other personal and property rights and interests of USSR citizens guaranteed by the USSR Constitution and the union- and autonomous-republic Constitutions;
- (c) the rights and legally safeguarded interests of state institutions, enterprises, collective farms, and co-operative and other public organizations.

The task of justice in the USSR is to ensure the strict and undeviating observance of laws by all institutions, organizations, officials and citizens of the USSR.

ARTICLE 3. *Tasks of the Court.* By its entire activity the court educates citizens of the USSR in devotion to the homeland and to the cause of communism and in strict and undeviating observance of Soviet laws, in concern for socialist property, in observance of labour discipline, in an honest attitude toward state and public duty and in respect for the rights, honour and dignity of citizens and for the rules of socialist society.

In applying measures of criminal punishment, the court aims not only at punishing criminals but also at reforming and re-educating them.

ARTICLE 4. *Administration of Justice by the Hearing of Civil and Criminal Cases by the Court.* Justice is administered in the USSR through:

(a) the hearing and settlement in court sessions of civil cases involving disputes affecting the rights and interests of citizens, state enterprises, institutions, collective farms or co-operative or other public organizations.

(b) the hearing in court sessions of criminal cases and the application of measures of punishment established by law to persons guilty of having committed a crime or the acquittal of innocent persons.

ARTICLE 5. *Equality of Citizens Before the Law and the Courts.* Justice is administered in the USSR on the basis of the equality of citizens before the law and the courts, regardless of their social, property or official status, nationality, race or religion.

ARTICLE 6. *Administering Justice in Strict Conformity With the Law.* Justice is administered in the USSR in strict conformity with the legislation of the USSR and the legislation of the union and autonomous republics.

ARTICLE 7. *Formation of All Courts on the Elective Principle.* In accordance with Articles 105–109 of the USSR constitution, all courts in the USSR are formed on the elective principle.

ARTICLE 8. *Collegial Hearing of Cases in All Courts.* Cases are heard collegially in courts.

Cases are heard in all courts of original jurisdiction by a judge and two people's assessors.

Appeal and protest cases are heard by a court collegium of a higher court composed of three members of that court.

Cases involving protests against court judgments, sentences, decisions and orders that have entered into legal force are heard by a court collegium of the USSR Supreme Court or a union-republic Supreme Court composed of three members of the court.

The presidium of a court hears cases with a majority of the presidium members present.

The plenum of a court hears cases with at least two-thirds of its members present.

ARTICLE 9. *Independence of Judges and Their Subordination Only to the Law.* In administering justice, judges and people's assessors are independent and are subordinate only to the law.

ARTICLE 10. *Language in Which Court Proceedings Are Conducted.* In accordance with Article 110 of the USSR constitution, court proceedings in the USSR are conducted in the language of the union or autonomous republic or autonomous province or, in cases specified in the constitutions of the union and autonomous republics, in the language of the national region or of the majority of the population of the area; persons who do not know this language are guaranteed the opportunity of fully familiarizing themselves with the materials of a case through an interpreter and also the right to speak in court in their native language.

ARTICLE 11. *Public Trial in All Courts.* In accordance with Article 111 of the USSR Constitution, trial of cases in all courts of the USSR and the union republics is public, unless otherwise provided for by the law.

ARTICLE 12. *Guaranteeing the Accused the Right of Defence.* In accordance with Article 111 of the USSR constitution, the accused is guaranteed the right of defence.

ARTICLE 13. *Lawyers' Collegiums.* Lawyers' collegiums function for the purpose of undertaking court defence and for rendering other legal assistance to citizens, enterprises, institutions and organizations.

Lawyers' collegiums are voluntary associations of persons practising law, and they function on the basis of regulations approved by the union-republic Supreme Soviets.

ARTICLE 14. *Participation of the Prosecutor in Court.* The USSR Prosecutor General and the prosecutors subordinate to him, on the basis of and under the procedure established by the legislation of the USSR and the union republics, participate in administrative sessions and court sessions in the hearing of criminal and civil cases, support the state's prosecution in court, bring suits to court and support them, and exercise supervision over the legality of and grounds for sentences, judgments, decisions and orders handed down by court agencies and over the carrying out of court sentences.

ARTICLE 15. *Public Accusers and Defenders.* Under the procedure established by the legislation of the USSR and the union republics, public accusation and defence in court may be carried out by representatives of public organizations.

Victims of a crime may also support an accusation in cases stipulated in the legislation of the USSR and the union republics.

ARTICLE 16. *USSR and Union-Republic Courts.* USSR and union-republic courts function in the USSR.

ARTICLE 17. *USSR Courts.* The USSR courts consist of the USSR Supreme Court and military tribunals.

ARTICLE 18. *Union-Republic Courts.* The following are union-republic courts: the union-republic Supreme Courts, the autonomous-republic Supreme Courts, the province, territory and city courts, the courts of the autonomous provinces and national regions, and the district and urban people's courts.

ARTICLE 19. *Procedure for the Election of District and Urban People's Courts.* People's judges of the district and urban people's courts are elected for a period of five years by citizens of the district or city on the basis of universal, equal and direct suffrage by secret ballot.

People's assessors of district and urban people's courts are elected for a period of two years at general meetings of workers, employees and peasants at their place of work or residence and at meetings of servicemen in military units.

The procedure for elections of people's judges and people's assessors is established by the legislation of the union republics.

ARTICLE 20. *Procedure for the Election of Province, Territory and City Courts and Courts of Autonomous Provinces and National Regions.* Province, territory and city courts and courts of autonomous provinces and national regions are elected by the respective Soviets for a period of five years.

ARTICLE 21. *Composition of Province, Territory and City Courts and Courts of Autonomous Provinces and National Regions.* Province, territory and city courts and courts of autonomous provinces and national regions are composed of a chairman, vice-chairmen, members of the court and people's assessors, and they function through

(a) a court collegium for civil cases;
(b) a court collegium for criminal cases;
(c) a court presidium.

ARTICLE 22. *Procedure for Election and Powers of the Autonomous-Republic Supreme Courts.* The autonomous-republic Supreme Court is the highest judicial body of the autonomous republic.

The autonomous-republic Supreme Court is charged with supervision over the judicial activity of all court agencies of the autonomous republic under the procedure established by the legislation of the USSR and the union republic.

The autonomous-republic Supreme Court is elected by the autonomous-republic Supreme Soviet for a period of five years.

ARTICLE 23. *Composition of the Autonomous-Republic Supreme Courts.* The autonomous-republic Supreme Courts are composed of a chairman, vice-chairmen, members of the Supreme Court and people's assessors, and they function through:

(a) a court collegium for civil cases;
(b) a court collegium for criminal cases;
(c) a presidium of the Supreme Court.

ARTICLE 24. *Procedure for Election and Powers of the Union-Republic Supreme Courts.* The union-republic Supreme Court is the highest judicial body of the union republic.

The union-republic Supreme Court is charged with supervision over the judicial activity of all court agencies of the union republic under the procedure established by the legislation of the USSR and the union republic.

The union-republic Supreme Court is elected by the union-republic Supreme Soviet for a period of five years.

ARTICLE 25. *Composition of the Union-Republic Supreme Courts.* The union-republic Supreme Courts are composed of a chairman, vice-chairmen, members of the Supreme Court and people's assessors, and they function through:

(a) a court collegium for civil cases;
(b) a court collegium for criminal cases;
(c) a plenum of the Supreme Court.

Presidiums may be formed in the union-republic Supreme Courts in accordance with the legislation of the union republics.

The competence of the presidiums and plenums of the union-republic Supreme Courts is established by the legislation of the union republics.

ARTICLE 26. *Procedure for Election and Powers of the USSR Supreme Court.* The USSR Supreme Court is the highest judicial body of the USSR.

The USSR Supreme Court is charged with supervision over the judicial activity of the court agencies of the USSR and the union republics within the limits established by the Statute on the USSR Supreme Court.

The USSR Supreme Court is elected by the USSR Supreme Soviet for a period of five years.

ARTICLE 27. *Composition of the USSR Supreme Court.* The USSR Supreme Court is composed of a chairman, vice-chairmen, members of the USSR Supreme Court and people's assessors, elected by the USSR Supreme Soviet, and the chairmen of the union-republic Supreme Courts, who are *ex officio* members of the USSR Supreme Court.

The USSR Supreme Court functions through:

(a) a court collegium for civil cases;
(b) a court collegium for criminal cases;
(c) a military collegium;
(d) a plenum of the USSR Supreme Court.

ARTICLE 28. *Military Tribunals.* The structure and competence and the procedure for the election of military tribunals are determined by the Statute on Military Tribunals.

ARTICLE 29. *Requirements for Candidates for Judge and People's Assessor.* Any citizen of the USSR who has the right to vote and who has reached the age of twenty-five by the day of elections may be elected a judge or people's assessor.

ARTICLE 30. *Equal Rights of People's Assessors and Judges in Administering Justice.* During the performance of their duties in court, people's assessors enjoy all the rights of judges.

ARTICLE 31. *Period in Which People's Assessors Are Called Up to Serve in Court.* People's assessors are called up to serve in court by turn for a period of not more than two weeks a year, except in instances in which an extension of this period is dictated by the need to complete examination of a court case begun with their participation.

ARTICLE 32. *Continuation of Pay for People's Assessors During Their Service in Court.* The pay of people's assessors who are workers or employees continues during the period they serve in court.

People's assessors who are not workers or employees are compensated for expenses incurred while performing their duties in court. The procedure for and amount of compensation are established by the legislation of the union republics.

ARTICLE 33. *Reports of People's Judges to the Voters.* People's judges report regularly to the voters on their work and the work of the people's court.

ARTICLE 34. *Accountability of Courts to the Agencies That Elected Them.* Province, territory and city courts and courts of autonomous provinces and national regions account to their respective Soviet.

Union- and autonomous-republic Supreme Courts account to their respective union- or autonomous-republic Supreme Soviet or, in the period between sessions, to the Presidium of the union- or autonomous-republic Supreme Soviet.

The USSR Supreme Court accounts to the USSR Supreme Soviet or, in the period between sessions, to the Presidium of the USSR Supreme Soviet.

ARTICLE 35. *Recall of Judges and People's Assessors Before the Expiration of Their Terms of Office.* Judges and people's assessors may not be deprived of their powers before expiration of their terms of office except on recall by the voters or by the agency that elected them, or because they have been sentenced by a court.

The procedure for recall of judges and people's assessors of USSR and union-republic courts is determined in accordance with the legislation of the USSR and the union republics.

ARTICLE 36. *Procedure for Holding Judges and People's Assessors Criminally Liable.* Judges may not be held criminally liable, removed from their posts in connection with this, or arrested except:

(a) with the consent of the Presidium of the union-republic Supreme Soviet in the case of people's judges and chairmen, vice-chairmen and members of province, territory and city courts, courts of autonomous provinces and national regions, and autonomous-republic Supreme Courts;

(b) with the consent of the union-republic Supreme Soviet or, in the period between sessions, of the Presidium of the union-republic Supreme Soviet in the case of chairmen, vice-chairmen and members of union-republic Supreme Courts, and also of people's assessors of these courts;

(c) with the consent of the USSR Supreme Soviet or, in the period between sessions, the Presidium of the USSR Supreme Soviet in the case of the chairman, vice-chairmen and members of the USSR

Supreme Court, and also of people's assessors of the USSR Supreme Court;

(d) with the consent of the Presidium of the USSR Supreme Soviet in the case of chairmen, vice-chairmen and members of military tribunals.

ARTICLE 37. *Disciplinary Responsibility of Judges.* Judges bear disciplinary responsibility under the procedure established by the legislation of the USSR for judges of USSR courts and by the legislation of the union republics of union-republic courts.

ARTICLE 38. *Execution of Court Judgments, Decisions and Orders.* Execution of judgments, decisions and orders in civil cases and execution of sentences, decisions and orders in criminal cases with respect to property judgments are carried out by court bailiffs attached to the courts.

Demands presented by court bailiffs in execution of court sentences, judgments, decisions and orders are binding on all officials and citizens.

ARTICLE 39. *Promulgation by the Union Republics of Laws on the Judicial System of the Union Republics.* On the basis of paragraph 'u' ['kh'] of Article 14 of the USSR constitution and in accordance with these Principles, the union-republic Supreme Soviets promulgate laws on the judicial system of the union republics.

Source: V. I. Vasiliev, i drugie, *Sbornik Zakonov SSSR*, 1938–1967 (Moscow, 1968), Vol. 2, p. 450.
Translation: CDSP, Vol. XI, No. 5, p. 8.

57. The Law on the People's Public Order Detachments

2 March 1959

Khrushchev's establishment of people's volunteer detachments, narodnye druzhiny, *in March* 1959 *was interpreted by some outside observers as an attempt to combat a crime wave : it was presented to the Soviet public as the implementation of official theories about popularizing state functions. Such groups had in fact been in existence in the 'thirties, when Komsomol members were expected to provide practical assistance for the militia.*

The new volunteer detachments, which soon absorbed over two million members, were evidently controlled by the local party authorities, and sometimes used for political purposes. To judge from press reports they declined in importance in the mid-'sixties, but were revived at the end of the decade. They were often associated with the drive against parasitism, and the so-called comrades' courts : see documents 58 *and* 60.

57. On the Participation of the Working People in the Preservation of Public Order in the Country

Decree of the Central Committee of the CPSU and the Council of Ministers of the USSR, 2 *March* 1959

The Soviet people have won great victories in all spheres of economic and cultural work. The working people's standard of living is steadily rising year by year. [Unemployment and poverty have long since been abolished in the USSR.] Thanks to the enormous work done by the Party, the government and public organizations in the communist indoctrination of the people, crime has declined sharply in our country and socialist legality has been strengthened. The overwhelming majority of Soviet citizens are working selflessly in various sectors of socialist construction; they have an honest approach to their public duty, sacredly observe Soviet laws, and respect the rules of socialist society.

At the same time, however, there are still individuals in our Soviet society who do not observe the norms of public behaviour, who appear in public places in an intoxicated state and who commit acts of hooliganism and other misdemeanours.

The Party Central Committee and the USSR Council of Ministers have noted that [there are major shortcomings in the struggle with violations of the public order.] One serious omission lies in the fact that the enormous force of public influence on violators of order is not being used to the proper extent.

Unseemly acts committed by individuals are rarely discussed at meetings of workers, collective farmers, employees, pupils and students and are not brought before the collective to be judged. [The militia, the prosecutor's office and the courts do not carry on enough prophylactic work to prevent crime, they are not sufficiently well linked with the public organizations, they do not devote the necessary attention to seeking out the causes and conditions which lead to crime, and do not bring them to the attention of the corresponding public and economic organizations. The administrative organs have not brought about the solution of all crimes or certainty of punishment for crimes committed. The hearing of criminal cases rarely takes place in public court sessions at enterprises, building sites, and in collective farms, and this reduces the court's educational significance. Public accusers are not brought in for court hearings. Materials on court hearings are seldom published in the local press.]

At present, given the growing awareness and political activity of the working people and the further development of Soviet democracy, the struggle against immoral and anti-social acts should be waged not only by administrative agencies, but principally by the extensive enlistment of the working people and public organizations in the cause of safeguarding public order in the country.

The experience of the young people's brigades for assisting the militia, the Young Communist League detachment headquarters, the voluntary detachments and the other forms of active participation by the working people in maintaining public order deserve encouragement.

Having generalized this favourable experience, the Party Central Committee and the USSR Council of Ministers decree that

1. In order to enlist the working people on a broad scale in safeguarding public order, the numerous proposals of the working people that voluntary people's detachments for safeguarding public order be established at enterprises and construction projects, in transport, in institutions, at state and collective farms, and in educational institutions and apartment house administrations be adopted.

The voluntary people's detachment for safeguarding public order shall be directed by district (city) headquarters consisting of representatives of Party and Soviet agencies, trade union and YCL organizations, and individual detachment commanders.

The volunteer detachments and district (city) headquarters must, as a rule, be headed by leading officials of the party organs.

The complements of these detachments shall be recruited on a strictly voluntary basis from among leading workers, employees, collective farmers, students, pupils and pensioners.

The voluntary people's detachments and the district (city) headquarters for the preservation of public order act in compliance with the statute approved for them, and work in contact with the administrative organs.

The draft of the temporary statute of volunteer people's detachments for the preservation of public order is to be approved, and the Central Committees of the Communist Parties and the Councils of Ministers of the union republics are charged with confirming it, with due regard for local conditions.

2. Bearing in mind the great public and state significance of attracting working people to the cause of preserving public order, the CC of the Communist Parties of the union republics, and the territorial, provincial, city and district party committees are obliged to organize people's volunteer detachments, and district (city) headquarters, and ensure that they work successfully in maintaining public order in the country. Extensive explanatory work on the importance of this measure and the necessity for actively supporting the people's volunteer detachments must be conducted amongst the public for this purpose.

3. The Central Committee of the YCL must ensure the active participation of the best Komsomol members and young people in the people's volunteer detachments.

4. Party and Soviet agencies and trade union and YCL organizations must adopt the measures necessary to inculcate in pupils, students and young people strong habits of observance of discipline and rules of conduct in schools, educational institutions, the family, on the street and in public places, and to organize, in an appropriate form, the explanation of Soviet laws to them.

5. Institutions of internal affairs, agencies of the prosecutor's office, justice agencies and the courts must intensify the struggle against antisocial phenomena and conduct public trials of malicious violators of public order directly at enterprises, construction projects and state and collective farms, ensuring the meticulous and skilful organization of such cases with the aim of increasing their educational significance, and enlisting the services of public accusers when necessary. The aforementioned agencies are also required to give every possible assistance to voluntary people's detachments in their work.

Pravda-Izvestia text only

The Party Central Committee and the USSR Council of Ministers have approved the draft of the provisional statute on voluntary people's detachments and have instructed the Communist Party Central Committees and Councils of Ministers of the union republics to approve it, taking local conditions into consideration.

The draft of the provisional statute on voluntary people's detachments provides that these detachments shall admit citizens of the USSR, generally not under the age of eighteen, on the basis of personal applications submitted to trade-union and YCL committees or other public organizations at their place of work or residence, and on the recommendation of a meeting of the collective of which they are members.

The main functions of the detachments will be to safeguard public order, combat hooliganism, and participate in the explanatory work carried out by public organizations among the people for observance of the rules of socialist society.

In all their activity the people's detachments shall be guided by the requirements of Soviet laws, shall be under the protection of these laws, and shall perform their work in contact with public organizations and administrative agencies.

The members of detachments shall have the duty of defending the citizens, honour and dignity, taking the necessary measures to stop violations of public order, and restraining the violators, primarily through persuasion and warning. The members of detachments shall perform their duties in their free time and shall carry identification cards and wear badges.

The draft of the provisional statute defines the structure of the voluntary people's detachments and their rights and duties as well as the duties and rights of detachment members.

The Party Central Committee and the USSR Council of Ministers, considering the enormous importance to the people as a whole and to the state of enlisting the working people in safeguarding public order, has instructed local party and Soviet agencies to carry out extensive explanatory work among the people on the importance of this measure.

The Party Central Committee and the USSR Council of Ministers have expressed their firm conviction that all workers and collective farmers and the Soviet intelligentsia will greet these measures approvingly and will participate actively in their implementation.

Source: M. T. Efremov, i drugie, *Spravochnik partiinogo rabotnika*, vypusk 3 (Moscow, 1961), p. 577; *Pravda* and *Izvestia*, 10 March 1959.

Translation: *Current Digest of the Soviet Press*, Vol. XI, No. 10, p. 3 for the *Pravda* and *Izvestia* version; the original decree became available later. The parts of the text which were not published in the daily press have been added in square brackets by the editor for their own interest.

58. Khrushchev's RSFSR Law Against 'Parasites'

4 *May* 1961

60. The Statute on Comrades' Courts

3 *July* 1961

The RSFSR 'anti-parasite' law was the culmination of a trend in union-republican legislation begun in Uzbekistan in May 1957. Khrushchev's original idea was to make certain categories of unemployed persons (or persons who had jobs only for the sake of appearances) liable to expulsion to specially assigned localities. Such persons were also dealt with by the extra-legal 'comrades' courts', established in the RSFSR on 3 July 1961 (Similar bodies had existed in the 'twenties, though they had fallen into disuse, see p. 305.)

These new attempts to 'popularize' justice encountered resistance amongst the more sober legal minds—which is probably why there was such a long delay in passing a 'parasite' law in the RSFSR. It may also explain the shifting of responsibility for judging and sentencing 'parasites' firmly back to the people's courts by a decree of 20 September 1965. Investigation, it will be noted, was kept in the hands of the professional organs.

58. On Strengthening the Struggle with Persons Avoiding Socially Useful Work and Leading an Anti-Social, Parasitic Way of Life

Approved by the decree of the Supreme Soviet of the RSFSR, 4 May 1961.

... Considering the wish of many thousands of toilers to strengthen the struggle with parasitic elements the Presidium of the USSR decrees:
1. It is ordered that adults capable of working, not wishing to perform their most important constitutional duty, the duty to work honestly in accordance with their abilities, and avoiding socially useful work, extracting unearned income from the exploitation of parcels of land, automobiles, living space, or committing other anti-social acts permitting them to lead a parasitic way of life, shall be subjected to banishment by order of a county (city) people's court to specially designated places for a term of from two to five years, with confiscation of the property acquired by non-toiling means, and shall be compelled to work at the place to which they are sent.

Persons who obtain work in enterprises, in state and public offices, or by becoming members of collective farms only for the sake of appearances, and who, while enjoying the privileges and advantages of workers, collective farmers and office workers, in truth undermine labour discipline, occupy themselves with private-enterprise activities, live on resources obtained by non-toiling means or commit other anti-social offences permitting them to live a parasitic way of life shall also be subjected to the same measures of influence, established by an order of a county (city) people's court, as well as by a sentence of the public issued by a group of toilers working together in a factory, shop, office, organization, collective farm and collective-farm brigade.

An order of a county (city) people's court, or the sentence of the public to banishment of a person leading a parasitic way of life, shall issue only if, in spite of a warning of public organizations or state organs, the person leading a parasitic way of life fails to stand on the road to an honest toiling life within the period set for him.

2. The order of a county (city) people's court with regard to a person avoiding socially useful work and leading an anti-social parasitic way of life shall be final and may not be appealed.

A sentence of the public to banishment must be confirmed by the executive committee of a county (city) soviet of toilers' deputies, whose decision shall be final.

3. Exposure of persons leading an anti-social parasitic way of life and verification of all facts relating to this circumstance shall be carried out by the organs of militia and of the prosecutor's office on the basis of the evidence they have, on the initiative of state and public organizations and the declarations of citizens. On completion of the verification the material with the sanction of the prosecutor shall be forwarded to the county (city) people's court or to the toilers' group for examination.

4. If on verification and examination of the evidence concerning the person leading a parasitic way of life, there is found in his acts indication of a crime, the case must be sent to the organs of the prosecutor's office.

5. An order of the county (city) people's court, as well as a sentence of the public on banishment shall be executed by the militia.

Persons refusing to work at the place of banishment, on recommendation of the organs of militia shall be committed by a county (city) people's court to correctional labour with retention of 10 per cent of their wages, and if they also refuse to do correctional labour the court may substitute for it deprivation of freedom in accordance with the procedure of Article 28 of the criminal code of the RSFSR. The time served in correctional labour or deprivation of freedom shall not be counted in satisfaction of the term of banishment.

Flight from the place of banishment or en route thereto shall be punished under Article 186 of the criminal code of the RSFSR.

6. If a person subjected to banishment proves by his exemplary behaviour and honest relationship to work that he has been rehabilitated, he may be freed before the end of his term, but not before at least half has been served, if public organizations so request the county (city) people's court at the place

of banishment and if the executive committee of the county (city) soviet of toilers' deputies at the place of prior residence agrees.

7. The Council of Ministers of the RSFSR is authorized to issue an order putting into effect the necessary measures required by this decree.

Source: Vedomosti Verkhovnogo Soveta RSFSR, 1961, No. 18, statya 273.

Translation: J. N. Hazard and Isaac Shapiro, *The Soviet Legal System*, (Parker School of Foreign and Comparative Law, Columbia University, New York, 1962), Part I, p. 160, slightly abridged.

59. The Extension of the Death Penalty to Counterfeiting and Terrorism in the Camps

5 *May* 1961

The early 'sixties saw a sharpening of the more formal penalties against law-breakers, including a much freer application of the death penalty. The law of 5 May 1961, directed against counterfeiters and labour-camp hooligans, was the first of an important series. On 1 July the death penalty was introduced for illegal currency transactions. In February 1962 other crimes, including attacks on militiamen and the people's volunteers, rape, and bribery were penalized more harshly and made subject to the supreme penalty (in the most serious cases).

It seems from newspaper reports that these measures were no empty threat. All this was, of course, in contradiction to the USSR Principles of Criminal Legislation, which stipulated that the death penalty was to be retained only as an 'extraordinary penalty' for such crimes as high treason, espionage, and pre-meditated murder under aggravated circumstances (Article 22).

59. On Strengthening the Struggle with Especially Dangerous Crimes

Decree of the Supreme Soviet of the USSR, 5 May 1961

To strengthen the struggle with especially dangerous crimes the Presidium of the Supreme Soviet of the USSR decrees:

1. The death penalty—shooting—may be applied: for theft of state or public property in unusually large quantities, for preparation for the purpose of sale or the sale of counterfeit money or bank notes as a business, and also with regard to especially dangerous recidivists and persons convicted of serious crimes who terrorize at places of deprivation of freedom prisoners who are on the road to reform, or who attack the administration or who organize criminal groups for this purpose, or who take active parts in such groups.

In connection with this, Article 22 of the Fundamentals of criminal legislation of the USSR and of the union republics shall read as follows:

A sentence of death by shooting, as an exceptional measure, may be applied, until such times as it has been fully abolished, in cases of treason, espionage, wrecking, terrorist acts, banditry, the preparation for the purpose of sale or the sale of counterfeit money or bank notes as a business, premeditated murder under aggravating circumstances provided for in the articles of the criminal laws of the USSR and of the union republics which establish responsibility for premeditated murder, theft of state and public property in especially large amounts, and in wartime or under conditions of battle—and for other especially serious crimes in circumstances especially provided for by legislation of the USSR.

The application of the death penalty—shooting—shall be permitted also with regard to especially dangerous recidivists and persons convicted for serious crimes, who terrorize at places of deprivation of freedom prisoners who are on the road to reform, or who attack the administration or organize criminal groups for this purpose, or who take active part in such groups.

The death sentence may not be passed on persons under the age of eighteen years at the time the crime is committed or on women who are pregnant at the time the crime is committed or at the time sentence is passed. The death sentence cannot be executed in the case of women who are pregnant at the time of execution.

2. Article 24, para. 2 of the Law on criminal responsibility for state crimes shall be amended to read:

'The same acts [counterfeiting] when committed as a business shall be punished by deprivation of freedom for a term of from ten to fifteen years with confiscation of property or death with confiscation of property.'

3. It shall be established that especially dangerous recidivists as well as persons convicted of serious crimes, who terrorize at places of deprivation of freedom prisoners on the road to rehabilitation or who attack the administration or who organize criminal groups for this purpose or who take active part in such groups — shall be punished by deprivation of freedom for a term of from eight to fifteen years or by death.

Source: *Vedomosti Verkhovnogo Soveta SSSR,* 1961 No. 19, statya 207.
Translation: J. N. Hazard and Isaac Shapiro, *The Soviet Legal System,* (Parker School of International and Comparative Law, Columbia University, New York, 1962), Part I, p. 159, extract.

60. Statute on Comrades' Courts

Approved by the Edict of the Supreme Soviet of the RSFSR,
3 July 1961

Tasks of Comrades' Courts and Procedure for their Organization

ARTICLE 1. Comrades' courts are elected public agencies charged with actively contributing to the inculcation in citizens of a spirit of a communist attitude toward labour and socialist property and the observance of the rules of socialist society, and with developing among Soviet people a sense of collectivism and comradely mutual assistance and of respect for the dignity and honour of citizens. The chief duty of the comrades' courts is to prevent violation of the law and misdemeanours detrimental to society, to educate people by persuasion and public influence, and to create an intolerant attitude toward any antisocial acts. The comrades' courts are invested with the trust of the collective, express its will and are responsible to it.

ARTICLE 2. Comrades' courts at enterprises, institutions, organizations and higher and specialized secondary schools shall be set up by decision of a general meeting of the workers and employees or of the students.

Comrades' courts at collective farms and in apartment buildings served by housing offices or apartment managements or united in street committees, as well as those in rural populated points and settlements, shall be set up by decision of a general meeting of the collective farm members, the apartment house residents or the citizens of the village or settlement, in agreement with the executive committee of the respective soviet.

In large collectives comrades' courts may be set up in enterprise shops, collective farm brigades, etc.

Comrades' courts may be set up in collectives numbering at least fifty persons.

ARTICLE 3. Comrades' courts shall be elected for a term of one year by open ballot at general meetings of the workers' collectives. Meetings to elect comrades' courts shall be called by factory, plant or local trade-union committees, the boards of collective farms or the executive committees of local soviets.

Those who receive a majority vote with respect to the other candidates and more than half of the votes of those present at the meeting shall be considered elected members of the court.

The number of members of the court shall be fixed by the general meeting. The members of the court shall elect from among themselves by open vote a chairman of the comrades' court, vice-chairman and a secretary of the court.

ARTICLE 4. Comrades' courts shall report on their work to general meetings of the working people's collectives.

A member of a comrades' court who fails to justify the trust placed in him may be recalled by a general meeting before expiration of his term. Election of new members of comrades' courts to replace those who have been recalled or have dropped out for other reasons shall be held in the manner stipulated in Articles 2 and 3 of the present Statute.

Cases Heard by Comrades' Courts

ARTICLE 5. Comrades' courts shall hear cases involving:

(1) violation of labour discipline, including: absence from work without valid reason; arriving at work late or leaving before the end of the

working day; poor-quality work, or idle time resulting from a worker's unconscientious attitude toward his duties; failure to observe industrial safety regulations and other rules of labour protection, except cases entailing criminal liability; damage to inventory, instruments or materials through negligence.

(2) appearance in an intoxicated state, or other unworthy conduct, in public places or at work;

(3) unworthy behaviour toward women, failure to fulfil the duties of bringing up children, unworthy behaviour toward parents;

(4) abusive language, and circulating false rumours slandering a member of a collective, when such acts are first offences; foul language;

(5) the damaging of trees and other greenery;

(6) the damaging of living and other premises or of communal equipment, when the loss is not substantial;

(7) violations of apartment or dormitory regulations; disputes between tenants over the use of auxiliary premises or apartment-house services or payment for communal services, or over establishment of a procedure for the use of land plots between joint houseowners;

(8) property disputes between citizens who are members of the same collective involving sums of up to fifty roubles, if the parties to the dispute agree to the hearing of the case in a comrades' court;

(9) other antisocial acts not entailing criminal liability;

(10) administrative and other minor violations of the law, if the militia agencies, prosecutor's office or court consider it possible to transfer the case to a comrades' court for hearing.

ARTICLE 6. Cases shall be heard in a comrades' court at the offender's place of work or place of residence.

ARTICLE 7. Comrades' courts may not hear cases of violation of the law or of civil-law disputes in which verdicts or court decisions have already been handed down.

A disciplinary penalty imposed by management does not exclude the possibility of examining the same misdemeanour in a comrades' court upon the initiative of a public organization or of the comrades' court itself.

Procedure for the Hearing of Cases by Comrades' Courts

ARTICLE 8. Comrades' courts shall hear cases:

(1) at the recommendation of factory, plant or local trade-union committees; of voluntary peoples' detachments for the preservation of public order; of street, apartment-house, precinct and block committees; and of other public organizations and citizens' meetings.

(2) at the recommendation of the executive committees of local soviets, or of their standing committees;

307

(3) upon reports of state agencies, the directors of enterprises, institutions, and organizations, and the boards of collective farms;

(4) upon materials submitted by a court or prosecutor, or by an inquiry agency with the consent of the prosecutor;

(5) upon citizens' applications;

(6) upon the initiative of the comrades' court itself.

ARTICLE 9. A comrades' court shall hear a case within fifteen days of the time it receives it. The time and place of the hearing shall be determined by the chairman of the comrades' court, and shall be widely publicized among citizens.

ARTICLE 10. When necessary, the hearing of a case by a comrades' court shall be preceded by a check on the material received.

Directors of enterprises, institutions and organizations, as well as other officials and citizens, must submit to a comrades' court upon demand the information and documents needed in a case.

The chairman of the court or a vice-chairman shall familiarize a person brought before the court with the existing materials and, if there are grounds for hearing the case in the comrades' court, shall establish who are to be summoned to a session of the court as witnesses. The person on trial shall have the right to ask the court to request and obtain additional documents and to summon witnesses.

It shall be mandatory for citizens to appear upon the summons of a comrades' court.

ARTICLE 11. Sittings of the comrades' courts and the carrying out of instructions connected with the hearing of a case by members of the court shall take place after working hours. Cases shall be heard in public by at least three members of a comrades' court.

A person brought before a comrades' court may challenge the presiding officer or members of the comrades' court if he has reason to believe that they have a personal interest in the outcome of the case. The full comrades' court hearing the case shall decide whether to grant or deny the challenge.

A comrades' court examines the existing materials and hears explanations by the offender, the victim and the witnesses. Those attending the hearing may, with the court's permission, ask questions or speak on the merits of the case being heard.

The comrades' court shall keep a record of the hearing.

ARTICLE 12. If a person who has been summoned to a comrades' court fails to appear in court, the court shall adjourn the hearing of the case, ascertain the reasons for his failure to appear and, depending on the circumstances established, set another time for hearing of the case. Should this person again fail to appear in court without valid reason, the comrades' court may hear the case in his absence.

In the case of a person who has been summoned to a comrades' court on the basis of materials received from a prosecutor's office, a county (city) people's court or an inquiry agency and who fails to appear in court, the materials shall be returned to these agencies for adoption of the necessary measures.

ARTICLE 13. The decision of a comrades' court requires a majority vote of the members of the court participating in the hearing of the case. The decision shall stipulate the substance of the violation and the measure of influence set by the court. The decision of the comrades' court shall be signed by those participating in it—the presiding officer and the members of the court—and shall be announced publicly and brought to general notice.

Measures of Public Influence to be Applied by the Comrades' Courts

ARTICLE 14. In hearing a case and adopting a decision, a comrades' court shall be guided by existing legislation, this Statute and its sense of public duty.

ARTICLE 15. A comrades' court may apply the following measures of influence to the offender:

(1) make the offender apologize publicly to the victim or the collective;
(2) administer a comradely warning;
(3) administer public censure;
(4) administer a public reprimand, with or without publication in the press;
(5) impose a fine of up to ten roubles if the offence did not involve a violation of labour discipline;
(6) place before the director of the enterprise, institution or organization the question of applying the following measures in accordance with existing labour legislation: transferring the offender to a lower-paid job or demoting him;
(7) raise the question of evicting the offender from his apartment if he is unable to get along with other tenants or is guilty of a predatory attitude toward housing facilities or of a deliberate failure to pay his rent;
(8) a comrades' court may, in addition to applying the measures of influence stipulated in paragraphs (1)–(7) of this article, oblige the offender to make compensation, in an amount not exceeding fifty roubles, for damage caused by his illegal acts.

ARTICLE 16. A comrades' court may confine itself to the public hearing of a case and not apply the measures of public influence specified in Article 15 if the offender, having sincerely repented, publicly apologizes to the collective or the victim and voluntarily compensates for damage done.

If there are no grounds for a conviction, a comrades' court shall acquit the person brought before it.

In hearing property or other civil-law disputes, a comrades' court shall satisfy the claim fully or in part or reject it, or terminate the case if there has been a reconciliation of the parties to the dispute.

The comrades, court shall inform public organizations and officials of the reasons and conditions uncovered by it which contributed to a violation of the law or other offence.

ARTICLE 17. If a comrades' court, in hearing a case, becomes convinced of the necessity of holding the offender criminally or administratively liable, it shall adopt a decision to turn the materials over to the appropriate agencies.

If a comrades' court in examining a property or other civil-law dispute comes to the conclusion that the case is too complex for it to resolve, it shall hand the case over to a county (city) people's court.

ARTICLE 18. The decision of a comrades' court shall be final. If the decision handed down is contrary to the facts in the case or to existing legislation, the appropriate factory, plant or local trade-union committee or local Soviet executive committee has the right to suggest that the comrades' court rehear the case.

ARTICLE 19. A decision of a comrades' court calling for compensation for damage or imposing a fine, or a decision involving some other property indemnity, must be carried out within the time specified in the decision. If the decision is not carried out within the specified time, the chairman of the comrades' court shall remand the case to a people's judge, who after checking the materials submitted and the legality of the decision shall issue a writ of execution to be executed by a court marshal.

If the decision of the comrades' court is illegal, the people's judge shall refuse to issue a writ of execution, giving the grounds for the refusal in his decision and informing the trade-union committee or the Soviet executive committee, so that it may decide whether the case should be heard again.

Money collected from persons in the form of fines goes into the state budget under a procedure established by law.

ARTICLE 20. The decision of a comrades' court to administer a comradely warning, public censure or public reprimand shall remain in force for one year. If the person with respect to whom the decision has been handed down does not commit a new violation of the law within this period, the penalty shall be considered removed.

Upon a petition of a public organization, the director of an enterprise or institution or the board of a collective farm, or on application by the person brought to the comrades' court, or on its own initiative, a comrades' court has the right to remove the above-stipulated penalties before expiration of a year. Decisions to this effect shall be brought to general notice.

Direction of the Comrades' Courts

ARTICLE 21. Comrades' courts at enterprises, institutions, organizations and higher specialized secondary educational institutions shall be under the direction of the factory, plant or local trade-union committees. Comrades' courts at collective farms and in apartment houses served by housing offices or apartment-house managements or united in street committees and also in rural populated points and settlements shall function under the direction of the executive committees of the local soviets.

ARTICLE 22. Technical services shall be supplied to comrades' courts by the administration of the enterprise, institution, organization, housing-office or apartment-house management or by the board of the collective farm or the executive committee of the rural or settlement soviet.

Source: Vedomosti Verkhovnogo Soveta RSFSR, 1961, No. 26, statya 371.
Translation: CDSP, Vol. XIII, No. 33, p. 8.

61. Brezhnev's Drive Against 'Parasites'

23 February 1970

The problem of 'parasitism' evidently re-emerged in the late 'sixties (see document 58). The most likely explanations were the general deterioration in the political atmosphere, higher labour mobility, and local unemployment. The reaction of the leadership was sharply to increase social and administrative pressures on the unemployed. The penalties for these misdemeanours which had been introduced a few years before were, of course, still in force.

61. On Measures for Intensifying the Struggle with Persons who Avoid Socially Useful Labour and Lead an Anti-Social, Parasitic Way of Life.

Decree of the Central Committee of the CPSU and the Council of Ministers of the USSR, 23 February 1970

The Central Committee of the CPSU, and the Council of Ministers of the USSR decree that

1. The Central Committees of Communist Parties of the union republics, *krai* and *oblast* committees of the Party, the Councils of Ministers of the union and autonomous republics, the executive committees of *krai* and *oblast* soviets of workers' deputies are obliged to conduct a decisive struggle against instances of refusal to partake in socially useful labour, and to regard this work as an important means of strengthening discipline, and an integral part of the communist education of the toilers.

It should be considered a particularly important task of party, Soviet and social organizations to educate young people in a spirit of respect for labour, intolerance of parasitism and idleness, and to end departures from the norms of communist morality. It is necessary to exhibit constant concern for the encouragement, in each labour collective, and at people's places of residence, of an intolerant attitude towards those who avoid socially useful labour; meetings of toilers, comradely courts, village gatherings and other means of social pressure should be extensively used for this purpose.

2. The All-Union Central Committee of the Trade Unions and the Central Committee of the Komsomol must ensure the active participation of trade-union and Komsomol organizations in the work of re-educating persons who avoid socially useful labour; these bodies must co-operate in establishing such people in production collectives and take steps to see that they are involved in social work.

3. It be proposed to the Councils of Ministers of union republics that they

set up a system for employing persons who refrain from socially useful labour, bearing in mind that the latter should, as a rule, be given work at their place of permanent residence, with due regard for labour requirements, and in accordance with direction orders from the local soviet of workers' deputies. These orders are binding on the directors of enterprises, building sites, institutions and organizations, regardless of the ministry to which they belong.

4. It be made obligatory for all executive committees of local soviets of workers' deputies to:

Ensure that persons avoiding socially useful labour should be systematically and quickly sought out and given obligatory employment;

Exercise control over the observance of the established rules for employing and housing these people, and for organizing trade training and educational work among them;

Take all the necessary measures for the extensive involvement of the public in the struggle against instances of idleness, and also for co-ordinating the efforts of state organs and public organizations in this matter.

It be considered expedient to place responsibility for the organization of this work on one of the members of the executive committee of the corresponding soviet of workers' deputies. In order to carry out the day-to-day work of locating, registering and placing persons who avoid socially useful labour, a full-time official should, when necessary, be appointed to the administrative commissions attached to executive committees of district and town soviets of workers' deputies, within the staff and wage allotment for the local soviets of workers' deputies.

5. The Central Statistical Office of the USSR, Gosplan USSR, the Ministry of Internal Affairs of the USSR, and the State Committees of the Council of Ministers of the union republics for the use of labour resources, be charged with working out a unified system for registering able-bodied persons who are not engaged in socially useful labour, and organizing a study of the reasons for their non-involvement in labour.

6. The Ministry of Internal Affairs of the USSR, the Procuracy of the USSR, the Supreme Court of the USSR and their local organs are charged with ensuring that persons who refrain from socially useful labour and lead an anti-social, parasitic way of life should be quickly brought to justice in the approved fashion.

The administrative organs must use the force of law more decisively against malicious idlers, effect constant control over their behaviour, avert criminal or other anti-social acts on their part, and afford the greatest possible help to the state organs and public organizations in employing and re-educating these people.

Attention must be drawn to the necessity for the strictest observance of socialist legality in decisions about bringing persons who avoid socially useful labour to justice.

7. The Council of Ministers of the union republics must take measures to extend the network of reception and transit centres and boarding establishments for old people and invalids.

8. By way of modification to sub-section 'I', paragraph 11 of the Statutes of the Soviet Militia, the heads of organs of internal affairs are granted the right, with the sanction of the procurator, to keep persons detained for vagrancy and begging at reception and transit centres for the period of time necessary to establish their identity and solve the problem of employing them, to send them to boarding establishments for old people and invalids, or arrange guardianship for them, or to bring them to justice in accordance with the law, but for a period of not more than thirty days.

9. The Committee of the Press of the Council of Ministers of the USSR, the Committee for Radio and Television attached to the Council of Ministers of the USSR, the Committee for Cinematography attached to the Council of Ministers of the USSR, and the editors of newspapers and journals must allow in their work-plans for systematic coverage of questions relating to the labour education of Soviet people and measures in the struggle against parasitism of various kinds.

It is necessary to reveal more effectively by press, radio, television and cinema the meaning and character of labour in a socialist society and the problem of combining social and personal interests correctly: the role of society and the collective in the education of people must be shown, and idleness and other anti-social phenomena castigated more severely.

10. It must be recognized as expedient to introduce the necessary changes and additions into existing legislation covering the responsibility of persons who avoid socially useful labour and conduct an anti-social, parasitic way of life.

Source: K. M. Bogolyubov, i drugie (eds.), *Spravochnik partiinogo rabotnika vypusk 10* (Moscow, 1970), p. 367.
Editor's translation.

Part IV

The Peasant and the Land

62. Lenin's Decree on the Land

26 October 1917, *OS*

The Decree on the Land has been described as one of Lenin's cleverest political moves: there is little doubt that it ensured initial peasant approval for the change of government in the capitals. Lenin in effect took over the Social Revolutionaries' programme of socialization, which implied an agricultural system based on individual small-holdings. This was distinct from the policy of nationalization and large-scale state-controlled farming which had been the Bolshevik aim until the eve of the Revolution. The Left SRs were persuaded to join the Bolshevik government partly as a result of this measure. Lenin justified his switch of policy by claiming that such a programme was acceptable within the framework of a socialist revolution.

62. Decree on the Land Issued by the Second All-Russian Congress of Soviets

26 October 1917, *OS*

1. Landed proprietorship is abolished forthwith without any compensation.
2. The landed estates, as also all crown, monastery, and church lands, with all their livestock, implements, buildings and everything pertaining thereto, shall be placed at the disposal of the *volost* land committees and the *uyezd* soviets of peasants' deputies pending the convocation of the Constituent Assembly.
3. All damage to confiscated property, which henceforth belongs to the whole people, is proclaimed a grave crime to be punished by the revolutionary courts. The *uyezd* soviets of peasants' deputies shall take all necessary measures to assure the observance of the strictest order during the confiscation of the landed estates, to determine the size of estates, and the particular estates subject to confiscation, to draw up exact inventories of all property confiscated and to protect in the strictest revolutionary way all agricultural enterprises transferred to the people, with all buildings, implements, livestock, stocks of produce, etc.
4. The following peasant mandate, compiled by the newspaper *Izvestia Vserossiiskogo Soveta Krestyanskikh Deputatov* from 242 local peasant mandates and published in No. 88 of that paper (Petrograd, No. 88, 19 August 1917), shall serve everywhere to guide the implementation of the great land reforms until a final decision on the latter is taken by the Constituent Assembly.

On Land

The land question in its full scope can be settled only by the popular Constituent Assembly.

The most equitable settlement of the land question is to be as follows:

(1) Private ownership of land shall be abolished for ever; land shall not be sold, purchased, leased, mortgaged, or otherwise alienated.

All land, whether state, crown, monastery, church, factory, entailed, private, public, peasant, etc., shall be confiscated without compensation and become property of the whole people, and pass into the use of all those who cultivate it.

Persons who suffer by this property revolution shall be deemed to be entitled to public support only for the period necessary for adaptation to the new conditions of life.

(2) All mineral wealth—ore, oil, coal, salt, etc. and also all forests and waters of state importance, shall pass into the exclusive use of the state. All the small streams, lakes, woods, etc., shall pass into the use of the communes, to be administered by the local self-government bodies.

(3) Lands on which high-level scientific farming is practised— orchards, plantations, seed plots, nurseries, hot-houses etc.—shall not be divided up, but shall be converted into model farms, to be turned over for exclusive use to the state or to the communes, depending on the size and importance of such lands.

Household land in towns and villages, with orchards and vegetable gardens, shall be reserved for the use of their present owners, the size of the holdings, and the size of tax levied for the use thereof, to be determined by law.

(4) Stud farms, government and private pedigree stock and poultry farms, etc., shall be confiscated and become the property of the whole people, and pass into the exclusive use of the state or a commune, depending on the size and importance of such farms.

The question of compensation shall be examined by the Constituent Assembly.

(5) All livestock and farm implements of the confiscated estates shall pass into the exclusive use of the state or a commune, depending on their size and importance, and no compensation shall be paid for this.

The farm implements of peasants with little land shall not be subject to confiscation.

(6) The right to use the land shall be accorded to all citizens of the Russian State (without distinction of sex) desiring to cultivate it by their own labour, with the help of their families, or in partnership, but only as long as they are able to cultivate it. The employment of hired labour is not permitted.

318

In the event of the temporary physical disability of any member of a village commune for a period of up to two years, the village commune shall be obliged to assist him for this period by collectively cultivating his land until he is again able to work.

Peasants who, owing to old age or ill health, are permanently disabled and unable to cultivate the land personally, shall lose their right to the use of it but, in return, shall receive a pension from the state.

(7) Land tenure shall be on an equality basis, i.e. the land shall be distributed among the working people in conformity with a labour standard or a subsistence standard, depending on local conditions.

There shall be absolutely no restriction on the forms of land tenure—household, farm, communal, or co-operative, as shall be decided in each individual village and settlement.

(8) All land, when alienated, shall become part of the national land fund. Its distribution among the peasants shall be in charge of the local and central self-government bodies, from democratically organized village and city communes, in which there are no distinctions of social rank, to central regional government bodies.

The land fund shall be subject to periodical redistribution, depending on the growth of population and the increase in the productivity and the scientific level of farming.

When the boundaries of allotments are altered, the original nucleus of the allotment shall be left intact.

The land of the members who leave the commune shall revert to the land fund; preferential rights to such land shall be given to the near relatives of the members who have left, or to persons designated by the latter.

The cost of fertilizers and improvements put into the land, to the extent that they have not been fully used up to the time the allotment is returned to the land fund, shall be compensated.

Should the available land fund in a particular district prove inadequate for the needs of the local population, the surplus population shall be settled elsewhere.

The state shall take upon itself the organization of resettlement and shall bear the cost thereof, as well as the cost of supplying implements, etc.

Resettlement shall be effected in the following order: landless peasants desiring to resettle, then members of the commune who are of vicious habits, deserters, and so on, and finally, by lot or by agreement.

The entire contents of this mandate, as expressing the absolute will of the vast majority of the class-conscious peasants of all Russia, is proclaimed a provisional law, which, pending the convocation of the Constituent

Assembly, shall be carried into effect as far as possible immediately, and as to certain of its provisions with due gradualness, as shall be determined by the *uyezd* soviets of peasants' deputies.

5. The land of ordinary peasants and ordinary Cossacks shall not be confiscated.

Chairman of the Council of People's Commissars,
VLADIMIR ULYANOV-LENIN.

26 October 1917.

Source: G. D. Obichkin, i drugie, *Dekrety sovetskoi vlasti*, Vol. I (Moscow, 1957), p. 17.
Translation: Yu. Akhapkin, *First Decrees of Soviet Power* (Lawrence and Wishart, London, 1970), p. 23.

63. War Communism in the Village: the Committees of the Village Poor

11 June 1918

From the spring of 1918 *the supply of food from the villages was a matter of great concern to the Bolsheviks. Lenin claimed that hoarding by 'kulaks' and 'speculators' was the cause of the shortages; in May the penalties for this sin were increased, and workers' detachments were formed to make enforced collections. The establishment of the village Committees of the Poor, described in this document, in June, was an associated measure: the Committees became a hallmark of the Bolshevik policy of War Communism in the countryside. The Committees were supposed to deprive the kulaks of their surpluses, and distribute industrial products brought in from the towns. Poor and generally less successful peasants were usually given the upper hand in these bodies, which caused considerable dissension in rural communities. The measure was strongly opposed by the Left Social Revolutionaries, and contributed much to their final split with the Bolsheviks.*

63. Decree on Organizing and Supplying the Village Poor

Passed by the All-Russian Central Executive Committee, 11 *June* 1918

1. *Volost* and village committees of the poor, organized by local soviets of workers' and peasants' deputies with the participation of the (local) food departments and under the general control of the People's Commissariat of Food and the All-Russian Central Executive Committee, shall be established everywhere ...

2. Both native and newly arrived inhabitants of the village may elect and be elected to *volost* and village committees of the poor, with the exception of notorious kulaks ... who possess grain surpluses and other food products, and owners of commercial and industrial enterprises using hired labour, etc.

> NOTE. Peasants employing labour on farms which do not exceed the consumption standard may elect and be elected to the committees of the poor.

3. The *volost* and village committees of the poor discharge the following duties:

(a) Distribution of food, goods of prime necessity, and farming implements.

(b) Assistance to local food departments in requisitioning surplus grain from kulaks and the rich ...

7. The distribution of grain, goods of prime necessity, and farming implements must accord with the standards set up by the *gubernia* food departments and conform to the general plans of the People's Commissariat of Food ...

8. For the time being and until the People's Commissar of Food makes special rulings, the basis of grain distribution shall be as follows:

(a) Grain is distributed among the village poor in accordance with the established standards and free of charge, at the expense of the state. The distribution is made out of the grain surpluses which have been fully requisitioned from the kulaks and the rich in accordance with the decision of the *gubernia* and *uezd* soviets ... and have been delivered to the state grain storehouses ...

10. *Volost* committees of the poor are to take charge of the more complicated agricultural machinery and to organize communal cultivation of the fields and harvesting for the village poor; no charge will be made for the use of such machinery in places where the *volost* and village committees of the poor give energetic support to the food departments in requisitioning the surplus from the kulaks and the rich.

11. The Soviet of People's Commissars will place at the disposal of the People's Commissariat of Food such money as may be needed from time to time to execute this decree.

> YA. SVERDLOV, Chairman of the Central Executive Committee.
> V. ULIANOV (LENIN), President of the Sovnarkom.

Source: G. D. Obichkin, i drugie, *Dekrety sovetskoi vlasti*, Vol. II (Moscow, 1959), p. 416. *Translation:* James Bunyan, *Intervention, Civil War and Communism in Russia, April–December, 1918* (John Hopkins Press, Baltimore, 1936), p. 472. Extracts.

64. The New Economic Policy in the Village

21 *March* 1921

War Communism in the village was abolished, and the New Economic Policy introduced, by the decree of 21 March 1921. Based on a resolution passed a few days before at the Tenth Party Congress, this decree radically changed the state-peasant relationship to the benefit of the latter. The new tax on the peasant was to be less than the requisitions to which he had been subject before, though it was still to take precedence over his own consumption needs. The 1919 Land Law was revised in May 1922 to permit limited leasing of land and hiring of labour. This was another significant concession to the peasantry, but these measures did not come in time to avert a massive famine later in the year.

64. On the Replacement of the Requisitioning of Food and Raw Materials by a Tax in Kind

Decree of the All-Russian Central Executive Council, 21 March 1921

1. In order to ensure correct and stable farming based on a freer disposition by the farmer of the products of his labour and of his economic resources, to strengthen the peasant economy and raise its productivity, and also to determine precisely the state obligations which fall on the peasants, requisitioning, as a means of state procurement of food supplies, raw material and fodder, is to be replaced by a tax in kind.
2. This tax must be less than the peasant has been liable to up to the present through requisitions. The tax must be calculated so as to cover the most essential needs of the Army, urban workers, and the non-agricultural population. The general sum of the tax must be constantly reduced as the re-establishment of transport and industry permits the Soviet Government to receive agricultural products in exchange for factory and hand-made products.
3. The tax is to be levied in the form of a percentage or partial deduction from the products raised on the peasant holding, with due regard for the harvest, the number of consumers in the household and the number of cattle there.
4. The tax must be progressive; the percentage deducted must be lower for the holdings of the middle and weaker peasants and urban workers. The holdings of the poorest peasants may be exempted from some and, in exceptional cases, from all forms of tax in kind.
   Industrious peasants who increase the sown area and the number of cattle on their holdings or who increase the general productivity of their holdings, receive benefits when paying the tax in kind.

323

5. The taxation law must be drawn up and published in such time and manner as to inform the peasants as exactly as possible about the obligations entailed for them before the beginning of spring work in the fields.

6. The delivery to the state of the products due ends within definite time-limits, precisely established by law.

7. The responsibility for paying the tax rests with each individual household, and the organs of the Soviet government are charged with prosecuting everyone who does not fulfil his obligations.

Communal responsibility is abolished.

In order to check the assessment and payment of the tax, organizations of local peasants are formed, consisting of groups of persons paying various tax rates.

8. All reserves of food, raw materials and fodder which remain with the peasants after the tax has been paid are completely at their disposition and may be used by them for improving and strengthening their holdings, increasing their personal consumption or for exchanging for industrial, hand-made or agricultural goods.

Exchange is permitted within the limits of local economic turnover, through co-operative organizations, markets and bazaars.

9. Those farmers who wish to deliver to the state the surpluses which remain in their possession after the tax has been paid must be provided with consumer goods and agricultural equipment in exchange for such voluntary delivery of surpluses. With this end in view, a permanent state reserve fund of agricultural equipment and consumer goods is being created, to include both domestic products and goods purchased abroad. Part of the state gold reserve and some of the procured raw materials are set aside for this purpose.

10. Supplies for the poorest rural dwellers are arranged by the state in accordance with special rules.

11. Consequent to the present decree, the All-Russian Central Executive Committee requests the Council of People's Commissars to issue the necessary detailed statutes within one month.

> President of the All-Russian Central Executive Committee,
> M. KALININ.
> Secretary of the All-Russian Central Executive Committee,
> ZALUTSKY.

Source: V. N. Malin and A. V. Korobov (eds.), *Direktivy KPSS i sovetskogo pravitelstva po khozyaistvennym voprosam*, Vol. 1 (Moscow, 1957), p. 225.
Editor's translation.

65. Stalin Justifies Collectivization
28 May 1928

66. The Elimination of the Kulaks Proposed
27 December 1929

67. The Collectivization Drive Accelerated
5 January 1930

68. Stalin Chides the Enthusiasts
2 March 1930

The four well-known extracts given below illustrated the steps taken to ensure rapid 'collectivization' of agriculture. Collectivization strongly resembled Lenin's early projects for nationalization, which the Bolsheviks had appeared to abandon when they came to power. The first formal declaration of this new onslaught on the peasantry was in a resolution of the Fifteenth Party Congress, which met in December 1927. It was said to be justified by difficulties of food supply, which Stalin described in his speech of 28 May 1928. The policy of annihilating the kulaks as a class was propounded in his speech of 27 December 1929, though he omitted to provide any economic definition of the term. As a result, up to five million people lost their property and were deported. Harsh repressive measures were used against all opponents of collectivization.

The resolution of 5 January 1930 set a much more rapid tempo for collectivization than most people had expected. Stalin's 'Dizzy with Success' speech may best be regarded as an attempt to shift the blame for the excesses of the preceding months from his own shoulders on to those of local party officials. It was immediately followed by a fall in the coverage of the collectivized sector, according to one authority, from 58 per cent of peasant households early in March to 21 per cent by September. The movement was to recover quickly, however.

65. On the Grain Front
Extract from Stalin's talk to students of the Institute of Red Professors, the Communist Academy, the Sverdlov University, on 28 May 1928

... The underlying cause of our grain difficulties is that the increase in the production of grain for the market is not keeping pace with the increase in the demand for grain. Industry is growing. The number of workers is growing. Towns are growing. And, lastly, the regions producing industrial crops (cotton, flax, sugar-beet, etc.) are growing, creating a demand for grain. All this leads to a rapid increase in our requirements as regards grain—grain available for the market. But the production of grain for the market is increasing at a disastrously slow rate. It cannot be said that we have had a smaller amount of grain stocks at the disposal of the state this year than last year, or the year before. On the contrary, we have had far more grain in the hands of the state this year than in previous years. Nevertheless, we are faced with difficulties as regards the grain supply. Here are a few figures. In 1925–26 we managed to purchase 434,000,000 poods of grain by 1 April. Of this amount 123,000,000 poods were exported. Thus, there remained in the country 311,000,000 poods of grain. In 1926–27 we purchased 596,000,000 poods of grain by 1 April. Of this amount 153,000,000 poods were exported. There remained in the country 443,000,000 poods. In 1927–28 we purchased 576,000,000 poods of grain by 1 April. Of this amount 27,000,000 poods were exported. There remained in the country 549,000,000 poods. In other words, this year, by 1 April, the grain supplies available to meet the requirements of the country amounted to 100,000,000 poods more than last year, and 230,000,000 poods more than the year before. Nevertheless we are experiencing difficulties on the grain front this year ...

Indeed, is it not a fact that as regards the area sown to grain crops we have already reached the pre-war mark? Yes, it is a fact. Is it not a fact that already last year the gross production of grain was equal to the pre-war output, i.e., 5,000,000,000 poods? Yes, it is a fact. How, then, is it to be explained that, in spite of these facts, the amount of grain we are producing for the market is only one-half, and the amount we are exporting is only about one-twentieth, of what it was in pre-war times? The reason is primarily and chiefly the change in the structure of our agriculture brought about by the October Revolution, the change from large-scale landlord and large-scale kulak farming, which provided the largest proportion of marketed grain, to small and middle peasant farming, which provides the smallest proportion of marketed grain. The mere fact that before the war there were fifteen to sixteen million individual peasant farms, whereas now there are twenty-four to twenty-five million peasant farms, shows that the fundamental basis of our agriculture is small peasant farming, which provides a minimum amount of grain for the market. The strength of large-scale farming, irrespective of whether it is landlord, kulak or collective farming, lies in the fact that large farms are able to employ machinery, scientific knowledge, fertilizers, increase the productivity of labour, and thereby produce a maximum quantity of grain for the market. On the other hand, the weakness of small peasant farming lies in the fact that it lacks, or almost lacks, these opportunities, as a result of which it is semi-consuming farming, yielding little grain for the market. Take, for instance, the collective farms and the state farms. They market 47·2 per cent of their gross output of grain. In other words, they supply for the market a larger proportion of their output than did landlord farming in pre-war days. But what about the small and middle peasant farms? They market only 11·2 per cent of their total output of grain. The difference, as you see, is quite striking.

Here are a few figures illustrating the structure of grain production in the past, in the pre-war period, and at present, in the post-October period. These figures have been furnished by Comrade Nemchinov, a member of the Collegium of the Central Statistical Board. They do not claim to be exact, as Comrade Nemchinov explains in his memorandum; they permit of only approximate calculations. But these figures are quite adequate to enable us to understand the difference between the pre-war period and the post-October period in regard to the structure of grain production in general, and of the production of market grain in particular (see the table below).

What does this table show?

It shows, firstly, that the production of the overwhelming proportion of grain products has passed from the hands of landlords and kulaks into the hands of small and middle peasants. This means that the small and middle peasants, having completely emancipated themselves from the yoke of the landlords, and having, in the main, broken the strength of the kulaks, have thereby obtained the opportunity of considerably improving their material conditions. This is the result of the October Revolution. Here we see the effect, primarily, of the decisive gain which accrued to the great bulk of the peasantry as a result of the October Revolution.

Period	Gross grain production		Market grain (i.e., not consumed in the rural districts)		Percentage of market grain
	Millions of poods	Per cent	Millions of poods	Per cent	
Pre-war					
1. Landlords	600	12·0	281·6	21·6	47·0
2. Kulaks	1,900	38·0	650·0	50·0	34·0
3. Middle and poor peasants	2,500	50·0	369·0	28·4	14·7
Total	5,000	100·0	1,300·6	100·0	26·0
1926–27					
1. State farms and collective farms	80·0	1·7	37·8	6·0	47·2
2. Kulaks	617·0	13·0	126·0	20·0	20·0
3. Middle and poor peasants	4,052·0	85·3	466·2	74·0	11·2
Total	4,749·0	100·0	630·0	100·0	13·3

It shows, secondly, that in our country the principal holders of grain available for the market are the small and, primarily, the middle peasants. This means that not only in respect to gross output of grain, but also in respect to the production of grain for the market, the USSR has become, as a result of the October Revolution, a land of small peasant farming, and the middle peasant has become the 'central figure' in agriculture.

It shows, thirdly, that the abolition of landlord (large-scale) farming, the reduction of kulak (large-scale) farming to less than one-third, and the change to small peasant farming with only 11 per cent of its output available for the market, under conditions of the absence in the sphere of grain-growing of any more or less developed large-scale farming in common (collective farms and state farms), was bound to lead, and in fact has led, to a sharp reduction in the output of grain for the market as compared with pre-war times. It is a fact that the amount of marketed grain in our country is now half of what it was before the war, notwithstanding the fact that gross output of grain has reached the pre-war level.

That is the underlying cause of our difficulties on the grain front ...

What, then, is the way out of the situation?

1. The way out lies, firstly, in the transition from the small, backward and scattered peasant farms to amalgamated, large-scale common farms, equipped with machinery, armed with scientific knowledge and capable of producing a maximum of grain for the market. The solution lies in the transition from individual peasant farming to collective, to common farming ...

According to the figures of the Central Statistical Board, the gross production of grain by the collective farms in 1927 amounted to no less than fifty-five million poods, with an average marketable surplus of 30 per cent. The widespread movement for the creation of new collective farms and for the expansion of the old collective farms that started at the beginning of this year should considerably increase the grain output of the collective farms by the end of the year. Our task is to maintain the present rate of development of the collective-farm movement, to combine the collective farms into larger units, to get rid of sham collective farms, replacing them by genuine ones, and to establish a system whereby the collective farms will deliver to the state and co-operative organizations the whole of their market grain under penalty of being deprived of state subsidies and credits. I think that if these conditions are adhered to we shall, in three or four years, be able to obtain from the collective farms about forty to fifty million poods of grain for the market ...

2. The way out lies, secondly, in expanding and strengthening the old state farms, and in organizing and developing new, large state farms. According to the figures of the Central Statistical Board, the gross output of grain in the existing state farms amounted in 1927 to no less than 45,000,000 poods, with a marketable surplus of 65 per cent. There is no doubt that, given a certain

amount of state support, the state farms could considerably increase the production of grain. But our task does not end there. There is a decision of the Soviet government, on the strength of which new large state farms (from 10,000 to 30,000 dessiatins each) are being organized in districts where there are no peasant holdings; and in five or six years these state farms should produce about 100,000,000 poods of grain for the market. The organization of these state farms has already begun. The task is to put this decision of the Soviet government into effect at all costs. I think that, provided these tasks are fulfilled, we shall in three or four years be able to obtain from the old and new state farms 80,000,000 to 100,000,000 poods of grain for the market.

3. Finally, the way out lies in systematically increasing the yield of the small and middle individual peasant farms. We cannot and should not lend any support to the individual large kulak farms. But we can and should lend support to the individual small and middle-peasant farms, helping them to increase their crop yields and drawing them into the channel of co-operative organization. This is an old task: it was proclaimed with particular emphasis as early as 1921, when the tax in kind was substituted for the surplus-appropriation system. This task was confirmed by our Party at its Fourteenth and Fifteenth Congresses. The importance of the task is now emphasized by the difficulties on the grain front. That is why this task must be fulfilled with the same persistence as the first two tasks, the task with regard to collective farms and the task with regard to state farms ...

Should not, in addition to these measures, a number of other measures be adopted—measures, say, to reduce the speed of development of our industry, the growth of which is causing a considerable increase in the demand for grain, which at present is outstripping the increase in the production of grain for the market? No, they should not. Not under any circumstances! To reduce the speed of development of industry would mean to weaken the working class; for every step forward in the development of industry, every new factory, every new works, is, as Lenin expressed it, 'a new stronghold' of the working class, which strengthens its position in the fight against the petty-bourgeois anarchy, in the fight against the capitalist elements in our economy. On the contrary, we must maintain the present speed of development of industry; we must at the first opportunity develop it still further in order to pour goods into the rural districts and obtain from them more grain, in order to supply agriculture, primarily the collective farms and state farms, with machines, in order to industrialize agriculture and to increase the proportion of its output for the market.

Should we, perhaps, as a measure of greater 'caution', retard the development of heavy industry and make light industry, which produces chiefly for the peasant market, the basis of our industry as a whole? Not under any circumstances! That would be suicidal; it would mean undermining our whole industry, including light industry. It would mean abandoning the slogan of industrializing our country, transforming our country into an appendage of the capitalist system of economy ...

Source and Translation : J. Stalin, *Problems of Leninism* (Moscow, 1947), p. 206 (extracts).

66. Problems of Agrarian Policy in the USSR (extracts)

Stalin's speech delivered at the conference of Marxist students of the agrarian question, 27 *December* 1929

VI. The class changes and the turn in the Party's policy

... The characteristic feature of our work during the past year is: (a) that we, the Party and the Soviet government, have developed an offensive on the whole front against the capitalist elements in the countryside; and (b) that this offensive, as you know, has brought about and is bringing about very palpable, *positive* results.

What does this mean? It means that we have passed from the policy of *restricting* the exploiting proclivities of the kulaks to the policy of *eliminating* the kulaks as a class. This means that we have made, and are still making, one of the most decisive turns in our whole policy.

Until recently the Party adhered to the policy of *restricting* the exploiting proclivities of the kulaks. As you know, this policy was proclaimed as far back as the Eighth Party Congress. This policy was again announced at the time of the introduction of the New Economic Policy and at the Eleventh Congress of our Party. We all remember Lenin's well-known letter to Preobrazhensky (1922), in which he again urged the necessity of pursuing this policy. Finally, this policy was confirmed by the Fifteenth Congress of our Party. And it is this policy that we have pursued until recently ...

But today? What is the position? Today, we have an adequate material base which enables us to strike at the kulaks, to break their resistance, to eliminate them as a class, and to *substitute* for their output the output of the collective farms and state farms. You know that in 1929 the grain produced on the collective farms and state farms amounted to no less than 400,000,000 poods (200,000,000 poods less than the gross output of the kulak farms in 1927). You also know that in 1929 the collective farms and state farms supplied more than 130,000,000 poods of grain for the market (i.e., more than the kulaks in 1927). And finally, you know that in 1930 the gross output of the collective farms and state farms will amount to no less than 900,000,000 poods of grain (i.e., more than the gross output of the kulaks in 1927), and their output of grain for the market to not less than 400,000,000 poods (i.e., incomparably more than the kulaks supplied in 1927).

This is the position today, comrades.

This is the change that has taken place in the economics of our country.

330

This is the change in the alignment of class forces that has taken place in recent years.

Now, as you see, we have the material base which enables us to *substitute* for kulak output the output of the collective farms and state farms. That is why our offensive against the kulaks is now meeting with undeniable success. That is how the offensive against the kulaks must be carried on, if we mean a real offensive and not futile declamations against the kulaks.

That is why we have recently switched from a policy of *limiting* the exploiting tendencies of the kulaks to a policy of *liquidating the kulaks as a class* ...

Source and translation: J. Stalin, *Problems of Leninism* (Moscow, 1947), p. 317 (extracts).

67. On the Rate of Collectivization and State Assistance for Collective-Farm Construction

Decree of the Central Committee of the VKP(B), 5 January 1930

1. In recent months the collectivization movement has taken another step forward and has embraced not only separate groups of individual households, but also entire *raiony, okruga* and even *oblasti* and *kraiya*. The movement is based on collectivization of the means of production of poor and middle-peasant households.

All the rates of development of the collectivization movement envisaged by the plan have been surpassed. By the spring of 1930 the sown area worked on a communal basis will be significantly more than 30 million hectares, i.e., the five-year collectivization plan, which envisaged a coverage of 22–24 million hectares for the collectives towards the end of the five-year period, will already be significantly overfulfilled this year.

We therefore have the material base for *replacing* large-scale kulak production by *large-scale* collective-farm production, and for making a mighty stride forward towards the creation of a socialist agriculture, not to mention state farming, the growth of which is significantly overtaking all the planned objectives.

This circumstance, which has a decisive significance for the whole economy of the USSR, has given the Party every right to switch, in its practical work, from a policy of limiting the exploiting tendencies of the kulaks to one of liquidating the kulaks as a class.

2. It may be established without any doubt on the basis of all this that within the limits of the five-year plan, instead of collectivization of 20 per cent of the sown area as envisaged by that plan, we can solve the problem of collectivizing the overwhelming majority of peasant households. At the same time the collectivization of such important grain areas as the Lower Volga, the Middle Volga, and the North Caucasus may be basically completed by the

autumn of 1930, or in any case by the spring of 1931; the collectivization of other grain areas may be basically finished by the autumn of 1931, or in any case by the spring of 1932 ...

Source: V. N. Malin and A. V. Korobov (eds.), *Direktivy KPSS i sovetskogo pravitelstva po knhozyaistvennym voprosam*, Vol. 2 (Moscow, 1957), p. 137 (extract).
Editor's translation.

68. 'Dizzy with Success' (Problems of the Collective-Farm Movement)
Stalin's article in Pravda, *2 March* 1930

Everybody is now talking about the successes achieved by the Soviet government in the sphere of the collective-farm movement. Even our enemies are compelled to admit that important successes have been achieved. And these successes are great indeed.

It is a fact that by 20 February this year, 50 per cent of the peasant farms of the USSR had been collectivized. This means that by 20 February 1930 we had *fulfilled* the estimates of the Five-Year Plan *more than twice over*.

It is a fact that by 28 February this year, the collective farms had *already* stored more than 3,600,000 tons of seed for the spring sowing, i.e., more than 90 per cent of the plan, or about 220,000,000 poods. It cannot but be admitted that the storing of 220,000,000 poods of seed by the collective farms alone—after the grain purchasing plan had been successfully fulfilled—is a tremendous achievement.

What does all this show?

It shows that *the radical turn of the rural districts towards Socialism may already be regarded as guaranteed* ...

But successes also have their seamy side; especially when they are achieved with comparative 'ease', 'unexpectedly', so to speak. Such successes sometimes induce a spirit of conceit and arrogance: 'We can do anything!' 'We can win hands down!' People are often intoxicated by such successes, they become dizzy with success, they lose all sense of proportion, they lose the faculty of understanding realities, they reveal a tendency to overestimate their own strength and to underestimate the strength of the enemy; reckless attempts are made to settle all the problems of Socialist construction 'in two ticks'. In such cases care is not taken to *consolidate* the successes achieved and systematically to *utilize* them for the purpose of advancing further. Why should we consolidate successes? We shall anyhow reach the complete victory of Socialism in 'two ticks', 'We can do anything!' 'We can win hands down!'

Hence, the task of the Party: to wage a determined struggle against this frame of mind, which is dangerous and harmful to the cause, and to drive it out of the Party...

Source and Translation: J. Stalin, *Problems of Leninism* (Moscow, 1947), p. 326 (extracts).

69. The Political Role of Machine-and-Tractor Stations

11 January 1933

At the time of collectivization the Soviet peasants' experience of motor-driven agricultural machinery was limited to a few hundred privately owned tractors, and, from the mid-'twenties onwards, to rare 'tractor columns'. The establishment of the nationwide MTS system as a state-owned share company on 5 June 1929 reflected the official view that collectivization should go hand in hand with mechanization. By 1934 the MTS had taken over most of the machinery available in the collective farms: by 1940, they were servicing over 90 per cent of the kolkhoz ploughland.

No less important was the political role of these organizations, as outlined in the law of 11 January 1933. The MTS formed the spearhead of the Party's drive to increase its influence in the villages, where party organizations were few and far between. The sovkhozy, or state farms, which were mentioned in the same measure, were numerically far less significant and contained only a small proportion of the ploughland.

69. The Aims and Tasks of the Political Departments of Machine-and-Tractor Stations and State Farms

[The resolution of the combined plenum of the Central Committee and the Central Control Commission of the All-Russian Communist Party (Bolsheviks), 11 January 1933

1. *The weakness of political work in the village and the necessity for creating political departments in MTS and state farms.*

... The machine-and-tractor stations and state farms, as large factories of socialist agriculture, are an extremely important lever for reconstructing agriculture in a socialist manner and continually strengthening Soviet influence on the collective farmers.

The machine-and-tractor stations and state farms have won for themselves a firm place in socialist agriculture as organizers of the system of socialized production. However, despite the extremely important organizational and economic role of the MTS and their influence on the technical re-equipment and socialist reconstruction of agriculture, their *political* influence on the broad masses of the collective farmers is still quite inadequate. Often the MTS do not have a political complexion. Inside them, criminal and negligent attitudes towards party and government tasks, a criminal attitude towards state property, and the theft and plunder of collective-farm and state property, all flourish together. Hostile class elements not infrequently penetrate into the MTS themselves and work from within to increase their anti-Soviet influence on the collective farmers.

This to a significant extent also holds good for the state farms ...

2. *The tasks of the political departments of the MTS and state farms.*

The political departments of the MTS and state farms must, by the promotion of mass political work in collective and state farms on the one hand, and the organizational and economic consolidation of them on the other, supplement the economic and technical work of the MTS and state farms in solving the tasks set for collective and state farms: these tasks are in the sphere of raising crop yields, improving livestock handling, the timely organization of the autumn and spring sowing, the timely organization of harvesting and milling, and the timely and complete fulfilment by collective farmers and state farms of all their obligations to the state.

The political departments of the MTS and state farms must ensure party watchfulness and control in all spheres of the work and life not only of the MTS and state farms, but also of the collective farms which the MTS serve. Providing good-quality seed for the sowing period, averting the theft of seed, supervising correct milling practices, conducting the struggle against thefts of milled grain, and the struggle against failure to appear at work, ensuring attentive care for collective- and state-farm livestock and property, driving all wrecking, anti-Soviet and anti-collective elements from collective and state farms, selecting our best, well-tried cadres for collective and state farms—all these and similar matters must be at the focus of attention of the political departments.

The political departments of the MTS and state farms must ensure political control and surveillance of the distribution and use of collective farmers and state-farm workers, bearing in mind that the preservation of public, collective-farm and state-farm property, not to mention the successes of collective and state farms, depend on who is working the sowing or harvesting machine, who is in the state-farm livestock section, and who is keeping tally of the grain and all collective- and state-farm property.

A primary task of the political departments of the MTS is to ensure the unconditional and timely fulfilment by the *collective farms* and *collective farmers* of their obligations to the state, and in particular to wage a decisive struggle against the theft of collective-farm property, a struggle against instances of sabotage of party and government measures in the sphere of state grain and meat procurements in the collective farms.

A primary task of the political departments of *state farms* is to ensure the unconditional and timely fulfilment by state farms of their obligations to the state, and in particular to wage a decisive struggle against attempts by certain directors and their assistants to set the narrow interests of the state farm against the general interests of the state, a struggle against the concealment of surpluses of production instead of giving them up to the state.

The political departments of the MTS and state farms must ensure the firm, correct and timely application of the laws of the Soviet government concerning administrative and penal measures against organizers of the plunder of public property and the sabotage of party and government measures in agriculture.

All these penal measures, including court decisions on the above-mentioned crimes, should be brought to the notice of the broad collective-farm masses and state-farm workers by the political departments, which should also promote widespread mass explanatory and educative work among collective farmers and state-farm workers around and on the basis of such facts ...

Source: Kollektivizatsia selskogo khozyaistva: vazhneishie postanovlenia kommunisticheskoi partii i sovetskogo pravitelstva, 1927-35 (Moscow, 1957), p. 432 (extracts). Editor's translation.

70. The 1935 Collective-Farm Charter

17 *February* 1935

This extremely important document was 'standard' for the whole country and was never open to significant modification by individual collective farms. It was the second charter of its kind, the first, a short and rather vague outline, having been approved in March 1930. By the beginning of 1935 some 87 per cent of all peasant households had been collectivized. The standard charter covered the whole range of the collectivized peasant's rights and duties: in many respects— such as residence rights, work obligations, payment for labour and social security —it placed the peasants in a position much inferior to that of the workers, who alone benefited from such protection as the republican labour codes had to offer. In addition the peasants were virtually excluded from trade-union membership. Like all documents of long standing the charter came to acquire its own body of laws. It was replaced by another version in 1969 (see document 79).

70. Standard Charter of an Agricultural Artel [1]

Approved by the Second All-Union Congress of Shock Workers of the Collective Farms and confirmed by the Council of People's Commissars of the USSR and by the Central Committee of the All-Union Communist Party (Bolsheviks) on 17 February 1935

I. Aims and Purposes

1. The toiling peasants of the village (settlement, hamlet, *khutor, kishlak, aul*) of ... ... in the district of ... ... voluntarily join together in an agricultural artel in order to establish, with common means of production and organized, common labour, a collective, i.e. a social farm, to ensure complete victory over the kulaks, and all the exploiters and enemies of the toilers, over want and ignorance, over the backwardness of small individual farming, to create high productivity of labour and, by this means, to ensure the well-being of the members.

The path of collective farming, the path of socialism, is the only right path for the toiling peasants. The members of the artel take upon themselves the obligation to strengthen their artel, to work honestly, to distribute the collective-farm income according to the amount of work done, to guard social property, to take care of collective-farm property, to keep the tractors and machinery in good order, to tend the horses carefully, to execute the

[1] Translated also as the Model or Exemplary Collective-Farm Charter or Statute. (Ed.)

tasks imposed by the workers' and peasants' government in order to make their collective farm a Bolshevik one, and all its members prosperous.

II. The Land

2. All bounds that have hitherto divided the land allotment of the members of the artel shall be abolished, and all individual allotments in the fields shall be converted into a single piece of land, which shall be for the collective use of the artel.

Land occupied by the artel (like any other land in the USSR) is the state property of all the people. Under the laws of the workers' and peasants' state, the use of the land shall be secured to the artel for an indefinite period, that is to say, for ever. The land may be neither sold nor bought nor let by the artel.

The executive committees of the district soviets shall issue to each collective farm a state title-deed securing the use of the land for an indefinite period and fixing the size and exact boundaries of the land used by the artel; this land may not be decreased, but may be increased, out of either the free state land reserve or surplus land occupied by independent [uncollectivized] peasants, always, however, preserving the land of the collective farm in one block.

A small tract of land shall be allocated from the collectivized landholdings for the personal use of each household in the collective farm in the form of a house-and-garden [private] plot (vegetable garden, orchard).

The size of plots assigned for individual use by households (exclusive of the site of the house) may vary from one-quarter of a hectare to one-half of a hectare and, in certain districts, to one hectare, depending upon regional and district conditions, as determined by the people's commissariats for agriculture of the union republics on the basis of directions issued by the USSR People's Commissariat for Agriculture.

3. The landholdings of the artel may in no case be diminished. It is forbidden to provide allotments from the artel's landholdings to members who have left the artel. Departing members may receive allotments only out of the free lands of the state land fund.

The land of the artel shall be divided into separate fields to correspond with the established system of crop rotation. Each field brigade is to work the same piece of land during an established period of crop rotation.

Collective farms which possess large stockbreeding farms may, in case of need, and if they have a sufficient amount of land, parcel out certain tracts of land to the stockbreeding farms for the cultivation of animal fodder.

III. Means of Production

4. The following objects shall be owned only collectively: all draught animals, agricultural implements (ploughs, sowing machines, harrows, threshing machines, mowing machines, etc.), seed reserves, forage necessary for collectively owned livestock, buildings needed for collective farming, and all establishments processing agricultural products.

The following objects shall not be socialized and shall remain in the personal use of the collective-farm household: dwellings, personal cattle and poultry, as well as buildings necessary for keeping such cattle.

When farming implements are pooled, minor implements needed for tilling the house-and-garden plots shall be left to the individual households.

The management of the artel may, if necessary, allot a few horses out of the total number of collectively owned draught animals to serve the personal needs of the members, but on the condition that these services are paid for. The artel shall organize a mixed stockbreeding farm or, if there are large numbers of animals, several specialized stockbreeding farms.

5. In the regions of cultivation of grain, sugar beets, cotton, flax, hemp, potatoes and vegetables, tea and tobacco, each household in the collective farm may have in its individual possession one cow, not more than two calves, one sow with sucklings or, if the management of the collective farm should think it advisable, two sows with sucklings, not more than ten sheep and goats taken together, an unlimited number of fowl and rabbits, and not more than twenty beehives.

In agricultural regions with well-developed stockbreeding, each household in the collective farm may have in its individual possession two or three cows with their calves, two or three sows with sucklings, twenty or twenty-five sheep and goats taken together, an unlimited number of fowl and rabbits, and not more than twenty beehives. Such districts are, for instance, the agricultural districts of Kazakhstan not bordering on nomadic districts, forest districts of White Russia, the Chernigov and Kiev provinces of the Ukraine, the districts of the Baraba Steppes and Altai districts of Western Siberia, the Ishim and Tobolsk groups of districts of the Omsk province, the hilly part of Bashkiria, the eastern part of Eastern Siberia, the agricultural districts of the Far Eastern area, and the Vologda and Kholmogory groups of districts in the northern area.

In non-nomadic or semi-nomadic stockbreeding regions, where agriculture is of small significance and stockbreeding plays the leading part in agriculture, each household in the collective farm may have in its individual possession four or five cows with their calves, thirty or forty sheep and goats in all, two or three sows with sucklings, an unlimited number of fowl and rabbits, not more than twenty beehives, and also one horse or one milking mare or two camels or donkeys or two mules. These districts include, for example, the stockbreeding districts of Kazakhstan bordering on nomadic districts, the stockbreeding districts of Turkmenistan, Tadzhikistan, Kara-Kalpakia, Kirghizia, Oirotia, Khakassia, the western part of Buryat Mongolia, the Kalmyk autonomous region, the hilly districts of the Daghestan autonomous republic, the Checheno-Ingush, Kabarda-Balkarsk, Karachaevsk and Ossetin autonomous provinces of the Northern Caucasus, and also the hilly parts of the Azerbaijan, Armenian, and Georgian soviet socialist republics.

In the districts of nomadic stockbreeding, where agriculture has almost no significance and where stockbreeding is the all-embracing branch of farming, each household in the collective farm may have in its individual possession eight or ten cows with their calves, 100 to 150 sheep and goats in all, an unlimited number of fowl, up to ten horses, five or eight camels. These districts include, for instance, the nomadic districts of Kazakhstan, the Nogai district, and the nomadic districts of Buryat Mongolia.

IV. The Work of the Artel and its Management

6. The artel undertakes to conduct its collective farming according to plan, observing exactly the agricultural-production plans drawn up by the agencies of the workers' and peasants' government, and its obligations towards the state.

The artel takes upon itself to fulfil exactly the programmes of sowing, fallow ploughing, weeding, harvesting, threshing, and autumn ploughing prescribed with regard to the conditions and peculiarities of collective farms, and also the state plan for the development of stockbreeding.

The management and all the members of the artel undertake:

(a) To increase the fertility of the fields of the collective farm by the introduction and observance of correct rotation of crops, deep ploughing, extermination of weeds, increasing and improving fallow and autumn ploughing, timely and careful hoeing of cotton plantations, the application of manure taken from the stockbreeding farms and from households belonging to the collective farms, the application of mineral fertilizers, extermination of pests, timely and careful harvesting without losses, tending and cleaning irrigation works, safeguarding forests, planting trees to shelter the fields and observing strictly all agricultural and technical regulations established by the local land authorities;

(b) To select the best seeds for sowing, to purify them from any admixture, to keep them safe from damage and pilfering, to store them in clean, well-ventilated premises, to increase purebred sowing;

(c) To increase the area sown by utilization of all land at the disposal of the artel, by the improvement and cultivation of waste land, by ploughing up virgin land, and by introduction of effective land distribution within the collective farm;

(d) To make full use, on a collective basis, of all draught animals and traction engines, implements and agricultural machinery, of seeds, and of all the other means of production which the artel possesses, and also of all tractors, motors, threshers, combines, and other machinery which the workers' and peasants' government supplies to the collective farms through the machine-and-tractor stations, to tend livestock and machinery correctly, and to make every endeavour to keep the animals and machinery in the collective farm in good order and condition;

(e) To organize stockbreeding farms and, in those localities where conditions are favourable, horsebreeding farms, to increase the number of animals, to improve the breeds and the fecundity of animals, to help members who work honestly on the collective farm to acquire cows and small cattle; to mate the cows, mares, etc. (not only those collectively owned, but also those which are individually owned by farm members) with improved and purebred bulls, stallions, etc., and to observe the established zoological, technical, and veterinary regulations with respect to stockbreeding;

(f) To increase the production of fodder, to improve meadows and pastures, to render assistance to members who conscientiously work in the socialized sector, and to ensure for them, where possible, the use of the pastures of the collective farm, and also to give them, so far as possible, fodder for the cattle owned by them individually, on account of the labour days credited to them;

(g) To develop all other branches of agricultural production in accordance with local natural conditions, and also to develop home industries in accordance with the conditions prevailing in the district, to care for ponds and keep them clean, to dig new ponds and stock them with fish;

(h) To organize the construction of communal farm buildings by communal labour;

(i) To improve the labour qualifications of the members, and assist them in training to become brigadiers, tractor drivers, combine operators, drivers, veterinary surgeons and sanitary experts, stablemen, sow herders, cowmen, shepherds, field laboratory assistants;

(j) To raise the cultural standards of the members, to introduce newspapers, books, radios, establish clubs, lending libraries, and reading rooms, build public baths and hairdressing shops, construct clean and airy field-camps, keep the village streets in good order, plant various trees, especially fruit trees, and to assist the members in improving and decorating their houses;

(k) To involve the women in the work of the collective farm and the social life of the artel, to appoint capable and experienced women members to managerial posts, and free women from domestic work as much as possible by establishing creches, playgrounds, etc., for their children.

V. Membership

7. Admission to membership shall be granted by the general meeting of the members, which confirms the lists of new members submitted by the board.

All toilers, women as well as men, who have attained the age of sixteen, may join the artel.

No kulaks or persons deprived of the franchise shall be admitted to the artel.

NOTE: From this rule shall be exempt:

(a) Children of the disfranchised who, for a number of years, have been engaged in publicly useful work and who are working conscientiously;
(b) Former kulaks and members of their families who, having been deported for their anti-soviet and anti-collectivist activities, have proved at their place of deportation, for a period of three years, by their honest work and support of the measures passed by the Soviet government, that they have reformed.

Individual peasants who sold their horses in the two years preceding admission to the artel, and who have no seed, shall be admitted to the artel on the condition that they undertake to refund the cost of a horse by instalments out of their income over a period of six years and surrender the required quantity of seed in kind.

8. Members may be expelled from the artel only by a resolution of the general meeting at which not less than two-thirds of the total number of the members are present. The number of members present at the general meeting and the number of votes cast for expulsion should be explicitly stated in the minutes of the meeting. If an expelled member appeals against his expulsion to the District Executive Committee, the case shall be decided finally by the presidium of the District Executive Committee of Soviets in the presence of the chairman of the artel and the appellant.

VI. Funds of the Artel

9. Members admitted to the artel shall pay an entrance fee of from twenty to forty roubles according to the size of their households. The entrance fee shall go to the indivisible fund of the artel.

10. From one-quarter to one-half of the value of the collectively owned property of the members (draught animals, machinery, farm buildings, etc.) shall go into the indivisible fund of the artel; the more well-to-do the

member, the larger the proportion of his property to go into the indivisible fund. The remaining portion of his property shall be considered to be the member's own contribution.

When a member leaves the collective farm, the board settles accounts with him and returns to him his contribution in money; the departing member may then obtain a land allotment only outside the land enclosure belonging to the artel. As a rule, accounts are settled at the end of the agricultural season.

11. Out of the crops and the animal products obtained, the artel shall:

(a) Fulfil its obligations towards the state with respect to deliveries of products and the return of seed loans; pay the machine-and-tractor station in kind for the work it has done in accordance with the contract, which has the force of the law, and fulfil other contracts entered into;

(b) Store seed for the next year's sowing and fodder for animals for the whole year, and create permanent, annually renewed seed and fodder funds of from 10 to 15 per cent of the annual needs, in order to insure itself against crop failure or fodder shortages;

(c) In accordance with the decision of the general meeting, create funds to assist disabled, old, or sick people and poor families of Red Army soldiers, and to support crèches and orphans; all these funds should not exceed 2 per cent of the total annual production;

(d) Fix the proportion of the products which, in accordance with the decision of the general meeting, are to be sold to the state or on the free market;

(e) Distribute all the remaining crops and animal products produced by the artel among its members according to the number of labour days credited to each member.

12. From its money income the artel shall:

(a) Pay to the state taxes established by law and insurance premiums;

(b) Defray expenses necessary to cover the current needs of production, such as current repairs to agricultural machinery and implements, the medical treatment of animals, pest control, etc.

(c) Defray administrative expenses of the artel to the extent of not more than 2 per cent of its total income in money;

(d) Assign money for cultural needs, such as training brigadiers and other staff, organizing crèches and children's playgrounds, installing radios, etc.

(e) Replenish the indivisible funds of the artel for the purchase of cattle, agricultural machinery, and building materials, and for the payment of wages to workers hired from outside for building operations; also for making regular payments to the agricultural bank for long-term credit; at the same time payments from the indivisible funds may be from 10 per cent, but not more than 20 per cent of the money income of the artel.

(f) The remaining cash proceeds of the artel shall be distributed among the members in accordance with the number of labour days credited to each member.

All sums received by the artel shall be entered in the books on the day when the money is received.

The board shall prepare an estimate of revenue and expenditures for the ensuing year, which estimate shall become effective only upon approval by the general meeting.

The board may make expenditures only in accordance with the appropriations provided for in the estimate; arbitrary shifting of funds from one item of the expenditure estimate to another shall not be permitted, and the board is obliged to obtain the consent of the general meeting in order to transfer funds from one item to another.

The artel shall keep its money in a current account at a bank or a savings bank. Debits to the current account shall be made only by order of the board; this order is valid when signed by the farm chairman and the accountant.

VII. Organization and Remuneration of Labour and Labour Discipline

13. All work connected with running the artel shall be performed by the personal labour of its members in accordance with the rules of internal organization approved by the general meeting. Non-members may be engaged for agricultural work only when they possess special knowledge and training (agronomists, engineers, technicians, and so forth).

The hiring of outside casual labour shall be permitted only under exceptional circumstances, when urgent operations cannot be performed in time by the farm members working at full speed, and for building operations.

14. The management shall create production brigades from the members of the artel.

Field brigades shall be formed for the period of crop rotation.

A field brigade shall work the same plot for the period of crop rotation. The management shall, by a special act, secure to each field brigade all necessary machinery, draught animals, and farm buildings.

Members of stockbreeding brigades are formed for a period of not less than three years.

The management shall secure to each stockbreeding brigade productive cattle, as well as implements, draught animals, and the buildings necessary for carrying on animal husbandry.

Work shall be distributed among the members of the brigade by the brigadier, who must make the best possible use of each member of his brigade, without permitting himself to be influenced by family or other personal considerations when allotting the work. He must take into account the qualifications, experience, and physical fitness of each member, and, in cases of pregnant women or nursing mothers, recognize the necessity of alleviating their work. A woman shall be free from all work for a period of one month before and one month after childbirth, and during these two months shall receive remuneration equal to one half of the average number of labour days she normally earns.

15. Agricultural work in the artel is performed on a piece-rate basis.

The board works out, and the general meeting confirms, the required output norms and the rates of remuneration in terms of labour days for all agricultural operations.

Such output norms are fixed for each operation according to what a conscientious collective farmer can produce with the draught animals, machinery, and soil at hand. Each operation, as, for instance, ploughing one hectare, sowing one hectare, or hoeing one hectare of a cotton plantation, threshing one ton of grain, digging out two hundredweight of sugar beets, gathering one hectare of flax, moistening one hectare of flax, drawing one litre of milk, and so on, is to be valued in fractions of a labour day in accordance with the labour qualifications required and the complexity, difficulty, and importance of the operation for the artel.

The brigadier shall, not less than once a week, compute all the work which has been done by a member, and, in accordance with the established remuneration, enter the number of labour days credited to him into his labour book.

The management shall display every month a list of members showing the number of labour days credited to each member during the preceding month.

The annual amount of work and the income earned by each member shall be certified by the brigadier and the chairman of the artel as well as by the accountant. The list showing the number of labour days earned by each member shall be publicly displayed not later than a fortnight before the date of the general meeting which confirms the distribution of the income earned by the artel.

Should a field brigade, by its good work, harvest crops from its plot exceeding the average obtained by the artel, or should a stockbreeding brigade, by its good work, show an increased output of milk per cow, fatten cattle more successfully, or ensure the preservation of all young animals, the management shall increase the remuneration of the members of that brigade by up to 10 per cent of the total labour days credited to them; the best shock workers in the brigade are entitled to a 15 per cent increase, and the brigadier and stockbreeding farm manager to a 20 per cent increase.

Should an agricultural brigade, as a result of bad work, gather crops from its plot below the average obtained by the artel, or should a stockbreeding brigade, as a result of bad work, show a poorer output of milk per cow, poorer fattening of cattle, or greater mortality among young animals, the management shall reduce the credit in labour days of the members of such brigades by up to 10 per cent.

The distribution of income among the members shall be made exclusively according to the number of labour days credited to each member.

16. Money may be advanced to a member during the year to an amount not exceeding 50 per cent of the sum credited to him for his work.

Advances in kind shall be made to the members of the artel by the board after the threshing has begun; from 10 to 15 per cent of the threshed grain left for the needs of the artel may be used for this purpose.

An artel in which industrial crops are cultivated need not wait for the completion of delivery of cotton, flax, sugar, tea, tobacco, etc. to the state before making money advances to its members; these are made not less than once a week in the course of delivery, to the extent of 60 per cent of the money received for the products delivered.

17. All members of the artel shall assume the obligation to take good care of the property of the artel and the state-owned machinery used in the fields of the artel, to work honestly, to observe the provisions of the charter, to carry out the resolutions of the general meeting and the orders of the board, to follow the rules of internal organization of the artel, to execute conscientiously the tasks and social duties imposed upon them by the board and brigadiers, and to observe labour discipline strictly.

Members who fail to take good care of, or neglect, the collective property, who fail to report for work without justifiable reason, who work badly, or who violate labour discipline or the charter, shall be punished by the board in accordance with the rules of internal organization. For example, such a member may be ordered to do poor work over again without credit in labour days, he may be warned, reprimanded, or reproved at the general meeting, his name may be put up on the blackboard, he may be fined up to five labour days, he may be demoted to a lower-paid job or suspended from work.

In cases where all the measures of an educational and penal nature applied by the artel fail, the board raises the question of expelling incorrigible members from the artel at a general meeting.

Expulsion shall be carried out in accordance with the procedure provided for in Article 8 of the present Charter.

18. Any dissipation of collective and government property or reckless handling of the property and livestock of the collective farm or MTS machinery shall be deemed by the artel a betrayal of the common cause of the collective farm and aid to the enemies of the people.

Persons guilty of such criminal disruption of the bases of collective farming shall be passed to the courts to be punished in accordance with all the severity of the laws of the workers' and peasants' state.

VIII. Management of the Artel

19. The affairs of the artel shall be managed by the general meeting of the members, and, in the intervals between the meetings, by the board elected by the general meeting.

20. The general meeting shall be the highest authority in the management of the artel. The general meeting shall:

(a) Elect the chairman and the members of the board of the artel and also the auditing committee; the auditing committee shall be confirmed by the District Executive Committee of Soviets;

(b) Admit new members to and expel members from the artel;

(c) Confirm the programme of annual production, the estimate of revenue and expenditures, the building programme, the output norms, and remuneration rates in terms of labour days;

(d) Confirm the contract with the machine-and-tractor station;

(e) Confirm the annual report of the board, accompanied by the conclusions of the auditing committee, and also the reports of the board on the most important agricultural campaigns;

(f) Confirm the size of the various funds to be put aside and the amount of produce and money to be distributed per labour day;

(g) Confirm the rules of internal organization governing the conduct of artel affairs.

The decisions of the board affecting the matters enumerated in the present section of the Charter shall be null and void if not confirmed by the general meeting.

A quorum for the general meeting shall be not less than one-half of the membership of the artel; this quorum may decide all matters except the election of a chairman and members of the board, the expulsion of members, and the size of various funds; for resolutions upon these matters the presence of not less than two-thirds of the membership is required.

Resolutions of the general meeting are passed by a majority in an open vote.

21. To run the business of the artel, the general meeting elects for a period of two years a board of from five to nine persons depending on the size of the artel.

The board functions as the executive organ of the artel and is responsible to the general meeting for the work of the artel and for the fulfilment of its obligations to the state.

22. For the day-to-day management of the work of the artel and its brigades, and for day-to-day checking on the execution of the decisions of the board, the general meeting elects a chairman of the artel, who is also chairman of the board.

The chairman is obliged to convoke the board not less than twice a month to discuss current business and take the necessary decisions.

Upon the recommendation of the chairman, and to assist him, the board elects a vice-chairman from among its members.

The vice-chairman follows the directives of the chairman in all his work.

23. Brigadiers and managers of stockbreeding farms are appointed by the board for a period of not less than two years.

24. The board appoints from among the members of the artel, or hires from outside, an accountant to keep accounts and records of property. The accountant keeps accounts and records in accordance with the prescribed forms and is absolutely subordinate to the board and to the chairman of the artel.

The accountant has no right to dispose of the funds of the artel independently, to make advance payments, or to expend the stocks of produce. This right belongs only to the board and the chairman of the artel. All orders for payment must be signed by the chairman or the vice-chairman of the artel in addition to the accountant.

25. The auditing committee verifies all the board's economic and financial activities, i.e., ascertains whether all revenues in money and in kind are duly credited to the artel books, whether the procedure prescribed by the Charter for expenditures is being followed, whether the property of the artel is kept properly, whether there has been any theft or waste of the property or funds of the artel, whether the artel meets its obligations to the state and whether the artel pays its own debts and collects debts from its debtors.

In addition, the auditing committee carefully ascertains how the artel settles its accounts with its members and brings to light any case of cheating, inaccurate accreditation of labour days, delay in distributing income for labour days, or any other violation of the interests of the artel and its members.

The auditing committee audits the accounts four times a year. The auditing committee reports to the general meeting on the annual accounts submitted by the board, this being heard by the general meeting immediately after the board's report.

The auditing committee is responsible to the general meeting of the members of the artel for its work.

Source: N. D. Kazantsev, i drugie, *Istoria kolkhoznogo prava*, Vol. I (Moscow, 1959), p. 427.

Translation: V. Gsovski, *Soviet Civil Law*, Vol. I (Michigan University Press, Ann Arbor, 1948), p. 441. The terminology has been somewhat modernized by the editor (with the removal of post-1936 amendments to Article 12).

71. Against Abuses of the Charter

19 *April* 1938

The kind of abuse described in this ominous decree evidently arose when the labour on the collective farms was comparatively plentiful, and farm or outside officials coveted the possessions or the land farmed by ordinary members. The measure is also interesting as a reflection of the power which the local party and state authorities wielded over the internal workings of the collective farm, and the ruthlessness with which they exercised it.

71. On Prohibiting the Expulsion of Collective Farmers from Collective Farms

Joint resolution of the USSR Council of People's Commissars and the Central Committee of the Communist Party, 19 *April* 1938

The USSR Council of People's Commissars and the Central Committee of the Party have several times warned the Party and the soviet organizations of the harm caused by the mass expulsion of collective farmers from collective farms. The Council of People's Commissars and the CC have pointed out several times that such a practice is anti-party and anti-state. Nevertheless, in many regions, provinces, and republics, unjustifiable expulsion has in fact taken place ...[1]

Experience shows that the boards and the chairmen of collective farms, instead of observing the Charter of the Agricultural Artel and barring any arbitrary treatment of the collective farmers, are themselves the perpetrators of unlawful acts. A checkup has established that, in the overwhelming majority of cases, expulsions from the collective farms are devoid of any grounds whatsoever and undertaken without any serious motivation and for the most unimportant reasons. The most frequent type of expulsion concerns members of families of which the father has left for temporary or permanent work in state enterprises. Such expulsion on the basis of family ties is contrary to the very principles of the Charter of the Agricultural Artel ...

Leading party and soviet workers in the localities, instead of moderating and correcting the harmful practice of expulsion, fail to take decisive steps to preclude arbitrary treatment of collective farmers, show a heartless and bureaucratic attitude towards the fate of collective farmers and their appeals against unlawful expulsion from the farms, allow persons who arbitrarily

[1] The passage omitted describes many instances of such expulsion.

mistreat collective farmers to go unpunished, and often reduce their own role merely to recording the fact of expulsion and submitting statistical reports on them to superior soviet agencies. Moreover, these officials themselves often induce the chairmen and boards of collective farms to tread the path of unlawful expulsion under the banner of purging the collective farms of socially foreign and hostile class elements.

The USSR Council of People's Commissars and the Central Committee of the Communist Party consider that such a practice is based upon the formalistic and heartless bureaucratic attitude of many collective-farm managers, as well as of local officials of the Communist Party and state agencies, toward the fate of living people, the individual members of collective farms. Such managers fail to realize that expulsion from a collective farm means that the person expelled is deprived of his source of subsistence; it means that he is not only exposed to public disgrace but also condemned to hunger. They fail to understand that expulsion from collective farms breeds artificial discontent and bad feeling among those expelled. It creates among many collective farmers a sense of insecurity about their status in the collective farm, and can only play into the hands of the enemies of the people.

The USSR Council of People's Commissars and the Central Committee of the Communist Party have therefore resolved that:

1. All purges in collective farms, under any pretext whatsoever, shall be prohibited.

2. Expulsion from collective farms of people from families, one member of whom has gone away to work temporarily or permanently in a state enterprise, shall be prohibited.

3. Expulsion for violation of internal farm rules shall be prohibited.

4. It shall be established that, in the future, expulsion from a collective farm may be applied only as an extreme measure against members who have proved themselves to be obviously incorrigible, subversive, or disruptive to the collective farm, only after all preventive and educational measures provided for in the Charter have been exhausted, and in strict observance of the procedure for expulsion set out in the Charter, i.e., by decision of a general meeting attended by at least two-thirds of the members of the artel.

However, even in such cases, considerable attention must be devoted to the appeal of the expelled member.

5. It shall be established that the decision of the general meeting ordering expulsion shall not take legal effect, and the expelled member shall retain all the rights of a farm member, until the district executive committee has finally examined the decision.

6. Chairmen and members of collective-farm boards, as well as district officials of the party and state agencies, are hereby warned that persons guilty of violating the present resolution shall be brought to justice as criminals.

Source: N. D. Kazantsev, i drugie, (eds.) *Istoria kolkhoznogo prava*, Vol. II (Moscow, 1958), p. 41.
Translation: V. Gsovski, *Soviet Civil Law*, Vol. I (Michigan University Press, Ann Arbor, 1948), p. 460. See the editor's note to document 70.

72. Stronger Controls on the Peasant (extracts)

27 May 1939

It was evident from the proceedings of the Eighteenth Party Congress in March 1939 that the Soviet leadership was not satisfied with the controls over the peasant, who was evidently still obsessed with the notion of individual farming and reluctant to accept the spirit of collectivization. The resolution reproduced below marked a new and harsher stage in the party drive against the private sector. As a result of the new restrictions described here the holdings of private plots were reduced in some areas by as much as half, and many of the remaining uncollectivized households were driven into neighbouring collectives. The new obligatory minimum of labour days apparently caused labour inputs to rise by 8 per cent for men and 15 per cent for women in the following year.

72. On Measures to Protect Public Lands in the Collective Farms from being Squandered

Joint resolution of the Central Committee of the Communist Party and the USSR Council of People's Commissars of 27 May 1939

The Central Committee of the Communist Party and the USSR Council of People's Commissars have established the occurrence of serious distortions of party policy in the sphere of collective-farm land tenure. These distortions violate the clause of article 2 of the Charter relating to the standard size of the house-and-garden plots assigned for individual use, in particular their expansion through the squandering and dissipation of collectively held fields for the benefit of individual farming.

The dispersion and seizure of the collective farms' socialized lands for the benefit of individual farming include various kinds of unlawful additions to house-and-garden plots, which are thus increased beyond the size provided for in the Charter, either on the pretext of feigned separations of families, where a household fraudulently obtains an additional plot for members who pretend to have split off from it, or by direct allocation of house-and-garden plots to collective farmers out of the collective farms' socialized lands.

As a result of such anti-collective and anti-state practices, the interests of the collective farm, which are founded on public, collectivized land, are sacrificed to private ownership and avarice, and to people who use the collective farms for the purpose of speculation and personal profit.

In a number of collective farms, the practice has arisen of transforming the house-and-garden plot into the private property of the households so that the individual member, rather than the collective farm, disposes of it at his own discretion, i.e., he rents it out or retains it for his own use, although he himself does not work in the collective farm ...

The Central Committee of the Communist Party and the USSR Council of People's Commissars have resolved:

1. The practice of district and regional organizations of the Party and state, of the boards of collective farms and state land agencies, which allows such violations of the Standard Charter of the Agricultural Artel regarding land tenure in collective farms as the criminal squandering of collectively held land for the benefit of individual members of collective farms, is hereby condemned as anti-party and anti-state.

2. The collectively held land of the collective farms is inviolable, and its acreage shall under no circumstances be diminished without the special permission of the USSR government; it may only be enlarged.

3. Any attempt to reduce the collectively held land for the benefit of individual husbandry, as well as any increase of private plots in excess of the norms stipulated in the Standard Charter of the Agricultural Artel, shall be regarded as a criminal act, and those guilty of it are liable to prosecution.

4. Secretaries of the district Communist Party committees, presidents of the district executive committees, and other party and state officials who tolerate the dissipation of collectively held land and the extension of private plots are liable to dismissal, expulsion from the Party, and prosecution as violators of the law.

5. Members of collective farms who permit the lease of the house-and-garden plots assigned for their personal use or transfer them to others shall be expelled from the collective farms and deprived of such plots.

6. Chairmen of collective farms who allow the hay in the collectively held fields, meadows, and forests to be mown privately by individual members of the collective farm or persons who are not members shall be expelled from the collective farms and prosecuted for violation of the law...

8. Fields used by an uncollectivized peasant household are to be limited as follows: in irrigated cotton-growing areas—to ten hundredths of a hectare; in non-irrigated cotton-growing areas—to half a hectare; in market gardening and beet-growing areas—to half a hectare; and in all other areas—to one hectare. The private plot used by an uncollectivized peasant household, including the land which is built on, is to be limited to ten hundredths of a hectare in irrigated areas and twenty hundredths of a hectare in all others.

All land in excess of these norms, fields as well as the house-and-garden plots of independent households, shall be merged with the land of the collective farms and used primarily to replenish the land reserve of collective farms assigned for house-and-garden plots.

The following are also to be used for building up a fund of land for house-and-garden plots in the collective farms: (a) the house-and-garden plots of false collective farmers who have long since severed their ties with the life of the collective farm and have in fact left it; (b) the house-and-garden plots of collective farmers who do not earn the established minimum of labour days and are therefore considered to have left the collective farm; (c) the house-and-garden plots of collective farmers who emigrate from regions with small landholdings to regions where land is abundant …

14. Since the collective farms contain not only honest workers who earn from 200 to 600 or more labour days annually, and who constitute the overwhelming majority of collective farmers, representing the main force of the collective-farm movement, but also a number of able-bodied collective farmers who earn less than 20–60 labour days a year and who nevertheless continue to be counted as collective farmers and hamper the collective farm, it has been considered appropriate to establish, from 1939, a mandatory annual minimum of labour days for each collective farmer, man or woman, as follows:

(a) One hundred labour days in cotton-growing regions;
(b) Sixty labour days in the Moscow, Leningrad, Ivanovo, Yaroslav, Gorky, Kalinin, Vologda, Tula, Riazan, Smolensk, Archangel, Murmansk, Kirov, Perm, Sverdlov and Chita regions, Khabarov and Primorsk provinces, and the Karelian, Komi, Mari, and Yakut autonomous republics, and in the highland grain-producing districts and the cattle-raising districts entered on a list by the USSR People's Commissariat for Agriculture;
(c) Eighty labour days for all other districts of the USSR.

The collective farms are hereby advised to rule that able-bodied collective farmers, men or women, who during the year earn less than the above-mentioned norm shall be considered to have left the collective farm and to have lost their right to membership of it.

15. In view of the fact that the land used collectively by the collective farms cannot be reduced, and since the reserves of land available for assignment to individual house-and-garden plots of statutory size are exhausted in farms already suffering from a shortage of land, it is necessary to resettle collective farmers from such farms in regions with an abundance of land (the Volga, Omsk, and Cheliabinsk regions, Altai province, Kazakhstan, the Far East, etc.).

A Resettlement Administration shall be established and attached to the USSR Council of People's Commissars for guidance in matters involving the resettlement of superfluous collective farmers to regions where land is abundant.

16. Families of workers and employees who live permanently on and belong to collective farms shall retain house-and-garden plots of the established size only when the able-bodied members of such families work in the collective farms and fulfil the required minimum of labour days.

17. A congress of collective farmers is to be convened in the autumn of 1939

to consider the question of amendments to the Charter of the Agricultural Artel.

Source: N. D. Kazantsev, i drugie, (eds.) *Istoria kolkhoznogo prava*, Vol. II (Moscow, 1958), p. 107.
Translation: V. Gsovski, op. cit., p. 475 (extracts). See the editor's note to document 70.

73. The Collective Farm System Re-established

19 *September* 1946

The occupation of a large part of European Russia and the Ukraine by the Germans during the war caused the collective-farm system to disintegrate. According to official sources, some 5½ million hectares of collective-farm land were misappropriated during these years; unproductive administrative staffs swelled far over official norms, many outsiders got themselves illegally registered as collective-farm members, and local officials frequently used their authority to spoliate farm property. The decree reproduced below reflected official dismay at these developments and heralded the reaffirmation of the former controls. Persons guilty of the misdeeds listed were now made specifically subject to criminal prosecution. The Council for Collective Farm Affairs (see Article 10) which was to serve as the main instrument in this cause was constituted a few days later under the chairmanship of A. A. Andreev.

73. On Measures for Liquidating Violations of the Charter of the Agricultural Artel in the Collective Farms

Decree of the Council of Ministers of the USSR and Central Committee of the VKP(B), 19 *September* 1946

The USSR Council of Ministers and the Central Committee of the All-Union Communist Party (Bolsheviks) have established, on the basis of material received and a check-up made in several regions, that the Charter of the Agricultural Artel is being seriously violated in the collective farms.

These violations consist of the improper use of labour days, the dissipation of the collectively held land, the spoliation of collective-farm property, abuses of power by district and other party and soviet officials, and the violation of the democratic basis of management of the affairs of the collective farm, in particular the principle that the boards and chairmen of the farms should be elected by and present accounts to the general meetings of the collective farmers.

Improper Crediting of Labour Days

Improper crediting of labour days in the collective farms takes the form of inflating the executive and service staff and an exceedingly high expenditure of labour days and money on administration and management.

The improper utilization of labour, caused by an unfounded and extravagant increase of administrative and managerial jobs, has resulted in many collective farms experiencing a shortage of able-bodied collective farmers for work in the fields and animal husbandry units. At the same time many people employed in various services do nothing but receive a higher pay than those employed on productive jobs.

Grafters and parasites frequently hide themselves in useless, artificially invented jobs, thereby avoiding productive work, eating up the savings of the collective farms and living on the labour of those collective farmers who work in the fields and tend the cattle.

The Charter of an Agricultural Artel is violated in many collective farms in consequence of improper settlements with the collective farmers. Some of the members may not receive in full the products and money due to them in accordance with the labour days they have earned, while others receive more than is due to them in accordance with the labour days earned.

The harmful practice of issuing products to individual collective farmers irrespective of the number of labour days earned, on the basis of a note from the Chairman, has become widespread.

Along with these irregularities, in many collective farms persons who have no relation to the farm whatsoever, such as duty officers, watchmen and messengers of the village soviets, chiefs of fire departments, and supplementary officials of the village soviets and district organizations, are kept at the expense of the collective farms and are credited with labour days at the request of the local government agencies. Moreover, barbers, shoemakers, tailors, and other workers, who serve personal needs of the collective farmers and should, therefore, be paid by them personally, are very often credited in the collective farms with labour days.

The harmful practice of crediting labour days for work done for various village and district organizations and offices (erection and repair of buildings, procurement of firewood and building material, loading of cargoes and the like) is also to be found.

Such instances of dissipation of labour days result in the devaluation of the labour day, the diminution of income available for distribution for it, and a fall in the collective farmer's interest in the collective work.

Seizure of Collectively Held Land

It is the duty of the soviet and party agencies and the land offices to protect the land held collectively by the collective farms from seizure, as the USSR Council of People's Commissars and the Central Committee of the Communist Party warned in the Resolution of 27 May 1939. However, the facts and verification show that this resolution has in fact been forgotten by many officials and the plundering of collectively held land has again acquired a mass character.

This takes the form of enlargement of the house-and-garden plots of collective farmers by means of unauthorized seizure or illegal additions effected by the board and the chairmen of collective farms to extend their own holdings to the detriment of the public sector.

The plundering of collective land also occurs through illegal assignment by local government and land authorities, and even by unauthorized seizure of collectively held land by all kinds of organizations and persons under the guise of creating on collective land various auxiliary enterprises and individual vegetable gardens for workers and employees. Such seizure of collective land frequently occurs with the connivance of the boards of the collective farms, and the presidents of village and district soviets. It is understood that illegal seizure of collective land of collective farms for enterprises of any kind diminishes the collective farms' land fund, undermines collective farming and encourages seizure of collective lands in the farms by various self-seeking elements.

The seizure of collectively held lands, as was stated in the above-mentioned Resolution of 27 May 1939, leads to a situation in which *the interests of the collective farm, which are founded on public collectivized land, are sacrificed to private ownership and avarice and to people who use the collective farms for the purpose of speculation and personal profit.*

Pilferage of Collective-Farm Property

Instances of abuse, involving the pilferage of property by district and other party and state officials, have been established. Pilferage of collective-farm property takes the form of removing from the collective farm, free of charge or at a low price, collective cattle, grain, seed, fodder, meat, milk, butter, honey, vegetables, fruits and the like. Some district officials of the party, state and land offices, instead of strictly protecting public property as the basis of collective farming, commit gross infractions of Soviet law and, by abuse of their official status, illegally dispose of collective-farm property and income in kind and money by forcing the boards and chairmen of the collective farms to give them, free of charge or at a low price, property, cattle, and produce belonging to the collective farms.

These facts show that some officials holding responsible jobs have chosen the path of arbitrary administration and lawlessness with regard to the collective farms, and have begun shamelessly to dig into the property of the collective farms as though into their own pockets.

It is easy to realize that such abuses undermine the welfare of the collective farms, corrupt the leading cadres on the collective farms and prompt them in turn to commit all sorts of illegal acts.

In addition, an irresponsible attitude toward the settling of accounts with the collective farms is to be found among a number of state and other organizations. They do not pay the collective farms on time for produce delivered or work done, and this weakens the farms' economy.

Violation of the Democratic Basis of Collective-Farm Management

The Council of Ministers and the Central Committee of the Communist Party have established the presence in the collective farms of serious violations of the Charter of the Agricultural Artel regarding the election of the leading bodies of these farms—the boards, chairmen, auditing committees—and regarding the regular convocation of general meetings and submission of accounts to the general meeting of the members by the chairmen and boards.

These violations are manifested in the fact that, in many collective farms, general meetings of members are no longer convened and the members are thereby deprived of the chance to participate in the affairs of the collective farms; in fact, all the business of the agricultural artel, including the distribution of income, economic plans, and disposition of all material resources, is decided only by the board and the chairman, who do not submit any report on their activities to the general meeting.

As a result of this violation of democratic principles, general meetings to elect the board, chairman, and the auditing commission are not convened for several years, and the terms of office and conditions for election of chairman and boards provided for in the Charter are not observed. The matter has reached such a point of outrage that chairmen are appointed and dismissed by the district party and state organizations without the knowledge of the collective farmers. All this leads to a situation in which the chairmen of the collective farms cease to feel themselves responsible to the collective farmers, are independent of them, and lose touch with them. This is a distortion of the fundamentals of the Charter of the Agricultural Artel and a violation of democratic relations between the leadership of the collective farms and the collective farmers that inflicts serious damage on the cause of consolidating the collective farms.

The USSR Council of Ministers and the Central Committee of the Communist Party consider the above-mentioned abuses and offences extremely harmful for the cause of collective farming and extremely dangerous for all socialist construction in our country.

The USSR Council of Ministers and the Central Committee of the Communist Party consider that the harmful practice of distorting party and state policy, a practice which is alien to Leninism, must be resolutely and irrevocably stopped.

The USSR Council of Ministers and the Central Committee of the Communist Party have resolved that:

1. The distortions of the policy of the Party and state in the organization of collective farms and violations of the Charter of the Agricultural Artel indicated in this Resolution are hereby condemned as anti-collective and anti-state and those guilty of such distortions shall be brought to justice as criminals.

2. The leaders of the party and state organizations in the union republics as well as the leaders of regional and provincial organizations must urgently liquidate violations of the Charter of the Agricultural Artel, restore the full effect of the Charter, and preserve the collective farms against encroachment on their property.

3. The practice of stealing labour days in the collective farms and the improper distribution of farm income shall be ended.

Within two months swollen administrative and service staff in the collective farms must be verified and reduced, together with the number of labour days used to pay them. Administrative and management expenses must be brought into accord with the Charter of the Agricultural Artel.

Persons who are not connected with the collective farms shall be deprived of credit in labour days, and the district soviet and party organizations are forbidden to ask the collective farms to pay for work which does not pertain to the farms in labour days.

4. The leaders of party and soviet organizations, and the leaders of regional and provincial organizations, are obliged to restore the full effect of the Resolution of 27 May 1939, 'On measures to protect public lands in the collective farms from being squandered' (SP SSSR, 1939, No. 34, Article 235).

Prior to 15 November 1946, in each collective farm, the size of the collectively held fields and house-and-garden plots must be checked up on the spot, and the data collated with the entries in the land-record books; the land illegally seized by individual collective farmers or by organizations and offices for auxiliary enterprises shall be taken away from them and restored to the collective farms.

Within the same period of time, complete documentation of the land records of the collective farms (acts, record books, and the like) shall be restored.

Article 2 of the Resolution of the USSR Council of People's Commissars and the Central Committee of the Communist Party of 7 April 1942, which was in effect during the war and permitted the councils of people's commissars of the union-republics regional and provincial executive committees to allow industrial enterprises, institutions, organizations and military units to till unused collective-farm land with the permission of the farms for the duration of the war is hereby repealed, and all land temporarily transferred on the basis of that decree shall be restored to the collective farms by 15 November 1946.

5. The officials of soviet, party and land offices and the chairmen of the collective farms who are guilty of dissipation or unlawful disposition of collective-farm property, collectively held land, or money, shall be dismissed and brought to justice as violators of the law and enemies of the collective-farm system.

It shall be the duty of the councils of ministers of the republics, regional and provincial executive committees, the central committees of the Communist Party of the union republics, and the regional and provincial committees of the Party to secure within a period of two months the restoration to the collective farms of the property, cattle and money unlawfully taken from them, and to report within one month to the Council of Ministers and the Central Committee of the Communist Party concerning steps taken against those guilty of seizing collective-farm property.

6. District and other organizations and officials are hereby forbidden under penalty of criminal law to demand grain, produce, or money from collective farms for the needs of organizations of any kind, for conducting conventions, conferences, celebrations, or the financing of local construction.

7. The leaders of the party and soviet organizations of the union republics and the leaders of the regional and provincial organizations must, within three months, bring the accounts of various organizations with the collective farms into proper order, liquidate all the debts of various organizations and institutions to the collective farms, and establish a method of timely and honest payment to the collective farms for their produce and work done in future.

8. The democratic procedure provided for in the Charter requires the calling of general meetings for discussing collective-farm business and making decisions about it, electing the boards and chairmen, and covers the accountability of the boards, chairmen and auditing commissions. This procedure, which has been violated in many collective farms, is to be restored.

The district party and soviet committees and land offices are strictly forbidden to appoint or dismiss chairmen of collective farms independently of the general meetings of collective farmers.

General meetings of members shall be held in all collective farms by 15 February 1947 to hear reports on the results of economic activities for 1946 and to conduct the elections of the boards, chairmen, and auditing commissions in all instances where their terms of office have expired or when the general meeting resolves to do so prematurely.

9. The Councils of Ministers of the republics, regional and provincial executive committees, the central committees of the Communist Parties of the union republics, and the regional and provincial party committees, are obliged to submit, by 1 January 1947, to the USSR Council of Ministers and the Central Committee of the Communist Party, a report on the execution of the present regulation.

10. A Council for Collective-Farm Affairs is to be created under the government of the USSR to establish strict supervision of the observance of the Charter of the Agricultural Artel, protect collective farmers from attempts to violate the Charter, and decide questions pertaining to the organization of collective-farm construction.

Source: N. D. Kazantsev, op. cit., Vol. II, p. 291.
Translation: V. Gsovski, op. cit., p. 487. See the editor's note to document 70.

74. The Khrushchev Amalgamation Drive

17 July 1950

The amalgamation of collective farms was intended not only to improve the economic organization of agriculture, but also to strengthen party control of this traditionally weak sector. As specifically stated, the decree did not permit any easing of the financial pressures on the peasant. The amalgamation campaign was led by N. S. Khrushchev, who in that year replaced A. A. Andreev as the Politburo member responsible for agriculture. It was stated at the Nineteenth Party Congress that the number of collective farms had fallen from a quarter of a million to 97,000. There was, however, little evidence of improvement in agriculture as a result.

74. On Measures Connected with the Amalgamation of Small Collective Farms and the Associated Tasks of Party Organizations

Decree of the Council of Ministers of the USSR, 17 July 1950

The Council of Ministers of the USSR decrees that:

1. With the object of removing small-strip farming, wedge farming[1] and other shortcomings in the use of land in amalgamated collective farms, the Councils of the Ministers of the republics, and the executive committees of *kraiya* and *oblasti*, may, at the request of *raion* executive committees, and with the agreement of the collective farms, approve plans for fixing new boundaries for amalgamated collective farms without reducing the overall amount of land at the disposition of small collective farms which have amalgamated, and also transfer to the amalgamated collective farms small plots (of up to 100 hectares) of state forest land or the land of other users which is hedged around by collective-farm land, with the knowledge of these land-users.

2. When amalgamating small collective farms, the size of the garden plots and the collective-farm household norms for personal holdings of cattle are, as a rule, to be preserved within the limits enjoyed in accordance with the statute before amalgamation.

A change in the size of the garden plot and such cattle-holding norms may be made within the limits of the norms set down in the statute of the agricultural artel, and within the limits of the stock of land available for garden plots in the amalgamated collective farms, at the decision of the general

[1] *vklinivanie* in Russian.

assembly of collective farmers, by a majority of not less than two-thirds of the votes cast.

3. When uniting small collective farms the amalgamated farm is to take over the new 1950 delivery obligations of all agricultural products to the state, these being calculated as the sum of obligations and the sum of contractual agreements of the collective farms which have been brought together.

The Ministry of Procurement, together with the Councils of Ministers of the republics, and the executive committees of the *oblasti* and *kraiya*, must establish for the amalgamated collective farms standardized state delivery norms covering agricultural products of all kinds, on the condition that the volume of procurement of agricultural products set for the collective farms before amalgamation is preserved.

4. When small collective farms are amalgamated, the state obligations of the farms so united with regard to loans from the Agricultural and State Banks, the tax on their income, the obligatory insurance of salaried staff, together with other obligations to the state or to co-operative enterprises, institutions and organizations, are to be taken over fully by the united collective farm. Obligations to the Agricultural and State Banks and notices of payment relating to the newcomers are reformulated in the name of the amalgamated collective farm in the course of one month after the *raion* executive committee has examined the decisions of the general assemblies of collective farms with regard to the union.

5. Councils of Ministers of union and autonomous republics, and the executive committees of *kraiya* and *oblasti*, are to be allowed to grant individual amalgamated collective farms, by way of exception, in the second half of 1950,

(a) with the agreement of the Agricultural and State Banks, an extension of not more than three months for the repayment of loans to the Agricultural and State Banks which are overdue on the day of union;

(b) with the agreement of the Agricultural Bank, an extension of time for repaying debts on contributions payable into the indivisible funds for past years still outstanding on the day of union, these debts to be covered in the fourth quarter of 1950 and the first quarter of 1951.

6. The Ministry of Forestry of the USSR and the Ministry of Agriculture of the USSR are obliged to present to the Council of Ministers of the USSR, within ten days, proposals for allotting to the Councils of Ministers of republics and the executive committees of *kraiya* and *oblasti*, in the second half of 1950, extra areas of forest suitable for felling to meet the construction needs of amalgamated collective farms.

7. The Councils of Ministers of the union and autonomous republics and the executive committees of *kraiya* and *oblasti* are to be permitted to call in, for a period of up to six months, land-use specialists working in various

institutions, organizations and enterprises, to determine land uses in amalgamated collective farms.

The wage which these specialists were receiving at their permanent place of work is to be maintained for them during their work in the amalgamated collective farms.

Source: V. N. Malin and A. V. Korobov (eds.), *Direktivy KPSS i sovetskogo pravitelstva po khozyaistvennym voprosam*, Vol. 3 (Moscow, 1958), p. 534.
Editor's translation.

75. Khrushchev Criticizes Agricultural Stagnation under Stalin

3 *September* 1953

Khrushchev's immense speech (which ran to well over thirty thousand words) marked another turning point in the history of Soviet agriculture. The parts which we have chosen for translation here contained his general comments on the sorry state of Soviet agriculture at the death of Stalin. Significantly, his explanations did not include any criticism of the collective-farm system as such, nor was there any suggestion that he or his colleagues were in any way to blame for the failures. The concessions made to the peasant at this plenum included tax reductions, a rise in the prices paid for above-quota grain deliveries to the state, a cut in the compulsory-delivery quotas for animal products and vegetables, and some easing of the pressure on private husbandry.

75. On Measures for the Further Development of Soviet Agriculture

From N. S. Khrushchev's report at the Plenum of the CC CPSU,
3 *September* 1953

I. The State of Agriculture and the Task of Creating an Abundance of Agricultural Products

The collective-farm system which was set up under the leadership of the Communist Party has decisive advantages over all kinds of private agricultural production, be it small-scale, or of a large-scale capitalist type. In place of the old rural system with 25 million dispersed private households, there has been created and consolidated a system of socialist agriculture which is the largest in the world. The socialist system of agriculture in our country now embraces 94,000 collective farms, 8,950 machine-and-tractor stations, and more than 4,700 state farms ...

However we must honestly admit that we use the enormous reserves hidden in large-scale socialist agricultural production badly. We have many backward and even neglected collective farms and whole regions. In many collective farms and regions the harvests of agricultural produce continue to be low. The efficiency of agricultural production, particularly of livestock rearing, animal feeds, potatoes and vegetables is growing very slowly. An obvious discrepancy has arisen between the growth rate of our large-scale socialist industry, the urban population, and the material well-being of the working masses on the one hand, and the present level of agricultural production on the other.

Several facts may be adduced by way of illustration. Between 1913 and 1952 the overall production of heavy industry in the USSR grew (in comparable prices) twenty-seven times; this includes the production of the means of production, which grew forty-seven times. The growth of socialist industry is linked with a speed-up in the growth of the urban population, the size of which increased more than three times between 1926 and 1952. As the wealth of socialist society increases the material well-being of the toilers registers a steady growth. At the present time the real wage of worker and employees in the USSR is several times higher than the pre-revolutionary level. This means that our country gets richer as every year goes by, the material sufficiency of the toilers increases, and naturally, at the same time, greater demands are made on agriculture.

Yet the rate of development of socialist agriculture clearly lags behind the rate of growth of industry and the growth of the population's requirements of consumer goods. Suffice it to say that whereas, between 1940 and 1952, industrial production grew 2·3 times, the overall production of agriculture (in comparable prices) rose only by 10 per cent ...

What are the reasons for the insufficient level of agricultural production in general and the lag in a number of important branches of agriculture?

The Communist Party has consistently followed a course of developing heavy industry to the greatest possible extent as an essential condition for the successful development of all branches of the national economy, and in so doing it has achieved major successes. Most attention was paid to solving this primary economic problem, and our main efforts and funds were devoted to it. Our best cadres worked in the cause of industrialization. We had no opportunity to ensure that heavy industry and agriculture, and light industry, developed simultaneously at a rapid rate. It was necessary to create the proper conditions for this. Now that has been done. We have a powerful industrial base, well-consolidated collective farms, and trained cadres in all spheres of economic construction.

But there are other reasons for the lag in a number of important branches of agriculture, reasons which are rooted in shortcomings of our work and in the shortcomings of agricultural management, that is, reasons which depend on us personally.

Among these are, firstly, the violation, in a number of branches of agriculture, of the principle of material interest.[1] The principle of the material interest of the enterprise and each worker individually in the results of their labour is one of the basic principles of socialist management. V. I. Lenin showed that the transition to Communism needs many years, and that in this period of transition the economy should be built 'not directly on enthusiasm, but with the help of enthusiasm which is born of a great revolution, on personal interest and personal gain, and on economic accounting

[1] Meaning financial interest or gain. (Trans.)

366

methods'. Otherwise, V. I. Lenin went on to show, 'You will not get to Communism, neither will you lead tens and tens of millions of people to Communism.'[1]

At the same time facts show that the principle of interesting and encouraging workers materially is not applied in many important branches of agriculture.

This in the first place applies to livestock-rearing. We have calculations which show that the return on the delivery and sale of cotton by the collective farms to the state per labour day spent on this work comprised from 17 to 36 roubles in the republics of Central Asia; it was 12 roubles for sugar-beet in the Ukrainian Republic, and about 18 roubles for the sale of technical crops throughout the USSR as a whole. In regions with a high level of mechanization, like, for example, the Northern Caucasus, the collective farms pay out 8 to 14 roubles per labour day spent on grain crops. At the same time the payment for a labour day spent on livestock-rearing comprises on average only 5 roubles for the delivery and sale of the product in the USSR as a whole, and is little more than 4 roubles in the Ukraine. Thus livestock-rearing is in a disadvantageous position as compared with other branches of agriculture.

As a result of the obvious predominance of manual labour in livestock-rearing the cost of production is high. Yet facts show that the existing procurement and purchase prices for livestock products do not encourage the material interest of collective farms and collective farmers sufficiently to develop livestock-rearing, and, given the present state of this, do not bring in to collective farms and collective farmers the income they should. The same may be said with regard to vegetables and potatoes.

Furthermore, in many collective farms violations of the most important provisions of the agricultural-artel statute are permitted. The basic principle of this form of production is the correct combination of the collective farmer's social and personal interests, involving the subordination of his personal interests to his social ones. Proceeding from that guiding principle, it was determined in the statute that each collectivized household in the farm would have the right to the personal ownership of a small plot, separate from the main and decisive social sector. This subordinate plot is essential so long as the public sector of the collective farm is insufficiently developed and cannot in full measure satisfy either the social needs of the collective farm or the personal requirements of the collective farmers.

In many collective farms this important principle has been violated. This could not but lead, and in fact has led, to a reduction in the number of cows, sheep and pigs on collective farmers' private plots.

The violation of the principle of the material interest of collective farms and collective farmers has become particularly evident in present conditions. Our industry is growing at a rapid rate. It is experiencing a shortage of

[1] V. I. Lenin, *Works* Vol. 33, p. 36.

labour. We have long since forgotten what unemployment was. Every year the wages of the workers at enterprises rise, and their living conditions improve. In such a situation, if work in the public sector does not bring the collective farmer the right income for his labour days, and if at the same time his personal interests in his private plot are impinged upon, then he may easily find another outlet for his labour—he can just go off to the town and work in a factory. This is the reason for the outflow of some of the rural population from backward collective farms.

A very important reason for the serious lag in certain branches of agriculture is the clearly unsatisfactory use of the powerful machinery with which the state has equipped and continues to equip the machine-and-tractor stations. In many branches of agriculture, manual labour still predominates. Though there is a high level of mechanization in working grain crops, sugar-beet and cotton, mechanization lags behind in such important branches as livestock-rearing, and the cultivation of potatoes, vegetables, flax, and many other crops. The tractors and other machines in many MTS are used badly.

An important cause of the serious lag in many branches of agriculture is the unsatisfactory management of the collective farms, machine-and-tractor stations, and state farms by party, soviet and agricultural organs, especially when it comes to selecting, distributing and training cadres for agriculture, and conducting party political work in the village.

Finally it is necessary to say something about the reasons for this; they depend on the collective farms themselves, on the chairman and collective-farm boards, and on the collective farmers. In many farms labour discipline is still very low, and not all collective farmers participate fully in collective-farm production. The labour of the collective farmers is not well organized everywhere. There are still many instances of a negligent attitude towards social property ...

II. On The State of Livestock-Farming and Measures for its Further Development

The most urgent tasks confront us in the sphere of livestock-farming, since the lag here is long drawn-out in character, and we will not be able to improve the position quickly without decisive measures.

Our livestock-farming was backward even before the war. In the post-war years a great deal of work was done to re-establish and develop it. Between June 1945 and July 1953 the number of horned cattle in the USSR rose by 11·3 million, that of sheep and goats by 53·9 million, and that of pigs by 25·1 million.

It might seem at first sight that with such growth figures, and they are indeed significant, there would be no grounds for alarm. But in fact that is not so.

Let me quote some data on the number of cattle in the   SSR:

(In millions, at the beginning of the year, over comparable areas)

Year	All Horned Cattle	Cows Alone	Pigs	Sheep and Goats	Horses
1916	58·4	28·8	23·0	96·3	38·2
1928	66·8	33·2	27·7	114·6	36·1
1941	54·5	27·8	27·5	91·6	21·0
1953	56·6	24·3	28·5	109·9	15·3

These data show that by the beginning of 1953 the number of cows was 3·5 million less than at the beginning of 1941, and 8·9 million less than at the beginning of 1928 . . .

Source: N. S. Khrushchev, *Stroitelstvo kommunizma v SSSR i razvitie selskogo khozyais-tva*, Vol. 1 (Moscow, 1962), pp. 8–20 (extracts).
Editor's translation.

76. State Pensions and Other Benefits for the Peasant
15 *July* 1964

The introduction of state pensions for collective farmers was a landmark in the history of Soviet social security, and one of the most positive things which Khrushchev ever did for the peasantry. The 1935 collective-farm statute stipulated that each farm should take care of its own old, sick and disabled, and no provision was made for them in the state schemes (though the peasants contributed to the national budget by providing underpriced agricultural produce). The poverty of most farms meant that there was usually no reserve for purposes of social security. It will be noted that pensions granted by this law were on average only half of those available to the workers. This distinction was lessened in subsequent years, but peasants have not at the time of writing reached workers' levels, nor is it yet normal for them to join trade unions. About eight million peasants were said to have been receiving pensions by the end of 1964.

76. On Pensions and Allowances for Collective-Farm Members
Law of the USSR, 15 *July* 1964

Under the guidance of the Communist Party of the Soviet Union, the Soviet people have achieved, particularly in the past ten years, enormous successes in communist construction and in the development of the country's productive forces and have created a mighty, comprehensively developed economy. This enables the Soviet state systematically to raise the living standards of the people and to satisfy their growing needs more fully.

The possibility now exists of introducing a more stable system of social security on the collective farms through the establishment of pensions for old age, disability and loss of breadwinner and maternity allowances for women collective-farm members.

The pension insurance for collective farmers must not have a levelling approach. The higher the labour productivity of the collective farmers, the more products per hectare of ploughland the collective farm produces and sells to the state and the higher its income and the level of its contributions to the pension fund, the bigger should the pensions to its collective farmers be. Those collective farmers who work well and make a larger contribution to public production should be better provided for.

The establishment of a state system of social security for collective farmers will be an important new stimulus for a further upsurge in the labour activity of the collective-farm peasantry and for an increase in the output of farm products.

With the growth of the national income, in particular the incomes of the collective farms, the sizes of the pensions envisaged by the present law will gradually be raised to the level of the state pensions granted to workers and employees.

The Supreme Soviet of the Union of Soviet Socialist Republics resolves:

I. General Provisions

ARTICLE 1. Collective-farm members are entitled to pensions for old age and disability.

Unemployable members of the families of deceased collective farmers, if they were dependants, are entitled to pensions for loss of breadwinner.

ARTICLE 2. Women collective-farm members are entitled to maternity allowances.

ARTICLE 3. Collective farmers and members of their families who are simultaneously entitled to different pensions will be granted the pension of their choice.

ARTICLE 4. The payment of pensions and allowances in conformity with the present law is ensured at the expense of the collective farms and the state without any deductions from the incomes of the collective-farm members.

ARTICLE 5. Pensions are not subject to taxation.

II. Pensions

ARTICLE 6. The following collective-farm members are entitled to old-age pensions: men who have reached the age of 65 and have worked at least 25 years; women who have reached the age of 60 and have worked at least 20 years.

ARTICLE 7. Women collective-farm members who have given birth to five or more children and reared them to the age of eight are entitled to old-age pensions when they reach the age of 55 and have worked at least 15 years.

ARTICLE 8. Old-age pensions for collective-farm members will be granted in the amount of 50 per cent of earnings up to 50 roubles a month plus 25 per cent of the remainder of their earnings.

The minimum old-age pension is fixed at 12 roubles a month.

The maximum old-age pension is fixed at 102 roubles a month, that is, at the level of the maximum old-age pension stipulated in the Law on State Pensions for workers and employees who live permanently in rural localities and who are engaged in agriculture.

ARTICLE 9. Collective-farm members with a Group I or Group II disability are entitled to a disability pension.

ARTICLE 10. Pensions for disability as a result of occupational injury or disease are granted to collective-farm members regardless of how long they have worked.

Pensions for disability as a result of non-occupational disease or injury are granted to collective-farm members if they have worked the following periods when they apply for a pension:

	Work record (in years)	
Age	Men	Women
Under 20	1	1
20–22	2	1
23–25	3	2
26–30	5	3
31–35	7	5
36–40	10	7
41–45	12	9
46–50	14	11
51–55	16	13
56–60	18	14
61 and older	20	15

ARTICLE 11. Disability pensions for collective-farm members are granted in the following amounts: for disabled persons in Group I—50 per cent of earnings up to 50 roubles a month plus 25 per cent of additional earnings; for disabled persons in Group II—40 per cent of earnings up to 50 roubles a month plus 25 per cent of additional earnings.

The minimum pension is fixed at 15 roubles a month for disabled persons in Group I and 12 roubles for disabled persons in Group II.

In cases of disability as a result of occupational injury or disease, 20 per cent is added to the pensions (including minimum pensions) computed according to the above-established norms.

Maximum disability pensions are fixed at the level of the maximum disability pensions stipulated in the Law on State Pensions for workers and employees who live permanently in rural localities and who are engaged in agriculture.

ARTICLE 12. Unemployable members of the family of a deceased collective-farmer who were his dependants are entitled to pensions for loss of breadwinner.

The following are considered unemployable dependants: (a) children, brothers, sisters and grandchildren under the age of 16 (18 in the case of schoolchildren) and older ones if they have suffered a Group I or Group II disability before reaching the age of 16 (18 in the case of schoolchildren); this includes only those brothers, sisters and grandchildren who do not have an employable parent; (b) a father, mother, wife or husband who has reached old age—65 years in the case of men, 60 years in the case of women—or has become disabled; (c) grandfathers and grandmothers if they have reached the age of 65 or 60, respectively, or are disabled, and if there are no persons obliged by law to maintain them.

Children and unemployable parents of the deceased who were not his dependants are entitled to a pension for loss of breadwinner if his death has deprived them of a source of sustenance.

Persons who adopt children are entitled to pensions on the same terms as parents, and adopted children on the same terms as children who are not adopted.

ARTICLE 13. The families of collective farmers who die as a result of occupational injury or disease are entitled to pensions irrespective of the length of time the breadwinner had worked.

The families of collective farmers who die as a result of non-occupational injury or disease are entitled to pensions if the breadwinner had worked the length of time necessary to qualify him for a disability pension.

ARTICLE 14. Pensions for loss of breadwinner are granted in the following amounts, according to the number of unemployable members in the family: three or more—50 per cent of the breadwinner's earnings up to 50 roubles a month plus 25 per cent of additional earnings; two—40 per cent of the breadwinner's earnings up to 50 roubles a month plus 25 per cent of additional earnings; one—30 per cent of the breadwinner's earnings up to 50 roubles a month plus 10 per cent of additional earnings.

The minimum pension is fixed at 15 roubles a month for three or more unemployable family members; at 12 roubles for two unemployable family members; and at 9 roubles for one unemployable family member.

In cases of loss of breadwinner as a result of occupational injury or disease, 20 per cent is added to the pensions (including minimum pensions) computed according to the above-established norms.

Maximum pensions for loss of breadwinner are fixed at the level of the maximum pensions for loss of breadwinner stipulated in the Law on State Pensions for the families of workers and employees who live permanently in rural localities and who are engaged in agriculture.

ARTICLE 15. The following will be counted in the work record in granting pensions: (a) work as a collective-farm member; (b) work as a worker or employee, service in the USSR Armed Forces and service in guerrilla detachments, as well as other periods subject to inclusion in the work record in granting pensions under the Law on State Pensions.

ARTICLE 16. Pensions are based on the actual average monthly earnings on the collective farm for any five successive years (to be chosen by the person applying for the pension) out of the fifteen years preceding the application for a pension.

In the case of collective farmers who have worked on the collective farm for less than five years and collective-farm families that have lost a breadwinner who had worked on the collective farm for less than five years, pensions are based on the actual average monthly earnings on the collective farm during the time worked.

ARTICLE 17. Collective-farm pensioners who, after receiving a pension, have worked on the collective farm for at least two years with higher earnings than those on which the pension was based will receive a new pension based on these higher earnings.

III. Maternity Allowances for Women Collective Farmers

ARTICLE 18. Women collective farmers are entitled to maternity allowances irrespective of how long they have worked.

Maternity leave is granted for 56 calendar days before delivery and 56 calendar days after delivery, and in the event of abnormal or multiple births for 70 days after delivery.

ARTICLE 19. Maternity allowances for women collective farmers are determined according to the same system and the same norms as those established for women workers and women employees.

IV. Funds for the Payment of Pensions and Allowances

ARTICLE 20. A central all-union social-security fund for collective farmers is set up through payments out of the incomes of the collective farms and annual allocations under the USSR State Budget to pay the pensions and allowances stipulated in the present law.

ARTICLE 21. Beginning in 1964, all collective farms will make monetary contributions to the central all-union social-security fund for collective farmers in amounts to be determined by the USSR Council of Ministers.

Funds subject to transfer to the central all-union social-security fund for collective farmers are excluded from the incomes of collective farms in levying the tax.

V. Final Provisions

ARTICLE 22. Collective farms that pay pensions to their collective farmers in excess of the amounts established in the present law may maintain the size of these pensions by making the corresponding additional payments out of the collective farm's funds.

ARTICLE 23. The USSR Supreme Soviet resolves to charge the USSR Council of Ministers with issuing, on the basis of the present law:

(1) rules governing the system of granting and paying pensions to collective-farm members;
(2) rules governing the granting and payment of maternity allowances to women collective-farm members;
(3) rules governing the central all-union social-security fund for collective farmers.

The rules governing the system of granting and paying pensions to collective-farm members should, in particular, stipulate the conditions for granting pensions:

to members of the collective farms of those republics and provinces in which collective farms were set up later than in other regions of the country;

to members of collective farms who joined the collective farms during the first years of collectivization but who, as a result of old age or disability, stopped working on the collective farms without having the work record necessary to qualify them for a pension.

ARTICLE 24. The present law takes effect 1 January 1965.

A. MIKOYAN, Chairman of the Presidium, USSR Supreme Soviet.

M. GEORGADZE, Secretary of the Presidium.

Source: K. U. Chernenko, i drugie, *Spravochnik partiinogo rabotnika*, vypusk 6 (Moscow, 1966).

Translation: CDSP, Vol. XVI, No. 29, p. 25.

77. Brezhnev Criticizes Agricultural Stagnation under Khrushchev

24 *March* 1965

In this section of his speech Brezhnev, now First Secretary of the Party, criticized his predecessor's management of agriculture, and disassociated himself from it in the accepted Soviet manner. Khrushchev's main reforms of agricultural administration—the splitting of the party apparatus into separate industrial and rural sectors, the establishment of territorial collective- and state-farm production boards, and the demotion of the Ministry of Agriculture—had already been annulled. Later in his speech Brezhnev went on to promise new concessions to the peasants, in particular better prices, lower and firmer delivery quotas, a little more freedom for the private sector, a reduction of taxation, and the cancellation of some debts. Though these measures by no means solved the problems of Soviet agriculture, they were followed by a definite improvement in the living standards and output of the collective farms.

77. The Basic Results of the Development of Agriculture in Recent Years

From L. I. Brezhnev's report at the Plenum of the CC CPSU, 24 March 1965

Comrades! Our agriculture is based on the most advanced social system, which has withstood the test of time and through the entire course of historical development has proved itself an irresistible, vital force. Relying on the socialist system, the Communist Party has done substantial work to develop agriculture.

The September 1953 plenary session of the CPSU Central Committee had great importance. It worked out the correct course in the sphere of agriculture. And it must be said bluntly that as long as its decisions were implemented we had definite results. A great deal was done to strengthen the collective and state farms organizationally and economically, to improve their material and technical base and to increase the material incentives of rural workers.

At the Party's appeal tens of thousands of specialists and organizers of agricultural production went into the countryside at that time. The ploughing up of virgin and idle lands had great importance in increasing grain production. In the first five years after the September plenary session the sown areas were substantially expanded, yields were raised and the gross and marketable output of agriculture increased.

Unfortunately, however, these positive results were not further consolidated and developed. We were faced with the fact that in the past few years agriculture had slowed in its development, and our plans for an upsurge in agricultural production remained unfulfilled.

According to the control figures, the gross output of agriculture during the seven-year plan (1959–1965) should have risen by 70 per cent; in fact, during the first six years the increase came to only 10 per cent. Whereas the gross output of agriculture grew by an average 7·6 per cent a year during the period 1955–1959, in the past five years its average annual rise has been only 1·9 per cent. The growth in the yields of basic crops has slowed down. Thus the average yield of grain crops increased by 1·7 centners in 1955–1959 as compared with the preceding five-year period, while in the period 1960–1964 it rose by only 0·8 centner.

A similar phenomenon is to be observed in animal husbandry. The increase in the number of cattle over the past five years was only half as great as in the preceding five years. As for the number of pigs, sheep and poultry, it has actually declined substantially during this time. The average milk yield per cow on the collective and state farms has decreased by more than 370 kg.

The data that have been cited make it possible to draw a conclusion: Whereas there was a notable upsurge in agriculture up to 1959, in the period since then it has to all intents and purposes begun to mark time.

What are the basic reasons for this situation?

First, a weak spot in the guidance of agriculture is the fact that the demands of the economic laws of development of a socialist economy were not fully taken into account and were frequently even ignored. I have in mind first of all such laws as those of planned and proportional development and of expanded socialist reproduction, as well as the principles of the combination of public and personal interests, material incentives and others. But, as we know, life sternly punishes those who do not take these laws into account, who scorn them and are guilty of subjectivism.

Actions of a purely wilful nature, especially in the fields of planning, price formation, financing and the extension of credits, increasingly came to the fore in the practice of agricultural guidance in the past few years. It cannot be considered normal, for example, that the purchase prices of a number of agricultural products do not even cover the cost of their production. As a result the collective and state farms suffer large losses.

The numerous and sometimes ill-conceived reorganizations gave rise to an atmosphere of nervousness and confusion, deprived managers of a long-range view and undermined their faith in their abilities. Instead of painstaking, thoughtful work and profound analysis of the state of affairs, the practice of administration by fiat, of issuing commands to the collective and state farms, was often permitted.

Second, agriculture was faced with very great tasks, but they were inadequately backed up by the necessary economic measures, particularly the correct determination of the level of prices for agricultural products and

377

goods needed for production, the allocation of the appropriate capital investments and the improvement of material and technical supply. Thus in the five years 1954–1958 state investments in agriculture amounted to 11·3 per cent of all investments in the national economy, while in the control figures of the seven-year plan (1959–1965) they were set at only 7·5 per cent.

In contrast to other branches of the national economy, construction on the state farms and particularly on the collective farms was not fully provided with materials and integrated equipment. Large amounts were frequently channelled into projects whose construction was not demanded by the urgent interests of production. As a result these expenditures did not yield an economic effect, and the national economy thereby suffered losses.

Third, practically nothing was done to raise farming standards or increase fertility. Many collective and state farms violated the crop rotation and failed to observe the elementary rules of agrotechnology. The central agencies issued various kinds of stereotyped instruction on tilling the soil, on determining the structure of sown areas and replacing one farming system by another, and on caring for and feeding livestock, without taking into account natural, economic and production conditions or local experience. All this prevented the planned management of the farms, reduced the role of the land agencies and did not contribute to the productive utilization of the land.

Finally, in speaking about the reasons for the lag in agriculture, we must also acknowledge that there have been serious shortcomings in the work of party, soviet and land agencies. Of course, the work of our cadres was made more complicated by the atmosphere of frequent reorganizations and changes. Nevertheless, we have not utilized all the possibilities at our disposal. We have done insufficient work with people, we have been lax in basing ourselves on specialists and on agricultural science, we have been unable to organize properly the generalization and dissemination of advanced experience.

Comrades! We encounter the consequences of mistakes in the guidance of agriculture in all zones of the country, but they have had a special effect in the regions of the non-black-earth belt. Take Smolensk Province, for example. In the past five years the gross output of agriculture there has risen by only 1 per cent. The province has not even reached its pre-war level of production of the most important types of crops.

The yields of crops in the province remain low. The milk yield per cow on the collective and state farms has declined by almost 400 kg. All the branches of agriculture except for flax are unprofitable.

The situation that has evolved cannot but arouse our serious concern about the state of affairs in agriculture. In this connection the Presidium of the CPSU Central Committee has drawn up and will submit for the consideration of the Central Committee's plenary session important economic

378

measures aimed at the organizational and economic strengthening of the collective and state farms.

We understand that an upsurge in agriculture is something that is vitally necessary to us for the successful construction of communism. In order to resolve this nationwide task, we must put a firm economic foundation under agriculture. V. I. Lenin regarded this question as one of the most important questions of the Party's economic policy, since it touches upon the very foundation of the Soviet state—the relationship of the working class and the peasantry.

We must correct the mistakes that have been made in agriculture more quickly and put an end to subjectivism. We must utilize on a broad economic basis material and moral incentives for the development of production. Great efforts and a decisive change in methods of work is demanded of party, soviet and economic agencies, of all of us ...

Source: Plenum TsK KPSS, 24–26 marta 1965, stenografichesky otchet (Moscow, 1965), p. 5.
Translation: CDSP, Vol. XVII, No. 12, p. 3 (extracts).

78. The Peasant Gets a Guaranteed Wage

16 *May* 1966

The introduction of a guaranteed wage illustrates another aspect of the Brezhnev leadership's concern to better the lot of the peasant, in formal terms at least. No less significant was the stipulation that labour payments were no longer to be made from the residue of the farm budget (i.e., only after state and other demands had been met, as in Article 11 of the 1935 Charter). This step may have been prompted not so much by humanitarian considerations as by concern over agricultural failure and rural depopulation (which was by then serious).

78. On Raising the Material Incentives of Collective Farmers for the Development of Socialist Production

Decree of the CC CPSU and the Council of Ministers of the USSR, 16 *May* 1966

The Central Committee of the CPSU and the Council of Ministers of the USSR note that there are serious shortcomings in the practice of distributing incomes in collective farms and making payments for collective farmers' labour. In many collective farms the level of these payments does not provide collective farmers with the necessary material incentives for the development of the public sector.

The Central Committee of the CPSU and the Council of Ministers of the USSR, attaching, as they do, great significance to raising the material incentives for collective farmers to develop social production in the collective farms, decree that

1. The collective farms be recommended:

To make, from 1 July 1966, a guaranteed payment for collective farmers' labour (in money or kind), on the basis of the tariff rates of the corresponding category of workers in state farms. The output norms are to be fixed with regard to concrete conditions, as applicable to the output norms obtaining for analagous work in state farms;

To effect (together with the guaranteed payment of collective farmers' labour for the volume of work done) payment to collective farmers on the final results of their labour (for the quantity and quality of production, or for the overall income received);

To allow for the necessary funds in money and kind for the payment of collective farmers in the collective farms' production and finance plans, and to use these funds for this purpose alone;

To make the guaranteed labour payments to collective farmers in money at least once a month, and in kind, depending on the times when products are received.

2. In distributing income within the collective farm money shall in the first instance be allotted for the payment of the collective farmers' labour.

Allocations to the indivisible and other public funds are to be made in amounts determined by the collective farms themselves, after money has been allotted for collective farmers' labour, obligatory payments to the state, and contributions to the centralized all-union fund for collective farmers' social insurance.

3. It should be recommended to collective farms that they create, in order to satisfy collective farmers' requirements of agricultural products, a guaranteed fund in kind for distribution according to labour. A certain proportion of the overall grain harvest and other agricultural products is to be set aside for that fund, so that the collective farmers may, if they so desire, receive, against their guaranteed wage payment, grain and other products, and also fodder for their own private cattle, in quantities determined by the general assembly of collective farmers.

4. The introduction of guaranteed payment for collective farmers' labour, and further improvements in their pay, are to be effected through increasing their output of agricultural products, a growth of productivity, the removal of existing shortcomings in fixing labour norms and tariffs, the removal of surplus managerial and service personnel, a sharp reduction in unproductive expenses, and strict attention to economy.

5. The Councils of Ministers of the union republics are obliged, in the course of a month, to work out, with the agreement of the Ministry of Agriculture of the USSR and the State Committee of the Council of Ministers of the USSR for Questions of Labour and Wages, approved recommendations for the payment of labour in collective farms.

6. The State Bank of the USSR is obliged, in cases where collective farms do not have enough funds of their own to ensure the guaranteed payment of collective farmers' labour, in accordance with point 1 of this decree, to grant such collective farms, in 1966–1970, credit for up to five years within the limits of the sums included in the collective farms' long-term credit plans.

This credit is granted to collective farms on the basis of applications examined and approved by the *raion* executive committees.

The extent of the credit is determined within the limits of the difference between the guaranteed-wage fund and the collective farms' own means as designated for this purpose in the production and finance plans.

The collective farms are to repay this credit beginning from the third year after it has been received, and in the first place after their payments into the budget.

In view of the fact that the collective farms' long-term credit plans for 1966 have already been brought to the notice of the autonomous republics, *kraiya*, *oblasti* and *raiony*, the Councils of Ministers of republics, the executive committees of *kraiya*, *oblasti* and *raiony* are to effect, with the object of ensuring guaranteed payments for collective farms, and in cases where it is necessary, the redistribution of long-term credit between autonomous republics, *kraiya*, *oblasti*, *raiony* and collective farms.

7. The Councils of Ministers of the union republics are obliged to ensure, in 1966, in connection with the introduction of guaranteed payments in the collective farms and the increase in collective farmers' incomes, a corresponding increase in the turnover of retail goods and the production of consumer goods from local resources.

8. The Central Statistical Administration of the USSR is obliged, in agreement with the Ministry of Agriculture of the USSR and the State Bank of the USSR, to work out and introduce from 1 August 1966 current monthly reports on the settlement of collective farmers' labour payments.

Source: K. U. Chernenko and M. S. Smirtyukov (eds.), *Reshenia partii i pravitelstva po khozyaistvennym voprosam*, Vol. 6 (Moscow, 1968), p. 111.
Editor's translation.

79. The 1969 Collective-Farm Charter

27 November 1969

Like so many basic laws in the Soviet state, the new Model Statute had a difficult birth. In March 1965 the Central Committee passed a resolution calling for a new statute, and a drafting commission was set up the following January under the chairmanship of Leonid Brezhnev. The draft statute appeared only in April 1969. It was approved by the Third All-Union Congress of Collective Farmers, with some amendments, in November 1969.[1]

The new statute differs from the preceding one in many details, but unfortunately retains both its form and spirit. It is designed for a situation in which virtually all the peasantry has already been collectivized, and the provisions for joining have consequently been simplified. The statute reflects such post-Stalin innovations as the monthly advances to farm members, improved systems of payment, and the provision of state social security. There is a superficial extension of intra-farm democracy and some liberalization of the organization, but not to the detriment of the old framework of control from above.

79. The Model Charter of the Collective Farm

Approved by the Third All-Union Congress of Collective Farmers, 25–27 November 1969

The collective-farm system is an integral part of the Soviet socialist society; this path, outlined by V. I. Lenin, tested by history and corresponding to the specific characteristics and interests of the peasantry, is that of the peasantry's gradual transition to communism.

Public ownership of the means of production, the advantages of large-scale collective farming and the day-to-day concern and assistance of the Party and the state have made it possible to bring about enormous social and economic transformations in the countryside. Thanks to the selfless labour of the collective-farm peasantry and the efforts of the working class and all the Soviet people, the collective farms have become large mechanized agricultural enterprises, their communal wealth has increased immeasurably, the living standard of the collective farmers has risen, and the difference between the city and the countryside are gradually being overcome.

The collective farm as a communal form of the socialist economy fully corresponds to the tasks of the further development of productive forces in the countryside, provides for the management of production by the collective-farm masses themselves on the basis of collective-farm democracy,

[1] Changes in and additions to the draft version are here shown in italics. Substantive passages dropped from the draft are enclosed in square brackets.

and makes it possible to combine correctly the personal interests of the collective farmers and the interests of society at large, of all the people. The collective farm is a school of communism for the peasantry.

Under the leadership of the Communist Party, the collective-farm peasantry, in close and indestructible alliance with the working class, is actively participating in the construction of communism in our country.

I. Goals and Tasks

1. The ... ... Collective Farm in ... ... District, ... Region, ... Province (Territory), ... Republic, is a co-operative organization of voluntarily associated peasants for the joint conduct of large-scale socialist agricultural production on the basis of communal means of production and collective labour.

2. The collective farm sets as its chief tasks:

to strengthen and develop the communal sector in every way, steadily to increase labour productivity and the effectiveness of communal production [and to instil in collective farmers the spirit of a communist attitude toward labour];

to increase the production and sale to the state of agricultural output by means of the intensification and further technical re-equipment of collective-farm production, the introduction of integrated mechanization *and electrification* and the broad implementation of chemicalization and land reclamation; *under the leadership of Party organizations, to conduct work on the communist upbringing of the collective farmers, on drawing them into public life and on developing socialist competition;*

to satisfy more fully the growing material and cultural requirements of the collective farmers, to improve their living conditions and gradually to transform rural villages into well-appointed settlements.

II. Membership in the Collective Farm and the Rights and Obligations of Collective-farm Members

3. Any citizen [of the USSR] who has reached the age of sixteen and expresses a desire to participate through his labour in the communal sector of the collective farm may be a member of the collective farm.

Admission to collective-farm membership is carried out by the *general meeting of collective farmers* [by the board of the collective farm], *upon the recommendation of the board of the collective farm and in the presence of the person submitting the application* [upon application from a prospective member; the decision of the board is ratified by a general meeting of the members of the collective farm, in the presence of the individual who submitted the application].

An application for admission to collective-farm membership is considered by the collective-farm board within one month's time.

A collective farmer's labour booklet—these are of a single form—is kept for each member of the collective farm.

4. A member of the collective farm has the right:

to receive work in the communal sector of the collective farm with guaranteed pay in accordance with the quantity and quality of the labour he contributes;

to participate in the administration of the collective farm's affairs, to elect and to be elected to its administrative bodies; to submit proposals for improving the collective farm's activity and for eliminating shortcomings in the work of the board and of officials;

to receive assistance from the collective farm in increasing his production skills and in acquiring a speciality;

to use a personal plot of land for conducting auxiliary farming, for the construction of living quarters and farm buildings, and also to use the collective farm's pastures, communally owned draught animals and transportation for personal needs, under the procedure that has been established on the collective farm;

to social security, cultural and everyday services and assistance from the collective farm in the construction and repair of living quarters and in the provision of fuel.

5. A member of the collective farm is obliged:

to observe the collective farm's charter and its regulations, to carry out the resolutions of general meetings and the decisions of the collective-farm board;

to labour conscientiously in the communal sector, observe labour discipline and master advanced methods and procedures of work;

to participate actively in the administration of the collective farm's affairs, to care for, protect *and strengthen* state and collective-farm property, not to tolerate mismanagement or a negligent attitude toward communal property, to utilize rationally and correctly land in communal and personal use.

6. Collective-farm membership is retained by individuals who temporarily leave the collective farm, in the following cases:

a tour of active military duty;

election to an elective position in a Soviet, public or cooperative organization;

enrolment in studies making it necessary to leave production;

assignment to work in an inter-collective-farm organization, departure for work in industry or another branch of the national economy for a period established by the collective-farm board.

Collective-farm membership is also retained by collective farmers who have stopped working because of old age or disability, if they continue to live on the collective farm.

7. A collective farmer's application to leave the collective farm must be considered by the collective-farm board *and the general meeting of collective-farm members* [with subsequent ratification of the board's decision at the next general meeting of collective-farm members], no later than three months from the day the application was submitted.

The collective-farm board settles all accounts with a former collective farmer as of the end of the economic year, no later than one month after the collective farm's annual report is approved.

III. The Land and its Use

8. In accordance with the USSR constitution, the land held by the collective farm is allotted to it for free and permanent use, i.e., in perpetuity.

The land allotted to the collective farm is *state property* [the property of all the people and of the state], i.e., it is the common property of the nation, and it cannot be the object of purchase or sale, rental or other transactions.

The executive committee of the district (or city) Soviet issues to every collective farm a state deed on the right to use of the land, indicating the dimensions and precise boundaries of the land allotted to the collective farm.

The land allotted to the collective farm is subdivided into land for communal use and land for personal plots. The personal plots are separated by natural boundaries from the land given over to communal use.

9. The collective farm is obliged to make the fullest and most correct utilization of the land allotted to it, constantly to improve this land, to increase its fertility; *to bring unused land into agricultural production*; to carry out measures for land irrigation and drainage, for combating soil erosion and *for creating field shelter-belt plantings*; to care for collective-farm land and strictly protect it from wasteful use; to observe established regulations for *the protection of nature and for* the use of forests, sources of water and useful minerals (sand, clay, stone, peat, etc.).

The board, executive and specialists of the collective farm are responsible for the highly productive use of the land.

10. A reduction in the area of the collective farm's land or changes in the boundaries of the collective farm's landholdings occasioned by state or public needs are carried out only when a general meeting of the collective farmers has given its consent and by decision of the appropriate state agencies. Moreover, the assignment for non-agricultural needs or irrigated or drained land, ploughland or plots of land occupied by plantings of perennial fruits and vineyards is prohibited, as a rule.

The collective farm is entitled to compensation for losses connected with a reduction in the area of collective-farm land or *the temporary occupation of this land* [changes in the boundaries of the collective farm's landholdings]. *Compensation for losses is carried out* in accordance with the procedure established by legislation now in effect.

IV. The Collective Farm's Communal Property

11. The collective farm's communal property, along with state ownership of the land, constitutes the economic basis of the collective farm.

The collective farm's communal property consists of enterprises, buildings, installations, tractors, combines and other machinery, equipment, means of transportation, draught animals and productive livestock, perennial plantings, land-reclamation and irrigation installations, output, money and other collective-farm property. *The collective farm's communal property also includes the property and resources of inter-collective-farm and state–collective-farm organizations and enterprises on the basis of shares.*

12. For the implementation of its activities and the further growth of the communal sector, the collective farm creates, utilizes in a planned and efficient way and replenishes fixed production assets and working capital. These assets are indivisible (they are not to be distributed among the members of the collective farm) and are used only for their designated purposes.

Fixed assets for non-productive purposes are also indivisible.

13. The right to dispose of the property and monetary resources of the collective farm belongs only to the collective farm itself and to its administrative agencies. *The collective farm does not permit the diversion of resources for purposes not connected with its activity.*

The acquisition, sale, withdrawal from use and writing off of fixed assets and other material assets is carried out according to the procedure established by the general meeting of collective-farm members and on the basis of legislation now in effect.

Collective-farm members who cause the destruction, spoilage or loss of collective-farm property [through their negligence or carelessness], as well as those guilty of the unauthorized use of tractors, motor vehicles, farm machinery or draught animals [or productive livestock] and those who cause material damage to the collective farm are obliged to compensate the collective farm for these actions.

The amount of actual damage is determined by the collective-farm board. Penalties for damage done *are exacted in the amount of the actual damage, but no more than one-third of the basic monthly earnings of the collective farm member, if the damage was caused by carelessness in work. When the damage is inflicted deliberately, and also in cases provided for by legislation, the collective-farm member is materially liable for the full amount or a higher amount. Penalties for damage done are exacted by the collective-farm board, while disputed cases are settled by the people's courts* [may be set by the collective-farm board, with consideration of the specific situation in which it was inflicted, in amounts up to one-third of the basic monthly earnings of the collective-farm member, and larger amounts may be fixed by the people's court. A decision by a collective-farm board setting a penalty for damage may be appealed to a people's court by the collective farmer involved].

V. The Production-Economic and Financial Activity of the Collective Farm

14. The collective farm conducts its economic activity according to a plan that is approved by the general meeting of collective farmers, employing the most progressive and scientifically substantiated forms and methods of the organization of production, which ensure the obtaining of maximum amounts of high-quality output with minimum expenditures of labour and resources.

In drawing up its plans, the collective farm proceeds from the necessity of the expanded reproduction of the communal sector, fulfilment of the plan for state purchases, contract agreements for the sale of agricultural products and the above-plan sale of grain and other output necessary to the state, and the satisfaction of the material and cultural requirements of the collective farmers.

15. The collective farm's production-financial activity is carried out on the basis of economic accountability and the wide application of moral and material incentives aimed at developing production and increasing the farm's profitability.

16. The board and all the members of the collective farm are obliged to ensure:

the rational conduct of agricultural production, by means of its intensification and specialization and the preponderant development of those branches for which the best natural-economic conditions exist;

an increase in the harvest yield of agricultural crops on the basis of an upswing in the standards of farming, *the observance of crop rotations, the improvement of seed growing, the systematic application of fertilizers, and the implementation of other measures;*

the all-round development of animal husbandry, an increase in the productivity of livestock and poultry, the improvement of pedigreed stock-breeding, the observance of zootechnical and veterinary regulations, and the creation of a firm and stable feed base for animal husbandry;

the introduction in production of new machinery and progressive technology, integrated mechanization, electrification and the achievements of science and advanced experience; the conduct of land reclamation and chemicalization;

the efficient use and maintenance of tractors, combines, motor vehicles and other machines, draught animals and productive livestock, buildings and installations;

the construction of production buildings and cultural and service facilities, dwellings and children's institutions, roads, water-supply and other installations, in accordance with plans for the development of the farm and the build-up of communities.

17. For the purpose of the fuller and more even utilization of manpower and local sources of raw materials and of increasing the profitableness of the communal sector, the collective farm creates and develops, *without detriment to agricultural production*, auxiliary enterprises and various sidelines [*promysly*]; it can enter into contractual relations with industrial enterprises and trade organizations for the creation on the collective farm of branches (shops) for the production of various articles and commodities by the collective farmers in the periods that they have free from agricultural work.

18. The collective farm may take part on a voluntary basis in the activity of inter-collective-farm and state–collective-farm enterprises and organizations, and it may join associations and unions.

19. By decision of the general meeting of collective farmers, the collective farm may pool part of its resources with the resources of local soviets, state farms and other state and co-operative enterprises and organizations for the construction [on the collective farm], on the basis of shares, of cultural and service facilities and public amenities and for other measures aimed at the development of collective-farm production and the improvement of cultural and everyday services for the collective farmers.

20. The collective farm concludes contracts with state, co-operative and public organizations for the sale of agricultural output, the purchase of machinery, materials, livestock and other property, for the sale of semi-finished products and articles made by auxiliary enterprises and sidelines, for the performance of various jobs and the provision of services, and also enters into other contractual relations in accordance with the goals of its activity.

21. The collective farm opens an account with an institution of the USSR State Bank for the settling of accounts and the safekeeping of monetary resources and makes all deposits and settles all accounts in accordance with established regulations.

The transfer or payment of monetary funds from the account that the collective farm keeps in an institution of the USSR State Bank is carried out on instructions from the collective farm board.

The collective farm may make use of state short-term and long-term credits.

The instructions of the collective-farm board for the transfer or payment of funds from the collective farm's account and the collective farm's obligations with respect to credits are valid if they bear the signatures of the chairman and the chief bookkeeper of the collective farm.

22. The collective farm keeps bookkeeping, operational and statistical records, introduces advanced methods and forms of record-keeping, compiles reports according to approved forms and submits them to the appropriate agencies within the established deadlines.

23. The collective farm is not responsible for the obligations and debts of collective-farm members. The members of the collective farm have no property liability where the obligations and debts of the collective farm are concerned.

VI. Labour Organization, Pay and Discipline

24. All work in the communal sector of the collective farm is performed by the personal labour of the collective farmers.

The hiring of specialists and other personnel from outside is permitted only in instances in which the collective farm does not have the appropriate specialists or in which agricultural and other jobs cannot be performed by the collective farmers themselves within the requisite time-period.

The collective farm introduces the scientific organization of labour and shows concern for the full and most rational utilization of manpower in communal production.

25. The length and detailed schedule of the working day on the collective farm, the procedure for granting days off and annual paid vacations, and also the minimum labour participation in the communal sector by able-bodied collective farmers, are governed by the collective farm's regulations.

26. The forms of the organization of production and labour—sectors, live-stock sections, brigades, teams and other production units—are established and applied by the collective farm in accordance with the specific conditions of the farm and the level of the mechanization, specialization and technology of production.

Collective farmers are selected for membership in production units *on the basis of the interests of the developmnet of the communal sector and* with consideration of their qualifications, work experience, skills, place of residence and personal desires.

Plots of land, tractors, machinery and equipment, draught animals and productive livestock, the necessary buildings and other means of production are assigned to the collective farm's production units [for a number of years].

The activity of the collective farm's production units is carried out on the basis of the intra-farm settling of accounts.

27. The chief source of the collective farmers' incomes is the communal sector of the collective farm. Payment for labour on the collective farm is carried out in accordance with the quantity and quality of the labour contribution by each collective farmer to the communal sector, according to the

principle of higher pay for good labour, for the best results. *Increases in the pay of collective-farm members are to be carried out on the basis of the preponderant growth of labour productivity.*

The collective farm employs piecework *and job-rate payment* for labour, for volume of work done or output produced, *time-rate pay*, a combination of time-rate and bonus pay, *or other systems of pay* [according to established pay scales and rates]. Work that is done poorly through the fault of the collective farmer is not paid for, or the amount of pay for it is reduced accordingly.

Output norms and pay scales for agricultural and other jobs are worked out and, when necessary, reviewed with the broad participation of the collective farmers and specialists, proceeding from the *standard output norms and with consideration of the* specific conditions of the farm, and are approved by the collective-farm board.

28. The collective farm establishes guaranteed pay for collective-farm members for work in communal production.

For the purpose of raising the material interest of the collective farmers in increasing agricultural output, improving its quality and lowering its unit cost, supplementary payments and other forms of material incentives are used, in addition to the basic pay.

Collective-farm members who fail to fulfil the established minimum for labour participation in the communal sector without valid reasons, *and also those guilty of absenteeism*, may, by decision of the collective-farm board, be partially or completely deprived of supplementary payments and other forms of material encouragement.

29. To satisfy the collective farmers' requirements for agricultural products, a payment-in-kind fund [for distribution according to labour] is created on the collective farm; a certain portion of the gross harvest of grain and other products, as well as of feed, is allocated to this fund. These products and this feed are issued *as pay* or sold to the collective farmers in quantities and under the procedure established by the general meeting of collective-farm members.

30. The collective-farm board ensures the prompt payment of the earnings due to the collective farmers. In the process, money is paid at least once a month, and produce in kind is issued as it is received.

The final settling of accounts with the collective farmers is carried out no later than one month after the collective farm's annual report has been approved.

31. The collective-farm board, guided by this Charter, draws up *regulations and* statutes on pay and on the intra-farm settling of accounts, which are ratified by the general meeting of collective farmers.

32. All jobs on the collective farm are performed with observance of the established safety rules and the requirements of production sanitation.

The collective farm allocates the necessary resources for the conduct of safety measures and production sanitation and for the acquisition of special clothing, special footwear and protective devices for issuance or sale to the collective farmers according to established norms.

33. Women collective-farm members are entitled to pregnancy and child-birth leave; pregnant women are given lighter work; women with breast-fed babies are provided with the necessary conditions for nursing their infants at the proper time, and they may be granted additional leave.

The collective farm establishes a shorter working day and other privileges for adolescents.

34. For the achievement of high results in production, the elaboration and introduction of rationalizers' proposals, effecting savings in communal resources, irreproachable work for many years in collective-farm production and other services to the collective farm, the general meeting of collective-farm members or the board employs the following measures of encouragement for collective farmers:

a declaration of gratitude;
the issuance of a bonus or the award of a valuable gift;
the award of a Certificate of Honour;
inscription on the Roll of Honour or in the Book of Honour;
conferral of the titles Honoured Collective Farmer and Distinguished Collective Farmer.

Other measures of encouragement may also be established, at the discretion of the general meeting of collective-farm members.

The titles of Honoured Collective Farmer and Distinguished Collective Farmer are conferred by decision of the general meeting of collective-farm members, in accordance with the regulations approved by the collective farm.

35. For violations of labour discipline, the charter of the collective farm *or its regulations*, the general meeting of collective farmers or the collective-farm board may impose the following penalties on the guilty parties:

censure;
a reprimand;
strict reprimand;
transfer to a lower-paying job [for a period of up to three months];
dismissal from the position held;
warning of expulsion from collective-farm membership.

Expulsion from collective-farm membership may be employed as an extreme measure against individuals who regularly violate labour discipline or the collective farm's charter, after other sanctions have been used against these individuals. A resolution of the general meeting of collective farmers on expulsion from collective-farm membership may be appealed to the executive committee of the district (or city) Soviet.

Individuals expelled from collective-farm membership are deprived of the rights of a collective-farm member as established by this Charter.

Penalties may be imposed on the chairman of the collective farm, the chairman of the inspection commission, members of the board and members of the inspection commission by the general meeting of collective farmers; penalties may be imposed on chief (senior) specialists, the chief bookkeeper and the leaders of production units by the general meeting or by the collective-farm board.

The procedure for imposing and removing penalties is determined by the collective farm's regulations.

VII. Distribution of the Collective Farm's Gross Output and Income

36. In the distribution of income, the following must be ensured: the correct combination of accumulation and consumption, the continuous growth of production assets, insurance funds and communal funds for cultural and everyday purposes, and a rising living standard for the collective farmers.

The material expenditures on the production of the collective farm's output (depreciation of fixed assets, outlays of seeds, feed, fertilizer, petroleum products, expenditures on current repairs, etc.) are reimbursed out of the collective farm's gross output.

The collective farm forms a fund for labour payments out of gross income received.

The collective farm uses its net income:

to pay taxes and to make monetary payments to the state;
to increase fixed assets and working capital;
to create a fund for cultural and everyday purposes and a fund for social security and material assistance to collective farmers;
for material incentives to collective farmers and specialists;
to form and replenish a reserve fund, and for other purposes.

Allocations for increasing fixed assets and working capital are mandatory; the amounts of the allocations are established annually, taking into account the requirements for resources to ensure the continued steady growth of communal production.

37. From the in-kind output of crop cultivation and animal husbandry, the collective farm:

creates a seed fund to cover the farm's total requirements;
fulfils the plan for the sale of agricultural products to the state, repays loans in kind, creates an in-kind stock of grain and other products for issuance *as pay* or sale to the collective farmers and, when possible, sells over and above the plan grain and other output needed by the state;

allocates feed for communally owned livestock and poultry to cover annual requirements, and also for issuance or sale to the collective farmers; forms insurance and carryover funds of seeds, fodder and foodstuffs; allocates products for public catering and for the upkeep of children's institutions and orphans; assigns a portion of products and animal feed for assistance to pensioners, invalids and needy collective-farm members.

The collective farm sells its remaining output to the consumers' co-operatives or on the collective-farm markets, or uses it for other needs at its discretion.

38. The collective farm uses the money obtained from the sale of output and other sources primarily for settling accounts with the collective farmers for their labour, to cover other production expenditures, to make payments to the state, to repay monetary loans, and to form and replenish the collective farm's public funds.

VIII. Social Security for Collective Farmers

39. Collective-farm members, in accordance with legislation now in effect, receive old-age and disability pensions and pensions for the loss of a bread-winner *through the resources of the centralized union social security fund for collective farmers*; in addition, women receive pregnancy and childbirth allowances [from the centralized union social security fund for collective farmers].

40. *In accordance with established procedure, collective-farm members receive allowances for temporary disability and passes to sanatoriums and rest homes, and also are granted other forms of social insurance, through the centralized social insurance fund for collective farmers.*

By decision of the general meeting, the collective farm can make supplementary payments to all forms of pensions established for collective farmers and can establish personal pensions for veterans of collective-farm construction and indi-viduals performing special services in the development of the collective farm's communal sector.

[By decision of the general meeting, the collective farm can, out of its own funds, pay collective-farm members allowances for temporary dis-ability, purchase passes for collective farmers to sanatoriums and rest homes and provide other forms of social insurance, and also make supplementary payments to all forms of pensions established for collective farmers.]

The collective farm gives material assistance out of its own resources to disabled collective-farm members who do not receive pensions or allowances. By decision of the general meeting of collective farmers, the collective farm can allocate resources for the construction of collective-farm and inter-collective-farm sanatoriums, rest homes, Young Pioneer camps and homes for the aged and invalids.

According to established procedure, the collective farm allocates resources to the centralized Union social security fund for collective farmers and to the centralized Union social insurance fund for collective farmers.

IX. Culture, Everyday Life and Public Services and Amenities

41. The collective farm takes steps to improve the cultural and everyday conditions of the collective farmers' lives *and displays day-to-day concern for strengthening the health of collective-farm members and their families and for their physical training.*

To this end, the collective farm:

builds and equips collective-farm clubs, libraries and other cultural-enlightenment institutions *and sports installations,* assists in the de-development of physical culture and sports, and sets up kindergartens and nurseries;

assists parents and the schools in the correct upbringing of children, maintains close ties with the schools, gives assistance to public education agencies in the production training of children, provides the schools with plots of land, machinery, seeds, fertilizer and means of transportation, and ensures the job placement of school graduates on the collective farm; when necessary, organizes public catering for collective farmers;

gives assistance to the public health agencies in conducting curative and preventive measures on the collective farm and provides collective-farm members with free and emergency transportation to take sick persons to medical institutions;

provides public services and amenities, electricity and radio service for the collective-farm communities and the collective farmers' homes *and assists in the organization of everyday services for collective-farm members;* under the procedure established by the collective farm, gives assistance to the collective farmers in the construction and repair of dwellings, and provides housing space for specialists working on the collective farm who are in need of it.

The collective farm concerns itself with raising the production skills and cultural and technical level of the collective-farm members; sends collective farmers, under established procedure, for study in higher and specialized secondary educational institutions and vocational-technical schools and in advanced training courses; *grants privileges provided by existing legislation to collective farmers who are successfully studying in correspondence and evening general-education and specialized educational institutions and who are conscientiously working on the collective farm* [creates conditions for collective farmers to take correspondence courses].

Collective farmers who graduate from educational institutions to which their

395

collective farm has sent them are obliged to return to work in their speciality on that collective farm.

X. The Auxiliary Farming of the Collective Farmer's Family (Collective-Farm Household)

42. The collective farmer's family (collective-farm household) may own a dwelling, farm buildings, productive livestock, poultry, bees, and small agricultural implements for work on a personal plot.

The collective farmer's family (collective-farm household) is granted the use of a personal plot of land, as a vegetable garden, an orchard or for other needs, up to 0·50 hectares in size, including land occupied by buildings, and up to 0·20 hectares on irrigated land.

The size of the personal plot, within the established norms, is defined by the collective farm's charter. At the same time, the sizes of existing personal plots established in accordance with the Charter of the Agricultural Artel previously in effect may be retained.

The personal plot of the collective farmer's family (collective-farm household) is granted by decision of the general meeting of collective-farm members, and its size is established with consideration for the number of members of the collective farmer's family (collective-farm household) and their labour participation in the collective farm's communal sector.[1]

In carrying out the compact build-up of rural communities, the collective farm allots personal plots of a smaller size to collective farmers near their dwellings (or apartments), granting them the remaining portion of the land plot outside the residential zone of the community. In so doing, the total land area allotted for use by the collective farmer's family (collective-farm household) must not exceed the size of the personal plot as stipulated by the collective farm's charter.

The use of personal plots in the sizes established by the collective farm is retained by collective farmers' families (collective-farm households) in instances in which all members of the family (collective-farm household) are unable to work because of old age or disability, in which the only able-bodied member of the family (collective-farm household) is called up for a tour of active military duty, is elected to an elective position, takes up studies or temporarily transfers to other work, with the consent of the collective farm, or in which only minors remain in the family (collective-farm household). In all other instances, the question of the retention of the personal plot is decided by the general meeting of collective-farm members.

A personal plot may not be transferred for use by other individuals or be cultivated with the use of hired labour.

The collective-farm board gives assistance to collective farmers, under the procedure established by the collective farm, in the cultivation of personal

[1] See the bracketed paragraph at the end of Article 43.

396

plots; this assistance is rendered primarily to families in which there are no able-bodied individuals.

The collective-farm board is obliged to exercise systematic control over the observance of the established sizes of personal plots. In the event of an unauthorized increase in the size of a personal plot, the excess land over the established norm is confiscated by the board and the harvest grown on this land is turned over to the collective farm, without compensation for expenses incurred during the illegal use.

43. The collective farmer's family (collective-farm household) may have one cow with a calf up to one year of age, one heifer or bull up to two years of age, one sow with pigs up to three months of age or two hogs that are being fattened, up to ten sheep and goats (combined), beehives, poultry and rabbits.

An increase in the norms for the keeping of personally owned livestock by a collective farmer's family (collective-farm household), or the replacement of some types of livestock by others in certain regions, taking national characteristics and local conditions into account, is permitted by decision of the union-republic Council of Ministers.

The number and types of livestock that a collective farmer's family (collective-farm household) may have within the established norms are defined by the collective farm's charter.

The collective-farm board gives the collective farmers assistance in the acquisition of livestock, furnishes veterinary service, and also provides feed and pastures for livestock.

The keeping of livestock over and above the norms established by the charter is prohibited.

[The size of the personal plot and the number of livestock that a collective farmer's family (collective farm household) may keep are established by the general meeting of collective-farm members, taking into account the number of members in the family and their labour participation in the collective farm's communal sector.]

44. By decision of the general meeting of collective farmers, the collective farm grants personal plots of land to teachers, physicians and other specialists who work in the rural locality and reside on the collective farm's territory. Workers, office employees, pensioners and invalids residing on the collective farm's territory may, when vacant land for personal plots is available, be granted personal plots by decision of the general meeting of collective farmers.

The collective farm may also permit the aforementioned individuals to use pastures for their livestock, under the established procedure.

XI. The Collective Farm's Administrative Bodies and Inspection Commission

45. The administration of the collective farm's affairs is carried out on the basis of broad democracy and the active participation of the collective farmers in the resolution of all questions of collective-farm life.

The collective farm's affairs are administered by the general meeting of collective-farm members; during the period between meetings, they are administered by the collective-farm board.

46. The general meeting of collective-farm members is the highest administrative body of the collective farm.

The general meeting:

adopts the charter of the collective farm and makes changes in and additions to it;

elects the board and the chairman of the collective farm and the inspection commission of the collective farm;

decides questions [approves decisions of the board] on the admission of collective-farm members and [decides questions of] *on* the expulsion of collective farmers from collective-farm membership;

adopts regulations for the collective farm and statutes on pay and on the intra-farm settling of accounts;

ratifies the collective farm's organizational-management plan and its long-range and annual production-financial plans;

hears reports by the collective-farm board and inspection commission on their activities;

approves the annual report of the collective farm and the sizes of the collective farm's in-kind and monetary funds;

approves decisions of the collective-farm board on the appointment and release of chief (senior) specialists and the collective farm's chief book-keeper;

decides questions of the collective farm's participation in inter-collective-farm and state–collective-farm enterprises and organizations, of its affiliation with associations and unions, and of the enlargement of the collective farm or its division into smaller units;

reviews questions of changing the size of the collective farm's land or the boundaries of the land it uses.

Decisions of the collective-farm board on the questions listed above are not valid unless approved by the general meeting of collective farmers.

The general meeting of collective farmers also considers other questions of the collective farm's activity.

47. The general meeting of collective-farm members is convened by the collective-farm board at least four times a year. The collective-farm board is also obliged to convene the general meeting of collective farmers if this is

requested by at least one-third of the collective farm's members *or by the inspection commission.*

The general meeting is empowered to decide questions if the meeting is attended by at least two-thirds of the collective-farm members.

Decisions are adopted at the general meeting of collective farmers by a simple majority of votes.

The collective-farm board notifies the collective farmers of the convocation of a general meeting at least seven days in advance.

48. On large collective farms, where the convocation of general meetings of collective-farm members is difficult, meetings of representatives may be convened to decide questions falling within the purview of the general meeting.

Representatives are elected at meetings of collective farmers in the brigades and other units of the collective farm. The norms of representation and the procedure for the election of representatives are *determined by the collective-farm board* [established by the general meeting of collective-farm members]. *Questions falling within the jurisdiction of meetings of representatives are given preliminary discussion at meetings of collective farmers in the brigades (units). The representatives report to brigade (unit) meetings on decisions adopted by the meetings of representatives.*

A meeting of representatives is empowered to decide questions if it is attended by at least three-fourths of all the representatives.

49. The collective-farm board is an executive and administrative body that is responsible to the general meeting of collective-farm members, and it exercises direction over all the organizational, production, financial, cultural, service and educational activities of the collective farm.

The collective-farm board organizes fulfilment of the plans for the production and sale to the state of agricultural output, *ensures the rational utilization of land,* expends material and monetary resources in a careful and thrifty way, and takes steps to strengthen production and labour discipline.

In its activity, the collective-farm board constantly relies on the broad collective-farm *aktiv*; it develops and supports creative initiative on the part of collective-farm members in perfecting the organization of communal production and raising labour productivity, shows constant concern for improving the working and living conditions of the collective farmers, and takes a sensitive and attentive attitude toward the consideration of their requests and proposals.

The collective-farm board is elected for a term of three years. The collective-farm board makes an annual report on its activity to the general meeting of collective farmers.

Meetings of the collective-farm board are convened when necessary, but at least once a month; the board is empowered to decide questions if the meeting is attended by at least three-fourths of the board members.

The board adopts decisions by a simple majority of votes.

50. The general meeting of collective farmers elects the chairman of the collective farm, who is simultaneously the chairman of the collective-farm board, for a term of three years.

The chairman of the collective farm exercises day-to-day direction over the collective farm's activity, ensures the fulfilment of the decisions of the general meeting and the board, and represents the collective farm in its relations with state agencies and other institutions and organizations.

The collective-farm board elects from its membership one or two vice-chairmen of the collective farm.

[The chairman of the collective farm or board members who fail to justify the trust placed in them may be removed before the end of their terms by decision of the general meeting of collective-farm members.][1]

51. The collective-farm board appoints a chief bookkeeper from among the collective-farm members or hires a person for this post under a labour contract.

The chief bookkeeper organizes the keeping of records and the compilation of reports on the collective farm and exercises day-to-day control over the safe keeping and proper expenditure of monetary resources and material assets. The chief book-keeper, together with the collective-farm chairman, signs the annual report of the collective farm and documents certifying the receipt and expenditure of monetary resources and material assets.

52. To guide individual branches of the collective farm's activity, the board appoints specialists from among the collective-farm members or hires persons for these posts under labour contracts.

Chief (senior) specialists bear responsibility for the condition of the branch that they guide and organize fulfilment of the production-financial plan. The instructions of chief (senior) specialists on questions falling within their purview are mandatory for collective-farm members and also for the officials of the collective farm.

53. For the broader participation of collective-farm members in the administration of communal production, meetings of collective farmers are convened in the brigades and other production units of the collective farm.

The meeting of the collective farmers of a brigade (or unit):

elects a brigade leader (unit leader), whose election must subsequently be approved by the collective-farm board;
reviews the plan assignment, reports by the brigade leader (unit leader) on work done, and other questions of production activity;
discusses measures for strengthening labour discipline and submits proposals to the collective-farm board on measures of encouragement or penalties.

Meetings are convened by the leader of the production unit, by the board, or by the collective-farm chairman.

[1] See the last paragraph of Article 56.

The meeting elects a brigade council (unit council). The leader of the respective unit is the chairman of the council. The rights and obligations of the council are defined by the collective-farm board.

The instructions of the brigade leader (unit leader) relating to production activity are mandatory for all the collective farmers working in the given unit. In his work, the brigade leader (unit leader) is subordinate to the board and the chairman of the collective farm, and in specialized questions to the chief (senior) specialists as well.

54. The inspection commission, which exercises control over the economic and financial activity of the board and the officials of the collective farm, is elected for a term of three years. The inspection commission elects a chairman from among its members.

The inspection commission is guided by the collective farm's charter and by legislation now in effect, is accountable to the general meeting of collective-farm members, and exercises control over observance of the collective farm's charter, the preservation of collective-farm property, the legality of contracts and economic transactions, the expenditure of monetary resources and material assets and the correct keeping of records, the compilation of reports and the settling of accounts with collective farmers, and also over the prompt consideration by the collective-farm board and officials of complaints and petitions from collective farmers.

The inspection commission conducts at least two inspections each year of the collective farm's economic and financial activity, carries out periodic checkups on the economic activity of the brigades and other production units, and offers its conclusions on the collective farm's annual report. Inspection documents are subject to ratification by the general meeting of collective farmers.

55. The inspection commission has the right:

> to check on the proper utilization and preservation of agricultural output, seeds and fodder, material-technical and monetary resources, draught animals and productive livestock, buildings, installations and other property; to demand that officials and members of the collective farm present the necessary documents for examination [to inspect warehouses and other buildings and enterprises of the collective farm];
> to submit proposals, based on the results of checkups and inspections, for consideration by the general meeting and board of the collective farm.

The proposals of the inspection commission are considered at the next general meeting; proposals submitted to the collective-farm board are considered within ten days.

56. The election of the board, the chairman of the collective farm and the inspection commission is done by open or secret ballot, at the discretion of the general meeting of collective farmers.

The number of members of the board and of the inspection commission is determined by the general meeting of collective-farm members.

The collective-farm chairman, the board members and the chairman and members of the inspection commission, if they do not justify the trust placed in them by the collective farmers, can be removed from office before the completion of their terms by decision of the general meeting of collective-farm members.

57. The collective farm creates the necessary conditions for the successful activity of public organizations [that, under the guidance of the Party organizations, perform work having to do with the communist upbringing of the collective farmers, their enlistment in public life, and the development of socialist competition].

58. An economic council or a bureau of economic analysis, a cultural and everyday-service commission *or other commissions* operating on a volunteer basis, as well as a mutual aid fund [and other organizations], may be set up on the collective farm.

XII. The Adoption and Registration of the Collective Farm's Charter

59. The collective farm's charter, adopted by the general meeting of collective-farm members on the basis of the Mode Charter, is presented for registration to the executive committee of the district (or city) soviet. Subsequent changes in and additions to the collective farm's charter are made by the same procedure.

60. The registered charter of the collective farm is filed with the collective-farm board, the district agricultural agency and the executive committee of the district (or city) soviet.

61. The collective farm is guided in its activity by the collective farm's charter and by legislation in effect.

The collective farm, as a socialist *agricultural* enterprise, enjoys the rights of a juristic person and has its own seal and banner.

Source: *Torzhestvo Leninskogo kooperativnogo plana, Materialy 3ego Vsesoyuznogo S'ezda Kolkhoznikov* (Moscow, 1969), p. 87.
Translation: CDSP, Vol. XXI, No. 50, p. 9.

Part V

The Worker and his Labour

80. Workers' Control of Enterprises Granted
14 *November* 1917, *OS*

81. Workers' Control Abolished
18 *October* 1918

82. The Principle of One-Man Management Established
5 *April* 1920

The problem of who was to run all the individual enterprises and institutions was the subject of considerable debate in the first years of Soviet power. The extracts from three documents given here illustrate what in fact happened. The Bolsheviks began by declaring, some three weeks after their coup, that elected workers' factory committees would take over the running of all the privately owned enterprises in the country. The committees would have their own centralized national structure, but would co-operate with the state authorities. (The trade unions, which were at that time suspect to Bolsheviks, were largely bypassed.)

This rather ramshackle system was quietly dismantled in October 1918, after the economy had been extensively nationalized. Lenin managed to get the principle of one-man control approved by the Ninth Party Congress in March 1920; he was now opposed by the unions, who favoured a collegiate system. The final step in the struggle was the approval of Lenin's resolution on complete trade-union subordination to the Party the following year (see document 27). One-man control has remained a central feature of all Soviet enterprises.

80. The Statute on Workers' Control
Approved by the Council of People's Commissars, 14 November 1917, OS

1. In order to provide planned regulation of the national economy, workers' control over the manufacture, purchase, sale and storage of produce and raw materials and over the financial activity of enterprise is introduced in all industrial, commercial, banking, agricultural, co-operative and other enterprises which employ hired labour or give work to be done at home.
2. Workers' control is exercised by all the workers of the given enterprise through their elected bodies, such as factory committees, shop stewards' councils, etc., whose members include representatives of the office employees and the technical personnel.
3. In every city, *gubernia* and industrial district a local workers' control council is set up, which, being an agency of the soviet of workers', soldiers'

and peasants' deputies, is composed of representatives of trade unions, factory and office workers' committees, and workers' co-operatives ...

6. The workers' control bodies have the right to supervise production, establish output quotas, and take measures to ascertain production costs.

7. The workers' control bodies have the right of access to the entire business correspondence of an enterprise; concealment of the same by the owners is punishable by a court of law. Commercial secrecy is abolished. The owners are obliged to present to workers' control bodies all books and accounts for both the current and previous fiscal years.

8. Decisions of workers' control bodies are binding upon the owners of enterprises and may be revoked only by higher workers' control bodies ...

12. The All-Russia Workers' Control Council works out general plans of workers' control, issues instructions and ordinances, regulates relationships between district workers' control councils, and serves as the highest instance for all matters pertaining to workers' control.

13. The All-Russia Workers' Control Council co-ordinates the activity of workers' control bodies with that of all other institutions concerned with the organization of the national economy.

Instructions on the relationships between the All-Russia Workers' Control Council and other institutions organizing and regulating the national economy will be issued separately.

14. All laws and circulars hampering the activity of the factory and other committees and councils of wage and salary earners are repealed.

In the name of the Government of the Russian Republic,

> Chairman of the Council of People's Commissars, VL. ULYANOV (LENIN).
> People's Commissar of Labour, ALEXANDER SHLYAP-NIKOV.
> Business Manager of the Council of People's Commissars, VL. BONCH-BRUYEVICH.
> Secretary of the Council, N. GORBUNOV.

Source: G. D. Obichkin, i drugie, Dekrety sovetskoi vlasti, Vol. I (Moscow, 1957), p. 83. Translation: Yuri Akhapkin, First Decrees of Soviet Power (Lawrence and Wishart, London, 1970), p. 36 (abbreviated).

81. Abolition of Workers' Control

Resolution of the Conference of Metal Workers, 18 October 1918

Having considered the question of the place which the organs of workers' control should occupy in nationalized enterprises, particularly in the State Combine of Metallurgical Works, the Conference hereby resolves:

1. The organization of the administrative bodies of these enterprises guarantees that the representatives of the trade unions of the proletariat and the regulative organs of the state will have a decisive influence in the management of the amalgamated workshops; the need for the previously existing special organs of workers' control is thereby removed.
2. In view of this fact workers' control shall cease functioning and its organs shall be dissolved as soon as the administrative organs of the amalgamated workshops have been fully established.

Source: Metallist (Moscow), No. 7, 1918, p. 18.
Translation: James Bunyan, *Intervention, Civil War and Communism in Russia, April–December,* 1918 (Baltimore, Johns Hopkins Press, 1936), p. 267.

82. The Organization of Industrial Management (one-man control)

Resolution of the Ninth Congress of the Russian Communist Party (Bolsheviks), 29 March–5 April 1920 ('On the next tasks of economic construction', section IX)

The basic task in setting up management is the creation of a competent, firm, energetic leadership, be it for an individual industrial enterprise or for a whole branch of industry.

The congress considers it necessary, with the object of achieving a simpler and more accurate organization of production management and also of saving organizational resources, to make the management of industry more individual, namely by the establishment of full and unconditional one-man control in workshops large and small, by progress towards one-man control in works management, and by a reduction of collegiums in the middle and higher levels of the administrative and production apparatus ...

In any case, the actual implementation, from top to bottom, of the oft-proclaimed principle of making a given person individually responsible for given work is an essential condition for any improvement of economic organization or growth of production. The *collegiate approach,* in so far as it is encountered in the sphere of discussion or decision-making, must give way unconditionally to *one-man control* in the sphere of execution. The usefulness of every organization must be measured by the strictness with which duties, functions and responsibility are distributed in it.

NOTE. The work of managements must be carefully checked by means of a special body attached to the VSNKh with the object of both continuously selecting the best staff and establishing, in practice, the best methods of combining workers and specialists in management procedures.

The organization of managerial bodies in industry, of both the collegiate and one-man types, must be effected through the agreement of the VSNKh bodies with the leading trade-union bodies involved ...

Source: KPSS *v rezolyutsiyakh*, chast' I (Moscow, 1954), p. 482 (extracts). Editor's translation.

83. M. Tomsky Comments on Strikes

22 *April* 1922

After they had assumed power the Bolsheviks adopted an extremely negative attitude towards strikes, which they declared impermissible. The re-establishment of private enterprise in the NEP period, however, reopened the issue in a particularly awkward form. Here M. Tomsky, erstwhile president of the Soviet trade unions, gives perhaps the fullest authoritative statement ever to be published.

No law specifically forbidding strikes has ever been passed in the USSR. One outside observer claims that the only legal basis for the ban is the Metal Workers' Union's first labour contract of January 1918, which stipulated that no strikes, including sit-down strikes, go-slows, and working to rule, were to be allowed.[1] Strikes have nevertheless been frequent at times, and were particularly characteristic of the 'twenties. News of isolated occurrences still reaches the West; serious strikes, which were evidently suppressed by force, took place in Temir Tau and Novocherkassk in the 'sixties.

83. M. Tomsky's Comments on Strikes

From his speech at the Eleventh Congress of the Party,
27 *March–22 April* 1922

... The trade unions cannot conduct a dual policy in defending the interests of the workers. A trade union cannot say: we are defending the interests of hired workers at private enterprises, but we are not defending them at state enterprises. People will leave such trade unions and will have nothing to do with them. Soviet power will be discredited, and people will say: the trade unions at private enterprises defend the interests of the workers, but at state enterprises they do not defend them, and conditions there are worse.

The policy must be uniform, so that a worker at a state enterprise can feel that in respect of the law he is in no worse a position than a worker at a private enterprise. The matter is determined by this approach.

Milyutin deals with strikes at enterprises in the corrections he made. What does he recommend? That at private enterprises strikes may take place, but at state enterprises they should be regarded as impermissible. It is time for us to give up this functionary's approach to strikes. Strikes exist not because they are considered permissible or impermissible, but as a consequence of many causes. You may consider strikes to be in principle impermissible, for example, in Moscow, but here you have thirty to forty strikes a month, and

[1] Margaret Dewar, *Labour Policy in the USSR*, 1917–28 (London, 1956), p. 28.

proportionately fewer in other towns. We for our part consider strikes to be impermissible when they are led by Mensheviks who, by arranging these strikes, conduct a political struggle against Soviet power. But in ninety-nine cases out of a hundred no politics at all are involved, and it is a question of concrete cases and questions which can be sorted out and arranged.

So there can be no dualism in the question of strikes, and there should be a single line. That line must consist in defining strikes as a method in the struggle for the improvement of the economic conditions of the workers. Approaching the matter in this way, we proceed from the idea that the working class in Russia is completely devoted to the development of the productive forces in the country, since that is the sole and most important condition for preserving its dictatorship. Without the development of the productive forces of the country there can be no improvement in the economic position of the working class.

At the same time the question of the development of the productive forces of the country is raised before the working class in a particularly acute form. Every force which Soviet power uses to develop the country's productive forces is progressive but not, of course, when it results in the creation of bun shops, coffee bars, and so on. In such circumstances is the working class interested in violating correct production, in interrupting or destroying the productive forces? No, it is not. The strike is therefore an unsuitable method of struggle in the given economic circumstances. But this brings us to the basic definition of the distinction between a strike at state and privately owned enterprises.

What is a strike at a privately owned enterprise under conditions of the dictatorship of the proletariat? In what matters may a clash take place? In economic matters. Under what conditions? When capitalists try to go beyond the framework established by Soviet power and use the Soviet business situation to re-establish the old relations, that is, when a distinct economic counter-revolution takes place. At this point the working class is involved in a clash, and things go as far as a strike. Since this is so, it is necessary to insist that we should not allow the old relationships between labour and capital to be restored. That is the first thing.

The second thing is a strike at a state enterprise. Whom is the strike against? Against Soviet power? No, against the servants of Soviet power who have not mastered the essence of Soviet power and the dictatorship of the proletariat, who have got out of control and do not understand the policy of Soviet power. At this point the proletariat gives its servant a good shake and sends him off along the proletarian path.

The third form of strike is when people try to turn a strike into a weapon of struggle against Soviet power, that is, into a counter-revolutionary action, which the union, the Party and Soviet power will regard as a counter-revolutionary action. This is what a strike is. Is it possible to say that in this case you have the right to strike, but that we are depriving you of the right to strike? Firstly, the Soviet republic does not forbid striking as such, by law, and that is done for a purpose. We have no law against strikes. Here the worker does not recognize the strike as a method of struggle, not because the law forbids it, but because he understands, as a result of his class-consciousness, the situation in which he lives and struggles.

Can we say that it is impossible to strike at state enterprises, but possible at private ones? Ask any worker and he will say: 'If it is possible to improve the situation by means of a strike, then why don't they allow strikes at state enterprises?' That means that the workers of private enterprises are in a better position, and can make use of the most effective weapon of struggle.

From this it follows that with regard to strikes we must always take into account their principal distinctions, their character, essence, and the forms of strike in each particular instance. But from this it follows that if we recognize that strikes as a method of struggle are not suitable at a given moment, or are not suitable for solving conflicts, then from that there follows a whole series of propositions which indicate that in this case it is the task of the union to solve conflicts in a peaceable manner, that is, through conciliation chambers, the arbitration courts or something else. And only then, when it is impossible to come to an agreement (which in fact cannot happen as far as state enterprises are concerned), can a strike take place under the control of the higher trade-union organizations.

But at this point other orthodox Communists, of whom my old friend Comrade Ryazanov is one, get annoyed and say: 'Pardon, but Tomsky is saying the same thing as Gompers,[1] Henderson,[2] and so on; conciliation chambers, arbitration courts, arbitration and so on—those are the same words, and the same tactics that Kolokolnikov and Grinevich[3] spoke of.'

That is quite true: the same words, and the same tactics, only in different circumstances. Legin in Germany says: 'The working class is interested in the development of German industry, because without the development of German industry there will be unemployed, and the economic position of the workers cannot be improved, and therefore striking, as a method of struggle, is unsuitable, and it is necessary to seek peaceful solutions in the talks with capital.'

This is a confusion of thought, since in that case it is a question of the well-being of German national industry, of bourgeois industry, while we are talking in conditions of the dictatorship of the proletariat, and it is a matter of our Soviet worker and peasant industry. The working class is

---

[1] S. Gompers, 1850–1924, an American trade-union leader whose views were hostile to Bolshevism.

[2] A. Henderson, 1863–1935, a prominent British parliamentarian and leader of the Second (Socialist Workers') International.

[3] P. N. Kolokolnikov and V. P. Grinevich (Kogan) were Mensheviks active in the Soviet trade-union movement at the time of the Revolution.

in power, it directs this industry, and although we are superficially saying the same thing as the opportunists in West Europe say, in fact they are different. Therefore that objection does not bear criticism ...

Source: XI S'ezd VRKP(B), stenografichesky otchet (Moscow, 1961), p. 237. Editor's translation.

84. The RSFSR 1922 Labour Code (extracts)

30 *October* 1922

This code, which replaced the first, largely inoperative, Labour Code of 1918, *was to be the basis of Soviet labour legislation for over three decades.*

It retained the liberal stipulations of the 1918 *document regarding limitations on hours of work, holidays, protection of female and juvenile labour, and social insurance, etc. There were also important innovations in the freer spirit of the NEP. The principle of labour service was replaced by voluntary engagement on contract; a new section dealt with the trade unions, now firmly under party control; and the demotion of the factory committees, which had been important after the Bolshevik coup, was reaffirmed. A supplementary decree of* 9 *November made it clear that labour legislation (including the Code itself) could be enacted only by the government. This was an important departure from a pre-revolutionary Bolshevik thesis.*

Here we have attempted to extract some of the more important provisions. Of course many hundreds of amendments were made (particularly in the mid-'twenties and 'thirties) before the Code was replaced in July 1970 *(see document* 92).

84. Labour Code of the RSFSR (1922 edition)

Approved by the All-Russian Central Executive Committee, 30 *October* 1922

I. General Provisions

1. The provisions of the Labour Code shall apply to all persons performing work for remuneration, including home-workers, and shall be binding on all undertakings, institutions, and businesses (whether State, military, public, or private, including those which give out work to be done at home), and also on all persons who employ others for remuneration.

   NOTE. The CPC shall issue a special Order determining the exemptions from the application of this Code in respect of home-workers.

2. The CPC, the CLD, or the PLC under their authorization, shall decide to what extent this Code shall be applicable in cases of persons called up for compulsory labour service (section 11).
3. The CPC shall be entitled to extend the application of this Code, as regards particular parts thereof, to certain classes of soldiers not on active military service.

4. Every labour contract or agreement which is less favourable in respect of labour conditions than the provisions of this Code shall be void ...

II. The Engagement and Supply of Labour

5. Work for citizens of the RSFSR is made available on the basis of voluntary hiring, through the organs of the People's Labour Commissariat, with the exceptions indicated in Article 9.
6. Persons seeking work are registered as unemployed at the local office of the People's Labour Commissariat.
7. The hiring of labour by all enterprises, institutions, and undertakings (state, public and private) without exception as well as by individual employers, is conducted through the competent offices of the People's Labour Commissariat in the following manner:

   (a) The demand for labour is sent in the name of the management of the enterprise, institution or individual employer to the corresponding office of the PLC;
   (b) If there are any persons present who are registered at the office of the PLC and who satisfy the terms of the vacancies announced, these persons are sent to work in the manner set down by the PLC in agreement with the All-Russian Central Council of Trade Unions;
   (c) Employers inform the PLC offices of their acceptance of persons sent to them by these offices or of their refusal to accept them, in accordance with the rules established by the PLC.

8. The employer bears responsibility for (a) any incorrect information he has given regarding the conditions of the work offered, (b) any failure to observe the employment obligations he has taken upon himself, or (c) any unreasonable refusal to accept labour which has been sent to him.
9. Workers may be invited to work independently of PLC offices, as long as they are subsequently registered at these offices, in the following instances: (a) in cases which involve political trust or special knowledge associated with the person taken on, and (b) in cases when labour cannot be provided by PLC offices within three days of a demand for it being received.
10. The managements of state, public and private institutions and enterprises provide PLC offices with periodic information on the movement of labour in the manner and periods determined by the People's Labour Commissariat.

III. Calling up of Citizens of the RSFSR for Compulsory Labour Service

11. In exceptional cases (fighting the elements, or lack of workers to carry out important state work), all citizens of the RSFSR, with the exceptions

mentioned in sections 12 to 14, may be called up for work in the form of compulsory labour service in accordance with a special decision of the CPC or of the officials authorized for this purpose by the said Council.

12. The following persons shall not be liable to be called up for compulsory labour service: (*a*) persons under eighteen years of age; (*b*) men above forty-five years of age and women above forty years of age.

13. The following persons shall be exempt from calling up for compulsory labour service: (*a*) persons temporarily incapacitated for work on account of illness or injury, during the period requisite for their recovery; (*b*) pregnant women, during a period of eight weeks before confinement, and women, during a period of eight weeks after confinement; (*c*) nursing mothers; (*d*) men disabled in employment or in the war; (*e*) women with children under eight years of age, if no one is available to take care of such children.

14. Additional exceptions and relaxations in respect of various kinds of compulsory labour service shall be specified by the CPC, the CLD, and the PLC, with due regard to health, family circumstances, the nature of the work, and conditions of life.

IV. Collective Contracts ...

V. Contracts of Work

27. A contract of work shall mean an agreement between two or more persons whereby one party (the employee) places his labour at the disposal of the other party (the employer) in return for remuneration.

A contract of work may be concluded whether a collective contract exists or not.

28. The terms of the contract of work shall be fixed by agreement between the parties. Any terms in the contract of work which render the conditions of work less favourable than those laid down in the labour laws, in the collective contract, or in the rules of employment which are in force in the particular undertaking or institution (cf. sections 4, 15, 19, 52–55), and likewise terms intended to limit the political and general civic rights of the worker, shall be void.

VI. Rules of Employment ...

VII. Standards of Output ...

VIII. Remuneration of Work

58. The amount of the employee's remuneration for his work shall be fixed by collective and individual contracts of work.

59. The amount of the remuneration shall not be less than the compulsory minimum wage fixed for a given period by the competent state authorities for the class of work in question.

60. The amount of the remuneration shall be fixed in the contracts either at a time rate, on the basis of the normal working day (sections 94 et seq.), or by the piece. The amount of remuneration for overtime shall be specially noted in the contract, and shall not in any case be less than one-and-a-half times the normal wage for the first two hours, and twice the normal wage for subsequent hours, and the same for work on rest days or holidays (sections 109 et seq.).

61. Young persons shall be paid for the reduced working day in the same way as employees of the same class working the full day. The PLC may prescribe the methods of calculation and the standards for the payment of young persons, according to the nature and conditions of each branch of economic activity.

IX Guarantees and Compensation ...

X. Hours of Work

94. The duration of normal hours of work, both in production and in the accessory work necessary to production, shall not exceed eight hours.

> NOTE. The People's Commissariat of Labour, in agreement with the All-Union Central Council of Trade Unions, shall specify the groups of responsible political trade-union or soviet workers whose work shall not be subject to the restriction of hours specified in the present section.

95. The duration of the hours of work shall not exceed six hours (*a*) for persons between 16 and 18 years of age; (*b*) for persons employed in intellectual or office work, other than those who work in direct connection with production, (*c*) for persons employed underground, as provided in the list of occupations drawn up by the PLC.

A reduced working day shall be fixed for persons employed in specially exhausting and unhealthy branches of production, in accordance with the lists and rules drawn up by the PLC.

96. The duration of working hours fixed in sections 94 and 95 shall be reduced by one hour in case of night work ...

103. Work extending beyond the normal hours of work (overtime work) shall not be allowed as a rule.

104. Overtime work shall be allowed only in the following exceptional cases:

(*a*) For the performance of work absolutely necessary for the protection of the Republic and the prevention of crises and dangers threatening the commonwealth;

(*b*) For the performance of absolutely necessary work in the public interest in connection with the water supply, lighting, drainage, communications, and the postal, telegraph and telephone services, to remedy any incidental or unforeseen derangements of their working;

(*c*) When absolutely necessary to complete work which has been begun and which it has proved impossible for technical reasons to finish during the normal hours of work owing to an unforeseen or incidental delay, if the suspension of the work which has been begun would entail any damage to raw materials or machinery;

(*d*) For the effecting of temporary repairs and adjustments of machines or apparatus, if the derangement caused by the defect entails the interruption of the work of a considerable number of employees.

NOTE. It shall be permissible to work overtime in the cases mentioned in this section only in pursuance of a resolution of the local assessment and disputes committee or in default thereof with the consent of the competent trade union and the approval of the labour inspector, and in exceptional cases on condition that the labour inspector is subsequently informed thereof.

105. Persons who have not attained the age of eighteen years shall not in any circumstances be allowed to work overtime.

106. The number of hours' overtime for each employee shall not exceed 120 hours a year; the time spent in overtime work shall not exceed four hours within two consecutive days.

NOTE. In special branches of economic activity which are of a seasonal character, the number of hours' overtime may be increased beyond the limit mentioned in section 106 by the PLC in agreement with the ARCTU.

107. Overtime shall not be worked to make up time lost in consequence of an employee's beginning work late.

108. All overtime work shall be entered in the employee's wages book, and likewise in the special overtime register, showing the time when the said work begins and ends and the remuneration received by the employee for overtime.

XI. Rest Periods

109. Every employee shall be granted an uninterrupted weekly rest period of not less than forty-two hours. Weekly rest days shall be fixed by the local labour sections in agreement with the trade-union councils, and may be assigned on Sunday or on any other day of the week, according to the national and denominational composition of the body of wage-earning and salaried employees in each locality.

110. Employees in undertakings, institutions, and businesses, who are unable to avail themselves of the general weekly rest days owing to the nature of their work, shall be granted the prescribed rest period on other free days which are suitable for leave for them. This provision shall apply also to persons working in undertakings which from their nature necessitate continuous work. In the last-mentioned undertakings special days of leave shall be fixed for each group of employees in place of the general rest days.

111. No work shall be done on the following days:

(*a*) 1 January—New Year's Day;
(*b*) 22 January—anniversary of 9 January 1905;
(*c*) 12 March—anniversary of the overthrow of the autocracy;
(*d*) 18 March — anniversary of the Paris Commune;
(*e*) 1 and 2 May—anniversary of the International;
(*f*) 7 and 8 November—anniversary of the October Revolution.

112. The labour sections, in agreement with the provincial trade-union councils, may fix not more than six special rest days in the year in addition to those specified in section 111; these festivals shall be made to harmonize with local conditions, the composition of the population, popular festivals, etc.

NOTE. The PLC in agreement with the ARCTU may draw up lists of the undertakings and institutions in which work must, from its nature, be carried on uninterruptedly on any of the rest days and festivals mentioned in the foregoing section.

113. On the eves of rest days and festivals (sections 109 to 111) the hours of work shall not exceed six hours; these days shall be paid for as full working days; where payment is by the piece, special remuneration shall be paid for the hours during which work is not done in pursuance of this section, at the rates in force for the classes of work in question.

NOTE. No deduction shall be made from the wages of persons paid by the month, in respect of festivals and the eves thereof.

114. Every person employed for wages who has worked uninterruptedly for not less than five-and-a-half months shall be granted ordinary leave once a year for not less than a fortnight. The ordinary leave for persons who have not attained the age of eighteen years shall not be less than a month.

NOTE. The uninterrupted continuance of work which gives a right to ordinary leave under section 114 shall not be deemed to be broken by transference from one undertaking or institution to another on the instructions of the management, or by the removal of the employee from one State undertaking or institution to another without interruption of his employment.

418

115. Persons employed in specially dangerous and noxious undertakings shall be granted an extra leave period of not less than a fortnight in addition to the leave specified in section 114.

A list of the industries and occupations carrying the right to extra leave shall be drawn up by the PLC.

XII. Apprenticeship ...

XIII. Work of Women and Young Persons

129. Women and young persons under eighteen years of age shall not be employed in particularly heavy and unhealthy work, or in work underground.

A list of specially heavy and unhealthy occupations shall be issued by the PLC in agreement with the ARCTU, together with provisions restricting the carrying of weights; separate lists shall be issued for women and young persons.

130. Women and young persons under eighteen years of age shall not be employed at night.

> NOTE. The PLC, in agreement with the ARCTU, may authorize the employment at night of adult women in branches of industry in which it is absolutely necessary.

131. The employment at night or on overtime of pregnant women and nursing mothers shall be absolutely prohibited.

132. A woman employed in manual work shall be exempt from work for eight weeks before and eight weeks after her confinement, and a woman employed in office or intellectual work shall be exempt from work for six weeks before and six weeks after her confinement (section 181).

> NOTE. A list of the office and intellectual occupations for which, in view of their special nature, the period of leave in connection with maternity is fixed at eight weeks before and eight weeks after confinement, shall be issued by the PLC.

133. A woman shall not be required to undertake work elsewhere than in the locality where she is permanently employed, without her consent thereto, from the fifth month of pregnancy onward.

134. In addition to the general breaks (section 100), further breaks shall be granted to nursing mothers for the purpose of nursing their children. The exact duration of these breaks shall be fixed in the rules of employment, provided that breaks for nursing shall always be granted at intervals of not more than $3\frac{1}{2}$ hours, and each break shall amount to at least half an hour.

The said breaks shall be included in the working hours.

135. Young persons under sixteen years of age shall not be employed.

NOTE. The labour inspector shall be entitled to give permission in exceptional cases for the engagement of young persons who have attained the age of fourteen years, in accordance with special regulations issued by the PLC in agreement with the ARCTU.

136. The working hours of persons under sixteen years of age who are already employed in undertakings or who are newly engaged under section 135 (note) shall be fixed at four hours a day.

137. The minimum number of minors to be employed in the various branches of industry shall be fixed by order for each industry by the PLC in agreement with the ARCTU.

XIV. Protection of Workers

138. An undertaking shall not be opened, brought into operation, or transferred to another building, without the approval of the labour inspection service or the officials entrusted with supervision in respect of industrial hygiene and technical requirements.

139. Every undertaking and institution shall take the necessary steps to remedy or mitigate injurious conditions of work, to prevent accidents, and to maintain workrooms in a proper sanitary and hygienic condition; in these matters they shall conform to the general and special binding orders issued by the PLC for the various branches of industry.

140. Machinery, transmission apparatus and benches shall be disconnected during breaks, except in cases where disconnection is impossible for technical reasons, or when they serve the purpose of ventilation, drainage, lighting, etc.

141. In all specially injurious work, or work in an abnormal temperature or in a damp place, or entailing physical uncleanliness, and likewise in cases in which considerations of general hygiene render it desirable, employees shall be provided at the employer's expense with special clothing and protective apparatus (goggles, masks, respirators, soap, etc.) according to the nature of the work and in accordance with the lists of occupation and regulations issued by the PLC.

146. Supervision over the strict observance of all the provisions of this Code, and of all the decrees, instructions, orders and collective contracts relating to working conditions and the protection of the life and health of employees, shall be entrusted to the labour inspection service and the technical and health inspection services, all of which are within the competence of the PLC, in respect of all undertakings, institutions, businesses and individual employers without exception.

147. The labour inspectors shall be nominated for a specified period by the trade-union councils, and their nominations shall be ratified by the People's Commissariat of Labour ...

XV. Trade Unions (Productive Unions) of Wage-Earning and Salaried Employees, and their Representative Bodies in Undertakings, Institutions and Businesses

151. The trade unions (productive unions) in which citizens employed for remuneration in state, public and private undertakings, institutions and businesses are organized, may appear before the various authorities in the name of wage-earners as parties to collective contracts, and may represent them in all matters relating to work and conditions of life.

152. The trade unions (productive unions) organized in accordance with the principles drawn up by the competent congresses of these bodies shall not be liable to registration by state offices, as prescribed for associations and unions in general, but shall be registered with the central federations to which they are affiliated in accordance with the conditions prescribed by the All-Russian Congress of Trade Unions.

153. Other associations not registered with central federations under section 152 shall not be entitled to style themselves trade unions (productive unions) nor to claim the rights of such unions.

154. Trade unions (productive unions) shall be entitled—

(*a*) to acquire and manage property;
(*b*) to conclude contracts, agreements, etc., of all kinds under the legislation in force.

NOTE. All the rights possessed by trade unions (productive unions) shall also be possessed by their central federations.

155. Under Article 16 of the Constitution of the RSFSR, all state authorities shall be bound to afford trade unions (productive unions) and federations thereof all requisite assistance by furnishing them with properly equipped buildings for the establishment of labour palaces and union offices, and affording them privileges in connection with the use of the postal, telegraph, telephone, railway and water transport services.

156. The principal body representing the trade unions in undertakings institutions and businesses, shall be the committee of wage-earning and salaried employees (factory, mining, building, local, etc., committee) or an authorized delegate of the union instead of the committee.

NOTE 1. The procedure of the election of the employees' committee in each undertaking, institution or business shall be laid down by the competent trade union (productive union).

NOTE 2. The organization and procedure of the committees of wage-earning and salaried employees in the military and naval departments shall be governed by a special order issued by the PLC in agreement with the RMCR and the ARCTU.

157. No other committee than that established by section 156 of this Code and approved by the competent trade union (productive union) shall have the rights specified in sections 158 to 160.

158. The duties of the committee (section 156) shall be as follows:

(*a*) It shall safeguard the interests of the wage-earning and salaried employees which it represents in relation to the management of the undertaking, institution or business, in respect of matters connected with the employment and conditions of life of employees.

(*b*) It shall represent the employees before the Government and other public authorities.

(*c*) It shall see that the legislative provisions concerning the protection of workers, social insurance, the payment of wages, and the regulations for hygiene and the prevention of accidents, etc., are faithfully carried out by the management of the undertaking, institution or business, and shall co-operate with the state authorities concerned with the protection of the workers.

(*d*) It shall take steps to improve the social and material situation of wage-earning and salaried employees.

(*e*) It shall co-operate in the regular carrying on of production in state undertakings, and participate in the regulation and organization of economic activities through the competent trade unions (productive unions).

159. The management shall be notified of the election of the committee and of the fact that it has entered upon its duties. The number of members of the committee of wage-earning and salaried employees, who shall be exempt from their regular work for the purpose of transacting the business of the committee, shall be fixed in accordance with the following rules:

if the undertaking, institution or business employs not more than 300 persons, one member;
if it employs more than 300 but not more than 1,000 persons, two members;
if it employs more than 1,000 but not more than 5,000 persons, three members;
if it employs more than 5,000 persons, five members.

Members of the committee shall be released from work by the management in pursuance of a resolution of the committee.

160. The members of the committee who are released for regular work on behalf of the committee shall receive remuneration corresponding to their qualifications, and not less in any case than the appropriate scheduled rate ...

XVI. Organizations for the Settlement of Disputes and Investigation of Complaints Respecting Contraventions of Labour Laws

168. Cases concerning the infringement of labour laws, together with all disputes which arise over the use of hired labour, are resolved on either an obligatory basis—at special sessions of the People's Court—or through conciliation proceedings in Rating and Conflict Commissions, Conciliation Chambers, or Arbitration Courts, which are organized on the basis of parity representation of the parties concerned. All these institutions function on the basis of their own particular sets of statutes ...

XVII. Social Insurance

175. The social-insurance system shall cover all employees, irrespective of whether the undertakings, institutions and businesses in which they are employed are state, public, co-operative, established under a concession or lease, of mixed character, or private, or whether they are employed by private individuals, and also irrespective of the nature and duration of their employment and the method of remuneration.

176. The social-insurance system shall comprise (a) the granting of sick benefit; (b) the granting of benefit in case of temporary loss of working capacity (illness, injury, quarantine, pregnancy, confinement, care of a sick member of the family); (c) the granting of supplementary benefits (for the nursing of children, medical requisites, funerals); (d) the granting of unemployment benefit; (e) the granting of invalidity pension; (f) the granting of old-age pension; (g) the granting of pensions to members of the families of employees in case of loss (death or total disappearance).

177. For the purpose of effecting social insurance, contributions shall be fixed as percentages of the wages paid. The amount of the insurance contribution shall be fixed by special orders of the CPC according to the degree of unhealthiness or danger of the undertaking.

> NOTE. The insurance moneys shall be reserved exclusively for the purpose of ensuring benefits for wage-earning and salaried employees, and shall not be used for any other purpose whatever.

178. The insurance contributions shall be borne by the undertakings, institutions, businesses and individuals employing workers; they shall not be imposed upon the insured persons nor deducted from their wages.

179. In the event of temporary loss of working capacity, irrespective of the reason therefor (Article 176, paragraph (b)) all insured persons are given benefits equal to the tariff rate of their work category in their given enterprise or institution at the moment when payment of benefits is made; in any case this sum is not to be less than the actual earnings of the incapacitated person up to the moment when he stopped work.

180. Benefit for temporary loss of working capacity shall be paid from the date of the loss of working capacity to the date of its recovery or that of the establishment of the existence of invalidity.

181. Pregnancy and maternity benefit shall be paid to the insured person during the whole period of her absence from work, within the limits specified in section 132 of this Code and the note thereto ...

185. The unemployment benefit is fixed by the corresponding offices at not less than one-sixth of the average wage in the locality, depending on the skill grading of the person unemployed and his length of hired service up to the time of loss of earnings.

> NOTE. The benefits for unemployed juveniles are fixed in accordance with their skill grading without regard to their length of service.

186. The length of time over which unemployment benefits are paid, depending on skill grading and length of service, is fixed by the corresponding offices, so that the period within which such benefits are payable is not less than six months.

187. All persons who have worked as hired hands and who have lost their ability to work as a result of injury, illness or old age have the right to social insurance. The Council of People's Commissars is granted the right to fix the term of service which gives the right to an old-age pension.

188. Pension norms for invalids and forms of payment are fixed by the competent offices in accordance with the nature and degree of incapacity of the invalid and his material position.

> The President of the All–Russian Central Executive Committee, M. KALININ.
> The People's Labour Commissar, V. SCHMIDT.
> The Secretary of the All–Russian Central Executive Committee, A. ENUKIDZE.

Moscow, The Kremlin, 30 October 1922.

Source: Kodeks zakonov o trude, 1922 goda (Moscow, undated).

Translation: Selection of Documents relative to the Labour legislation of the USSR (HMSO, Cmd. 3775, London, 1931). Extracts. The full HMSO version is accurate but incorporates later changes. Articles 5–10, 168, 179, 185–188 have been translated by the editor to bring the text presented here into conformity with the 1922 version.

85. New Controls on Labour

9 *October* 1930

86. The Clamp-Down on Absenteeism

15 *November* 1932

87. The Abolition of the People's Commissariat of Labour

23 *June* 1933

These three measures illustrate the unfavourable changes which took place in the legal rights of the workers and the organization of the labour market in the first years of the planning era. Whereas the 'twenties had in general been years of industrial labour surplus, serious deficits began to become apparent in 1929. The policy of restricting entry to the labour market (using trade-union membership as a sort of filter) was replaced by labour direction and planned placement. The new policy entailed the abrupt abolition of unemployment benefits and pressure on the unemployed to take any work offered them. 'Absenteeism' was now defined much more strictly.

The abolition of the Commissariat of Labour in 1933 meant the disappearance of the labour exchange, and removed such protection of the workers' interests as the Commissariat had afforded. A few of its functions were transferred to the trade-union organizations. The Commissariat reappeared (as the State Committee for Labour and Wages) only in 1955, by which time the absenteeism rules had become inoperative. Unemployment benefits have never been re-introduced, though efforts were being made in the early 'seventies to bring them in under the guise of retraining bonuses.

85. On the Immediate Placement of the Unemployed and Suspension of Payment of Unemployment Insurance

Decree of the People's Commissariat of Labour, 9 October 1930

The People's Commissariat of Labour decrees as follows:

1. In view of the great shortage of labour in all branches of State industry, insurance bureaux are requested to discontinue payment of unemployment benefit. No provision for the payment of unemployment benefit has been made in the Budget of Social Insurance for the supplementary quarter October–December 1930.
2. Labour exchanges are instructed to take all necessary measures in order that the unemployed be immediately sent to work, and of these the first to be sent are persons entitled to draw unemployment benefit.

3. Unemployed persons are to be drafted not only to work in their own trades, but also to other work necessitating special qualifications.

At the same time labour exchanges should, according to local conditions (or the needs of any particular trade), extend their activities in the training and retraining of unemployed.

4. No excuse for refusal of work, with the exception of illness, supported by a medical certificate, should be considered. Refusal of work carries with it removal from the registers of the labour exchanges.

Medical certificates should be issued to the unemployed by medical boards and medical control boards. Unemployed in possession of medical certificates will receive benefits under the heading of unemployment benefit, but this benefit will come out of the sums allocated for temporary incapacity.

5. Personal responsibility for the due and correct execution of the present decree is placed upon the heads of the labour exchanges (and, in districts where these do not exist, on the directors of labour organizations) and upon the chairmen of insurance bureaux.

6. Article 1 of the present decree is to be put into force by telegraph.

Source: Izvestia, 11 November 1930.
Translation: Selection of Documents relative to the Labour legislation of the USSR (HMSO, Cmd. 3775, London, 1931), p. 165.

86. On Dismissal for Absence from Work Without Valid Reason

Decree of the Central Executive Committee of the Council of People's Commissars of the USSR, 15 November 1932

Having in view that the existing Labour Code (paragraph 'f' of Article 47 of the Labour Code of the RSFSR and the corresponding paragraphs of the Labour Codes of other union republics) permits the dismissal of a worker for absenteeism from work without sufficient reasons, if such absenteeism occurred for a total period of three days during a month, which, under the present condition of the absence of unemployment, tends to encourage absenteeism, infringes the normal process of production and is detrimental to the interests of the toilers generally, the Central Executive Committee and the Council of People's Commissaries resolve:

1. To cancel paragraph 'e' of Article 47 of the Labour Code of the RSFSR and the corresponding paragraphs of the Labour Codes of the union republics.

2. To order that a worker be dismissed from the services of a factory or establishment even in case of one day's absenteeism from work without sufficient reasons and be deprived of the food-and-goods card issued to him as a member of the staff of the factory or establishment and also of the use of lodgings which are allowed to him in the houses belonging to the factory or establishment.

3. To instruct the governments of the allied republics to amend their Labour Codes accordingly.

> President of the Central Executive Committee of the USSR,
> M. KALININ.
> Chairman of the Council of People's Commissaries of the USSR, V. MOLOTOV (SKRYABIN).
> Secretary of the Central Executive Committee of the USSR,
> A. YENUKIDZE.

Source: Izvestia, 16 November 1932.
Translation: Slavonic and East European Review, Vol. XI, No. 33, July 1934, pp. 692-3.

87. On Uniting the People's Commissariat of Labour of the USSR and the All-Union Central Council of Trade Unions

Decree of the Central Executive Committee of the USSR, the Council of People's Commissaries and the AUCCTU, 23 June 1933

In order to meet the requests of the workers' trade-union organizations and to secure the better execution of duties imposed on the People's Commissariat for Labour of the USSR, the Central Executive Committee of the USSR, the Council of People's Commissaries of the USSR, and the All-Union Central Council of Trade Unions resolve:

1. To amalgamate the People's Commissariat for Labour of the USSR, together with all its branches and departments, including the Department of Social Insurance, with the apparatus of the All-Union Central Council of Trade Unions, centrally as well as locally, and to charge the All-Union Central Council of Trade Unions with the duties which formerly had been carried out by the People's Commissariat for Labour and by its local branches.
2. To instruct the All-Union Central Council of Trade Unions to prepare, in a month's time, a project of concrete measures in correspondence with this decree and to present this project to the Council of People's Commissaries of the USSR.

> President of the Central Executive Committee of the USSR,
> M. KALININ.
> Chairman of the Council of People's Commissars of the USSR, V. MOLOTOV (SKRYABIN).
> Secretary of the All-Union Central Council of Trade Unions, N. SHVERNIK.

Source: Izvestia, 24 June 1933.
Translation: Slavonic and East European Review, Vol. XIII, No. 37, p. 436.

88. Labour Discipline Strengthened

28 December 1938

89. Hours Lengthened and Freedom to Change Work Lost

26 June 1940

The decrees reproduced below illustrate the pressure which Stalin exerted on the worker prior to the outbreak of war. Though partly explicable by the imminence of hostilities, they were not formally rescinded until the mid-'fifties. The decree of December 1938 *intensified labour discipline to an extreme degree, a fact ill-concealed by the social-security provisions which were tacked on to it. 'Lateness' was defined early in January* 1939 *as a period not exceeding twenty minutes : persons who arrived after that were subject to immediate dismissal. The formal introduction of the eight-hour day in* 1940 *meant the abandonment of the six- and seven-hour day which, when implemented, had been a real achievement in the field of Soviet labour : the seven-day working week meant six days at work and one day off, replacing a five-on, one-off pattern. The restrictions on changing jobs without the permission of the management, the incredibly strict interpreta-tions of 'absence', and the concept of correctional labour at one's work-place were characteristic features of Stalin's labour policies.*

88. On the Consolidation of Labour Discipline, Improvement of the Practice of Social Security, and Suppression of Abuses in this Field

Decree of the Council of People's Commissars of the USSR, the CC VKP(B) and the AUCCTU, 28 December 1938

The USSR Council of People's Commissars, the Central Committee of the All-Union Communist Party (Bolshevik) and the All-Union Central Council of Trade Unions resolve:

1. To oblige the managements of enterprises and establishments (offices) along with trade-union organs to lead a determined struggle against all violators of labour discipline and internal labour regulations, against shirkers, idlers, and self-seekers—against all who have a dishonest attitude toward their labour obligations, be they workers (wage-earners) or employees (salaried workers).

The law requires the dismissal of a worker or employee for absence without sufficient reason. This measure is directed against parasites who do not want to work but try to live at the expense of the state, at the expense of the people. The requirements of the law regarding the dismissal of slackers should be carried out without fail.

The eight-, seven-, and six-hour day, depending on the conditions of the job, is established by law and accepted by the working class. In addition, the overwhelming majority of workers have a seven-hour working day. The state demands, and the working class supports the requirement, that the duration of the working day, established by law, be observed precisely and without any violations; that where the six-, seven-, and eight-hour day is prescribed, work should be carried out in full conformity with the law, namely, a full six-, seven-, or eight-hour day. Tardiness, early departure for and late return from lunch, leaving work before the scheduled time, and also loafing on the job—all these constitute a rude violation of labour discipline, and a violation of the law, which undermines the economic and defensive might of the country, and the well-being of the people.

A worker or employee coming late to work without sufficient reason, or leaving early for lunch or returning too late, or leaving the enterprise or establishment before the scheduled time, or loafing during working hours, is subject to administrative penalties: reproof or reprimand, reprimand with a warning of dismissal, transfer to another, lower-paying job for a period up to three months, or demotion to a lower-grade job.

A worker or employee committing three such infractions in one month or four infractions in two consecutive months is subject to dismissal as a shirker and violator of labour law and labour discipline.

2. To establish that managers of enterprises, establishments, workshops and sections are subject to dismissal and penal prosecution if they do not promote measures for strengthening labour discipline or avoid taking measures against shirkers, idlers and self-seekers in conformity with the present decree and the decree of 15 November 1932 of the Central Executive Committee and the USSR Council of People's Commissars, 'Respecting Dismissal for Absence Without Sufficient Reason' (Collection of Laws, USSR, 1932, No. 78, Article 475).

3. Workers and employees desiring to leave their jobs are obliged to give one month's notice to the management of the enterprise or establishment.

4. In a case when a worker or employee is dismissed for inadequate reasons, remuneration for his enforced absence is calculated at the rate of the average wage earned, but not for more than twenty days, and the managements of enterprises and establishments, factory committees, local trade-union committees, and the Appraisement and Conflict Commissions are obliged to examine complaints of illegal discharge within three days from the day the complaint was lodged, and the legal organs, within five days.

5. Workers and employees—members of trade unions—who are temporarily incapacitated, are entitled to compensation (not counting compensation for pregnancy and child birth) in the following manner—depending on the length of continuous service in a given enterprise or establishment—

(a) For continuous service in one and the same enterprise or establishment	6 years or over	100% of earnings
(b) For continuous service in one and the same enterprise or establishment	3–6 years	80% of earnings
(c) For continuous service in one and the same enterprise or establishment	2–3 years	60% of earnings
(d) For continuous service in one and the same enterprise or establishment	up to 2 years	50% of earnings

6. Juveniles, up to eighteen years of age, are entitled to compensation as in Article 5 in the following manner—depending on the length of continuous service in a given enterprise or establishment: continuous work—two years or over—80 per cent of earnings; up to two years—60 per cent of earnings. In addition, time spent in factory-and-workshop training is calculated in the length of service...

12. On the basis of Article 31 of the Decree of 17 November 1937 of the Central Executive Committee and the Council of People's Commissars of the USSR, 'Concerning the Preservation of the Housing Fund and Improvement of Housing in Cities' (USSR Laws, 1937, No. 69, Article 314), it is established that workers and employees who are assigned dwelling space in connection with their work in the house of a state enterprise, office, or economic organization (or in a house leased by such enterprises or establishments), are liable to compulsory administrative eviction within ten days, without any living quarters being provided for them, in the event of their departure from the enterprise or establishment, after the promulgation of this resolution, either as a result of voluntary departure or dismissal for violation of labour discipline or committing a crime...

13. The right to a normal holiday is granted to workers and employees after eleven months' continuous work in the same enterprise or establishment.

14. Female workers and female employees, in cases of pregnancy and birth, are granted thirty-five calendar days' leave before the birth of a child and twenty-eight calendar days' leave after the birth besides the established annual leave. Compensation for pregnancy and birth leave is paid at established rates at state expense. The pregnancy and birth leave is granted and compensation paid to those female workers and female employees who have worked continuously in the same enterprise or establishment for at least seven months.

15. Priority rights to rest homes are granted to those workers and employees who have worked in the same enterprise or establishment for more than two years...

26. The present Resolution goes into effect on 1 January 1939.

Chairman of the Council of People's Commissars, V. MOLOTOV.

430

Secretary of the Central Committee of the All-Union Communist Party (Bolshevik), J. STALIN.
Secretary of the All-Union Central Council of Trade Unions, N. SHVERNIK.

Source: Izvestia, 29 December 1938.
Translation: J. Meisel and E. S. Kozera, *Materials for the Study of the Soviet System* (George Wahr Publishing Co., Ann Arbor, 1950), extracts. The preamble and more detailed pension provisions have been omitted.

89. On the Transfer to an Eight-Hour Working Day, and Seven-Day Working Week, and on the Prohibition of Unauthorized Quitting of Enterprises and Institutions by Workers and Employees

Edict of the Supreme Soviet of the USSR, 26 June 1940

In accordance with the proposal of the All-Union Central Council of Labour Unions, the Presidium of the Supreme Soviet of the USSR decrees:
1. The duration of the working day for workers and clerks in all government, co-operative and social enterprises and offices shall be increased:

> from 7 to 8 hours—in enterprises working with a 7-hour working day;
> from 6 to 7 hours—for work on a 6-hour working day, except for trades having dangerous conditions of work in accordance with a list approved by the Council of People's Commissars of the USSR;
> from 6 to 8 hours—for clerks in offices;
> from 6 to 8 hours—for persons over 16 years of age.

2. Work in all government, co-operative and social enterprises and offices shall be changed from a six-day week to a seven-day week, the seventh day of the week—Sunday—being a day of rest.
3. Voluntary withdrawal of a worker or clerk from government, co-operative and social enterprises and offices, as well as voluntary transfer from one enterprise or office to another, is forbidden.
    Only the director of an enterprise or chief of an office can permit withdrawal from an enterprise or office or transfer from one enterprise or office to another.
4. The director of an enterprise and chief of an office shall have the right and is required to give a worker or clerk permission to leave an enterprise or office in the following situations:

> (a) When a worker or clerk, in the opinion of a medical commission, cannot perform his former work because of an illness or condition as an invalid, and when the management is unable to provide him with other

suitable work in the same enterprise or office, or when a pensioner, to whom an old-age pension is payable, wishes to leave work;

(b) When a worker or clerk must stop work in view of the fact that he has been admitted to a higher or middle special school.

Vacations for women workers and clerks during pregnancy and after giving birth shall be preserved in accordance with existing legislation.

5. A workman or clerk who voluntarily leaves a state, co-operative or public enterprise or office, shall be tried by a court, and in accordance with the sentence of the People's Court shall be imprisoned for terms from two to four months.

For absenteeism without satisfactory reason, workers and clerks of state, co-operative and public enterprises and offices shall be tried by a court, and in accordance with the sentence of the People's Court shall be penalized by correctional labour at their place of work for terms up to six months with withholding of their wages in amounts up to 25 per cent.

In view of the above, compulsory dismissal for absenteeism without satisfactory reasons shall be done away with.

People's Courts shall be ordered to review all cases referred to in the present Article in not less than five days and shall put the sentence into effect immediately.

6. A director of an enterprise or chief of an office who does not prosecute persons guilty of voluntary departure from an enterprise or office or guilty of absenteeism without satisfactory reasons shall be held responsible before a court.

A director of an enterprise or chief of an office who hires persons who conceal the fact that they departed voluntarily from an enterprise or office shall be held responsible also before a court.

7. The present decree shall come into force on 27 June 1940.

Source: *Vedomosti Verkhovnogo Soveta SSSR*, 1940, No. 20.

Translation: J. N. Hazard and M. L. Weisberg, *Cases and Readings on Soviet Law* (Parker School of Foreign and Comparative Law, Columbia University, New York, 1950), p. 146.

90. Khrushchev Restores Freedom of Employment

25 April 1956

Although only one of several measures aimed at liberalizing the Soviet labour market in the mid-'fifties, this was perhaps the best known. 'Unauthorized' quitting had, it seems, become widespread despite all restrictions, yet the removal of the legal bonds which had bound the worker for so long had a symbolic significance. Criminal responsibility for absenteeism had evidently been removed in 1951 *(see Article* 8d*), but this measure does not seem to have been published. Changing jobs without authorization was subsequently to entail only the temporary loss of certain social-insurance rights. Half-day working on Saturdays and on the eves of public holidays had been introduced on* 8 *March of that year, and working hours were to be further shortened in subsequent years.*

90. On the Annulment of Criminal Responsibility of Workers and Employees for Unauthorized Departure from Enterprises and Institutions and for Absence Without Valid Reasons

Edict of the Presidium of the Supreme Soviet of the USSR, 25 *April* 1956

As a result of the growth in the consciousness of the toilers and the rise in their material well-being and cultural level, there has been an improvement of discipline at enterprises and institutions.

In these circumstances the existing criminal responsibility of workers and employees for unauthorized departure from enterprises and institutions and for repeated or long-term absence without valid reason is not necessary, and can be replaced by measures of a disciplinary and social character.

The Presidium of the Supreme Soviet of the USSR decrees:

1. To annul the criminal responsibility of workers and employees for unauthorized departure from enterprises and institutions and for repeated or extended absence without valid reason.

2. To release from their sentences persons found guilty of unauthorized departure from enterprises and institutions and of absence without valid reason.

3. To halt proceedings in cases of unauthorized departure from enterprises and institutions and cases of absenteeism which have not been examined by courts up to the publication of this Edict.

4. To annul the convictions of citizens who have been sentenced before or who have served terms in prison for unauthorized departure from enterprises and institutions and for absenteeism, and also of those released from their sentences on the basis of this Edict.

5. Workers and employees who are leaving their jobs at their own wish are

obliged to inform the management of the enterprise or institution of this two weeks beforehand.

6. Workers and employees who leave their work at their own wish lose their uninterrupted service rating and have the right to temporary disability benefits only after they have worked at their new job for not less than six months.

This rule does not apply to:

(a) Workers and employees who are released as a result of illness, chronic ill-health, or to take up an old-age pension;
(b) Persons who have ceased work as a result of admission to a higher or middle special educational institution, or to a research degree course;
(c) Persons who leave as a result of their husband or wife being transferred to another area;
(d) Pregnant women and mothers who have children less than a year old, if they transfer to work at their place of residence;
(e) Persons who leave for other valid reasons covered by decrees of the Council of Ministers of the USSR.

7. The director of an enterprise or the head of an institution applies one of the following measures in cases of absence of a worker or employee without valid reason:

(a) A disciplinary fine in accordance with the internal labour organization rules, or in accordance with the statutes of enterprises and institutions where special disciplinary regulations are in force;
(b) Deprivation of the right to receive percentage allowances on retirement for a period of up to three months, or a reduction of the one-time payment on retirement of up to 25 per cent;
(c) Dismissal from work with a note in the labour book of the person concerned to the effect that he was 'dismissed for absence without valid reason'.

The dismissed person loses his uninterrupted service rating and obtains the right to temporary disability benefits only after he has worked not less than six months at his new job.

Instead of applying the above measures the director of an enterprise or the head of an institution may at his discretion pass the material on absence without valid reason for examination by a comradely court.

8. The following measures have been annulled:

(a) The Edict of 26 June 1940, 'On the transfer to an eight-hour working day and a seven-day working week, and on the prohibition of un-authorized quitting of enterprises and institutions by workers and employees', excepting Articles 1 and 2.

(b) The Edict of 17 July 1940, 'On the prohibition of unauthorized quitting by tractor and combine-harvester drivers, working in the MTS'.

(c) The Edict of 19 October 1940, 'On the manner of obligatory transfer of engineers, technicians, craftsmen, employees and qualified workers from some enterprises and institutions to others'.

(d) The Edict of 14 July 1951, 'On replacing criminal responsibility of workers and employees for absenteeism, except in cases of repeated or long-term absenteeism, by measures of a disciplinary and social character'.

(e) The Edict of 13 November 1952, 'On introducing changes and additions into the Edict of the Presidium of the Supreme Soviet of the USSR of 17 July 1940 "On the prohibition of unauthorized quitting by tractor and combine-harvester drivers working in the MTS" and that of 19 October 1940, "On the manner of obligatory transfer of engineers, technicians, craftsmen, employees and qualified workers from some enterprises and institutions to others"'.

Source: D. S. Karev (ed.), *Sbornik zakonodatel'nykh aktov o trude* (Moscow, 1956), p. 74. Editor's translation.

91. A National Minimum Wage Reintroduced, with Tax Concessions

8 September 1956

This law marked a new era in the Soviet incomes policy for workers and employees. The last general minimum wage had been fixed in December 1927, *and although improvements were made for some workers in* 1937 *and* 1946, *there was no longer a state minimum in existence by the time Stalin died.*[1] *The introduction of a new set of minimum rates, and some less important changes in direct taxation, reflected the egalitarian trend which Khrushchev was to promote in this field. New general minima were introduced over the period* 1959 *to* 1962, *and again in January* 1968. *The tax changes mentioned in Article* 6 *were covered by a separate law of the same date, but an edict of* 18 *December* 1957 *freed the categories of persons involved from direct taxes altogether.*

91. On Raising the Wages of Low-paid Workers and Employees

Decree of the Council of Ministers of the USSR, the Central Committee of the CPSU, and the All-Union Central Committee of Trade Unions,
8 September 1956

With the object of improving further the material well-being of the toilers, the Council of Ministers of the USSR, the Central Committee of the CPSU, and the All-Union Central Committee of Trade Unions decree that:

1. Henceforth, from 1 January 1957 until the implementation of measures for a general regularization of the wages of workers and employees, the wages of low-paid workers and employees are to be raised, and fixed as follows:

(a) for workers and employees engaged directly at industrial enterprises, construction sites, transport and communication enterprises—at not less than 300 to 350 roubles a month;

(b) for the remaining workers and employees, and also for junior service personnel and the security staff of industrial enterprises, building sites, communications and transport enterprises in towns and workers' settlements—at not less than 300 roubles, and in rural localities at not less than 270 roubles a month.

This wage increase covers workers and employees who have a tariff rate or salary lower than the level indicated.

[1] N. G. Aleksandrov, i drugie, *Zakonodatelstvo o trude, Kommentarii* (Moscow, 1954), p. 88. Edition for restricted circulation.

2. Payments to workers and employees for fulfilment of their output norms, premiums, payments for overtime, work on holidays and night work, supplements and retirement bonuses, and also supplements for work in regions of the Far North and localities equated thereto, in desert or mountain regions, are to be made over and above the wage rates indicated in paragraph 1 of this decree.

These payments are calculated on the basis of the rates and salaries operative at enterprises, in organizations and institutions.

3. Ministers and heads of administrations of the USSR and Councils of Ministers of the union republics are entrusted with fixing, within a month, with the agreement of the State Committee of the Council of Ministers of the USSR for Questions of Labour and Wages, and that of the AUCCTU, a minimal wage for particular branches of the economy within the limits indicated in paragraph 1, clause (a) of this decree.

4. In cases where workers and employees have worked less than a full month the wage is to be fixed proportionately to the time which they have worked in that month.

5. The payment of the labour of apprentices at enterprises, building sites and in organizations and institutions is to be made in accordance with existing rules.

The payment of labour of workers and employees who give instruction in connection with retraining is to be made in accordance with paragraph 1 of this decree.

6. It is recognized as being necessary to abolish, from 1 January 1957, the levy of income tax and the tax on bachelors, single Soviet citizens and citizens with small families among workers, employees and apprentices who receive a wage or grant of less than 370 roubles a month. The draft law on raising the untaxable wage minimum for workers and employees is to be submitted to the Presidium of the Supreme Soviet of the USSR for approval.

7. The economic plan and the state budget for 1957 are to provide for the expenditure incurred through measures connected with raising the wages of low-paid workers and employees to the sum of 8 milliard roubles; this will ensure that wages are raised on average over the whole group of workers and employees indicated by approximately 33 per cent.

Source : D. S. Karev (ed.), *Sbornik zakonodatel'nykh aktov o trude* (Moscow, 1956), p. 157. Editor's translation.

92. The 1970 All-Union Principles of Labour Legislation
15 *July* 1970

These All-Union Principles of Labour Legislation set out, in formal terms, the fundamentals of labour law, social insurance and trade-union rights for the whole country. As such the Principles are intended to serve as a framework for a new set of republican labour codes.

The Principles took no less than eleven years to complete, the first draft, produced in 1959, *having been shelved. The new document contains numerous post-Stalin provisions on hours and conditions of work and social insurance. The Principles remain, however, basically conservative in character, and do not embrace a number of liberal proposals which were made in the press prior to their adoption. Thus there is no provision for redundancy or unemployment payments, labour discipline rules are stringent, and the worker is not afforded any new means of protection against the management. The general and final provisions have been omitted from the text presented here, and sections on labour protection and settlement of disputes have been abridged.*

92. Principles of Labour Legislation of the USSR and Union Republics
Approved by the Supreme Soviet of the USSR, 15 *July* 1970

I. General Provisions

ARTICLE 1. *The Aims of Soviet Labour Legislation.* Soviet labour legislation regulates the labour relations of all workers and employees; promoting the growth of labour productivity and the efficiency of social production, and on this basis raising the living standards and cultural level of the working people; promoting the strengthening of labour discipline, and gradually making work for the benefit of society into a prime vital need of every able-bodied person.

The labour legislation establishes a high standard of working conditions and thoroughgoing protection of the labour rights of workers and employees.
ARTICLE 2. *Fundamental Labour Rights and Duties of Workers and Employees.* The right of citizens of the USSR to work is ensured by the socialist organization of the national economy, the steady growth of the productive forces of Soviet society, the elimination of the possibility of economic crises and the eradication of unemployment.

Workers and employees exercise the right to work by concluding a labour contract for work at an enterprise, institution or organization. Workers and employees have the right to state-guaranteed pay commensurate with the quantity and quality of the expended labour; the right to leisure in accordance with the laws limiting the work-day and the work-week and providing annual paid vacations; the right to healthy and safe working conditions; the right to free occupational training and free training to raise their qualifications; the right to unite in trade unions, to participate in the management of production and to enjoy social security at state expense in the form of state social insurance in old age and also in cases of illness or disability.

It is the duty of all workers and employees to observe labour discipline, manifest care for public property and meet the work quotas set by the state in conjunction with the trade unions.

ARTICLE 3. *Regulation of the Labour of Collective-Farm Members.* The labour of collective-farm members is regulated by the collective-farm statutes adopted on the basis of and in conformity with the Model Collective-Farm statutes and with the legislation of the USSR and of the union republics pertaining to collective farms.

ARTICLE 4. *Labour Legislation of the USSR and the Union Republics.* The labour legislation of the USSR and of the union republics consists of the present Principles and other acts of USSR labour legislation and the codes of labour laws and other acts of union-republic labour legislation promulgated in conformity with these Principles.

The labour of workers and employees, in matters covered by the present Principles, is regulated by:

USSR legislation,

USSR and union-republic legislation,

union-republic legislation.

The jurisdiction of the USSR and of the union republics in the regulation of the labour of workers and employees is delineated according to the rules of Article 107 and other articles of the present Principles.

Questions of the labour of workers and employees which are not covered by the present Principles are regulated by legislation of the USSR and the union republics.

ARTICLE 5. *Labour-Contract Conditions Running Counter to Labour Legislation Are Invalid.* Conditions of labour contracts impairing the position of workers and employees in comparison with the USSR and union-republic labour legislation or otherwise running counter to this legislation are invalid.

II. The Collective Contract

ARTICLE 6. *Conclusion of the Collective Contract and Its Scope of Operation.* The collective contract [or collective agreement] is concluded by the factory committee, plant committee or local committee of the trade union, on behalf of the collective of workers and employees, with the administration of the enterprise or organization.

The conclusion of the collective contract should be preceded by discussion and approval of its draft at meetings (conferences) of the workers and employees.

The collective contract applies to all workers and employees of the enterprise or organization, regardless of whether they are members of the trade union.

ARTICLE 7. *Contents of the Collective Contract.* The collective contract should contain the basic provisions on questions of labour and earnings as established for the given enterprise or organization, in conformity with the legislation in force, and also provisions on working hours, leisure, payment of labour, material incentives and labour protection which have been worked out by the administration and the trade union's factory, plant or local committee within the scope of the rights granted them; these provisions being of a normative nature.

The collective contract establishes the mutual obligations of the administration and of the collective of workers and employees in meeting production plans, improving the organization of production and labour, introducing new technology and raising labour productivity, improving the quality and reducing the unit costs of output, developing socialist competition, strengthening production and labour discipline, raising the qualifications of personnel, and training personnel directly on the job.

The collective contract should contain the obligations of the administration and of the trade union's factory, plant or local committee in regard to drawing workers and employees into the management of production; improving labour quotas, forms of payment and material incentives; protecting labour; granting privileges and advantages to outstanding workers; improving housing conditions of the working people and cultural and everyday services to them, and developing educational and mass-cultural work.

III. The Labour Contract

ARTICLE 8. *The Parties to the Labour Contract; Its Contents.* The labour contract is an agreement between a working person and an enterprise, institution or organization, according to which the person undertakes to perform work in a particular speciality, skill or position, in conformity with internal labour regulations, while the enterprise, institution or organization undertakes to pay the working person a wage or salary and to provide the working conditions called for by labour legislation, by the collective contract and by agreement between the parties.

ARTICLE 9. *Guarantees in Hiring.* Ungrounded refusal to grant employment is forbidden.

In accordance with the constitution of the USSR any direct or indirect restriction of rights and any establishment of direct or indirect advantages in granting employment on the grounds of sex, race, nationality or attitude toward religion is not allowed.

ARTICLE 10. *Duration of the Labour Contract.* Labour contracts are concluded:

(1) for an indefinite term;
(2) for a definite term of no more than three years;
(3) for the time required to complete a definite job.

ARTICLE 11. *Probation Period.* When concluding a labour contract, the parties may stipulate a trial period to verify the suitability of the worker or employee for the job.

The limits of duration of the probationary period are established by legislation of the USSR and the union republics.

ARTICLE 12. *Prohibition Against Demanding the Performance of Work Not Stipulated in the Labour Contract.* The administration does not have the right to demand that a worker or employee perform work not stipulated in the labour contract.

ARTICLE 13. *Transfer to Another Job.* Transfer to another job at the same enterprise, institution or organization, as well as transfer to work at another enterprise, institution or organization or to a different locality, even though the employing enterprise, institution or organization moves there, is permitted only with the consent of the worker or employee, except in cases provided for in Articles 14 and 56 of the present Principles.

ARTICLE 14. *Temporary Transfer to Other Work in the Event of Production Necessity or Shut-down.* In the event that production necessity requires the enterprise, institution or organization to transfer a worker or employee to work not stipulated in the labour contract, the administration has the right to transfer the person for a period of up to one month to other work at the same enterprise, institution or organization or at a different enterprise, institution or organization, but in the same locality, and with payment according to the work performed, but not less than the average earnings for the previous work. Such a transfer is permitted to prevent or eliminate a natural calamity or industrial mishap or for the rapid elimination of their consequences; to prevent accidents, shut-down [*prostoi*—idle time], destruction of or damage to state or public property and in other emergency cases or to replace an absent worker or employee. The duration of transfer to other work to replace an absent worker or employee may not exceed one month in the course of a calendar year.

In the event of shut-down [idle time], workers and employees may be transferred, with consideration of their specialities and qualifications, to other work at the same enterprise, institution or organization for the full time of the forced idleness or to another enterprise, institution or organization, but in the same locality, for a period up to one month. If transferred to lower-paid work because of such idle time, workers and employees who meet the output quotas retain their average earnings for the previous work, while

441

those who do not meet the output quotas or who have been transferred to work paid by the hour retain their base wage or salary.

The transfer of skilled workers to unskilled work is not permitted in cases of forced idleness or the temporary replacement of an absent worker or employee.

ARTICLE 15. *Grounds for Terminating a Labour Contract.* The following are grounds for terminating a labour contract:

(1) agreement between the parties;

(2) expiration of the term (points 2 and 3 of Article 10), except in cases in which the labour relations actually continue and neither of the parties has demanded their termination;

(3) the call-up or enlistment of the worker or employee into military service;

(4) dissolution of the labour contract at the initiative of the worker or employee (Article 16), at the initiative of the administration (Article 17) or at the demand of a trade-union body (Article 20);

(5) transfer of the employed person to other work, with his consent, or his or her acceptance of an elective office;

(6) refusal of the worker or employee to accept a transfer to another locality if the enterprise, institution or organization moves there;

(7) entry into legal force of a court sentence (except suspended sentence) of the worker or employee to deprivation of freedom, or to corrective labour other than at his or her place of work, or to some other punishment that precludes the possibility of keeping his or her job.

ARTICLE 16. *Dissolution of the Labour Contract at the Initiative of the Worker or Employee.* Workers and employees have the right to dissolve a labour contract of indefinite term upon giving the administration two weeks' written notice.

A labour contract signed for a definite term (points 2 and 3 of Article 10) may be cancelled by the worker or employee before expiration of the term in the event of illness or disability preventing performance of the work called for by the terms of the contract; in the event of violation by the administration of labour legislation or the collective or labour contract, or for other valid reasons.

ARTICLE 17. *Dissolution of the Labour Contract at the Initiative of the Administration.* The administration of the enterprise, institution or organization may dissolve a labour contract of indefinite term, or a labour contract of definite term before expiration of the term, only in the event of:

(1) closing down of the enterprise, institution or organization or a reduction in its staff;

(2) unfitness of the worker or employee for the position or for the work

because of insufficient skill or a state of health preventing continuation of the work;

(3) regular failure by the worker or employee, without valid cause, to perform the duties imposed on him by the labour contract or by internal labour regulations, provided he or she had previously incurred disciplinary punishment [i.e., imposed by the administration] or public punishment [i.e., imposed by public organizations of the shop, enterprise, institution or organization.—Trans.];

(4) absence without valid cause (including appearance at work in a state of intoxication);

(5) failure to appear at work for four consecutive months as a result of temporary disability, except in case of maternity leave, if USSR legislation does not establish a longer period for retention of the job or position in the case of some specific illness. If a worker or employee has been disabled by an industrial accident or occupational illness, his or her job or position shall be held for him or her until he or she is again capable of work or permanent disability is established;

(6) the return to work of the worker or employee who had formerly held this job.

Dismissal on the grounds set forth in points (1), (2) and (6) of the present article is permitted if it is not possible to transfer the person, with his or her consent, to another job.

ARTICLE 18. *Prohibition Against Dissolution of a Labour Contract at the Initiative of the Administration Without the Consent of the Trade Union's Factory, Plant or Local Committee.* Dissolution of a labour contract upon the initiative of the administration of the enterprise, institution or organization is not permitted without the prior consent of the trade union's factory, plant or local committee except in cases stipulated by USSR legislation.

Dissolution of a labour contract in violation of the terms of the first part of the present article is illegal, and the person discharged has the right to reinstatement in his job (Article 91).

ARTICLE 19. *Severance Pay.* When a labour contract is terminated upon the grounds set forth in points 3 or 6 of Article 15 or points 1, 2 or 6 of Article 17 of the present Principles or as a result of the administration's violation of labour legislation or of the collective or labour contract (second part of Article 16), workers and employees receive a severance payment in the amount of two weeks' average earnings.

ARTICLE 20. *Dissolution of a Labour Contract Upon the Demand of a Trade-Union Body.* Upon the demand of a trade-union body (no lower than borough or district level), the administration is required to annul the contract of a management official or to remove him or her from the post held if he or she has violated labour legislation, does not meet the obligations set forth in the collective contract, manifests bureaucracy, or resorts to red tape.

The demand of the trade-union body may be appealed by the official or the administration to a trade-union body of higher rank; such body's decision shall be final.

IV. Working Hours and Time Off

ARTICLE 21. *Normal Work-Week.* The normal working hours for workers and employees at enterprises, institutions and organizations shall not exceed forty-one per week. The work-week will gradually be reduced as the economic and other conditions necessary for this are established.

ARTICLE 22. *Shorter Work-Week.* Shorter working hours have been established for:

(1) workers and employees aged 16 to 18 — 36 hours per week; and persons 15 to 16 (Article 74) — 24 hours per week;
(2) workers and employees engaged in jobs with harmful working conditions — not more than 36 hours per week.

In addition, USSR legislation establishes a reduced work-week for various categories of employees (teachers, physicians and others).

ARTICLE 23. *The Five-Day and Six-Day Work-Week and Daily Hours of Work.* A five-day work-week with two days off is established for workers and employees. Under the five-day work-week, working hours per day (or shift) are determined by the internal labour regulations or the shift schedules confirmed by the administration in agreement with the trade union's plant, factory or local committee, with due observance of the established length of the work-week (Articles 21 and 22).

At enterprises, institutions and organizations where the nature of production or the conditions of work make the introduction of the five-day work-week inexpedient, a six-day work-week with one day off is established. Under the six-day work-week, the length of the working day shall not exceed seven hours for the 41-hour week, six hours for the 36-hour week, and four hours for the 24-hour week.

ARTICLE 24. *Working Hours on the Day Before a Public Holiday and Before Weekends.* On the day before a public holiday (Article 31) the work-day of workers and employees, except those covered by Article 22 of the present Principles, is reduced by one hour in the case of both the five-day and six-day work-week.

On weekends the work-day in the case of the six-day work-week may not exceed six hours.

ARTICLE 25. *Working Hours at Night.* For night work the length of the daily work (or shift) is reduced by one hour. This rule does not apply to workers and employees for whom shorter hours are already provided (the second part and point 2 of the first part of Article 22).

The length of night work is the same as that of daytime work when this is

444

necessitated by production conditions, in particular in continuous production and also in shift work under the six-day work-week with one day off.

The time from 10.00 p.m. to 6.00 a.m. is considered night-time.

ARTICLE 26. *Part-Time Work.* Upon agreement between the worker or employee and the administration, either at the time of hiring or subsequently, a partial work-day or a partial work-week may be established. Remuneration in these instances is proportionate to the time worked or is dependent upon output.

ARTICLE 27. *Restriction of Overtime Work.* As a rule, overtime work is not permitted.

The administration may resort to overtime work only in exceptional cases provided for by legislation of the union republics. Overtime work may be done only with the permission of the trade union's factory, plant or local committee.

Overtime work should not exceed four hours for each worker or employee in the course of two consecutive days, nor 120 hours in a year.

ARTICLE 28. *Cumulative Tally of Working Time.* At continuously operating enterprises and at institutions, organizations, individual production units, shops, sectors, departments and in certain types of work where the daily or weekly length of working time established for the given category of workers or employees cannot be observed because of the conditions of production (or work), a cumulative tally of working time may be introduced with the consent of the trade union's factory, plant or local committee, provided that total working time during the accounting period does not exceed the normal number of working hours (Articles 21 and 22).

ARTICLE 29. *Break for Rest and Meals.* Workers and employees are granted a break for rest and food no longer than two hours in duration. The break is not included in the working time.

In jobs in which breaks cannot be established because of production conditions, the worker or employee should be given an opportunity to eat during work-time. The list of such jobs and the order and place for such meals are determined by the administration in agreement with the trade union's factory, plant or local committee.

ARTICLE 30. *Days Off.* Under the five-day work-week, workers and employees are granted two days off per week, and under the six-day work-week, one day.

The duration of the weekly continuous leave should be no less than 42 hours.

Work on days off is forbidden. Individual workers and employees may be called in to work on these days only with the permission of the trade union's factory, plant or local committee and only in exceptional instances determined by legislation of the union republics. For work on a day off, a compensatory day of leave is granted within the next two weeks.

If it is impossible to grant a compensatory day of leave (if the worker or employee has meantime been discharged or in other instances provided by legislation), work on the day off is paid double.

ARTICLE 31. *Public Holidays.* Work is not done at enterprises, institutions and organizations on the following public holidays:

1 January—New Year's Day,
8 March—International Women's Day,
1 and 2 May—Day of International Solidarity of the Working People,
9 May—Victory Day,
7 and 8 November—Anniversary of the Great October Socialist Revolution,
5 December—USSR Constitution Day.

Work which cannot be stopped because of technical and production conditions (continuously operating enterprises, institutions or organizations), work called for by the need for services to the public, and also emergency repair and loading–unloading work are permitted on holidays.

ARTICLE 32. *Annual Vacations.* All workers and employees are granted annual vacations with retention of their jobs (or positions) and average earnings (Articles 33 and 34).

The vacation schedule is established by the administration in agreement with the trade union's factory, plant or local committee.

The substitution of monetary compensation for vacation is not permitted except in case of the discharge of a worker or employee who has not taken his vacation.

ARTICLE 33. *Length of Vacation.* Workers and employees are granted an annual vacation of at least fifteen working days, with gradual increase in the length of vacation. The procedure for calculating the length of the annual vacation is determined by USSR legislation.

Workers and employees under eighteen are granted an annual vacation of one calendar month.

ARTICLE 34. *Additional Vacation Time.* Additional annual vacation time is granted:

(1) to workers and employees engaged in jobs with harmful working conditions;

(2) to workers and employees engaged in various branches of the national economy and having a long record of employment at one enterprise or organization;

(3) to personnel with unregulated working hours;

(4) to workers and employees working in the Far North or equivalent localities;

(5) in other instances provided by legislation.

ARTICLE 35. *Unpaid Leave.* The administration may grant a brief leave without pay to a worker or employee, upon his or her application, for family reasons or other valid reasons.

446

V. Earnings [Wages, Salary], Guarantees and Compensation

ARTICLE 36. *Payment According to Labour. Minimum Wage.* In accordance with the USSR Constitution, the labour of workers and employees is paid according to its quantity and quality. Any reduction whatever in the amount of pay because of sex, age, race or nationality is forbidden.

The monthly earnings of a worker or employee may not be lower than the minimum wage set by the state.

ARTICLE 37. *Pay Setting. Establishment of Wage and Salary Scales.* Pay is set by the state with the participation of the trade unions.

Workers are paid on the basis of wage scales adopted centrally. The evaluation of jobs according to definite pay categories and the awarding of qualification ratings to workers is carried out by the administration of the enterprise, institution or organization in agreement with the trade union's factory, plant or local committee and in conformity with the scale-qualification handbook.

The work of employees is paid on the basis of the salary scale adopted centrally. Salaries of employees are established by the administration of the enterprise, institution or organization in accordance with the position and qualifications of the employee.

Higher than normal pay is established for heavy work, work with harmful working conditions and work in localities with severe climatic conditions.

ARTICLE 38. *System for Remuneration of Labour.* Workers and employees are paid for their labour by a time rate or piece rate.

To increase the workers' and employees' material interest in meeting and exceeding production plans, in raising the efficiency and profitability of production, in increasing labour productivity, in improving the quality of products and in saving resources, the time-plus-bonus and piece-plus-bonus systems of pay may be introduced.

The administration of the enterprise, institution or organization, in agreement with the trade union's factory, plant or local committee, establishes the system of payment by the hour or by the piece and also confirms the regulations on bonuses for workers and employees.

Workers and employees of enterprises and organizations may receive, in addition to payment under the systems of labour remuneration, additional payment according to the totals of the year's work, from the fund formed out of the profits secured by the enterprise or organization. The amount of remuneration is determined in the light of the results of the worker's or employee's labour and the total length of his continuous employment by the given enterprise or organization.

ARTICLE 39. *Output Quotas (Time Norms), Operation Norms, Normatives for Number of Personnel, and Piece-Rate Calculation.* Output quotas (time norms), operation norms, and normatives for the size of staffs of workers and employees are in keeping with the level reached in technology, scientific organization of labour and production, and advanced work-experience. These norms and normatives are subject to replacement with new ones as technological, economic and organizational measures to increase labour productivity are put into effect. The introduction and revision of norms and normatives is handled by the administration of the enterprise, institution or organization in agreement with the trade union's factory, plant or local committee.

Uniform or model (interbranch, branch or departmental) norms and normatives may be established for similar types of work (jobs).

In the piece-rate wage system, rates are based on the established categories of work (jobs), the scale rates (wages) and the output quotas (or time norms).

Under the hourly-rate system, norms are set for workers and employees for operating the machines or units assigned to them or else the workers and employees are given standardized production assignments to be accomplished in a certain period of time. Normatives may be established for the numbers of workers and employees required for the performance of various functions or amounts of work.

ARTICLE 40. *Overtime Pay.* On the hourly-rate system overtime work is compensated at time-and-a-half for the first two hours and at double time for subsequent hours.

On the piece-rate system, and also in branches of the national economy having uniform wage-rates established for both piece-rate workers and hourly-rate workers, overtime draws extra pay in the amount established by USSR legislation.

ARTICLE 41. *Payment for Work on Public Holidays.* Work on public holidays (second part of Article 31) is paid at a double rate.

If the worker or employee who works on a public holiday so desires, he may be granted a day of leave in lieu of this day.

ARTICLE 42. *Payment for Night Work.* Work at night (Article 25) is remunerated at a higher rate set by USSR legislation.

ARTICLE 43. *Payment for Work in the Event of Failure to Meet Output Quotas, in the Event of Defective Output and in the Event of Forced Idle Time.* If output norms are not met, if defective products are produced, or if idle time occurs, through no fault of the worker or employee, payment is made in the amounts determined by USSR legislation.

Monthly earnings in such cases may not be lower than the established minimum wage (Article 36).

Output that is completely defective (total rejects) through the worker's or employee's own fault and idle time through his or her own fault are not subject to payment. Output that is partially defective through his or her fault is paid at a reduced rate, depending upon the degree of serviceability of the items produced.

ARTICLE 44. *Retention of Pay Upon Transfer to Other, Lower-Paid Work.* If a worker or employee is transferred permanently to other, lower-paid work, he retains his previous average earnings for two weeks from the date of transfer.

ARTICLE 45. *Intervals for Payment of Earnings.* Earnings are paid at least once in each half month.

For certain categories of workers and employees, other intervals for the payment of earnings may be established by legislation of the union republics.

ARTICLE 46. *Guarantees to Workers and Employees Elected to Elective Office.* Workers and employees released from their jobs because of election to elective office in state bodies and also in party, trade-union, Young Communist League, co-operative or other public organizations are restored, upon completion of their term in office, to their former jobs (positions) or, if these are no longer available, given other equivalent work (positions) at the same or, with the person's consent, another enterprise, institution or organization.

ARTICLE 47. *Guarantees to Workers and Employees During Performance of State or Public Obligations.* While fulfiling state or public obligations, workers and employees are guaranteed retention of their jobs (positions) and their average earnings while fulfilling their state or public obligations, if USSR legislation provides that these obligations may be carried out during working hours.

Workers and employees summoned to fulfil the obligations stipulated by the USSR Law on Universal Military Duty are granted guarantees and privileges in accordance with that law.

ARTICLE 48. *Guarantees and Compensation During Business Trips and During Transfer to Work in Another Locality.* Workers and employees have a right to reimbursement of expenses and other forms of compensation in connection with official business trips, transfer to new jobs in another locality or acceptance of jobs or assignment to work in another locality.

Employees sent on business trips retain their jobs (positions) and their average earnings for the entire duration of the business trip.

ARTICLE 49. *Guarantees in the Imposition on Workers and Employees of Material Responsibility for Loss Caused to the Enterprise, Institution or Organization.* For loss caused to the enterprise, institution or organization in the course of performance of work duties, the workers or employees through whose fault the loss was incurred bear material responsibility in the amount of the direct actual loss, but no greater than one-third of their monthly wage or salary.

Material responsibility greater than one-third of the monthly wage or salary, but no more than the full amount of the loss incurred, is imposed only in cases stipulated in USSR legislation.

With the written consent of the worker or employee, the administration of the enterprise, institution or organization may order compensation to be levied for the loss in the amount provided for in the first part of the present article. The final deadline for the administration order for withholding the sum from pay is two weeks from the date that the loss caused by the worker or employee was discovered. If the worker or employee does not give written consent, the sum may not be withheld from his or her pay, and the question of reimbursement of the loss is reviewed, upon application of the administration, by the district or borough (city) people's court.

ARTICLE 50. *Restrictions on Withholding From Earnings.* Withholding from earnings is permitted only in instances stipulated by legislation of the USSR and union republics.

At each payment of earnings the total of all withholdings may not exceed 20 per cent or in cases specially stipulated by legislation of the USSR and union republics 50 per cent, of the earnings due in payment to the worker or employee.

When withholding from earnings under more than one writ of execution, at least 50 per cent of the earnings must be reserved to the worker or employee.

The limitations established in the second and third parts of this article do not extend to withholdings from the earnings of persons serving a term of corrective labour.

Withholding is not permitted from severance pay, compensation payments and other payments exempted by legislation from withholding.

VI. Labour Discipline

ARTICLE 51. *Obligations of Workers and Employees.* Workers and employees are obliged to work honestly and conscientiously, observe labour discipline, carry out the administration's orders promptly and exactly, raise labour productivity, improve the quality of output, observe technological requirements and the regulations on labour protection, safety and industrial cleanliness, and preserve socialist property and strengthen socialist ownership.

ARTICLE 52. *Maintaining Labour Discipline.* Labour discipline at enterprises, institutions and organizations is maintained through a conscientious attitude toward work, by persuasion and also by encouragement of conscientious work. If necessary, disciplinary measures and public influence are brought to bear on individual unconscientious workers or employees.

ARTICLE 53. *Obligations of the Administration.* The administration of an enterprise, institution or organization is obligated to organize the work of its workers and employees correctly, create conditions for the growth of labour productivity, maintain labour discipline and production discipline, strictly observe labour legislation and labour-protection regulations, pay close heed to the needs and requirements of its workers and employees and improve their living and working conditions.

ARTICLE 54. *Internal Regulations. Rules on Discipline.* The work routine at enterprises, institutions and organizations is determined by the internal labour regulations established by the administration in agreement with the trade union's factory, plant or local committee on the basis of the model regulations adopted in the established procedure.

In some branches of the national economy certain categories of workers and employees are subject to rules on discipline.

ARTICLE 55. *Encouragement of Achievements in Work.* The following measures are employed to encourage exemplary performance of work duties, achievements in socialist competition, raising labour productivity, improving the quality of output, long and irreproachable service, innovations in work and other accomplishments on the job:

(1) a public commendation,
(2) a bonus,
(3) a gift of value,
(4) a certificate of merit,
(5) entry in the Honour Book or Honour Roll.

The internal work regulations and rules on discipline may provide for other measures of encouragement also.

Measures of encouragement are issued by the administration jointly or by agreement with the trade union's factory, plant or local committee.

Workers and employees who perform their work duties successfully and conscientiously are granted advantages and privileges in the sphere of social, cultural and everyday services and in housing (passes to sanatoriums and rest homes, improved housing, etc.). Such employees are also given preference in promotion.

For distinctive achievements in work, workers and employees are recommended to superior bodies for encouragement—for awards of Orders, medals, certificates of merit, badges, and honorary titles, including the title of an outstanding worker in a given trade.

ARTICLE 56. *Penalties for Breach of Labour Discipline.* The administration of an enterprise, institution or organization imposes the following disciplinary penalties for breaches of labour discipline:

(1) reproof,
(2) reprimand,
(3) severe reprimand,
(4) transfer to lower-paid work for a period of up to three months or demotion to a lower position for the same period,
(5) dismissal (points 3 and 4 of Article 17).

Legislation on disciplinary liability and the rules of discipline may also provide other disciplinary penalties for certain categories of workers and employees.

The administration has the right to refer a case of breach of labour discipline to a hearing by a comrades' court or a public organization instead of imposing disciplinary penalties.

VII. Labour Protection

ARTICLE 57. *Maintaining Healthy and Safe Working Conditions.* Healthy and safe working conditions are provided at all enterprises, institutions and organizations.

Maintenance of healthy and safe working conditions rests with the administrations of enterprises, institutions and organizations.

The administration is obliged to introduce modern safety equipment to prevent industrial accidents and to provide sanitary and hygienic conditions to ward off occupational illnesses among workers and employees.

VIII. Women's Labour

ARTICLE 68. *Work at Which Women May Not Be Employed.* It is forbidden to employ women in heavy work, in work with harmful working conditions, or in jobs underground except certain ones (non-manual labour and work in health and other services).

ARTICLE 69. *Restrictions on Assigning Women to Night Work, Overtime, or Business Trips.* It is not permitted to assign women to night work except in branches of the economy where this is called for by particular necessity, and then only as a temporary measure.

It is not permitted to assign pregnant women, nursing mothers or women with children under one year of age to night work, overtime, work on days off, or business trips.

It is not permitted to assign women with children aged one to eight to overtime work or to business trips, without their consent.

ARTICLE 70. *Transfer of Pregnant Women, Nursing Mothers and Women With Children Under One Year of Age to Lighter Work.* On the basis of a medical certificate, a pregnant woman is transferred to other, lighter work for the duration of pregnancy, with retention of her previous average earnings.

Nursing mothers and women with children under one year of age, if unable to perform their former work, are transferred to other work with retention of the previous average earnings until the infant is weaned or until the child reaches the age of one year.

ARTICLE 71. *Leaves for Pregnancy and Childbirth.* Women are granted leaves for pregnancy and childbirth, from 56 calendar days before childbirth until 56 calendar days following it, with payment of state social insurance benefits during this period. In the event of complications during childbirth or the birth of two or more children, a leave of 70 calendar days is granted following childbirth.

In addition to the leave for pregnancy and childbirth, a woman may, on request, be granted additional leave without pay until the child reaches the age of one year.

ARTICLE 72. *Breaks for Nursing an Infant.* Nursing mothers and women

452

with children under one year of age are granted, apart from the common break for rest and meals, additional time for nursing the baby.

These breaks are granted at least every three hours, for at least 30 minutes each.

Breaks for nursing a child are included in working time and are paid at the mother's average rate of earnings.

ARTICLE 73. *Guarantees to Pregnant Women, Nursing Mothers and Women With Children Under One Year of Age Regarding Employment and Prohibition Against Discharging Them.* It is forbidden to refuse women employment or to reduce their earnings on account of pregnancy or nursing a child.

Dismissal of a pregnant woman, a nursing mother or a woman with a child under one year of age at the initiative of the administration is not permitted except in cases of complete dissolution of the enterprise, institution or organization, dismissal then being permitted with obligatory provisions of another job.

IX. Young People's Labour

ARTICLE 74. *Age at Which Employment Is Permitted.* Persons under 16 years of age may not be employed.

However, in exceptional cases, with the agreement of the trade union's factory, plant or local committee, persons who have reached the age of 15 may be employed.

ARTICLE 75. *Jobs in Which the Employment of Persons Under 18 Is Prohibited.* Employment of persons under 18 years of age in heavy jobs and in jobs with harmful or hazardous working conditions, as well as in jobs underground, is prohibited.

ARTICLE 76. *Medical Examinations of Persons Under 18.* Persons under 18 may be hired only after a medical examination and thereafter they must take an obligatory medical examination each year until they reach the age of 18.

ARTICLE 77. *Remuneration of the Labour of Workers and Employees Under 18 With Reduced Working Hours.* Workers and employees under 18 with reduced working hours are paid the same sum as workers and employees of the corresponding category with a full work-day.

The labour of workers and employees under 18 hired for piece-rate jobs is remunerated at the piece rates established for adults, with additional payment at the scale rates for the time by which their work-day is shorter than the work-day of adults.

ARTICLE 78. *Prohibition Against Assigning Workers and Employees Under 18 to Night-Time or Overtime Work.* It is forbidden to assign workers and employees under 18 to night-time or overtime work or to work on days off.

ARTICLE 79. *Vacations for Workers and Employees Under 18.* The annual vacations for workers and employees under 18 (Article 33) are granted during the summer or, at their request, at any other time of the year.

ARTICLE 80. *Obligatory Quotas for Hiring and Training Young People.* All enterprises and organizations are set quotas for hiring and training young people who have completed general-education, vocational or technical schools and also for other persons under 18.

ARTICLE 81. *Provision of Work According to Speciality and Qualifications for Young Workers and Specialists Graduated from Educational Institutions.* Young workers graduated from vocational or technical schools and young specialists graduated from higher or specialized secondary educational institutions are granted work in keeping with the speciality or qualification they have acquired.

ARTICLE 82. *Restrictions on the Dismissal of Workers and Employees Under 18.* Dismissal of workers and employees under 18 at the initiative of the administration other than with observance of the general rules on dismissal is permitted only with the consent of the district or borough (city) Committee on Affairs of Minors; and, further, dismissal on the grounds cited in points 1, 2 and 6 of Article 17 of the present Principles is permitted only in exceptional instances and is not permitted unless another job is found for the person being dismissed.

X. Privileges for Workers and Employees Who Combine Work and Study

ARTICLE 83. *Organization of Industrial Training and Creation of the Necessary Conditions for Combining Work and Study.* For the occupational training of workers and employees, particularly of young people, and for raising their qualifications, the administration of enterprises, organizations and institutions organize individual, brigade, course and other forms of industrial training at the expense of the enterprise, organization or institution.

The administration is obligated to create the necessary conditions for combining work and study for workers and employees who are undergoing industrial training or studying at educational institutions without interrupting their employment.

Successful completion of industrial training by workers and employees, their general-educational and occupational preparation, and also their acquisition of a higher or specialized secondary education must be taken into consideration in raising qualification ratings or granting promotions.

ARTICLE 84. *Privileges for Workers and Employees Studying at General and Vocational-Technical Educational Institutions.* Workers and employees studying at general-education or vocational-technical schools without interrupting their employment are placed on a shorter work-week or shorter work-day while continuing to receive their regular earnings under the established rules; they are also granted other privileges.

ARTICLE 85. *Privileges for Workers and Employees Studying at Higher or Specialized Secondary Educational Institutions.* Workers and employees taking examinations for admission to higher or specialized secondary educational institutions are granted leave without pay.

Workers and employees studying in evening or correspondence divisions of higher or specialized secondary educational institutions are granted paid leaves in accordance with the established rules for leave in connection with their study, as well as other privileges.

XI. Labour Disputes

ARTICLE 86. *Agencies Examining Labour Disputes.* Labour disputes are examined by:

(1) committees on labour disputes that are formed at enterprises, institutions and organizations and consist of an equal number of representatives of the trade-union committee and representatives of the administration;
(2) factory, plant and local committees of the trade unions;
(3) district or borough (city) people's courts.

The labour disputes of certain categories of personnel are examined by superior agencies (Article 94).

ARTICLE 87. *Committees on Labour Disputes.* The committees on labour disputes are the mandatory primary bodies for examining labour disputes arising at enterprises, institutions or organizations between workers or employees, on the one hand, and the administration, on the other, with the exception of disputes subject by law to examination directly in the district or borough (city) people's courts or other agencies.

The committee arrives at a solution through agreement between the parties concerned.

ARTICLE 88. *Examination of Labour Disputes by Factory, Plant and Local Committees of Trade Unions.* The factory, plant and local committees of the trade unions examine labour disputes at the request of workers or employees if the parties have failed to reach agreement in the committee on labour disputes or if the workers or employees appeal against this committee's decision. The factory, plant or local committee may uphold the committee's decision or overrule it and hand down its own ruling on the substance of the dispute.

The factory, plant or local committee of the trade union, upon its own initiative or upon a complaint by the Prosecutor, overrules a committee decision that contradicts existing legislation and renders its own judgement on the substance of the dispute.

ARTICLE 89. *Examination of Labour Disputes in District or Borough (City) People's Courts.* Labour disputes are examined in district or borough (city) people's courts:

(1) upon the petition of workers or employees if they disagree with the ruling of the factory, plant or local committee of the trade union, or upon the administration's petition if it believes the ruling of the factory, plant or local committee is in contradiction to existing legislation;

(2) upon the petition of workers or employees if they disagree with the decision of the committee on labour disputes composed of the trade-union organizer and the manager of the enterprise, institution or organization, if this committee has failed to bring the parties concerned to agreement, or if there is no factory, plant or local trade-union committee or trade-union organizer at the enterprise, institution or organization.

Furthermore, labour disputes are heard directly in the district or borough (city) people's courts without prior reference of the case to the committee on labour disputes or the factory, plant or local committee:

(1) upon the petition for reinstatement by workers or employees who have been dismissed on the initiative of the administration of the enterprise, institution or organization, except when the personnel in question hold positions included in the special list (Article 94);

(2) upon the administration's petition for reimbursement by workers or employees for loss suffered by the enterprise, institution or organization ...

XII. Trade Unions. Participation of Workers and Employees in Management of Production

ARTICLE 95. *Right of Workers and Employees to Unite in Trade Unions.* In accordance with the USSR constitution, workers and employees are guaranteed the right to unite in trade unions.

Trade unions function in accordance with the statutes that they adopt and are not subject to registration with state agencies.

State agencies, enterprises, institutions and organizations are obligated to co-operate with the trade unions in every way in their work.

ARTICLE 96. *Rights of Trade Unions.* Trade unions represent the interests of the workers and employees in the areas of production, labour, everyday life and culture.

Trade unions participate in the drafting and realization of state plans for development of the national economy; and in the solution of questions of the distribution and utilization of material and financial resources, they draw workers and office employees into the management of production, organize socialist competition and mass technical creativity, and help strengthen production discipline and labour discipline.

The establishment of working conditions and earnings, the application of labour legislation, and the utilization of public consumption funds in instances stipulated by laws of the USSR and union republics and decisions of the USSR Council of Ministers and union-republic Councils of Ministers are functions of the enterprises, institutions and organizations and their superior agencies which are performed jointly or in agreement with the trade unions.

Trade unions exercise supervision and control over the observance of labour legislation and labour-protection regulations and they inspect housing and everyday services for workers and employees.

Trade unions administer state social insurance and also the sanatoriums, clinics, rest homes, cultural, educational, tourist and sports institutions under their jurisdiction.

Trade unions as represented by the All-Union Central Council of Trade Unions enjoy the right of legislative initiative.

ARTICLE 97. *Right of Workers and Employees to Participate in the Management of Production.* Workers and employees have the right to participate in the discussion and solution of industrial-development problems and to submit proposals for improving the work of enterprises, institutions and organizations, and also proposals on questions of social-cultural and everyday services.

Workers and employees participate in the management of production through the trade unions, other public organizations, people's control agencies, general meetings, production meetings and conferences and various forms of public activity of workers and employees.

The administrations of enterprises, institutions and organizations are obligated to establish conditions necessary for workers' and employees' participation in the management of production. The officials of enterprises, institutions and organizations are obliged to examine promptly the criticisms and proposals made by workers and employees and inform them of the measures taken.

ARTICLE 98. *Relationship Between the Trade Union's Factory, Plant or Local Committee and the Administration.* The relationship between the trade union's factory, plant or local committee and the administration of the enterprise, institution or organization is determined by the USSR law on the rights of trade unions' factory, plant or local committees.

Enterprises and organizations are obliged to allocate monetary funds to the trade unions for mass-cultural and physical-culture activities.

ARTICLE 99. *Additional Guarantees to Elective Trade-Union Officials.* Workers and employees elected to the trade union's plant, factory, local or shop committee and not released from their production jobs may not be transferred to other work or subject to disciplinary penalties without the prior consent of the trade union's factory, plant or local committee, and in the case of chairmen of these committees and trade-union organizers without the prior consent of the superior trade-union body.

Dismissal at the administration's initiative of chairmen or members of factory, plant or local committees who have not been released from production jobs may take place only with the consent of the superior trade-union body in addition to observance of the general procedure for dismissal. A trade-union organizer may be dismissed at the administration's initiative only with the consent of the superior trade-union body.

XIII. State Social Insurance

ARTICLE 100. *Coverage of All Workers and Employees by Social Insurance. Social Insurance Funds.* All workers and employees are subject to mandatory state social insurance.

State social insurance of workers and employees is at state expense. Premiums for social insurance are paid by the enterprises, institutions and organizations without any deductions from workers' and employees' earnings. Failure of an enterprise, institution or organization to pay the insurance premiums does not deprive the workers and employees of the right to benefits under state social insurance.

ARTICLE 101. *Types of Benefits Under Social Insurance.* Workers and employees and, where applicable, members of their families also, are entitled under state social insurance to:

(1) benefits for temporary disability and, in addition, for women, benefits for pregnancy and childbirth;
(2) benefits upon the birth of a child; benefits for burial;
(3) pensions for old age, disability and loss of the breadwinner, and also the longevity-of-employment pension benefits established for certain categories of personnel.

State social-insurance funds are used also for sanatorium and health-resort treatment of workers and employees, for the facilities afforded them at clinics and rest homes, for medicinal (special-diet) food, for maintaining Young Pioneer camps and for other measures under state social insurance.

ARTICLE 102. *Benefits for Temporary Disability, Pregnancy and Childbirth.* Benefits for disability are paid in the event of illness, bodily injury, temporary transfer to other work because of illness, the need to nurse a sick family member, quarantine, sanatorium and health-resort treatment and prosthesis, in an amount up to the full earnings. In the event of illness or bodily injury, the benefit is paid until ability to work is restored or until permanent disability is established.

Benefits for pregnancy and childbirth are paid during the entire leave for pregnancy and childbirth, in an amount of from two-thirds to full earnings.

ARTICLE 103. *Pensions for Old Age, Permanent Disability, and Loss of the Breadwinner.* Pensions to workers and employees for old age or permanent disability and pensions to members of their families in the case of loss of the breadwinner are fixed in accordance with the USSR Law on State Pensions.

XIV. Supervision and Control over the Observance of Labour Legislation

ARTICLE 104. *Agencies of Supervision and Control Over the Observance of Labour Legislation.* Supervision and control over the observance of labour legislation and labour-protection regulations are exercised by:

(1) state agencies and inspection services which are specially authorized to do this and which function independently of the administrations of enterprises, institutions, organizations and their superior agencies;

(2) trade unions and the technical and legal labour inspection services under their jurisdiction — in accordance with the regulations adopted by the All-Union Central Committee of Trade Unions with regard to these inspection services.

The soviets of working people's deputies and their executive and administrative agencies exercise control over the observance of labour legislation in the manner prescribed by USSR and union-republic legislation.

Ministries and departments exercise internal departmental control over the observance of labour legislation in respect to the enterprises, institutions and organizations under their jurisdiction.

Supreme supervision over the precise execution of the labour laws by all ministries and departments, enterprises, institutions and organizations and their officials rests with the USSR Prosecutor-General.

ARTICLE 105. *Liability for Violation of Labour Legislation.* Officials guilty of violating labour legislation and labour-protection regulations, of failing to meet their obligations under the collective contract and labour-protection agreements or of obstructing the work of trade unions bear liability in the manner established by USSR and union-republic legislation.

Source: K. M. Bogolyubov, i drugie (eds.), *Spravochnik partiinogo rabotnika,* vypusk 11 (Moscow, 1971), p. 283.
Translation: CDSP, Vol. XXII, No. 34, p. 1. Slightly abridged.

Note on Translation

I have been glad, in compiling this volume, to use the work of many translators, past and present. This has meant some unevenness, and occasional discrepancies between texts. My response, as noted in the introduction, has been to iron out the most eye-catching variations, without attempting to achieve anything like uniformity of terminology. The translations are not, after all, presented merely for their linguistic qualities, and most readers will be satisfied if the sense and texture of the Russian are reproduced reasonably well in English. My policy has likewise been to retain the transliteration used in the original translations, and avoid pointless letter-switching. The glossary is intended to help where there might be some confusion: apart from the explanation of words which have specific Soviet connotations, I have included English and Russian equivalents of certain terms, and the initialled forms of some of the less obvious official bodies.

I decided it was pointless to include footnotes on all the many persons mentioned in the text: the biographies of most are easily accessible. Details have however been provided on a few individuals who did not belong to the Soviet leadership.

As far as my own translations are concerned, my aim has been to achieve a degree of readability without sacrifice to the real meaning of the original. I have retained the Russian forms for administrative divisions. Square brackets have been used to mark editorial changes, and textual omissions are shown by ellipsis dots, in the accepted manner.

The older translations require special comment. Most of these were very creditable pieces of work, done long before many now generally accepted conventions had materialized. Many of the Soviet originals were themselves badly drafted, or written in long-winded and tortuous prose (a characteristic which is, incidentally, still in evidence). The quality of translation inevitably suffered. I have, in such cases, replaced outdated terms, and modified occasional infelicities and flaws, while preserving as far as possible the body of the first translator's work.

English spellings have been standardized (for instance, the 'ize' ending is used throughout), and the spellings of texts originally published in the USA have been anglicized. Typographical presentation has also been standardized, obvious printers' errors corrected, and full points eliminated from all abbreviations, but any substantial modifications have been noted at the end of the relevant document.

Bibliographical Note

Full bibliographical details of sources used have been given at the end of each document, and other bibliographical references are given in footnotes. In the case of works which came out in Moscow the publishers' names have not been given; these publishing houses are all state-owned and their names are not usually needed for bibliographical purposes.

The abbreviated title *CDSP* for *Current Digest of the Soviet Press* is used on several occasions: full details will be found on p. 108.

Glossary

administration, common translation of *upravlenie*, understood as a directorate or similar organizational entity.

aktiv, a group of persons who give their time (and enthusiasm) for this work on a part-time voluntary basis.

All-Russian, term used frequently in the early years of Soviet power to denote the RSFSR.

allotment, identical with 'plot'.

ARCTU, All-Russian Council of Trade Unions.

artel, a community formed in accordance with Soviet law for production purposes.

AUCCTU, All-Union Central Council of the Trade Unions (VTsSP S).

aul, Central Asian or Caucasian-type rural settlement.

autonomous republic, one of twenty internal administrative areas inhabited by a basically indigenous ethnic group.

Belorussia, identical with White Russia, one of the union republics, q.v.

board, small managerial body, common translation of *pravlenie*.

borough, occasional translation for urban *raion*, or district.

brigade, a small group of workers or peasants formally responsible for a given job, headed by a 'brigadier'.

bureau (*buro*), a small body of persons elected or nominated to perform managerial or administrative functions.

candidate, probationary or junior member of an organization.

CC, Central Committee (of the Party).

CCC, Central Control Commission (TsKK), the highest body with verification functions in the Party, and for a period, state administration, 1921–34.

CEC, Central Executive Committee (TsIK), the leading body of the Congress of Soviets, 1917–36.

chairman, identical in Russian with *president*.

city (*gorod*), identical with *town, urban*; there is no distinction between city and town in Russian.

clerk, occasional translation of *sluzhashchii*, or *employee*.

CLD, *see* STO.

collective (*kollektiv*), an informal group of people who live or work together.

collegium, a small group of responsible officials formed to advise in the running of an organization.

commissar, commissary, commissioner, head of a people's commissariat (or ministry), 1917–46. Subsequently the terms ministry, minister, etc., were used.

Communist, specifically a member of the Communist Party.

consultative, or deliberative (voice). Used to describe the right to take part in discussion (without the right to vote on it). Usually confined to probationary members of an organization.

control (*kontrol*), a term which may in Russian embrace control, supervision and verification.

Council for Labour and Defence (STO), a body which existed from 1920 to 1937 with co-ordinative economic functions.

CPC, Council of People's Commissars; *see also* KPK.

CPSU, until 1918, Russian Social Democratic Workers' Party (Bolsheviks), RSDRP(B): 1918–25, Russian Communist Party (Bolsheviks), RKP(B): 1925–52, All-Union Communist Party (Bolsheviks), VKP(B). Since 1952, the Communist Party of the Soviet Union (KPSS).

decision (of an organizational body), common translation of *reshenie* or *postanovlenie*.

decree, common translation of *postanovlenie*, *dekret*.

district, common translation of *raion* (urban or rural). *See also* borough.

ECCI, Executive Committee of the Communist International.

edict, common translation of *ukaz*.

employee, *sluzhashchii*, any white-collar or non-manual worker.

fabkom, factory or works committee.

Glavlit, Main Administration for Affairs of Literature and Publishing; *see* document 13, p. 71.

gorkom, town (party) committee.

gorod, town, city.

GPU, State Political Administration; *see* document 44, p. 237.

gubernia, the basic administrative unit in the USSR (below republican level) until the administrative reorganization of 1929–30. In 1917 there were fifty-six of them in the RSFSR.

hectare, 2·47 acres.

household (*dvor*), the legal administrative unit among the peasantry and in the collective farm, comprising both the individuals in a family and their common dwelling.

ispolkom, local executive committee.

izvestia, news, information. A common title for Soviet periodicals.

khutor, individual farmstead (Ukraine, Belorussia, Baltic areas).

kishlak, Central-Asian-type rural settlement, originally for winter use by nomads.

kolkhoz, collective farm.

Komsomol, Communist League of Youth (VLKSM).

KPK, Commission for Party Control.

krai, an extremely large administrative unit in the Asiatic parts of the USSR, usually translated as 'territory'.

kraikom, territorial party committee.

kulak, rich and proverbially anti-Soviet peasant: the term was never given an economic definition.

labour-day, a work-unit used on the collective farm: a day's labour could rate as more or less than one 'labour-day', depending on how demanding it was.

levada, enclosed pasture land.

MTS, machine-and-tractor station.

narodny komissariat (NK), People's Commissariat (of a given branch of the administration or economy).

NEP, New Economic Policy.

NKVD. People's Commissariat of Internal Affairs.

obkom, provincial (party) committee.

oblast, basic subdivision of the larger republics, usually translated as 'province'. There are at present about a hundred *oblasti* in the USSR.

OGPU, Unified State Political Administration (secret police); *see* document 46, p. 245.

okrug (national *okrug*), one of some ten small administrative units inhabited by a basically indigenous ethnic group.

OS, Old Style, of dates according to the Julian Calendar used in Russia up until 14 February 1918 (New Style). In the twentieth century 'old style' dates lagged behind the Gregorian (new style) calendar by thirteen days.

Partorg, a party organizer (low grade).

Party, the, primarily the CPSU. In Soviet documents sometimes with, and sometimes without, a capital letter. Union republics are formally credited with their own 'Parties'.

Plenum, a full session of the leading or inner body of a Soviet organization.

PLC, People's Labour Commissariat.

president, *see* chairman.

Presidium, the leading body in the Supreme Soviets and many other Soviet organizations: a group of persons elected to run a meeting.

private plot, an area of land allotted for the use of a Soviet citizen, primarily the peasant: 'private' only in the sense of being available for personal use.

protocol (*protokol*), a document recording the speeches or decisions made at a meeting.

province, see *oblast*.

raiispolkom raion, executive committee.

raikom, raion, committee (party).

raion, subdivision of the *oblast* and of certain large towns. At present they number about 4,000. Usually translated as 'district' or 'region'.

revision, sometimes means auditing or accounting.

RKP(B), *see* CPSU.

RMCR, Revolutionary Military Republican Council.

RSDRP(B), *see* CPSU.

RSFSR, Russian Soviet Federative Socialist Republic.

SNK, Council of People's Commissars.

Soviet, 'council' in Russian.

sovkhoz, state farm.

Sovnarkhoz, literally, economic council—a name with several connotations in Soviet history.

Sovnarkom, Council of People's Commissars.

SR, Social Revolutionary (person or party).

stage, the period of attachment to an organization or enterprise; a probationary period.

stanitsa, Cossack village.

STO, Council for Labour and Defence, q.v.

SZ SSSR, USSR collection of laws.

territory, *see krai*.

town, township (*gorod*).

TSIK, Central Executive Committee, q.v.

uezd (*uyezd*), a subdivision of a *gubernia* until 1929–30. There were 476 of them in the RSFSR in 1917.

ukaz, edict.

union republic, one of the fifteen Soviet administrative entities with an external frontier.

USSR, Union of Soviet Socialist Republics (SSSR).

vedomosti, record, gazette. A common title for Soviet periodicals.

VKP(B), *see* CPSU.

volost, a subdivision of the *uezd* until 1929–30. In 1917 they numbered over 10,000.

VSNKh, Supreme Economic Council, 1917–32, 1963–5: All-Russian Economic Council, 1960–65.

VTsIK, All-Russian Central Executive Committee, leading body of the All-Russian Congress of Soviets, 1917–37.

VTsSPS, *see* AUCCTU.

wedgefarming (*vklinivanie*), working narrow strips of land.

YCL, *Komsomol*, q.v.

zemstvo, a type of local administrative body established by the reform of 1864 and abolished by the Bolsheviks.

List of Document Titles

16. On Improving the Work of the Soviets of Workers' Deputies and Strengthening their Ties with the Masses. *Decree of the Central Committee of the CPSU, 22 January 1957.*

17. Law on Further Improving the Organization of Management of Industry and Construction. *Passed by the Presidium of the Supreme Soviet of the USSR, 10 May 1957.*

18. On the Method of Publishing and Implementing Laws of the USSR, Decrees of the Supreme Soviet of the USSR, Edicts and Decrees of the Presidium of the Supreme Soviet of the USSR. *Edict of 19 June 1958.*

19. On the Work of the Soviets of Workers' Deputies of the Poltava Oblast. *Decree of the Central Committee of the CPSU, 16 November 1965.*

20. On the Formation of Permanent Commissions of the Soviet of the Union. *Decree of the Soviet of the Union, 3 August 1966.*

21. Report on Results of Elections to Union-Republic and Autonomous-Republic Supreme Soviets and Local Soviets. *Data on election results published from materials received from the Presidiums of the Union-Republic Supreme Soviets, 20 June 1971.*

PART II THE PARTY

22. On the Organizational Question. *Decree of the Eighth Congress of the RKP(B), 18–23 March 1919.*

23. Statute of the Russian Communist Party (Bolsheviks). *Approved at the Eighth Conference of the RKP(B), 2–4 December 1919.*

24. On the Organizational Question. *Resolution of the Ninth Congress of the VKP(B), 29 March–5 April 1920.*

25. Demands of the Kronstadt Insurgents, Expressed in the Resolution of the General Meeting of the Crews of the Ships of the Line. *Kronstadt, 28 February 1921.*

26. On the Unity of the Party. *Decree of the Tenth Congress of the RKP(B), 8–16 March 1921.*

27. On the Syndicalist and Anarchist Deviation in our Party. *Decree of the Tenth Congress of the Russian Communist Party, 16 March 1921.*

28. Letter to the Congress ('Lenin's Testament'). *Dictated 23 December 1922–4 January 1923.*

29. On the Opposition. *Decree of the Fifteenth Congress of the VKP(B), 2–19 December 1927.*

30. Resolution of the Joint Meeting of the Politburo of the Central Committee and the Presidium of the Central Control Commission on Intra-Party Affairs, 9 February 1929. *Approved by the joint plenary session of the Central Committee and the Central Control Commission of the All-Union Communist Party (Bolsheviks), 23 April 1929.*

31. On Party Purges. *Resolution of the CC and of the CCC of the VKP(B), 28 April 1933.*

PART III LEGALITY, THE COURTS AND THE POLICE

469

by a Tax in Kind. *Decree of the All-Russian Central Executive Council, 21 March 1921.*

65. On the Grain Front. *Extract from Stalin's talk to students of the Institute of Red Professors, the Communist Academy and Sverdlov University, on 28 May 1928.*

66. Problems of Agrarian Policy in the USSR. *Stalin's speech delivered at the conference of Marxist students of the agrarian question, 27 December 1929.*

67. On the Rate of Collectivization and State Assistance for Collective-Farm Construction. *Decree of the Central Committee of the VKP(B), 5 January 1930.*

68. 'Dizzy with Success' (Problems of the Collective-Farm Movement). *Stalin's article in Pravda, 2 March 1930.*

69. The Aims and Tasks of the Political Departments of Machine-and-Tractor Stations and State Farms. *The resolution of the combined plenum of the Central Committee and the Central Control Commission of the All-Russian Communist Party (Bolsheviks), 11 January 1933.*

70. Standard Charter of an Agricultural Artel. *Approved by the Second All-Union Congress of Shock Workers of the Collective Farms and confirmed by the Council of People's Commissars of the USSR and by the Central Committee of the All-Union Communist Party (Bolsheviks) on 17 February 1935.*

71. On Prohibiting the Expulsion of Collective Farmers from Collective Farms. *Joint resolution of the USSR Council of People's Commissars and the Central Committee of the Communist Party, 19 April 1938.*

72. On Measures to Protect Public Lands in the Collective Farms from being Squandered. *Joint resolution of the Central Committee of the Communist Party and the USSR Council of People's Commissars of 27 May 1939.*

73. On Measures for Liquidating Violations of the Charter of the Agricultural Artel in the Collective Farms. *Decree of the Council of Ministers of the USSR and Central Committee of the VKP(B), 19 September 1946.*

74. On Measures Connected with the Amalgamation of Small Collective Farms and the Associated Tasks of Party Organizations. *Decree of the Council of Ministers of the USSR, 17 July 1950.*

75. On Measures for the Further Development of Soviet Agriculture. *From N. S. Khrushchev's report at the Plenum of the CC CPSU, 3 September 1953.*

76. On Pensions and Allowances for Collective-Farm Members. *Law of the USSR, 15 July 1964.*

77. The Basic Results of the Development of Agriculture in Recent Years. *From L. I. Brezhnev's report at the Plenum of the CC CPSU, 24 March 1965.*

the Council of Ministers of the USSR, the Central Committee of the CPSU, and the All-Union Central Committee of Trade Unions, 8 September 1956.

92. Principles of Labour Legislation of the USSR and Union Republics. *Approved by the Supreme Soviet of the USSR,* 15 *July* 1970.